PERSONAL VIDEOCONFERENCING

AF815254

The publisher offers discounts on this book when ordered in quantity. For more information please contact:

Special Sales Department
Manning Publications Co.
3 Lewis Street
Greenwich, CT 06830
or
lee@manning.com
Fax: (203) 661–9018

Copyediting: Margaret Marynowski
Typesetting: Dorothy Marsico
Internal Design: Stephen Brill
Cover Design: Diana Coe

Copyright © 1996 by Manning Publications Co.
All rights reserved.

No part of this publication may be reproduced, stored in a retrieval system, or transmitted, in any form or by means, electronic, mechanical, photocopying, or otherwise, without prior written permission of the publisher.

Recognizing the importance of preserving what has been written, it is the policy of Manning Publications to have the books they publish printed on acid–free paper, and we exert our best efforts to that end.

Many of the designations used by manufacturers and vendors to distinguish their products are protected as trademarks. Wherever these designations appear in this book, and we have been aware of the trademark claim, they have been typeset in initial caps or all caps.

Library of Congress Cataloging in Publication Data

Rosen, Evan.
Personal videoconferencing / Evan Rosen.
p. cm.
Includes bibliographical references and index.
ISBN 1-884777-28-7
1. Videoconferencing. 2. Business communication—Technological innovations. 3. Videoconferencing—Equipment and supplies.
I. Title.
HF5734.7.R67 1996
284.3'54—dc20 96-28265
CIP

1 2 3 4 5 6 7 8 9 10 — BB — 00 99 98 97 96

Printed in the United States of America

Personal Videoconferencing

EVAN ROSEN

MANNING
Greenwich
(74° w. long.)

col•lab•ic•ate (kŏ **lab** ik kayt), *v.* to collaborate and communicate

This book is dedicated to my parents, Gerald and Lois Rosen, for encouraging me to collabicate.

Contents

About the Author

Evan Rosen is a principal with Impact Video Communication, a San Francisco-based communications consulting and training firm. He is also a frequent seminar, workshop and keynote speaker on videoconferencing and other media topics. Evan has worked with leading corporations in planning and implementing personal videoconferencing, group videoconferencing, intranets, store-and-forward video and other emerging communication and collaboration technologies. As a consulting member of the Personal Conferencing Work Group, Evan worked with other industry pioneers to shape the personal videoconferencing industry.

Evan is also an accomplished business and technology journalist. His work has ap-peared on CNN and CBS, and he has held news positions at KICU-TV in San Jose, WTOL-TV in Toledo, WABC-TV in New York, WXYZ-TV in Detroit and KODE-TV in Joplin, Missouri. Evan's articles have appeared in publications including *The New York Post*, *Teleconferencing Business*, and *Telemarketing and Call Center Solutions*. He has received numerous communications awards including an Emmy nomination, an Associated Press award and two awards from Women In Communications. He holds a B.A. in history from the University of Michigan—Ann Arbor. He can be reached through e-mail at `erosen@impactvid.com`.

Preface

I'm a curious creature, in part because my parents took me many places when I was growing up and encouraged me to ask questions. One of those outings is perhaps my earliest childhood memory. It was a visit to the 1964 World's Fair in New York City. The fair itself is a blur. What I do remember vividly is what seemed to be an amazing invention at the AT&T pavilion. It was a telephone that could see. I tried using Picturephone, but sadly the invention was touch and go. I could see only myself through the "Vu-self" option and not the woman using the other unit someplace else at the fair. Her image flickered away moments before my turn came. I was determined, however, to get another turn. Throughout high school, college, and a career in broadcast journalism, another turn never came.

The next opportunity to use a phone that could see finally arrived some thirty years later. However, the video phone was really not a phone at all. It was a personal computer with videophone capability. Not only could I communicate with clients and others through video face to face, but also I could collaborate on documents and share applications. These capabilities were particularly valuable in the communications consulting and training business, because I was working with many clients that are geographically dispersed. I realized the value of face to face contact, but I simply was unable to visit all of my clients each week. The phone filled the gaps, but these professional relationships required more. Personal videoconferencing worked in many situations.

As Impact Video Communication's clients began demanding new approaches to uniting dispersed workgroups and better ways of communicating and collaborating, I became more involved with the development of emerging communication and collaboration technologies. Increasingly, speaking engagements filled my calendar, and editors were asking me to write articles. I was forced to produce increasing amounts of material to fulfill these obligations. That's why I turned to the Internet. I posted a request in a telecommunications newsgroup. The request was for users of desktop videoconferencing to relate their experiences. One of the responses came from publisher Marjan Bace. "Do you think a book would be doable?" wrote Marjan. A virtual relationship evolved, and that relationship has produced this book.

Acknowledgments

Many personal videoconferencing pioneers have graciously contributed their time to this project. They have helped revolutionize the way people work and live. The author wishes to acknowledge the following people and companies for their contributions:

Ernie DeNigris, Steven Plavny, John Slevin, Pat Mallon, Marvin Lurie, Taya Harmon, and Barbara Sweeney of AT&T; Joseph Jesson of Amoco, David Connolly, and Joe Carter of Andersen Consulting; Susan Squires of Andersen Worldwide; Ken Pickar of Allied Signal Aerospace; Frank Casanova, Eric Hoffert, Suzanne Hampton, John Harriman, Min Wang, and Larry Wood of Apple Computer; Jim Elacqua of Arnold, White and Durkee; Surendar Magar of Array Microsystems; Martha Gorman of Bassett Healthcare; Stephen Scullen of the Bank of Boston; Kimberly Scholtz of Beaupre & Co.; Ray Sollars and John Kimball of Boeing; James Slaby of Bay Networks; Charlie Judice of Bell Atlantic; Bob Anderson of British Petroleum; Laurie Bauer of Best Buy; Jennifer Forbes of Beneficial; Tom Little of Boston University; Dr. Robert Rainer of the Bowman Gray School of Medicine; Bennet Bayer and Grant Mason of Casio Phone Mate; Kristi Moushon of Caterpillar; Dave Holt and John Loeliger of Chromatic Research; Adam Stein of Cisco Systems; Peter Thorp and Connie Thanasoulis of Citibank; Mia Bradway and Jim Ross of CLI; Hussein ElBadaly of Consolidated Edison; Nancy Pearce of COS; Tim Bigley and Margherita Brodbeck Roth of Credit Suisse Holdings; Mike Bellefeuille and Cindy Scott of Corel; Steve Erde of Cornell University; Sarah Dickinson of Dickinson & Associates; Rebecca Taylor of DataBeam; Michael Black and Linda Goff of Datapoint; Suzanne Snygg of Dataquest; Marcy Kaplan and Bill Weber of DVC/BCR Enterprises; Ken Pine of Dolch; Stan Marder of

Duck Corporation; Joe Parkinson, Chris McNiffe, Kevin Deierling, Robin Chirico, and Stacey O'Connell of 8×8; Bill Muller of Ernst & Young; Patricia Napier and Karen Usher of the European Teleconferencing Federation; Fiona Perrin of Enigma Publishing; Peter Price of Eisys; Stuart Johnstone of EscapeSoft; Larry Shaw of the Exploratorium; Al Chambers, Guisseppe Delena, Rex Greenslade, and Dawn Looney of Ford Motor Company; David Kelley of Frebon International; Bill Smalley of the Fulton County Courts; John Meyer of Funrise Toy; Bernadette Brugman of GE Capital; William Ray of the Glasgow Electric Plant Board; Abbey Bernstein of Grant/Jacoby; Joe Horzepa of Horizon Consultants; Phil Karp of Hyperion Capital Management; William Randle of Huntington Bancshares; Tom Hall of Hughes Aircraft/Computer Sciences Corporation; Van Romine of the Institute for Telework; Scott Hudson of the Georgia Institute of Technology; Bill Young of Impact Video Communication; Anthony Iorio of ITT; Tom Manley of INET Marketing; Jerrie Rea of Incite; Jack Toto and Keith Wimberley of InSoft; Jeff Charles of the Institute for the Future: Charles Morrison of Informedia Interactive; Sudhir Bhagwan, Pat Gelsinger, Frank Gill, Andrew Grove, Victoria Pierce, Jon Jackson, James Johnson, Jeff Thompson, Seth Walker, and Janet Woodworth of Intel; Bob Davis and Michael Zeug of Iterated; Scarlett Moore of Johnson & Johnson; Heather Jameson of Ketchum; Ace Allen of KU Medical Center; David Dirks of Lawrence Livermore National Laboratories; Kevin Pitts of Link-VTC; Louis Belt of Laidlaw Environmental Services; Sheila Silveira of Lam Research Corporation; Mort Herman of Lucent Technologies Microelectronics and George Ralston of Lucent Technologies; Jay Crookston, Patricia Garriga, Cal Jackson, and John Rushing of MCI; Blake Irving and Dennis Riley of Microsoft; Randy Schnack of Midwest Information Systems; Rick Hanson of Magma Copper; Harry Mott of Mott 4 Productions; Dr. Ray Jarris of Maritime Health Services; Leonard Rubin of the Manhattan District Attorney's Office; Judith Hamilton of National Semiconductor; Bruce Gilbaugh of NASA; Michael Kleper of the National Technical Institute for the Deaf; Rich Herndon of Netsurf; Noreen Cardinali of the New Jersey Department of Transportation; Fred Campo of Northrop Grumman; Peter Lee of Novacor Chemicals; Barry Fishman of Northwestern University; Jerry Lange of NYNEX; Ron Howard of the Oklahoma County Courts; Randall Yuen of Oppenheimer; Rajesh Shakkarwar of Opti; Tom Brady, Michael Powell, Herb Yee, Dan Theobald, and Rebecca Weill of Pacific Bell; Christine Perey of Perey Communications; Fred Parnon of Parnon & Pratt; Toni Alonso of Pfizer; Norman Gaut, Rich Baker, and Kevin Flanagan of PictureTel; Judy Estrin of Precept; Stephen Shao of Project DIANE; Phillip Russell of Purdue University; Steve Trustman of PVCI; Shykeh Gordon of RADVision; Steven Bennett of Reuters America; Brad Thorney of Rockwell International; John Griffin and Doug Marlowe of RSI Systems; Dr. Roger Stronell of RTI; Dale Harris of Stanford University; Jim Berry and

Barry Hess of Sandia Laboratories; Bob Leader of SAP Software; Bruce Quigley of Smith Micro Software; Ellen Grace Henson and Jamie Schein of Silicon Graphics; Ellen Isaacs of Sun Microsystems; Henry Musard of SEMCO; Timothy Binkley of the School of Visual Arts; Martin Levetin of Socket Communications; Susan Bregman, Brooke Jarabek, and Rob Slemmons of Sprint; Steven Friedland and Marty Waldron of Stone Marriccini Patterson; Ruth Ann Burchnall of Stress Engineering; Daniel Flohr and Joe Vitetta of Target Technologies; Gil Bassak of Teleconferencing Business; Sigram Schindler, Stephan Wenger, and Robert White of Teles; Keith DeStasio, Leon Schilmoeller, and Laura Sutton of 3M; Ray Palmer of TRW; Jack London and Gregg Reich of the Thomas Jefferson University Cancer Center; Mike Cebula of US Bank; Paul Ekman of the University of California; Judith Olson of the University of Michigan; Jim Emal of the University of Nebraska; Bob Greenberg of the University of Tennessee; Lt. Richard Stakelum of the US Navy; Asaf Mohr and Tony Zuccarino of VDONet; Ron Shields of VideoLAN; Mike Clifford and Katie Phillips of VCON; Bill Sullivan of Vic Hi Tech; Jim Rowe of VideoTwist; Michael Barron of Virtual Realty; Paul Costa of Videssence; David Cunningham of VIEWnet; Staffan Ericsson, Anthony Antonuccio, and Mary Campbell of VIVO Software; Tom Stevenson, Charles Sauer, Karen Lee, Sheri Goodwin, and Vicki Newton of VTEL; Sharon Leighty, Amy Reiber, and Travis Kringlen of Vyvx; Olivier Garbe of Winnov; Christopher Miner of Workstation Technologies; Peter Knight of the World Bank; David Down of Williams Pipeline; Pennie Turgeon of Worcester Polytechnic Institute; Lois Wong of Xerox; Brian Gilpin, Allen Helvajian, and Eric Hughes of Wells Fargo; Forrest Milkowski, Tracy Wemett and Cindy Sesnick of White Pine Software; and Bob Mirani of the Yankee Group.

Also thanks to Ray Brady, Gil Gordon, Gerald Linderman, Judith Lasater, Eugene Lisansky, Bob Rowe, Jack Nilles, Chip Drake, Alan & Sue Morris, Dave Gilbert, Linda Joyce, Pat Huff, Mike Konczal, Glen Mazzone, Joe Spencer, Rich White, David Ragan, John Walsh, Mary Lindsay, Jim Malone, Jim Srodes, Marilyn Babb, Marny Stanier and Russ Reissinger.

And a very special thanks to: Hedley Rainnie of 8×8; Ralph Ungermann of First Virtual Corporation; Frederick Hirzel of Vocal Technologies; Sarkis Zartarian of Applied Communication Concepts; G.A. Ford and Fred Haisch of AT&T Laboratories; and Mark St. Pierre of Ascom Nexion for reviewing the manuscript, and to Christine Traut of Andersen Worldwide for her constant input through regular personal videoconferences.

Also to Marjan Bace, Lee Fitzpatrick, Mary Piergies, Ted Kennedy, Stephen Brill, and the staff of Manning Publications and Prentice Hall for their commitment to the project. Also to Diana Coe of kō Design studio for designing the cover, to Margaret Marynowski for copyediting the book, and to Dottie Marsico for handling production.

The author is deeply indebted to Katherine Hirzel of Impact Video Communication for coordinating the photographs and illustrations, for researching many areas, and for providing support throughout this project.

Introduction

The traditional approach to writing a book is to borrow countless concepts from many people. While contributors may receive credit if their ideas are written, verbal contributions are less likely to be acknowledged. Such an approach would approximate hypocrisy in a book about using technology to collaborate and communicate. I would be cheating the reader if I were simply to distill the thoughts of contributors into my own analysis.

The research for this book relies largely on interviews plus personal experience consulting to corporations in strategic approaches to personal videoconferencing, intranets, group videoconferencing, media and presentation training, and collaboration. These specific areas are increasingly becoming interrelated as advanced networks and technologies emerge. Because the input of hundreds of people helped produce *Personal Videoconferencing*, the book is peppered with quotes from these collaborators. Therefore, the narrative style is closer to a documentary than to a book.

I used personal videoconferencing technology often in researching the book. I have never met many of the collaborators in person, yet because we worked together through real-time video I feel a bond with them. Some contributors enjoyed virtual meals with me as we begged and borrowed time for research sessions. They shared their thoughts over lunch or breakfast through personal videoconferencing. Because of time differences, I was frequently eating a muffin and drinking coffee on the West Coast of the United States while a collaborator on the East Coast was enjoying a sandwich or salad.

Frequently, books about technology are geared towards either a lay audience or a technical group. This book attempts to bridge that gap. As we go forward, technicians and engineers must learn more about the practical uses of technology so that they can design tools that compliment human behavior. Similarly, professionals from many walks must gain more knowledge about how technology works. Technology has invaded almost every professional's life, and the real world has grabbed hold of almost every technologist. No longer, for example, can an engineer successfully remain steeped in theory. The Internet and the speed of information are playing a major role. No longer do technical people communicate and collaborate only with each other. There is less segregation from one profession to the next. A doctor may help write the software that aids in patient diagnosis and care, and a software engineer must learn more about medicine, education, marketing or other specialized professions if he or she is to design effective software.

My objective in writing this book is to stimulate discussion and generate new ideas about *collabication*, the marriage of collaboration and communication. The book is presented in four parts. Part 1 describes why personal videoconferencing is taking hold now, successes and mistakes users are experiencing, and how individuals and organizations are using personal videoconferencing to achieve results. Part 2 details the technology and the history of personal videoconferencing. Part 3 provides practical information for professionals interested in implementing the technology in organizations. Part 4 looks ahead to the future impact of personal videoconferencing at home and at work as well as describing how using the technology effectively can boost careers. The appendix provides system requirements and other useful information about specific personal videoconferencing systems.

Reading a book—even one that impacts your career—should be a pleasure rather than a chore. So, grab a cool drink, a warm cup of tea, or whatever makes you comfortable and begin the journey.

PART I

THE DEATH OF DISTANCE

1

Shifting Cultures: A Ripe Time for New Tools

The best approach to understanding the power and pitfalls of personal videoconferencing is to step back from the technology. Personal videoconferencing is about culture and people. The technology serves as nothing more than a tool that helps us adapt to a fundamental change in the way we live and work. We are moving from a culture of competition to one of collaboration. While business requires competing, our approach is changing. Working with others to achieve business objectives is becoming more accepted than working alone. In fact, collaborating is becoming increasingly important to competing effectively and boosting the bottom line. Collaboration's first cousin is communication, an age-old critical element in achieving personal and professional objectives. Collaboration and communication are becoming intertwined, as the word collabication suggests. Tools such as personal videoconferencing can help advance collabication, but technology is only part of the answer. The cultural shift requires rethinking jobs, organizational structures, and lifestyles. Before we discuss personal videoconferencing, it is essential to examine the trends that have created a demand for more powerful communication and collaboration tools.

Workers Without Time

Nobody has any time. Yesterday, people could take days to answer business letters and memos, so there was little expectation of immediacy. Today, because technology lets us respond right away, there is no excuse for delay. This means that since business must be done now, it is difficult for many professionals to catch their breath. Forget about a leisurely lunch. Most businesspeople are lucky if there is time to grab a sandwich and eat at their desk. In this fast-paced world, the standard is to arrive early and leave late. Then, hit the highway and face the traffic. In many metropolitan areas, an hour and fifteen minutes each way is a typical commute.

Time increasingly taps professionals on the shoulder, and life is a race to beat the clock. Time-to-market governs revenue. "Face time" with clients helps one understand their business needs and keep the accounts. Travel time allows face time. Billable hours can determine professional value. Quality time with family helps raise children well and preserve the marriage. Everything and everybody chips away at the most precious commodity. They take it all and then some, so there is no time left.

People strive to create more time. They look to gadgets for freedom, but in many cases, technology has enslaved them. Fifty to a hundred e-mail messages can pile up in a day. Then there are the twenty voice mail messages. That's not to mention the stack of faxes and snail mail. There is no time to return all of the calls and respond to all of the paper. E-mail goes unanswered, or the sender receives an inadequate response. Professionals want to clear their plates, but the helpings are coming far faster than anybody can chew.

Many professionals would like to hash things out and get tasks done. However, the decision-making and problem-solving process prevents rapid resolution. That process often involves scheduling multiple meetings to discuss issues, retreating to separate work spaces to develop solutions, faxing documents back and forth, and initiating numerous follow-up phone calls. Resolving a single problem can take weeks. Multiply this process by the dozens of problems most professionals address in a month, and paralysis can develop. Stress overwhelms these professionals, and productivity suffers. Traditional tools are falling short, and professionals are demanding more efficient ways of getting things done. The demands of the workplace require new methods of communication and collaboration. Such methods must permit immediate problem solving and prevent work from piling up.

Shifting priorities

Many professionals are refusing to wait for new tools. The punishing pace of their jobs is forcing them to rethink their goals. What mattered most yesterday matters less today. To regain time, professionals are cashing out. They are giving up paychecks and scaling back lifestyles. To some, time is worth more than money. A 1995 poll conducted by the Harwood Group found that 28% of Americans voluntarily reduced their income over the previous five years to reflect changes in priorities. Advancing through corporate ranks is holding less luster, and the trappings of success are becoming less of a priority. Some people are choosing to buy and earn less. Researchers call this trend "voluntary simplicity" or "downshifting."

In Seattle, a simple living study circle has formed. A *New York Times* headline reads "The Simple Life Lures Refugees From Stress." People are trading in large homes for condos, abandoning household clutter, cutting credit card balances, and rejecting consumerism. For increasing numbers of people, the goodies they are giving up are worth far less than the sacrifice keeping them requires. What's more, people are finding simplicity feels better. The Harwood Group poll shows that 15% of respondents said they would be much more satisfied with their lives if they had nicer things in their homes. Sixty six percent said more time with family and friends would give them the most satisfaction.

Even captains of industry are giving up power to achieve balance in their lives. Former American Express President Jeffrey Stiefler walked away from prestige and a yearly pay-out of more than $4 million. After climbing the corporate ranks, Stiefler's goals shifted away from his work and towards his family. After putting in a full day plus commuting from the American Express headquarters in Manhattan to his house in Greenwich, Connecticut, Stiefler rarely made it home before 8 pm. Stiefler told the *Wall Street Journal* that he almost never had dinner with his three sons, and he saw them for only 15 minutes a day. After leaving American Express, Stiefler pursued a better lifestyle and helped raise his sons.

The threat of losing top-notch professionals has forced employers to respond. To preserve their investment in people, companies are giving in to the demand for more balanced lives. Tenet Healthcare, the nation's second largest hospital company, has moved its corporate headquarters from Santa Monica, California to Santa Barbara on the Pacific coast. The reason is that several executives live in Santa Barbara and were tired of commuting to greater Los Angeles. The Tenet relocation is a case of lifestyle shaping corporate policy.

Some of the biggest concessions to balance are coming in the most competitive fields. Take law, for example. Increasing numbers of law firms are letting lawyers choose a slow road, rather than the fast track to becoming a partner. Some law firms are permitting those who have made partner to work part time, and compensation reflects the shortened work weeks. For some lawyers, working within the traditional framework is falling short, despite the commitment of some firms to encouraging balance between work and family. This trend has given rise to the Legal Research Network. The Los Angeles-based firm has recruited lawyers with changing priorities, partners on maternity leave, and retired judges. They work from home on projects, avoiding the grind of a major law firm. These lawyers have expertise in specific areas. Since there is no need to pay a team of junior generalists to research each project from scratch, LRN can deliver legal services at half the fees of major firms. Meantime, some leading New York "white shoe" law firms are fading away. Mudge Rose Guthrie Alexander & Ferndon, the firm that once counted among its ranks Richard Nixon and former Attorney General John Mitchell, is now merely a memory. The firm closed its doors in 1995 after 126 years in business. The demise of Mudge Rose was due in part to the firm's loss of partners and clients, as well as its failure to keep pace with a changing business environment.

The lack of balance among members of Congress has prompted the Speaker of the House to establish the Family Quality of Life Advisory Committee. Besides members of Congress, the bipartisan group includes their children and spouses. The Speaker pledged to stick to schedules that would give members more time with their families. This has involved early adjournment on some Fridays and scheduling no votes before 5 pm on some Mondays, creating longer weekends. Also, members are increasingly bringing their children to work and are taking "potty breaks" between votes. Fifteen-hour days persist, but balance has become a Congressional objective. Because priorities are shifting, people are searching for new tools to help them balance work and family.

Rethinking the Corporation

Corporate structures are changing. Dictating policy from headquarters, for example, falls short as companies globalize. Decisions are increasingly made at outposts, rather than at the head office. As companies increasingly operate multiple facilities in different cities and countries, local managers become empowered. They know the local markets and culture, so they decide how to develop solutions that meet demands. Globalization distributes departments, scattering them among several locations. A team leader may work in one city, while the team members work in many other cities or rural areas. Staying in touch requires travel plus the endless e-mail, fax, and phone cycle. Distributed work teams and globalization require new tools and better networks to achieve results.

Yesterday, corporations practiced paternalism. Though prosperity came and went, managers stayed. The mantra was take care of the flock, despite inefficiency. The three-martini lunch prevailed. Then came alcohol awareness and tax law changes. Next came the push for productivity and an increasing hunger for corporate profits. Companies gobbled up competitors, then trimmed the fat. Positions without measurable bottom-line benefits to the corporation dried up, and corporate reengineering teams slashed and burned their way to efficiency. Companies turned to "outsourcing," surrendering activities to independent firms that specialize in everything from cleaning the restrooms to supporting information systems. Diversification was out, and core competency was in. Accounting and management consulting firms are seizing on this trend in marketing their products. Deloitte & Touche, LLP has run national newspaper ads promoting "cosourcing," a blend of outsourcing and collaboration.

As a new era dawns, alliances and partnerships are on a roll. The relationship economy governs profits. Corporations that are thousands of miles apart geographically and zillions of miles apart culturally are joining forces. Each brings a complimentary competency to the table. The potential benefits of these relationships can be huge, but achieving results requires managing relationships. This is tough when professionals must bridge a cultural divide. Traditional relationship management tools such as face-to-face meetings, the phone, and e-mail fall short. Frequent face-to-face meetings zap time and contribute to mounting hotel and airfare bills, while the phone and e-mail are both one dimensional. The relationship economy requires a relationship medium.

Corporate refugees and downsized professionals

The drive for efficiency and higher profits has caused corporations to consolidate departments and positions. Downsizing has forced professionals to leave what they had perceived as the security of their employers. Survivors are squeezed to work harder and faster, and those who reject this environment become corporate refugees. Whether these professionals flee corporations or leave under protest, many must consider new ways of earning a living. The relationship economy applies to these individuals, as well as to corporations. Just as companies form alliances and partner with one another, professionals partner with other individuals and firms. This lone eagle may deliver his or her expertise to several companies, working on projects rather than as part of a process. He or she may form alliances with other lone eagles who have complimentary skills. These virtual work teams form for a specific purpose, and then dissolve.

The trend towards contract work has benefited both individuals and companies. The individual gains balance between work and family, more control over work schedule, and greater choices on where to live and work. Companies can increase profits through lower benefit costs, decreased training dollars and the decreased need for real estate. When AT&T announced its trivestiture and a resulting 40,000 layoffs, the company suggested that people should think of employment differently. "Jobless, but not workless," was the way AT&T officials were quoted as describing the emerging environment. Professionals are increasingly becoming agents, rather than employees. This trend has demanded more effective collaboration and communication tools.

The trend towards contracting, coupled with increased corporate acceptance of telecommuting, is boosting the number of home-based workers. Forty-six million people in the United States worked at home in 1995, according to IDC/LINK Resources. The statistics include self-employed people, corporate telecommuters, and corporate after-hours homeworkers. The after-hours group includes prospective corporate refugees who are getting their feet wet before taking the plunge. So important is the trend away from corporate offices and towards the home office that marketing people have invented a category to describe this marketplace segment: SOHO, which stands for small office/home office. Anne Klein has marketed its Anne Klein II line of casual wear to this segment. The clothing maker's newspaper inserts demonstrate the need for less formal clothing as women work at home. "This is the time of the un-office," proclaims the add, which includes pictures of women working on laptop computers, changing diapers and blending work activities with those at home.

Clogged highways and polluted air are pushing some states to mandate that corporations help reduce road travel. Telecommuting is a major part of that equation for many employers. Though the federal government has reversed its requirement that eleven states meet commute trip reduction levels, some of those states have enacted their own laws. New Jersey's Air Traffic Congestion and Air Pollution Control Act mandates that 3600 work sites reduce the number of commuting cars on the road between 6:30 and 9:30 AM, when the most ozone is created. To comply with the law, employers can choose from a menu of options, including telecommuting.

Beyond government mandates, studies and statistics are convincing increasing numbers of employers that telecommuting increases worker productivity. Many home-based workers can put in time when they are at peak performance, which for some is during the wee hours—and for others may be during typical commuting hours. Equally persuasive are the savings on office space and real estate costs. Without a commute and with blurring boundaries between work and leisure time, home-based workers tend to put in more hours. Even so, many companies stop short of widespread telecommuting programs, because managers still want to see and interact with their team members. Some turn to compromise solutions including suburban telecommuting centers and "hoteling."

Hoteling lets professionals who spend most of their time in the field drop in at a temporary office. They call ahead to make a reservation. Then a concierge books a cubicle, puts a nameplate on the door, sets pictures of family members on the desk and activates voice mail. For many organizations, however, the culture of control prevails, and managers want to keep closer tabs on their teams. For these companies, hoteling—and certainly telecommuting—fail to fit the corporate culture. Companies that are less governed by a culture of control find that telecommuting raises other kinds of problems. Some people who work from home feel isolated, cut off from the camraderie that the traditional workplace offers. The telecommuting experience requires addressing both management concerns and worker isolation. Part of the solution involves implementing richer collabication tools that can unite dispersed teams.

Exit the middleperson

The power of information is squeezing the middleperson. Lower-level people within organizations can gain immediate access to information through intranets or internal webs, and they can bypass the chain-of-command by using e-mail to communicate directly with senior management. Senior executives must no longer rely on middle managers to keep them posted on what's happening at the operations level. E-mail provides a direct link.

While researching this book, I encountered an efficient public relations account executive doing work for a large videoconferencing vendor. The PR account executive was trying to arrange for me to interview any of several senior executives. The administrative staff—essentially middlepeople—insisted all of these executives were "out of town," "unavailable," or "traveling." The aggressive PR person stuck to her objective. She sent an e-mail to all of the senior executives. The only one who answered her query was the CEO. He promptly responded that he would enjoy doing the interview, and the next morning he and I conducted an interview that lasted over an hour and a half. E-mail effectively cut out the gatekeepers and middlepeople.

No longer do organizations need middle managers to filter information for employees. Intranet webs and groupware are creating collective knowledge. The more people know, the more competitive the organization becomes. With fewer middlepeople, corporate hierarchies are flattening. To encourage collaboration and communication, the American Diabetes Association has eliminated job titles. This move has reduced chain-of-command concerns, as staffers solve problems and get things done.

Alcoa has structurally revolutionized the executive suite to emphasize productivity and an open exchange of information instead of hierarchy and bureacracy. The company's senior executives, including CEO Paul O'Neill, work in open cubicles. The executive floor also includes a "communications center" designed to encourage interaction and ad-hoc meetings. The center includes televisions, fax machines, magazines, tables, and chairs. There is also a kitchen where executives can microwave food and sit around tables and talk. This kind of approach is nothing new in Silicon Valley and other technology centers, but it is revolutionary in most traditional corporations.

The decline of the middleperson goes beyond large organizations. In a way, doctors and lawyers are middlepeople. They study for years in school, gain experience in their practices, and deliver that information in the form of treatment or advice to clients. When they run into problems, they consult specialists. Often primary care physicians serve as gatekeepers, determining if and when a patient may see a specialist.

Traditionally, patients relied on doctors for all of their information on symptoms. Now with an Internet connection and a few clicks of a mouse, they can research their symptoms themselves. In a 1995 survey conducted by America Online, 26% of those responding said that AOL's Health and Medical Forum had helped them avoid at least one unnecessary doctor's visit. Fifty-one percent of those responding said the forum had increased their confidence in discussing with their doctors the benefits, risks, and costs of medical procedures.

Internet access and use of on-line services are also impacting law. As people research legal issues on-line, attorneys are knocked off of a pedestal. Doctors and lawyers may have expertise and years of experience, but the mystique of their professions will fade away unless they work harder in providing greater expertise and value to their clients.

The stakes are increasingly too high for doctors and lawyers to work in a vacuum. They need immediate access to information and the ability to share information with colleagues in other cities and countries. This means they need better tools to communicate and collaborate efficiently so that they can provide better services. Also, many patients demand enhanced tools and greater access. They increasingly want to consult directly with specialists, without a middleperson serving as the gatekeeper. They also may wish to form virtual support groups with other people who experience similar symptoms. In many cases, the ability to look a fellow patient in the eye and communicate in real time, regardless of distance, makes a difference.

The Mobile, Global Society

Business globalization has uprooted professionals and their families. Transfers have yanked divorced parents from their children, creating a geographical divide. Court decisions are reinforcing this trend. One decision will likely have a significant impact on divorced couples in California, the US's most populated state. The California Supreme Court decided in a 1996 case that once a judge awards custody, the parent wishing to move bears no burden of establishing that the move is necessary. This means that it is getting harder to keep children and their parents close to one another. The impact of relocation goes beyond the relationship between parents and children. Other family members suffer as well. Increasingly, children see their grandparents only on holidays, and they fill in the gaps between visits by using the telephone, letters, and photographs. This helps maintain relationships, but enriching relationships requires more.

The distributed family problem gets even worse when professionals take jobs in other countries. In such cases, families can stay apart for years. The busy professional who lacks family time finds that his or her children mature quickly. They leave for college, take jobs in other cities or countries, and may never return to live where they grew up. The challenge is to encourage quality family relationships, despite the impact of a mobile and global society. Communication is critical when travel is impossible. One-dimensional tools like the phone, letters, and e-mail help, but quality interaction requires more. If a divorced parent could help a child with homework using a media-rich communication and collaboration medium, both would gain back some of what distance stole. Just as distributed work groups require better tools, fragmented families demand higher impact communication methods that will unite them.

The pervasive, powerful PC

PCs are everywhere. Components have become near commodities, and economies of scale have led to mass production. By the late 1990s, Intel estimates that 100 million PCs will ship worldwide each year. That's more than either television sets or cars. In part, because of home PCs, children watch less television than they used to. Nielsen Media Research reports that television viewing hours among children under eleven dropped 18% between 1984 and 1995. A *New York Times* poll conducted in 1996 showed that 33% of children under 12 spent "a lot or some" time using a personal computer. As the PC becomes pervasive, the role of the computer continues to evolve. It has moved well beyond word processing functions and can now serve as an entertainment and communications center. As the PC becomes a window on the world, users exchange e-mail and participate in chat groups globally. Accessing the World Wide Web lets PC users communicate with companies, research topics of interest, and shop.

In the wired world, anybody can contact anybody else at any time and find out just about anything. People are getting used to communicating with strangers through their computers. On-line communities are growing. People meet on-line, form in-person relationships, and then get married. The President of the United States has advocated Internet access in every school.

Classes are learning from experts on-line, and children are developing electronic pen pals. The PC is driving interaction among people.

The convergence

As the role of the PC evolves, the computer, communications and consumer electronics industries are converging (Figure 1–1). The PC can act as a television, a stereo, and a phone. Multimedia PCs are seducing television viewers with visual stimulation. In fact, the PC/TV has emerged, allowing viewers to flip back and forth between the Internet and TV shows. If users prefer to access the Internet on part of the monitor and watch TV on another part, that is possible also. Many of these systems come with both a wireless keyboard and a remote control, and both devices can control the cursor. People are getting used to interacting with their PCs. The convergence is turning the personal computer into a window on the outside world. Like the telephone, the PC offers 2-way communication. Like the television, the medium delivers video. Add to these capabilities the ability to design graphics, create animation, edit videotape, and capture and manipulate images. The PC has proven it does it all, so people constantly expect their computers to do even more.

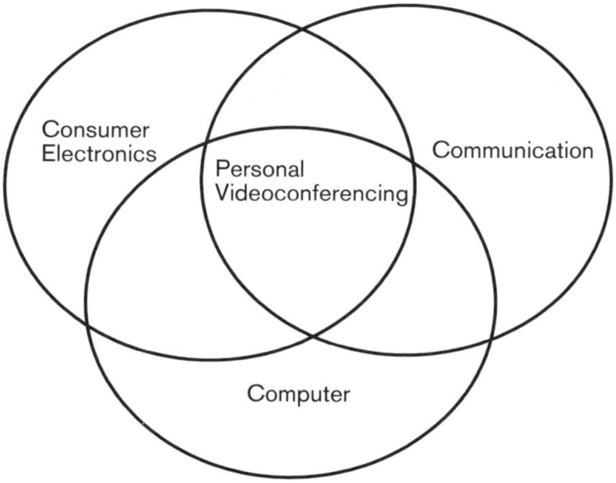

Figure 1–1: The convergence

Meantime, chip companies strive to create a demand for more processing power. The more capabilities users demand that their PCs perform, the more

MIPS—millions of instructions per second—microprocessors must provide. Processing video requires the most MIPS. Chip companies have invested heavily in refining PC-based video technologies to increase the demand for their microprocessors. Scores of other companies have invested heavily in video technology, believing that people will want to communicate visually through their computers. For these companies, the stakes are high. Mass market acceptance of PC-based video telephony will drive profits. The convergence is pushing the PC to become an increasingly rich communication medium.

Whatever happened to the paperless office?

Part of the promise of the PC revolution was the paperless office. People are still waiting. According to *Windows Magazine*, American business produces about 90 billion documents a year. Then business reproduces these documents to generate about a trillion copies. The advent of network printing is boosting the efficiency of reproduction, and the paper keeps piling up. While the PC allows users to create and store electronic documents, distributing those documents has required hard copies. The cycle of copying, printing, faxing, and overnight mail persists. As people dig their way through the piles on their desks, they demand more efficient distribution of documents. The quest for the paperless office continues as companies face mounting storage costs. Paper-filled file cabinets take up precious real estate, and spending time filing decreases efficiency. With the rise of the home office, storage also becomes an issue. In many telecommuting environments, a spare bedroom has been converted into an office. Because space is tight, the paper has to go. People demand tools that allow them to share and collaborate on documents electronically and in real-time, regardless of distance. Enrich such tools with real-time video communication, and a media-rich virtual workspace emerges. This cuts down copying, printing, faxing and overnight mail, and brings us one step closer to the paperless office.

Urban refugees and the rise of rural living

The impact of technology has historically moved people from place to place. The Industrial Revolution pulled people off the farm and into the factory. As the rural exodus continued and agribusiness grew, the family farm suffered. More people left rural areas to seek work in cities. Now, however, the pendulum is swinging the other way as we move into what Nicholas Negroponte has termed the *post-information age*. In this age, information is customized and distributed to individuals regardless of time and place. As technology links people globally and the self-employment rate rises, people are returning to rural areas. The most rapidly growing states in the 1990s have been the more rural ones. Nevada, Idaho, Arizona, Colorado, Utah, Hawaii, Washington, New Mexico, Georgia, and Oregon are the US Census Bureau's top 10 population growth states. Since 1990, personal income in nonmetropolitan areas has been growing faster than in metropolitan areas, according to the Center for the New West. Urban refugees are increasingly taking root in rural areas, where they find lower housing costs, less pollution, less crime, and a nicer setting. Taxes and insurance are also lower in rural areas.

With the rise of home-based consultants and contractors, it increasingly matters less where the home is located. Since the PC is the centerpiece of most work, a professional can just as easily use that computer from a house in the mountains as from a downtown office. With the growth of the Internet, it is easier for geographically dispersed project teams to stay in touch. However, maintaining effective working relationships requires more than e-mail, faxes, and the phone. If the objective is to eliminate the impact of distance while providing the freedom to live and work from anywhere, rural professionals require richer tools.

Urgency and the Web generation

Children of the 1950s who grew up watching *I Love Lucy* and calling their friends on rotary dial phones entered a working world in which secretaries typed letters that took days to deliver. The MTV generation, which grew up in the early 1980s, joined a working world that demanded more. They wrote their own letters on personal computers and then faxed them to their destinations. The pace was picking up. The Web generation, which came of age in the mid 1990s, enters an emerging work world in which information travels at lightning speed. The fax is a relic. E-mail is in. This generation does homework on powerful PCs while checking out the World Wide Web. Immediate information and results seem natural. So does leveraging collective knowledge through the Internet and corporate intranets.

Visiting an internal Web site with a few mouse clicks makes more sense to the Web generation than placing a call to an internal specialist and waiting for a call back. Since the Webites grew up playing interactive video games at home, interacting with a PC becomes a breeze. After participating in on-line chat groups, adding an inexpensive camera to a computer seems like a logical next step. Real-time video communication is more of an evolution than a revolution.

Backdrop of the Video Age

Every generation that has grown up since the 1950s is part of the video age. This age has given rise to visual immediacy. In this age, television has shaped the world's social, political and economic climate. The video age has evolved from a store-and-forward environment to a real-time bombardment of information and images. In the early days of television news, newscasts included day-old film. Then came advances in satellite and microwave technology, and live delivery became the standard.

Now a swelling television universe is narrowcasting shows to audiences with special tastes. One of those channels is C-SPAN, which broadcasts debate on the floor of the House of Representatives, as well as committee hearings and other government-oriented programming. People are getting used to looking in on their members of Congress whenever they choose. The Gulf War, the world's first 24-hour television war, sensitized viewers to video immediacy. Now people demand the ability to watch a missile attack in real-time, rather than as file tape on a news broadcast.

The video age has grown increasingly personal. Since camcorders can be bought for the price of a mid-range TV, people are putting their own video on their television screens. Videos of summer vacations and holiday gatherings can be played on the VCR and viewed in the living room. In effect, everybody can be on TV. Not only are people are getting used to seeing themselves on camera, but also they are getting used to hearing their own voices. As recently as the 1970s, telephone answering machines were in a handful of homes. The sound of one's voice played back often provoked giggles, blushes, and even denials that the recording sounded anything like them. Much has changed. Today voice mail is a standard business tool, and professionals are comfortable leaving voice messages for individuals they have never before spoken with or met.

Amateur videographers are harnessing the power of the visual medium. An amateur videotape of Los Angeles police officers beating motorist Rodney King tarnished the image of an entire police department. Television stations encourage amateur videographers to hunt for news. When the amateurs find news and shoot it, the stations air the tape. At almost every parade, rally or other event, some amateur videographer is capturing the action.

Surveillance cameras are everywhere. George Orwell's vision of a society controlled through video as described in the book *1984* has arrived in a way. The difference is that we stop short of caring. Cameras watch us in banks, in stores, in malls, in airports, and in lobbies. Police departments are even installing surveillance cameras on streets. Redwood City, California police use video cameras downtown so they can listen for gunfire and see who fires the shots. Baltimore police use video to monitor every street in a 16-block area, 24-hours a day. A video system watches and records everything that happens on those streets. Roving security cameras also play a role. Dana Hills High School in Dana Hills, California assigns camera-carrying supervisors to videotape the cafeteria. The idea is to discourage students from breaking rules and to present proof when they step out of line. On increasing numbers of picket lines, both labor and management representatives videotape one another. Video has saturated society.

Personal videoconferencing defined

Against the backdrop of the video age emerges personal videoconferencing. Personal videoconferencing includes desktop, laptop, palmtop, TV set-based videoconferencing, and real-time video kiosks. These are primarily personal communication devices. Unlike more costly group videoconferencing systems that corporations typically deploy in conference rooms, personal videoconferencing serves primarily one person in his or her office, at home or on the road. Although there are times that two or three people may squeeze into a frame, the technology is designed for one. TV set-based videoconferencing is perhaps an exception, because several people can participate from a living-room couch.

Personal videoconferencing is often referred to as simply *desktop videoconferencing*. However, this description is too narrow given the development of increasingly smaller portable computers that are by no means limited to the desktop. The term *personal videoconferencing* more accurately reflects anytime, anyplace communication and collaboration. Throughout this book, however, *desktop videoconferencing* and the broader term *personal videoconferencing* are at times used interchangeably.

The promise of personal videoconferencing

We have discussed many social and economic trends. Now we will address how personal videoconferencing impacts those trends. Personal videoconferencing permits people to communicate through video face-to-face while simultaneously sharing documents, electronic whiteboards, and applications. Conferencing need not include video. In some cases, the ability to share documents, applications, and whiteboards in real time with audio is enough. Despite the limitations of the technology that this book discusses, the world is increasingly ready for personal videoconferencing. Social and economic trends have played a major role in preparing personal videoconferencing users for the cultural shift that is inevitable when applying the technology. The video age has stoked the coals. The impact of introducing personal videoconferencing to somebody's desktop or other personal space is significant. However, the prevalence of video has made the communication transition more of a shift than a shock. As recently as the 1960s and 1970s, fear of appearing on camera helped stunt the market growth of AT&T's Picturephone. Since then, the world has changed. The video age has made cameras inescapable. Like it or not, people have grown accustomed to the electronic eye.

Personal videoconferencing promises to give professionals more time. The technology helps prevent problems and work from piling up. Sharing documents and meeting through video face-to-face lets team members make decisions and solve problems on the spot. Because each participant has all of his or her files and work available on a PC, there is less of a need to delay decisions. Follow-up work never disappears, but it does diminish. The endless cycle of e-mail, voice mail, overnight mail, and faxes declines.

The technology also offers an opportunity to help balance family and work life. This is a benefit both to the individual and the corporation. The individual can live anywhere and work from home, a telecommuting center, a satellite office, shared workspace, or from anywhere that compliments a chosen lifestyle. Without time spent commuting and without having to show up at a company office, parents can more easily attend a child's soccer or little league game or help with homework. Meantime, personal videoconferencing lets these individuals collaborate with other work team members through a powerful medium that decreases the impact of distance.

Companies can remain competitive by using personal videoconferencing to attract and keep the best professionals regardless of location. Personal videoconferencing expands the hiring pool by linking companies with workers globally. No longer is it necessary for employees to be located near a company office to collaborate effectively with colleagues. Also a benefit to companies is that the burn-out syndrome decreases as professionals gain the flexibility to work from whatever location they choose. Other benefits to companies, professionals, and society include clearing the highways, reducing air pollution, reducing the need for corporate real estate, and saving employees the time and expense of commuting. Also, corporate refugees who work from home as contractors can join virtual work teams more effectively. They can complete projects faster by sharing virtual workspaces and communicating more closely through personal videoconferencing.

Managing the distributed workforce

Personal Conferencing provides an essential tool for managing the decentralized corporation. Managers can now visit four cities in a morning from the comfort of their offices or cubicles. All of the files, notes and information an electronic meeting may require is at the manager's fingertips. As downsizing forces out middlepeople, corporate leaders can be briefed instantly by conferencing with operations people. Personal videoconferencing gives the senior manager unfiltered access to the people doing the work, regardless of location. As more work is outsourced to contractors, personal videoconferencing unites internal and external members of teams. This requires managing relationships. A corporation can stay close to its law firm, marketing firm, public relations firm, accounting firm, and consultants through real-time communication and collaboration. An organization can also use the technology to develop more effective joint ventures. Personal videoconferencing provides the relationship medium for a relationship economy.

Personal videoconferencing offers perhaps the best opportunity yet to push paper out of offices. Since the technology allows people to collaborate on documents and then save the finished product, there is less need to exchange paper. This reduces desktop clutter and the time and money spent printing, faxing, and mailing. The reduction of paper contributes to the increased efficiency that globalization and decentralization require.

Enriching lives

The technology reduces the distance between separated families. Divorced parents in other cities can see and hear their children talk. They can help their kids with homework and other projects. Personal videoconferencing can reduce the pain of separation. Professionals who leave their homelands to gain career opportunities can stay closer to their parents than they can on the telephone. Personal videoconferencing enhances the one-dimensional interaction that the phone and e-mail offer. The technology delivers a richer medium that relationships require.

Personal videoconferencing makes rural living more viable. The PC has seduced urban refugees with the promise of "any time, any place" communication. However, video and data conferencing capability allow the PC to deliver what it promises. The technology lets professionals participate in virtual work teams and develop closer relationships with clients. They can do this while breathing clean air, avoiding high crime rates, paying less to live, and enjoying beautiful surroundings. The technology lets people make more choices. They can choose where they want to live, which hours they want to work, and increasingly the people with whom they work. More choices empower people.

Before we get Carried Away

Personal videoconferencing is by no means a panacea. In many cases, there is still no substitute for the face-to-face meeting. Shaking a colleague's hand and enjoying lunch with a business associate often accomplish more than videoconferencing can. However, the technology can successfully fill in the gaps between face-to-face encounters. In many cases, in-person meetings may be impossible or impractical because of cost and time restraints. In these situations, personal videoconferencing may provide richer interaction than the phone or e-mail.

Personal videoconferencing stops short of replacing other technologies. E-mail, fax, the phone, and voice mail are all important to doing business. Personal videoconferencing compliments these technologies with another communication and collaboration option. This option does wonders in some situations, but can also become overkill in many instances. Establishing a video link to verify somebody's mailing address, for example, is less efficient than sending an e-mail message. Scheduling a meeting can be done at least as efficiently on a voice call as on a video call. Personal videoconferencing is simply one option as people select which medium fits the situation.

It is important to think of personal videoconferencing as part of a palette of emerging communication and collaboration tools. These tools include store-and-forward video, such as video mail, and corporate intranets or internal Webs. Personal videoconferencing can never exist in a vacuum. Some situations may require the impact of video without the real-time component, and therefore video mail works better. An example of this would be a brief project status update. Video mail adds a video and voice component to e-mail, and therefore enriches store-and-forward communication. In many instances, intranets and groupware may be more appropriate than personal videoconferencing. These technologies let people share knowledge and collaborate without a real-time component. Each collaborator can contribute on his or her schedule. If a project manager wants to research his or her company's media campaigns, for example, visiting intranet web sites to read an archive of news releases may be far more efficient than establishing several personal videoconferences with the marketing or corporate communications department.

The rise of collabication

Collaboration + Communication
= *Collabication*

The word *collabication* is a contraction of *collaboration* and *communication*. Collabication describes the dual nature of many media-rich tools, including personal videoconferencing. The personal videoconferencing industry is now embracing communication and collaboration. The industry is recognizing the shift in work patterns that the technology encourages. BCR Enterprises has launched *Virtual Workgroups*, a magazine devoted to electronic collaboration. Applied Business Telecommunications has started an annual Collaboration Summit, which precedes its DeskCon conference. BCR Enterprises now includes keynotes and break-out sessions with titles like "Virtual Workgroup Dynamics: The Theories and Practice" in its DVC Conference & Exhibition schedule. Besides focusing on communication and collaboration, the industry is also shifting attention toward applications. Initially, the industry refrain was that users would determine applications. That notion has changed, and the industry is now paying more attention to the ways that professionals can apply desktop videoconferencing to boost productivity.

As the personal videoconferencing industry matures, companies are investing in trade shows and maximizing attendance. BCR Enterprises, for example, bought the DVC Conference & Exhibition in late 1995. The company used its marketing muscle to double attendance the next year. The show was born in 1994 when Bill Weber, a trade show organizer and California political activist, and his colleague Steve Ohr were running another trade show in Taipei, Taiwan. During a San Francisco television talk show in the late 1970s, Weber had advocated replacing every telephone with a video phone to reduce travel and ease the energy crisis. Over lunch in Taipei some fifteen years later, Weber and Ohr discussed growing industries that might produce successful shows. DVC emerged as their number one pick.

As the DVC conference was taking shape, the producers of the TeleCon exhibition and conference were also moving towards the desktop. TeleCon, which focused on teleconferencing and room videoconferencing, began adding desktop videoconferencing exhibits in the early 1990s. Desktop videoconferencing had become so important by the Fall of 1996 that the theme for TeleCon XVI in Anaheim, California was "Connecting to the Desktop." The same year, the International Teleconferencing Association (ITCA) was promoting *telecollaborative communications* as the theme of its exhibition in Washington, DC. TeleCon's producers, Applied Business Telecommunications, had also launched DeskCon in 1994. DeskCon focused strictly on desktop videoconferencing.

Despite an expanding personal videoconferencing industry and social trends that encourage use of the technology, barriers to universal deployment persist. First world nations like the US are less developed technologically than they may seem. One in twenty US households has no telephone, according to the US Census Bureau. The figures mirror economic status and ethnicity. One in five Native American households is without phone service. More than half of US households have no PC. Linking the world through desktop video is many years away. Meantime, the impact of personal videoconferencing may widen the gap between the technology haves and have-nots. Gaining the ability to communicate and collaborate with anybody, anywhere in real time through video becomes a powerful edge. The haves will sustain the ability to earn a living while maintaining closer relationships with their families. The have-nots increasingly will find that they are cut-off from opportunities.

Personal videoconferencing is changing how we work and live. Popular culture has been promising real-time video communication for decades. *The Jetsons* and *Star Trek* on television and the film *2001 Space Odyssey* raised our expectations. Video phones always seemed nifty in the movies. The power of the PC partnered with the impact of personal videoconferencing is producing a more complex environment than the movies portrayed. Though a debate persists about the need for real-time video, ultimately that conflict will fade away. Video is here to stay in almost every way. Personal videoconferencing is no exception. It is worth considering, however, what the technology will give us and what it will take from us. In the broadest sense, what matters most is whether personal videoconferencing furthers democracy or damages it. The technology probably does both. We lose some privacy and gain some freedom. On the Bill of Rights scorecard, that means personal videoconferencing is a wash.

Personal videoconferencing gives us time. That time is ours to spend on achieving more at work or with our families. However, the technology delivers that payoff only if we understand the limits and the potential of personal videoconferencing. We can solve problems through real-time video communication and collaboration, but only if we master the medium. Success requires determination, creativity, and humor.

2

Collaborating Through Conferencing

With or Without Video

Television news professionals call certain kinds of stories "Hey Martha" stories. A Hey Martha is the two-headed chicken that dances, or the high-diving champion who is a dog. These stories are called Hey Marthas, because they prompt the viewer to call out to his wife, "Hey Martha, come here and look at what they're showing on the news." A Hey Martha story may fall short of delivering the most important news of the day, but the report is certainly the most memorable.

Likewise, video can be considered the Hey Martha or the Gee Whiz feature of desktop conferencing. Being able to communicate with somebody face-to-face through a computer screen makes some jaws drop. For some professionals, however, video may deliver more expressions of "wow" than productivity. Some users of desktop conferencing regard the ability to see a coworker as less essential than the ability to collaborate through document conferencing, whiteboarding, and application sharing. Video in this use model is the sizzle, but not the steak. If video is used at all, it is only to wave hello and goodbye. According to Barry Fishman, who runs the CoVis Project at Northwestern University, "In two thirds of instances that we want to use conferencing, video is irrelevant. Audio is important to us. Screen sharing is important to us."

Frank Casanova, Director of the Apple Computer Advanced Technology Group Exploratory Products Laboratory, observes that there is a peculiar paradox when it comes to the value of video for personal videoconferencing. The paradox is that there was little interest in desktop videoconferencing until reasonable bandwidth became more available and until compression techniques were refined. However, the bandwidth and capability to conduct screen-to-screen, real-time collaboration with audio had been available for many years before personal videoconferencing. But, says Casanova, "If you ask people which of the three capabilities of videoconferencing they'd give up first, video, audio, or collaboration windows, the answer is almost always video." Ken Pickar, Senior Vice President of Engineering and Technology for Allied Signal Aerospace, agrees. "People get the most excited when they share a common space," explains Pickar. "What is most valuable is when they're both doodling on a whiteboard that could contain a PowerPoint or Excel program, some other common software, or an engineering drawing."

Ellen Grace Henson, Ambassador of Visual Communications for Silicon Graphics, agrees that real-time video usually takes a back seat to screen-to-screen collaboration. "In actual usage, except for very specific requirements, the perceived need for interactive, real-time video drops off quickly," Henson insists. Part of the reason, according to Henson, is that video demands more CPU processing power and network bandwidth than other conferencing capabilities. Henson also believes, however, that as the quality of video increases and the cost of processing and transmission goes down, the value of video increases.

Despite the emphasis on real-time collaboration for many applications, there is also a convincing argument that effective collaboration requires face-to-face interaction. When we are working closely with somebody, it often becomes necessary to see their facial expressions. Facial expressions tell us, for example, whether a colleague understands or agrees with us. Sometimes organizations approach personal videoconferencing believing the video is unnecessary, but professionals ultimately embrace face-to-face communication. "In consulting, the first reaction is almost always that we really don't need video," says Bob Leader of SAP Software. "But almost 100% of the time after they've had a chance to use it, they understand the video. Being able to see facial expressions, body language, acceptance, things you could see only if you were standing in front of them makes a real difference."

Tom Hall, a contractor who manages videoconferencing for Hughes Aircraft, agrees that video makes a difference. "The videoconferencing part of it is as important as the file sharing," says Hall. "Our teams are so far apart that the ability for them to see each other is important. Despite the limitations of the technology, you see enough of the body language that it brings the teams together," according to Hall.

In an Op-ed column in the January 15, 1996 *New York Times*, writer Rose Moss discusses the limitations of non-video collaborative technology. Her point is that hallway conversations and other casual encounters in physical settings are important to productivity and happiness. "We are gregarious animals. We want to see what other people look like when we talk to them," writes Moss. "Sometimes technology gives clues: we can sometimes tell when someone we're talking to on the phone is smiling. But in hallways we pick up nuances like eye contact, closeness, or withdrawal." Some of these attributes of face-to-face communication are apparent on video. They help make the argument that video is of value to desktop conferencing.

Some personal videoconferencing users believe that there is a danger in using collaborative functions such as document conferencing as a way to avoid real-time video communication. Christine Traut, Application Strategies Manager for Andersen Worldwide, believes screen-to-screen collaboration can produce results, if users approach conferencing properly. However, "Some people who are not very social will tend to hide behind collaboration," according to Traut.

Toni Alonso, Video Services Manager for Pfizer, believes video is critical for all users, but that collaborative functions are less useful to senior management. "Desktop videoconferencing is more for the worker bee and not for the executive. The executive will have it there for status and talking heads, not collaborative features," Alonso insists.

In a paper entitled "Telepresence: Integrating Shared Task and Person Spaces," William A. S. Buxton of the University of Toronto insists that graceful transitions are important between video face-to-face encounters and nuts-and-bolts collaboration. Buxton also points out that the application determines whether video or collaborative functions will dominate the desktop videoconference. For example, in negotiating, the activity is mainly in the shared space of the participants themselves, where we are "reading each other, for information about trust and confidence," Buxton writes. However, in preparing a budget using an electronic spreadsheet, "the visual channel is dominated by the task space." Buxton's paper can be found on the Web at

`http://www.dgp.toronto.edu/OTP/papers/bill.buxton`

The Andersen Worldwide Study

A 1994 comprehensive study by Susan E. Squires and Thomas O. Schrader of Andersen Worldwide compared the value of non-video desktop conferencing with desktop videoconferencing. Researchers used statistical sampling techniques to select 54 participants from a pool of 1200. They conducted the study at Andersen Worldwide's Professional Development Center in St. Charles, Illinois. Half of the participants used Intel ProShare with video, and the other half used ProShare without video. The participants were unaware that there were two groups. The study revealed that 75% of those in the video group and 65% of those in the non-video group said they would prefer video. However, only 33% of the video group reported that the ability to see the other person enhanced communication.

Christine Traut of Andersen Worldwide believes the video group would have been more confident in the technology as a communication enhancement if the ProShare systems had been configured differently. Traut says the video participants were able to view both the remote party and themselves in separate windows. The ability to see oneself, Traut believes, can be distracting because users become either self-conscious or fascinated with themselves. Also, both the local and remote video windows were set at "Always on Top," meaning the video can occupy a more prominent screen position than collaborative features.

The study also addressed the impact of the technology on working patterns. When asked if desktop conferencing would encourage working with colleagues, non-video users were more likely to answer "yes" while video users were more likely to respond "not sure." The perceived benefits of the technology also varied between the two groups. According to a report on the study, "Video users were more likely to cite relationship building and less likely to note improved productivity as a benefit. Non-video users, on the other hand, cited improved productivity and access to expertise as benefits four times more often than did video users." However, 72% of all participants responded that the technology encouraged colleagues to work together more often. 84% of all participants indicated that the technology improved the quality of communication between colleagues.

Participants represented all four personnel classifications within the firm: partners, managers, seniors, and staff. An interesting result of the study was that seniors were more likely than the others to indicate that they preferred the non-video conferencing package. Susan Squires, the Andersen evaluation consultant and anthropologist, says this result is probably tied to the role seniors play within Andersen. She says seniors do Andersen's detailed work and supervise others who carry out the day-to-day implementation of projects. The position of seniors in the Andersen hierarchy may be comparable to floor supervisors in a manufacturing plant or staff sergeants in the army. "Seniors probably don't need a face-to-face with anyone to negotiate anything," Squires explains. "They're more concerned with work plans and assigning tasks."

Managers and partners, however, focus on selling and negotiating. They constantly must communicate externally and internally. Therefore, Squires believes, their role within the firm explains why they were more likely than seniors to favor video. The staff included mostly recent college graduates in their 20s. "They played with the video and thought it was a fabulous toy. But they didn't think of their job responsibilities when they used it," according to Squires.

The study's interviews and other soft data indicated that participants across-the-board were likely to minimize video windows during nuts-and-bolts collaboration. Also, seniors and managers were the most successful at using the collaboration software, primarily because their PC experience was greater than that of partners or staff.

The University of Michigan Study

Researchers at the University of Michigan's Collaboratory for Research on Electronic Work (CREW) have also investigated the value of video. Judith S. Olson, Gary M. Olson, and David K. Meader detail one study in a paper entitled "What Mix of Video and Audio is Useful for Remote Real-time Work?" AT&T, Ameritech and the National Science Foundation sponsored the project. During the study, 36 groups of 3 professionals spent an hour and a half designing an Automated Post Office. All of the groups used ShrEdit, a collaborative text-editing tool. Half the groups used video and audio to communicate, while the other half used only audio.

Analysis of questionnaires showed that without a video connection, the quality of the discussion was inferior. The study also found that collaborating using high-quality video was as good as a face-to-face encounter. However, the study found that remote work without video falls short compared with a face-to-face session. Also, collaborators in the study perceived that video added value. The researchers also discovered that remote workers collaborating without video appreciated the experience less. According to the paper, "They were less able to tell how their other group members were reacting to things said." The paper concluded that, "Adding video to remote work has some value in terms of the work accomplished by the groups, and has a clearer effect on the satisfaction of the group members." Additional information can be found on the Web at

`http://www.crew.umich.edu`

The Sun Microsystems Laboratories Study

In 1992, Sun Microsystems Laboratories evaluated the importance of video to desktop conferencing during a fourteen-week study. Ellen Isaacs and John C. Tang published the results in a paper entitled "Why Do Users Like Video? Studies of Multimedia-Supported Collaboration." According to the paper, the study deployed a desktop conferencing prototype (DCP) that linked collaborators in Billerica, Massachusetts with others in two buildings in Mountain View, California. Previously, the software development group had worked together in neighboring cubicles in Billerica. Researchers set the default frame rate for the study to 5 frames per second, and there was only one instance out of 72 that the collaborators chose to increase the rate to 10 frames per second.

First researchers studied the interactions of the collaborators without the use of DCP. Next, the researchers introduced the DCP to the work environment. In the third stage, the researchers removed the video from the DCP and studied the impact on the collaborators.

The study indicated that without video capability, use of desktop conferencing dropped off. According to the Isaacs and Tang paper, "Interviews with the team indicated that they strongly liked the video because they could see each others' reactions, monitor if they were being understood, and engage in more social, personal contact through video." The study also showed that video was particularly valuable in understanding pauses. If a collaborator looked up at the ceiling during a pause, it was clear that the person was considering how to respond. Leaning forward indicated that a collaborator had failed to hear what the remote collaborator had said. In contrast, without video a pause tended to confuse a collaborator.

The Sun study also showed that the average number of e-mail messages per day dropped significantly when researchers implemented the DCP. When researchers removed the video from the DCP, the average number of e-mail messages per day nearly doubled. Interviews with the collaborators indicated that they sometimes chose to answer an e-mail with a desktop videoconference. According to the Isaacs and Tang paper, "One member said that he sometimes started composing a reply e-mail message, but then realized that he could respond with a desktop conference instead and discarded the unfinished e-mail reply." Additional information on Sun Microsystems Laboratories can be found on the Web at

`http://www.sunlabs.com`

To See or Not to See: The Big Debate

As the Japanese telecommunications giant NTT moved toward video telephone service in the early 1970s, some NTT executives doubted the value of video. Masao Miyake, the managing director for construction and installation, according to the November 22, 1971 issue of *Electronics*, believed that "Video phones will be used more to transmit drawings, documents, and pictures of products than for face-to-face conversation." This viewpoint may be partially rooted in culture in that the Japanese place a premium on face-to-face meetings, and they have been slower in warming up to all forms of videoconferencing.

As Intel formed its Personal Conferencing Division in the early 1990s, the company's executives debated the value of video in personal conferencing. Although Intel ultimately decided to move forward with a videoconferencing product, many executives felt document conferencing and application sharing along with audio conferencing were the killer features. People who wished to collaborate through their computers, some Intel people believed, had little desire to see each other. Besides, group systems already provided videoconferencing solutions that provided better video.

Ultimately, the video believers prevailed and Intel delivered the ProShare Video System. However, the company also offers non-video versions of ProShare for those who simply require document conferencing, whiteboarding, and application sharing capability. Other companies, such as DataBeam, also provide non-video conferencing software solutions. In fact, DataBeam delivered to market in mid 1995 the first multipoint document conferencing product based on the T.120 standard. The product called *FarSite* supports multipoint conferencing among users in different network environments, including point-to-point modems, local area networks (LAN) and bridging services. DataBeam has made deals with VIVO Software, Microsoft, and others to bundle FarSite into other products. Desktop conferencing without video is often categorized as data conferencing. Data conferencing is the simultaneous transmission of voice and data from personal computers. This can be achieved over Plain Old Telephone Service (POTS) or higher bandwidth connections such as Integrated Services Digital Network (ISDN).

Collaborative Meeting Tools

Desktop conferencing with or without video lets collaborators hold virtual work sessions and meetings. These meetings can be desk-to-desk, floor-to-floor, building-to-building, city-to-city, country-to-country, and even space to Earth through the use of satellite technology. Desktop conferencing software includes virtual meeting and collaborative tools. These tools replace—and in many cases enhance—aspects of in-person meetings and post-meeting follow-up.

Application and file sharing

Application sharing allows two or more desktop videoconferencing users to collaborate on PowerPoint presentations, spreadsheets, graphic design programs, and other software in real time. The application runs on only one computer, but appears to run on all the PCs involved in the session. All the participants can use keyboard and mouse controls in sharing the application.

Document conferencing

Document conferencing lets two or more desktop videoconferencing users simultaneously write and edit a legal brief, X-ray, news release, annual report, or any other document. This is similar to distributing a document at a meeting and letting each person review and mark up their own copy. Usually document conferencing is achieved when one collaborator cuts and pastes the document from an application onto the shared whiteboard.

Whiteboarding

Whiteboarding lets desktop videoconferencing users create a shared workspace similar to a white board on the wall of a meeting room. Collaborators can use electronic highlighters, pens, and other markers as visual aids to the virtual meeting. As one collaborator highlights a portion of text, for example, the same highlighted image appears on the other person's computer screen. Xerox has brought whiteboarding to group conferencing through its LiveBoard product. LiveBoard's 67-inch screen lets participants share a workspace using infrared pens. Desktop PCs running MeetingBoard software can connect with LiveBoard.

Turning the Video On and Off

Northrop Grumman uses desktop videoconferencing to link design engineers in New York with hands-on maintenance professionals in Florida. According to Fred Campo who runs the technology integration lab for Northrop Grumman, the two groups will approach a collaborative session by arranging a desktop videoconference by phone or through a scheduling system. The teams will begin their collaborative session with real-time, interactive video to discuss the design problem. When everyone understands the problem, the collaborators turn off the video. They then play back stored video of the wiring harness or other problem part. The engineer will pause the video, put it in a white board and circle problem areas. Then both teams will share a computer aided design (CAD) application to make sure they have carried out the plans properly. After the nuts and bolts of collaboration, the teams turn the video back on. "We close the session with real-time, talking-head video and plan our next move," says Campo.

What is Collaborating?

The Random House Dictionary of the English Language defines *collaborate* as "to work, one with another; cooperate, as on a literary work." The Oxford American Dictionary defines *collaborate* as "to work in partnership." Desktop conferencing requires that we fine tune these definitions. Traditionally people have viewed collaboration as a vague concept of working together, and the word *collaborate* undoubtedly means different things to different people. To some, *collaborate* might mean getting verbal or written input. To others, *collaborate* might mean sharing expenses or trade secrets to produce a product. Still to others, *collaborate* may mean joining with others to solve problems or achieve specific objectives. Michael Schrage, author of *No More Teams! Mastering the Dynamics of Creative Collaboration*, says collaboration is the process of shared creation. He says the value comes from the interaction, rather than from the individuals. Schrage says better communication and teamwork have little to do with collaboration. Desktop conferencing makes collaborating more tangible, because the technology provides tools to accomplish objectives. We can define *collaborate* as "to share virtual workspace."

Learning to collaborate

The new definition of *collaborate* intensifies the meaning of the word. Previously, we could assume people knew how to collaborate, because the concept of "working together" was sufficiently vague. People could work together in whatever way worked for them. Companies could promote collaboration as a positive objective, like productivity or creativity, and employees could meet that objective in many different ways. Because of desktop conferencing, collaboration now requires specific skills. Besides the mechanics of learning document conferencing and application sharing, collaboration requires behavioral changes or adjustments in the way in which we relate to one another. Making changes on a document and faxing the revisions to somebody, waiting for their revisions, and then viewing the latest version requires far fewer human relations skills than making changes together in real time.

The intensity of real-time collaboration raises such issues as how we react when somebody changes our work on our own computer screen and whether it works if we both make changes to a document simultaneously. Should one person go first and then pass the baton? Do we compete for the upper hand in laying out a page or marking up an X-ray? Companies and individuals are unable to escape dealing with these issues. The human factors can make the difference between boosting productivity and boosting friction between coworkers. Guidelines are evolving that govern successful relationships in the virtual workspace. Successful and productive relationships lead to mastering the art of collaboration. People who master collaboration through desktop conferencing could be called power collaborators.

The Collabicators

Collaborators that use video as well as application sharing and document conferencing could be called *collabicators.* The collabicators emerged from the ranks of early desktop conferencing adopters. Early users realized the new medium differed dramatically from other kinds of collaboration. *Collabication* represents the merged skills that the dual medium requires. The law firm of Arnold, White & Durkee was one early user that quickly learned to collabicate. This Houston-based firm leapt forward with desktop conferencing, in part because the firm represented Intel in intellectual property cases. The firm implemented both ProShare video systems and non-video ProShare versions. The ability to share legal briefs with clients screen-to-screen transformed the firm's practice. No longer was the endless cycle of overnight mail, faxes, phone calls, and meetings necessary. The client and the lawyer could work on briefs together. So powerful was this application that a senior partner with minimal interest in technology for the first time began using a personal computer.

The shift

The collabicators discovered that desktop conferencing combined with intranets, the Internet, and other emerging information technologies helps create a new communication standard. The technology provides additional access, and therefore eases hierarchies. As people of many levels within an organization collaborate from their desktops, position becomes less relevant and productivity becomes more important. When project team members work together in person, somebody often sits at the head of the table. Usually, that person is either in charge or is perceived to be the head person, whose opinions count the most. When an employee works with his or her boss, the boss often sits behind a desk in a larger chair. This amplifies the boss's position and tends to stifle differing views.

Collabicating through desktop conferencing, however, means nobody sits at the foot of somebody else's desk. Aside from conference control features, there is no head chair. The collabicators work together using the same tools to complete a project efficiently. The focus is on productivity, rather than on pulling rank. Of course, there are limits to this paradigm, because desktop conferencing is sparking evolution—rather than revolution—in collaborative work patterns. The boss's opinion still may hold more weight. However, without the trappings of position, the boss may become more receptive to differing views. Also desktop conferencing encourages simultaneous input, rather than second-guessing and follow-up criticism. Therefore all collaborators, senior as well as junior people, have a stake in the document, product, or project that comes out of a collaborative session.

Professionals who insist on looking out for number one at the expense of the team may see their fortunes decline, because of the paradigm shift that technology reinforces. "We have all kinds of problems where people don't like to collaborate," says Fred Campo who runs the technology integration lab for Northrop Grumman. "They're used to being superstars. And in a collaborative environment, there are no superstars." The superstars of the millennium may be the power collaborators. Says Bill Muller, Visual Communications Manager for Ernst & Young LLP, "As we evolve from individual-oriented to team-oriented organizations, that's going to drive the use of collaborative-oriented tools, desktop videoconferencing being one of them."

Pete Griffin, Corporate Technical Consultant of Tandy Corporation, believes desktop videoconferencing can prompt a shift in the way corporate users view senior managers. When you enter the CEO's office, according to Griffin, there is an atmosphere that indicates that the person occupying the office is the boss. "When you're talking to the chairman on video, you don't have the environmental reinforcement that he's in charge," says Griffin. "Desktop videoconferencing equalizes people more quickly."

Griffin also believes that implementing the technology can change the corporate culture from a regimented one to one that includes more give and take. However, Griffin doubts the technology will change militaristic managers, and his view is that those managers are less likely to use desktop videoconferencing. "The person who has been successful operating by giving orders and not looking for feedback doesn't need this," explains Griffin. "The person who is leading by example and wants input does need desktop videoconferencing."

The move towards collabication is a major cultural shift—in corporations, in schools and in society. Schools and parents have conditioned generations that written work should be the author's alone. "In class they gave you a bad grade for collaborating. They called it cheating," says Sarkis Zartarian of Applied Communication Concepts. Teachers claimed blackboards as their own. Corporate managers owned the whiteboard. Desktop conferencing is changing this approach to education and business. Author Michael Schrage compares the new shared visual workspace to the napkin often used for joint planning at a bar or restaurant or on an airplane. The napkin is now officially sanctioned in the form of a shared electronic whiteboard, and leading corporations now teach employees collaboration techniques.

Changing how we work

G.A. (Gerry) Ford, videoconferencing department head at AT&T Laboratories (formerly part of AT&T Bell Laboratories), observes that achieving market acceptance for desktop conferencing is much harder than that of fax technology. The reason is that there is a far greater learning curve. While both technologies have had a major impact on productivity, desktop conferencing requires far more from the user. First off, the desktop conferencing user must become familiar with using programs on a PC. Then the user must learn the mechanics of sharing documents and applications. The final part of the equation is that the user must learn the less tangible collaboration skills that make conferencing effective. There is a major difference between gaining these skills and learning how to drop a page in a fax machine, dial a number, and press the start button.

"Using fax didn't take a major change in the way we work," says Ford. "People have to change their personal processes to make this (desktop conferencing) work." Therefore, according to Ford, "Changing The Way People Work...Together" is more than just a marketing slogan for AT&T's WorldWorx network services. Jay Crookston, networkMCI Conferencing's VP for US Sales, agrees that conferencing users face a learning curve. "There's mayhem in an electronic meeting, for example, when everybody starts futzing around with the tool bars," says Crookston. "We have to counsel, coach, and consult our customers so that this technology doesn't overwhelm them." Dennis Riley, who runs Microsoft's desktop videoconferencing lab, believes that using the technology involves a major cultural shift. "It's a whole new way of thinking. It requires a whole new way of working," says Riley. "I look at it as migrating from Windows 3.1 to Windows 95, to Windows NT. It's a whole new operating system for business."

Muller, of Ernst & Young, believes a major shift in work practices is necessary before widespread adoption of screen-to-screen collaboration is likely. "We have to develop collaborative computing behaviors before collaborative computing is really going to take off," says Muller. Ernst & Young uses desktop videoconferencing primarily as a cost-effective alternative to room videoconferencing, linking home-based consultants to Ernst & Young offices. However, screen-to-screen collaboration has been slower to catch on at Ernst & Young. "We are a store-and-forward society," says Muller. "We produce our work, ship it off, and get it back." Muller believes there is a big difference in comfort level between store-and-forward and real-time collaboration. Leonard Rubin, who implemented desktop videoconferencing at the Manhattan District Attorney's Office, agrees. "You have less time to reflect when you're doing it in real time. It requires a different way of thinking. There's more pressure to act more quickly."

Steve Bennett, Area Videoconferencing Coordinator and LAN manager for Reuters America, believes the immediate nature of collaboration through personal videoconferencing offers a major advantage. "The company that latches on to this is going to be out there in the forefront of getting things done," says Bennett. "You won't be in a scenario where you're spending more time transmitting the document for changes. Through desktop videoconferencing you can make the changes in real time. There's a big difference. You minimize the waiting time for changes." Tom Manley, President of INET Marketing and also Senior Systems Analyst with Lockheed Martin, agrees. "We're becoming much more efficient, because we're able to share visual information much more immediately. It's much more powerful to be able to visualize what's going on." Manley says that using desktop videoconferencing for collaborating on spreadsheets means a major shift in habits. "Even with e-mail, which is almost instantaneous, there's still a lag time. Now you're making the numbers work immediately," explains Manley. "We don't have that luxury of the float. So, I think it will definitely change the way we work."

Desktop conferencing allows a collaborator to get an immediate reaction to his or her work from another collaborator. That reaction may come in many forms. These may range from such subtle reactions as facial expressions, to more obvious reactions, like verbal feedback or document mark-up. Welcoming these forms of immediate reaction from colleagues may require adjustment. "When you store-and-forward, you're not there at the time they are evaluating your work, so it's not as threatening," Muller of Ernst & Young insists.

Lt. Richard Stakelum of the US Navy believes that real-time collaboration will cause a shift away from e-mail. Stakelum compares the change to that which occurred when the telephone replaced the telegraph. The telegraph allowed people to receive a message, read it, think about it, compose a response, then send it. The telephone revolutionized that process, forcing people to think while they communicated rather than before they responded. Likewise, Stakelum feels that screen-to-screen conferencing will force people to make decisions faster. "If somebody sends something in e-mail, it might take days before I get back," says Stakelum. "If I'm collaborating in real time, it's immediate." Despite adjusting to the immediacy of conferencing, Stakelum believes the collaborative shift is on balance positive. "One problem many businesses are having is inundation with e-mail." Often, Stakelum points out, communication goes unanswered because the e-mail stack gets too high. Conferencing is harder to avoid, and encourages collaborators to solve problems more quickly.

The shift towards conferencing requires collaborators to be on their toes, if you ask Bob Leader of SAP Software. Leader says that store-and-forward communication allows people to muddle through more easily than conferencing. "E-mail and fax allows you to be not as prepared," Leader explains. "Real-time collaboration means you must have all the pieces of the puzzle. It's the more immediate nature of it." Toni Alonso, of Pfizer, agrees that the technology spotlights organizational skills. "Desktop videoconferencing is extremely effective, if you have an agenda, and the materials prepared, and the files ready. You must have your screen set up exactly how you want it. People who are very prepared take less time and are most effective," says Alonso.

Compared with the overnight mail, fax, and phone routine, desktop conferencing gives managers and other professionals more information before they make decisions, according to Louis Belt, Regional Network Administrator for Laidlaw Environmental Services. Belt believes professionals often make decisions before they should, because they base their decisions on partial information. They may be waiting for another fax or phone call, but they grow impatient. "If you get some of the facts, you start pondering," says Belt. "Then if you get additional information, you try to make it fit whatever conclusion you've already reached." Desktop conferencing can provide all information at the same time, avoiding any tendency for a decision-maker to jump the gun. Says Belt, "With desktop conferencing, all the data is there immediately. It's much easier to make an objective decision."

Electronic collaboration often requires creating drafts of documents, building ideas, and refining them with the input of others. However, many people hesitate to share work in progress, and are comfortable only in presenting a finished product. Judith Hamilton, National Semiconductor's videoconferencing project manager, believes that many people invest their egos in their work, and therefore have trouble collaborating effectively. "When others correct erroneous conclusions, the people receiving that feedback can't handle it. They shut down," says Hamilton. Hamilton believes that people must learn to be more sensitive about how to give and receive feedback, so that they can effectively use collaborative tools. "We've had to create workshops and put words on paper indicating that if you want to say this, say it this way," says Hamilton.

Desktop videoconferencing is also changing the nature of some professions. Architecture is one example. Architect Marc Arnold, of the San Francisco-based firm Stone Marraccini Patterson, says, "It used to be for an architect to go to a meeting, that person would send drawings to the print room. With desktop videoconferencing, you have to load the drawings in ahead of time." Arnold says while desktop videoconferencing may boost efficiency for his firm, the architect must take more time to plan a video meeting.

Ralph Ungermann, founder and CEO of First Virtual Corporation and a Silicon Valley luminary, believes that end-users will warm up to desktop conferencing as the quality of the experience goes up. First Virtual Corporation is a networking company that specializes in bringing ATM to the desktop. Ungermann's view is that users will demand that desktop conferencing become nearly identical to a meeting before they will embrace the technology. Ungermann believes the faster and more comprehensive collaborative tools become and the higher the bandwidth for video, the more enthusiasm will develop for desktop conferencing.

Ungermann is also among those who believe desktop conferencing is having a major impact on work habits, and that guidelines must evolve. "You've got to define when you use it, how you use it, and when you don't use it," says Ungermann. Ungermann says one work practices trend he has seen in companies that use desktop videoconferencing heavily is that professionals use the technology to virtually "camp out" around their boss's desk. Successful users show their boss documents, get the boss's input, and transcend hierarchy by collaborating screen-to-screen instead of sitting at the foot of the boss's desk. These professionals have mastered the technology to achieve both group and personal results. They would likely fit the model of the power collaborators.

Though many industry analysts believe technology goes far in making small businesses bigger, the inverse may also be true. Blake Irving, Group

Manager of Microsoft's Personal Systems Division, says desktop videoconferencing "makes the benefits of having a small business smaller." In Irving's view, the technology shrinks Fortune 1000 businesses by uniting dispersed work groups and speeding decision making. "The communication benefits that small businesses used to have are changing rapidly," according to Irving. He points out that the combination of e-mail, voice mail and desktop videoconferencing have enriched the communication options available to large companies. Now floor-to-floor and building-to-building communication is easier. "I regularly have virtual hallway chats with a ton of folks, and I resolve issues with people I've never met face-to-face," Irving says.

Computer collaboration versus face-to-face

Desktop conferencing provides screen sharing tools that are different from collaborative tools available during face-to-face encounters. However, the question arises whether computer collaboration can provide the synergy of face-to-face collaboration, particularly when no video is used. Tora K. Bikson and J.D. Eveland of the Rand Corporation have addressed these issues in a paper called "The Interplay of Work Group Structures and Computer Support." The paper was published in the 1990 book *Intellectual Teamwork*. The paper describes a study of recent corporate retirees divided into an electronic group and a traditional group. Though the primary electronic tool available was RANDMAIL, an e-mail system, the study provides insight into all forms of computer collaboration.

The study concluded that "Electronically supported groups develop a richer communications structure with less hierarchical differentiation, broader participation, and more fluctuating and situational leadership structures." The study also found that electronic collaborators feel more involved in their work, get greater satisfaction from projects, and identify more with the products of group work. The study also found a significant learning curve exists in mastering computer collaboration. During the learning period, there is low productivity. Each new electronic collaboration tool requires this low-output period. However, according to the Bikson and Eveland paper, "As mastery of the tools is gained, output rises quickly and makes up for—and may surpass—the learning period lag."

The Andersen Center for Strategic Consulting in Palo Alto, California provides technology-based solutions for companies seeking to overcome the constraints of time and place. The center has worked with desktop conferencing and groupware with a focus on telecommuting and uniting dispersed work groups. However, Senior Manager Dave Connelly of the Andersen Center says PC-based collaboration has its limitations for many Andersen clients. Connelly says senior executives have stopped short of embracing the PC as a substitute for face-to-face meetings. "Culturally, they still want a handshake. They still want a face-to-face. These are mostly male, in their 50s, making a couple of million bucks a year," explains Connelly. "When we talk to lower-level people, they are far more interested in desktop videoconferencing. They're intrigued, but they are not sure that it will work."

When there is a need to build trust and pave the way for a close business relationship, desktop videoconferencing may fall short. Ken Pickar, Senior Vice President for Engineering and Technology for Allied Signal Aerospace, believes it is important to sort out which meetings must be in-person. "There are certain kick-off meetings that must be face-to-face. I want to minimize those through technology. But I haven't seen anything that accomplishes that well," according to Pickar.

Some industry leaders say people who are new to desktop videoconferencing often use the technology when a face-to-face meeting or some other collaboration medium may work better. Blake Irving, of Microsoft, says "You find gratuitous use of the technology. As folks start trying it out, they find out that desktop videoconferencing is not appropriate for replacing every face-to-face communication. Over time, they start ramping down." Irving says he experienced this phenomenon when he began using the technology. The longer he used desktop videoconferencing, however, the more he returned to face-to-face encounters for certain kinds of communication.

Irving believes that desktop videoconferencing is most useful for longer collaborative sessions, but less appropriate for replacing short, casual phone calls. To make his point, Irving uses the analogy of typefaces. "In the early days, you saw weekend publishers using tons of fonts on a page. Now they're using one or three, maximum. People have gotten smarter in the use of fonts and more targeted in the appropriate use." Likewise, Irving believes that desktop videoconferencing users will become more choosey about when to select conferencing as the best communication medium.

Tom Manley, of INET Marketing and Lockheed Martin, believes substituting desktop videoconferencing for the telephone should work almost every time. "I can't imagine any type of verbal communication that wouldn't work for desktop videoconferencing," insists Manley. "When would the added bonus of the video not be appropriate? Maybe you wouldn't want somebody to see you in your bathrobe." Manley qualifies his view, though, by saying that if something is not appropriate for strictly verbal communication, then it's probably not appropriate for desktop videoconferencing. An example of this, he says, would be a contract that requires a signature. In this situation, overnight mail or a face-to-face meeting would be more appropriate.

Collaborative security guidelines

Desktop videoconferencing can pose serious security problems, unless the user takes precautions. If you share Program Manager in Windows, for example, the remote user has access to every file and application on your computer. Jim Elacqua, Senior Partner with the law firm Arnold, White & Durkee takes steps to eliminate risk. "As a precaution, I shut down my e-mail system and take everything off my screen that is private to my clients. With a few preferences, you can secure your network," says Elacqua.

Collaborating, now or later

As groupware such as Lotus Notes and Microsoft Exchange coexists with personal videoconferencing on the desktop, we must choose which method of collaborating fits the specific situation. Store-and-forward approaches with or without video may work better in some instances, while real-time collaboration with or without video may fit the bill in other situations. Leon Schilmoeller, Manager of LAN Messaging and Groupware for 3M, believes both approaches can be important to product development and review. Schilmoeller says store-and-forward makes sense during the "actual constructive work" of the project, and also during peer review and input. This way, principal contributors in different time zones and with varying schedules can view the work and comment conveniently. Real-time collaboration works best, according to Schilmoeller, in resolving major differences. In this fashion, all of the collaborators can hash out the issues at once.

Conferencing with or without video should be thought of as one element of a collaborative computing environment, according to Ellen Grace Henson, Ambassador of Visual Communications for Silicon Graphics. InPerson is the conferencing product included in Mindshare, the Silicon Graphics collection of collaborative capabilities. Mindshare includes other tools like Media Mail, a video store-and-forward capability. Mindshare also provides the ability to easily create Web pages for publishing and browsing, integrated digital media presentation software, and media creation tools. Henson believes that the ability to mail video desktop-to-desktop can be a powerful collaborative tool that compliments real-time exchanges. "Conferencing technology becomes more valuable when you combine it with other collaborative capabilities," she explains. Using Media Mail, for example, to send a video clip to a colleague allows the coworker to evaluate the clip and to respond when he or she is ready. This provides an alternative to real-time collaboration. Ronald Baecker of the Computer Systems Research Institute of the University of Toronto in a paper called "New Paradigms for Computing in the Nineties" pointed out that the most effective collaborative work includes both real-time and off-line interaction. However, according to Baecker, most collaborative technologies have been developed as either synchronous or asynchronous, but rarely both. More information on Baecker is available on the web at

`http://www.dgp.utoronto.ca`

Fred Campo, of Northrop Grumman, provides an easy equation for determining whether e-mail or desktop videoconferencing fits the situation best. Campo says "If it requires sending e-mail back and forth more than twice, real-time conferencing is necessary."

3

Communicating Through Conferencing

The Personal Videoconferencing Generation

One of many reasons why Picturephone failed to take off in the 1960s was that people were uncomfortable appearing on camera. Tape recorders were still a novelty in the 1960s, and many people disliked even hearing their voices played back, much less seeing themselves on camera. Sensitivity to the visual medium has evolved as technology advances have impacted cultures worldwide. Home video cameras, security cameras, corporate video, MTV, and an explosion in the number of cable television channels have all contributed to video awareness. The question is whether that awareness translates into a greater comfort level on camera.

Fred Haisch, currently an AT&T Laboratories technical manager, was one of 300 engineers on the Picturephone team. Haisch believes human factors such as comfort level on camera still provide a barrier to worldwide acceptance of personal videoconferencing. However, Haisch feels technology users have made significant progress since the Picturephone days. "We're used to talking on answering machines, and we don't mind hearing ourselves recorded," says Haisch. "People have camcorders too, so people are more comfortable seeing and hearing themselves on recorded media."

When researchers in the 1920s wanted to develop a telephone that could see, the telephone itself was in its infancy. Telephone users thought that talking to somebody without seeing them was strange. This notion was partially responsible for the stilted style of voice that many people used on the telephone. Early users tended to speak slowly and formally, overenunciating syllables. This formality is apparent in new users of various audio and visual technology. Beginning television news reporters, for example, often appear "stiff" on camera and speak with pronunciation precision that is anything but natural and conversational. This happens, because the new technology, or our new exposure to existing technology, can make us feel like we are being judged.

The new television reporter, the new telephone user, the new tape recorder user, or the new personal videoconferencing user often feels like the technology distorts them. Therefore the tendency is to create a persona that seems more appropriate for the occasion of using the new device. This tendency can make the new technology user appear unnatural, forced, or phoney. When answering machines first appeared, for example, people often used formal greetings that included their first and last names, and specific instructions about how to leave a message. Now, greetings are more likely to include music, first names only, and a more conversational delivery. Because of these creative approaches, answering machine users are more likely to maximize the potential of the technology. Likewise, voice mail users are now more likely to update their greetings daily with information about their schedules and whereabouts. They are more likely to request a detailed message, and people leaving voice mails are more likely to describe why they are calling, rather than simply requesting a call back. This approach helps maximize the medium, because certain kinds of problems can be solved without a synchronous conversation. As the new user gets more accustomed to almost any technology over time, he or she grows less conscious of the medium and becomes more natural.

Julius P. Molnar, former Executive Vice President of AT&T Bell Laboratories, described the evolution of user comfort level in a 1969 issue of the *Bell Laboratories Record*. "Once the novelty wears off and one can use Picturephone without being self-conscious, he senses in his conversation an enhanced feeling of proximity and intimacy with the other party," Molnar wrote. "The unconscious response that party makes to a remark by breaking into a smile, or by dropping his jaw, or by not responding at all, adds a definite though indescribable 'extra' to the communication process."

The Value of Video

The debate continues over the value of seeing the person you are calling. For some use models, screen-to-screen collaboration without video may do the trick. For some situations, there is undoubtedly no substitute for a face-to-face meeting. Even with full-frame, television-quality video, something still seems missing from videoconferencing compared with an in-person encounter. Howard Rheingold addresses this phenomenon in *The Virtual Community*. Rheingold writes that an Indian researcher at Xerox EuroPARC in Cambridge told computer guru John Barlow that what video fails to deliver is the *prana*. The prana is *the life force*, or literally, *the breath*. Nevertheless, the value of being face-to-face with a colleague through video is unbeatable in certain cases. The introduction of *The Virtual Community* is available at

`http://www.well.com/user/hlr/vcbook/vcbookintro.html`

Ralph Ungermann of First Virtual Corporation uses the example of his company's Italian business partners. Ungermann and his colleagues at FVC's Santa Clara, California headquarters have developed close relationships with the people who are physically a continent away. Ungermann and others have not only productive meetings with the Italian group, but also they have social get-togethers through personal videoconferencing. Sharing a virtual beer and some laughs has gone a long way in developing business relationships. "Business is about people," explains Ungermann. "Seeing people and looking them in the eye and sharing stuff is important every day."

For Lt. Richard Stakelum of the US Navy, desktop videoconferencing replaces much of what has been lost in business communication. "We've gone almost full circle," explains Stakelum. "Originally, we were meeting face-to-face and were fully collaborating in business. When computers came in, we were often trying to accomplish through e-mail what we previously did face-to-face. This insulated many people and in some cases prevented us from communicating effectively." Stakelum believes desktop videoconferencing allows people to regain many of the face-to-face business relationships that have been lost. "The computer is still there to help you," says Stakelum. "But now we can communicate face-to-face through it."

Christine Traut, Manager of Application Strategies for Andersen Worldwide, says desktop videoconferencing has helped her form closer alliances. "If you asked me who my closest colleagues are at work, most are people that I video with," according to Traut. For Traut, video is critical to desktop conferencing. However, she stresses that it can be a turn-off to think of using the technology as performing, being on stage, or on television. The key is being natural. Traut says she has successfully used desktop videoconferencing to communicate with phone company technical support people. "To suddenly see the face of some tech support person, everything that can happen in a face-to-face encounter starts happening. Some people even flirt, which just doesn't happen as often or as powerfully on the telephone." Traut also believes that the "warm and fuzzy" feeling that a customer gets after a positive desktop videoconferencing experience with a company representative has the potential to generate better corporate image results than a multimillion dollar television advertising campaign.

Dr. Judith Olson of the University of Michigan believes that desktop videoconferencing can have a reassuring impact on the user. She describes a business trip to the Netherlands during which she had to prepare for a desktop videoconference with executives in Ann Arbor. She practiced by conducting a desktop videoconference from the Netherlands with a colleague at the University of Michigan. Her remote colleague was sitting in an office in front of an open door. Olson could see another colleague walking down the hall, and she motioned him to join in the encounter. "It had a huge emotional effect on me in that I was home again. For me to be a bit lonely and be able to come home was very valuable," explains Olson.

When the personal computer first became a communication tool, professionals began substituting e-mail for face-to-face or phone encounters. This was a boost for those who are uncomfortable with social interaction. Personal videoconferencing may shift the pendulum the other way. "E-mail is more in the mind than in the heart," says Traut. "When you have to read and write on the net, it's an introvert's paradise. As soon as you add video, it becomes the captain of the football team's medium." Traut believes the medium is important to anybody who counts on socializing for business success, particularly sales people. She also believes office politicians and networkers can have a field day with the technology. "Video makes me feel related to people across distance. I feel like I do when I say hello to people in the corridor at work."

A study by Bellcore indicates that videoconferencing users demand high-quality video. The results show that the satisfaction of both business customers and consumers increases significantly with bandwidth. At 128 kbps, 40% of business customers and 54% of consumers surveyed responded that the video was satisfactory. At 384 kbps, 88% of business customers and 89% of consumers surveyed indicated they were satisfied. David Dirks, Videoconferencing Project Manager at Lawrence Livermore National Laboratory, says he finds that video quality is critical to users. "Some feel that unless I can see their pupils dilate and see them sweat, real communication isn't going on."

Perfecting the Virtual Meeting

It is debatable whether desktop videoconferencing will ever supplant the face-to-face meeting, or whether such a switch would be desirable. However, researchers at telecommunications network providers, as well as hardware manufacturers, are working on ways to make virtual meetings more like face-to-face meetings. *Telepresence* is a term that describes making videoconferencing more like a face-to-face encounter.

Undoubtedly, there are significant differences between personal videoconferencing and face-to-face meetings. Personal videoconferencing lacks the sense of touch, so that a handshake is impossible. While adding real handshake capability to the technology may require nothing less than a leap of faith, other service upgrades will go far in minimizing the differences between virtual meetings and face-to-face ones. Improved audio compression algorithms are making desktop videoconferences sound far better than the phone and much like in-person meetings. In fact, sound is so critical to telepresence that there are those who believe it is more important than video in making people feel like they are sitting across from one another. "Sound is number one, and video quality is secondary," according to Steve Trustman of Personal Video Communications, Inc. (PVCI), the top reseller of PictureTel desktop units in North America. "If the sound is not perfect and it doesn't sound like the person's in the room with you, an executive is not going to use it," says Trustman. Studies support Trustman's view. A 1992 Sun Microsystems Laboratories study detailed in a paper by Ellen Isaacs and John C. Tang indicates that "Our experiences confirm that audio is relatively more important than video in supporting collaboration."

The level of minimum video quality required depends entirely on the application. In high-level meetings in which nuances of nonverbal communication become critical, for example, speeds above 384 kbps are needed. When a professional wants to collaborate with a colleague, 128 kbps—or even POTS—may do the trick. "I'm much more interested in being able to converse with 100 people at 128 kbps than 12 people at 384 kbps," according to Industry Analyst Christine Perey of Perey Communications and Consulting. However, "There are some things I do where I want to read all the body language because I'm giving people my money or my life, in the case of legal work," explains Perey.

The eye contact dilemma

A universal stumbling block to virtual meetings through personal videoconferencing is the lack of proper eye contact that systems allow. Some users feel that the video windows of some systems are too small to provide the ability to see the remote user's eyes. Even if the window is large enough, however, there are other issues involving proper eye contact. Because the camera is normally mounted on top of the monitor, it is nearly impossible to maintain adequate eye contact with a remote user. The dilemma is that if we look at the image of the remote user's eyes, from that person's perspective our eyes appear to be looking elsewhere. However, if we look directly into the camera—appearing to the remote user that we are looking into his or her eyes—we are unable to see that person's eyes directly because we are looking away from the image on the monitor.

The ideal solution to this dilemma would allow both parties to maintain eye contact easily without having to look into a camera. Research teams are working on solutions at the Centre for Human Communications at BT Laboratories in Ipswich, U.K., Lucent Technologies Bell Laboratories, NTT's Interdisciplinary Research Laboratories in Tokyo, and at ATR Communications Systems Research Laboratories in Kyoto.

A Bell Labs research team delivered a paper addressing eye contact issues at the Society for Information Display 1995 conference in Orlando, Florida. The paper indicates, "Although it can be argued that users will adjust to the differences or learn to look at the camera, good terminal-design practice has the equipment adapting to the user whenever possible instead of vice versa." Bell Labs is working on a rear-projection system in which a video camera is mounted behind and literally looks through the monitor. This set-up captures the image of the desktop videoconferencing user at eye level.

BT Laboratories is developing a "View Through the Screen" system in which a camera placed above an angled screen captures the user's reflection in the screen. When the image is transmitted, the user appears to be looking directly at the person at the far end.

Placing the camera behind the screen, however, raises a host of privacy issues. This type of design may conjure up images of big brother in the George Orwell book *1984*, which describes an authoritative government that spies on its subjects through cameras hidden in television sets, among other places. Privacy and reciprocity features would likely become even more important to a behind-the-screen camera placement approach. These features would prevent people from feeling somebody was monitoring them without their knowledge or without their ability to look at the other person.

Other attempts to address the eye contact problem involve a solution similar to the teleprompter, which is the device that allows television anchors to read the news while seeming to look the viewer in the eye. In his paper entitled "Telepresence: Integrating Shared Task and Person Spaces," William A. S. Buxton of the University of Toronto details a Reciprocal Video Tunnel. The technique was implemented by William Newman of Rank Xerox EuroPARC. The system uses mirrors to reflect the image of the monitor over the camera lens. In this way, the desktop videoconferencing user can see the other person while looking into the lens. According to Buxton's paper, "By adopting teleprompter technology from the broadcast industry, this problem of eye contact can be largely overcome."

Bridging the cultural gap

As desktop videoconferencing makes the world smaller by uniting physically separated people, the technology may also increase awareness of cultural differences. Direct eye contact, for example, is appropriate when doing business in the United States or Western Europe. However, many other cultures regard direct eye contact as rude. In Japan, for instance, it is often considered more acceptable to look at somebody at nose or mouth level while addressing them. These cultural differences may have impact both in the use and design of desktop videoconferencing systems. If we wish to make a Japanese colleague feel comfortable, perhaps we should look at a spot just under the camera rather than directly into the lens. National Semiconductor has had extensive cross-cultural experience with desktop videoconferencing. "The Japanese are very reluctant to make a commitment on camera," says Judith Hamilton, videoconferencing project manager. "That culture is particularly self-conscious about using cameras and technology. They turn off their preview mode, because they are so embarrassed."

Dr. Judith Olson of the University of Michigan says that cultural differences in dress can make a major difference in the success of a desktop videoconference. "If you see engineers in Mexico wearing open-collared brown shirts and sun glasses, you are sure that they are not engineers and you behave differently," says Olson. This phenomenon applies to differing corporate cultures as well. Olson tells the story of a multipoint videoconference she and her colleagues had with a Silicon Valley company and a major management consulting firm. The academics were wearing tweed, the management consultants were wearing white shirts and power ties, and the high-tech crowd was wearing tee shirts with political statements on them. The videoconference bombed, and it took a year to patch up the relationship.

Olson points out that for face-to-face meetings, it is proper etiquette to dress in clothes that are appropriate to the culture that we are visiting. The distinction of who is the visitor is blurred, however, during a desktop videoconference. The most appropriate approach to cultural differences may be for all participants to meet part way in terms of dress and habits. The impact here is that use of the technology could encourage the world to become more homogeneous.

Time differences can make cross-cultural communication even more difficult. Olson tells the story of a videoconference she conducted from the Netherlands with executives in Ann Arbor, Michigan. It was a holiday in the Netherlands, and she had to persuade a systems person to open a building and wait while she conducted the videoconference. Meantime, it was a work day in Ann Arbor. "The executives were rattling on amongst themselves. I was getting short with them, because the systems person wanted to go home." Olson says she believes that no technology can eliminate time zone differences.

Keeping up with multipoint

Multipoint desktop videoconferences pose special communication concerns. In many multipoint approaches, one speaker has the floor. As other participants interject or even as stray noise is audible, the camera becomes *hot* at the site where the noise comes from. This is called voice-activated switching. "You get tennis neck from watching screens go back and forth," according to

Steve Bennett, Area Videoconferencing Coordinator and LAN Manager, for Reuters America. For this reason, Bennett believes a "montage" approach to desktop videoconferencing is the answer. Such an approach provides the ability to view all of the conference participants on one or more screens. This scenario resembles the classic television game show "Hollywood Squares," in which three rows of star contestants fill the screen, tic-tac-toe style. However, a montage approach can require greater bandwidth, depending on the implementation.

Some manufacturers of multipoint bridges (MCU), which allow multisite desktop videoconferences, have incorporated a montage-like capability into their products. VideoServer has billed itself as the first company to deliver a product that lets users view more than one other site at a time, without expensive systems integration work. The Continuous Presence product released in late 1995 is an add-in card to VideoServer's Multimedia Conference Server (MCS). Continuous Presence allows a desktop videoconferencing user to view and hear up to four other sites during a multipoint call. The product accomplishes this without requiring any additional bandwidth. Christine Traut of Andersen Worldwide calls Continuous Presence a "Brady Bunch" approach because of the opening of the TV show that displays a series of squares containing video clips of family members on one screen.

William A.S. Buxton and his colleagues at the University of Toronto have worked on telepresence solutions to multipoint desktop videoconferences. The Hydra system is a series of small monitors with a lens beneath each. The units, about 2 feet tall and four inches wide, are placed across the desktop. Each unit represents another person participating in the desktop videoconference. "It is potentially much easier to maintain awareness of who is visually attending to whom, and to take advantage of conversational acts such as head turning," according to Buxton's paper on telepresence. In another paper, however, Marilyn M. Mantei of the University of Toronto points out the limitations of Hydra. Mantei writes that the system requires "enormous" bandwidth and that "Its implementation in a large-scale communication system would be very difficult."

Uniting the Distributed Work Group

The study of media spaces has provided insight into how distributed work groups communicate through desktop videoconferencing. A media space is an electronic environment, allowing physically distant groups to work together. A media space usually includes a continuous video and audio link.

Bellcore, Xerox Palo Alto Research Center (PARC), the University of Toronto, Rank Xerox Research Centre, and the Ontario Telepresence Project are among the organizations that have conducted media space trials. Both the premise and conclusion of many of these trials is that informal communication is critical in organizations. Informal communication is spontaneous, and includes chance meetings like water cooler encounters. However, this kind of exchange can be more rich with information than a prearranged conference. Informal communication is particularly important in developing and sharing a corporate or organizational culture. There is concern that distributed work groups may miss out on informal communication; and therefore, organizations have conducted studies to evaluate whether media spaces can bridge the gap.

The Xerox PARC media space

Xerox PARC created and conducted a media space between 1985 and 1988. During the trial, the Systems Concepts Laboratory (SCL) was geographically split between Palo Alto, California and Portland, Oregon. The objective was to unite the 20-person work group through technologies supporting collaboration. Sara A. Bly, Steve R. Harrison, and Susan Irwin of Xerox detailed the media space trial in the January, 1993 issue of *Communications of the ACM*. The article points out that Picturephone and a work of video art called "Hole-in-Space" influenced the birth of the SCL media space. Video artists Kit Galloway and Sherri Rabinowitz created "Hole-in-Space," which was a video and audio link between Century City, California and Lincoln Center in New York City. The link allowed strangers walking along to interact with others more than three thousand miles away through chance encounters. The work of art seemed to suggest that casual encounters improved communication.

In creating the media space, Xerox set up two nearly identical physical environments. Both the one in Palo Alto and the other in Portland included offices that surrounded a common area. During the trial, the technology and the work activity evolved together in that researchers would add hardware and change the configuration, for example, as requirements changed. Ultimately, video and audio connections linked eight offices in Palo Alto, six offices in Portland, and several common areas or lounges in both locations. A video switch allowed participants to constantly change the configuration so that it would support their work activities. Public-to-public, private-to-public, and private-to-private video and audio connections were all part of the mix. When privacy was essential, users generally switched off microphones rather than cameras. Meetings were often videotaped, so that participants as well as those unable to attend could review what transpired. Media space participants also sent one another PARC-o-grams, which were video memos delivered via mail service.

Participants used the Xerox media space both for meetings and chance encounters. Researchers passing through the common area often greeted researchers at the remote site. Even when nobody appeared in the video shot of the remote common area or somebody's office, the audio provided plenty of information about the activities. Discussions could be heard as one might here cubicle-to-cubicle talk while sharing the same physical workspace.

Among the findings of the Xerox media space project was the need for a shared electronic writing space. Focusing the camera on a wall-based whiteboard allowed remote collaborators to show one another their work, but stopped short of letting the participants work on a document together. The realization of the need for a shared electronic whiteboard and subsequent prototypes contributed to the development of such tools that are now part of desktop videoconferencing systems.

Problems associated with the Xerox media space included half-duplex audio, which meant only one site could be heard at one time. This interfered with natural communication, which normally includes some interruption. Far-end camera control made some participants uncomfortable, because they felt watched. Researchers found that the media space was no replacement for face-to-face communication, but that the model nevertheless helped link physically separate work groups. According to the article by Bly, Harrison and Irwin, "Sometimes frustrations of not having the ability to interact as we would face-to-face caused us to embark on some new path. Sometimes the need to communicate more fully was answered by an airplane trip tempered by the realization that a media space, even when limited, offered a much richer environment than no cross-site connection." Among the most significant findings of the Xerox media space project was that over 70% of the communication involved casual, "drop-in" encounters, and that this kind of communication would never have occurred without the video link. More information on Xerox PARC is available on the Web at

`http://www.parc.xerox.com`

Bellcore's Cruiser

Bellcore conducted another kind of media space trial for four months in 1990. For the project, Bellcore used a desktop videoconferencing prototype called Cruiser. The system, designed by Robert Fish, Robert Kraut and Robert Root of Bellcore, is described in the January 1993 issue of *Communications of the ACM*. Fish, Kraut, Root, and Ronald E. Rice of Rutgers University wrote the article. Participants in the trial included summer interns and their mentors, totaling 23 people. The video and audio links involved two parties at a time, and the system included no document conferencing or application sharing. Besides *cruises* or video calls, users could initiate *glances*, which were one-second, video-only links. The system itself initiated *autocruises*, at random times. The idea of the autocruises was to simulate walking down the corridor and randomly seeing and stopping to talk with others.

The system included such privacy safeguards as the *reciprocity rule*, which meant that if one person could see and hear a user, that user could likewise see and hear them. Also users could initiate a *private* command, which notified others that calls would not be accepted. Other features included an *active directory*, showing the availability of all users and a *call history*.

Results of the study indicated that users rarely engaged in conversation during an autocruise, and that 40% of users indicated they found that feature the most objectionable. Participants also indicated that they used the cruiser system primarily for greeting and scheduling, rather than problem-solving and decision-making. Ninety percent of respondents reported that a major problem was an inability to share documents and other work tools while using the cruiser. Therefore, participants collaborated on work primarily during face-to-face encounters. According to the article in *Communications of the ACM*, "Our experience with the Cruiser system suggests that even communication systems intended for informal communication must also support sustained task-focused work and must allow graceful transition to it."

Other interesting findings of the Bellcore cruiser experiment were that participants felt the system was most useful for routine information exchange, like project status checks and staying in touch. More complicated, challenging, or "socially sensitive" tasks required face-to-face encounters. However, the participants preferred the cruiser to the phone or memos for these kinds of exchanges. Most of the participants were concerned about privacy before the study, but after the cruiser experiment they had fewer privacy worries. One concern, however, was that participants were unable to see others who might be in the room at the remote end. Because the cameras had a fixed and relatively narrow field, it was impossible to see anybody in the room other than the person in front of the camera.

After the trial, Bellcore updated the cruiser system to include multiparty connections, application sharing, and *The Gallery*. The Gallery provided a "less intrusive" way to communicate workstation to workstation. Like the Xerox PARC Portholes, the feature let users keep a gallery of still images on their screens of other users or places. This allowed users to check the availability of other users without initiating a video call. Researchers also updated Cruiser with a Virtual Auditorium feature that allowed desktop broadcasting and enabled the audience to communicate through video with each other. More information on Bellcore is available on the Web at

`http://www.bellcore.com`

RAVE at Rank Xerox

The RAVE media space at Rank Xerox Research Centre in England was a descendent of the Xerox PARC media space. The system provided safeguards, allowing users to control their level of accessibility. One system feature was a 5-second glance into the offices of other participants. As people used these glances, the system provided sounds of doors opening and closing. This safeguard ensured that participants knew when others were glancing at them. RAVE researchers confirmed that technology-based interaction such as desktop videoconferencing is more formal and less interactive than face-to-face communication.

The RAVE study also found that the design of videoconferencing systems has a major impact on behavior. Dr. Judith Olson of the University of Michigan, who participated in the study, says that participants and others would often walk into the commons area without knowing there was a camera present. Researchers experimented by putting the camera inside the eyes of a mannequin, so that people would feel as if they were talking to somebody when they addressed the camera. They ultimately removed the camera from the mannequin and placed a monitor nearby, so that participants could see themselves on camera. Olson relates the story of a night watchman who needed to fix his trousers and so removed them in the commons late at night. He was embarrassed to learn that researchers burning the midnight oil witnessed the event. More information on Rank Xerox is available on the Web at

`http://www.xerox.com/RXRC/home.html`

CAVECAT and VOODOO

The University of Toronto has made significant progress in creating and improving media spaces. The Computer Audio Video Enhanced Collaboration and Telepresence (CAVECAT) media space allowed both multipoint and "private" connections. However, the system informed all other users if a private video meeting was taking place. The idea was to simulate the physical office situation in which somebody's office door is closed, but perhaps others can see who is meeting through a window. CAVECAT gave researchers an opportunity to perfect the "virtual open office." A later-generation media space called VOODOO allowed participants to view their colleagues through a series of small windows on their computer screens. The default shot is long, but participants can choose a tighter shot to engage in more intimate interaction. A paper by Jim Li and Marilyn Mantei called "Working Together, Virtually" describes VOODOO. The paper points out that "The worker knows that viewing of others is reciprocal and that preventing someone from viewing oneself is done only by relinquishing the privilege of seeing the other person." Also, the system filters out typing sounds to prevent colleagues from disturbing one another.

The Ontario Telepresence Project

Another important media space experiment is the one that the Ontario Telepresence Project (OTP) conducted for three years ending in 1994. The mandate of the $4.8 million project was to gain insight into the social impact of technology by testing advanced media space systems. Both public and private money funded the research. As part of the project, researchers conducted trials on the sites of participating companies. One of those companies was Provitel, which was encouraging the use of the VISIT desktop videoconferencing system. The trial included both VISIT and a prototype called Telepresence Media Space System (TMS). Besides real-time video communication and collaboration capabilities, TMS also included video mail, video receptionist, and video recording of conferences capabilities. TMS also used several cameras and monitors, and provided doorway glances into offices. This allowed an opportunity for the office inhabitant to invite in the visitor. This capability was designed to be less intrusive than initiating a close-up, screen-to-screen encounter.

Gale Moore of OTP and Ken Schuyler of Provitel describe their project experiences in a paper entitled "Videoconferencing 1990's Stye: Sharing Faces, Places and Spaces." The paper points out that there were social as well as technical factors that impeded effective communication. For example, the group within Provitel had a voice-driven rather than text-driven culture. Participants reported that they regularly responded to voice mail, but that they were slower in responding to e-mail. Also, the mobile nature of the work required that participants leave their offices frequently. Therefore, both VISIT and TMS were overly restrictive as they required participants to remain on Provitel premises. The researchers found that organizational culture had a major impact on effective communication using desktop videoconferencing. We will look at cultural and other deployment issues in Chapter 8.

A paper distributed by Corel Corporation and written by OTP researchers called "Facts, Lies and Videoconferencing" discusses the value of using a separate monitor for desktop videoconferencing. According to the paper, "The electronic visitor occupies a space of their own within the room as they would if they were present, and the computer screen can be used to share documents, spreadsheets, or other objects." This prevents the remote party from getting buried under documents and applications running on the PC.

Montage and finding the right time

Researchers at Sun Microsystems Laboratories built on the findings of many media space experiments by deploying Montage. Montage is a prototype that helps collaborators determine opportune times to interact. John C. Tang and Monica Rua describe the prototype in a 1994 paper called "Montage: Providing Teleproximity for Distributed Groups." The system uses electronic *glances* to determine whether a collaborator is in his or her office. If the collaborator is out, Montage provides alternatives that include browsing the person's on-line calendar, sending the collaborator an e-mail, and sending an electronic note that appears on the collaborator's screen.

Montage can be compared to peering into somebody's office to see whether they are busy. The Tang and Rua paper describes this process as the "pre-interaction negotiation" that precedes the decision whether to have a conference. According to the paper, "Since much of the negotiation about whether to have an interaction occurs through visual cues, video is a natural channel for enabling users to accomplish this negotiation." When one participant *glanced* to see if another collaborator wanted to join him for lunch, for example, he saw that the other person was on the phone. That person gave him a one-minute sign language cue. Had the participant used the phone to invite the collaborator, he would have gotten voice mail and would likely have missed arranging the lunch meeting.

Forum and desktop broadcasting

The Sun Microsystems Laboratories team has also focused on desktop broadcasting or one-to-many communication. The prototype system called Forum lets a presenter broadcast video, audio, and slides, and the system allows audiences to ask questions. Forum also lets the presenter poll the audience anonymously and lets the audience exchange written comments to the speaker and with one another. Ellen A. Isaacs, Trevor Morris, Thomas K. Rodriguez, and John C. Tang describe Forum in a 1995 paper called "A Comparison of Face-to-Face and Distributed Presentations." They delivered the paper at the 1995 Conference on Computer-Human Interaction in Denver. The study found that Forum attracted larger audiences than face-to-face talks, but that the attention span of Forum audiences was shorter. What accounts for the shallow interest in Forum presentations, according to the paper, is the other applications on the computer and other activities in the office that compete for the user's attention. "Having an on-line presentation like this is wonderful!" the paper quotes one user as saying. "I can choose to focus on areas of importance and tune out to get more worth-while work accomplished."

The study showed that interaction between the presenter and the audience was greater in face-to-face encounters than through Forum. The paper indicates that in-person audiences asked more follow-up questions than did Forum audiences, creating more of a back-and-forth and less of a lecture. This reduced both the effectiveness and the satisfaction of the presenter.

Additional information on computer supported cooperative work (CSCW) is available on the web at

```
http://www.demon.co.uk/jrac/cscwdir.html
```

The Meaning of Facial Expressions

Facial expressions have a major impact on communication. The more clearly we can see expressions through desktop videoconferencing, the more effective our exchange becomes. Despite the insistence of some that document conferencing and application sharing are more useful than video, ultimately we communicate more effectively if we can see how the other party is reacting. Facial expressions can indicate, for example, confusion, understanding, agreement, or objection.

Paul Ekman of the University of California School of Medicine in San Francisco has devoted his career to studying facial expressions as indicators of emotion. Much of Ekman's research has focused on the physiological changes that facial action causes. Expressions of anger and fear, for example, accelerated the heart rates of Ekman's research subjects. Ekman and Wallace V. Friesen are the creators of the Facial Action Coding System (FACS), which objectively measures facial expressions for counselors and researchers studying interpersonal relations and others seeking to improve interpersonal communication skills. The FACS breaks down expressions into *action units* which include such actions as *inner brow raiser* and *lip presser*. According to Ekman, people can deceive others convincingly by misrepresenting their emotions through speech. Some facial expressions are also essentially lies, but contain what Ekman and his associates call *leakage*. Leakage is the clues to people's true feelings that are included in misleading facial expressions. "We can't control our facial expressions very well," says Ekman. "When we try, we often look worse. Some people are good. They typically go into acting or sales."

Ekman wrote in the April, 1993 issue of the American Psychologist, "When attention is focused on these often-brief, fragmentary signs of emotional expression, they can betray a lie by contradicting the emotion the person verbally claims to be feeling." In other words, people can try to fake it, but their facial expressions usually give some indication of their true feelings away. This is particularly apparent on video playback. The ramifications of this research for desktop videoconferencing are that conferences can be constantly under the microscope. Store-and-forward video, including video mail, reinforces the impact of facial expressions, because these displays of emotion are potentially a permanent record.

Ekman is also working with NTT and others on technology that would allow full-frame videoconferencing over POTS without compression. The technique involves encoding facial codes or muscle movements, and sending the information over phone lines in binary code along with a freeze-frame of the face. Software at the remote end would then decode and reanimate muscle movements. Ekman expects the technology will deliver 90% of facial expressions that people see. "If you were negotiating a really complex deal, it won't be good enough," says Ekman.

Stored video capability allows all participants to review videoconferences as often as they like. This permits the opportunity to examine the nuances in nonverbal as well as spoken communication. These nuances include facial expressions, body language, voice tone, and voice inflection. This capability can impact business dynamics in that we may wish to scrutinize a potential business partner's facial expressions and to detect their degree of honesty, stability, or other qualities. This, of course, works both ways, in that our own body language, voices, and even dress can be scrutinized.

Toni Alonso, Video Services Manager for Pfizer, believes that facial expressions count for more during a desktop videoconference than during a group or room videoconference. "The facial expressions that are blurred on a room system are magnified on the desktop, because on the desktop you tend to focus the camera from the neck up instead of from the table up," explains Alonso. "Frown lines are very obvious. Question marks on foreheads are more apparent." Unlike some corporate cultures that may emphasize collaborative functions over video interaction, Pfizer's culture endorses face-to-face communication. Pfizer's business is making and selling pharmaceutical drugs. "It's important for us to be there when doctors are administering drugs to a patient. This is how the corporate culture evolved to emphasize seeing the expressions on people's faces."

Bill Muller of Ernst & Young believes personal videoconferencing users must sharpen presentation skills to become effective through the medium. "End users must understand that they are on TV," says Muller. "They must sit erect, smile, and use camera close ups in order to get their message across." Muller's point about camera close-ups is important. A tight shot of a face is more intimate, and therefore more powerful. If you are watching a Presidential news conference on television, for example, are the President's words more powerful if spoken during a wide shot of the room or during a close-up on the President's face? The answer is certainly the latter. People want to be able to see the facial expressions of others, and personal videoconferencing is no exception. If we remain on a long or wide shot throughout a desktop videoconference, it can be interpreted that we are trying to avoid scrutiny.

Louis Belt, Regional Network Administrator for Laidlaw Environmental Services, agrees that desktop videoconferencing requires additional communication skills. "Some people will make a positive comment while making a negative gesture," says Belt. "People learn to be more genuine or better actors." Belt explains that facial expressions have become important as Laidlaw reengineers the company and manages projects and emergencies using desktop videoconferencing. "You know it if they're rolling their eyes, and that's important," according to Belt.

Some desktop videoconferencing users believe the technology offers video quality inadequate to enhance communication. Ken Pickar, Senior Vice President for Engineering and Technology for Allied Signal Aerospace, says the ability to view nonverbal communication is limited through the technology. "Using the low bandwidth, you get frozen faces. Occasionally you get someone throwing their head back laughing." Pickar says the technology is inadequate for both management meetings and performance evaluations. He finds that he can pick up just as much information about the attitude of the other person through a voice call. "If someone's annoyed, you can tell in their voice as well as their face."

The Dilemma of Guidelines

The notion of personal scrutiny through desktop videoconferencing conjures up all sorts of frightening images, including the absence of privacy in the video age portrayed in George Orwell's book *1984*. The danger of emphasizing the significance of body language, voice quality, dress, and personal communication approaches is that the user becomes so overwhelmed by the ramifications of the technology that he or she overlooks the potential benefits and avoids desktop videoconferencing. For this reason, corporate users are balancing the need for effective communication guidelines with the need to avoid overwhelming end users with rules that can turn them off to the technology.

Credit Suisse, which uses VTEL S-Max systems and Intel ProShare, takes the less-is-more approach to desktop videoconferencing guidelines. "We try not to post rules," says Tim Bigley of Credit Suisse. "We just want people to talk and act the way they want." Bigley says that many in his company are aware of dress guidelines that are commonly endorsed elsewhere, such as avoiding loud plaids. However, Credit Suisse avoids embracing these guidelines. "If people have to dress differently to do videoconferencing, it doesn't make any sense," Bigley explains. Though there are no formal guidelines, many Credit Suisse users have determined their own personal guidelines for on-camera comfort and confidence. "Some people who are going bald don't like the camera on top of the computer looking down on their heads," says Bigley. The solution for these users is placing the camera beside—rather than on top of—the monitor.

Some organizations that have implemented videoconferencing without addressing effective communication practices have later found it necessary to tackle these issues. When Leonard Rubin introduced desktop videoconferencing at the Manhattan District Attorney's Office, the idea was to replace face-to-face interviews between police officers and prosecutors. Rubin and his staff assumed communication through the technology was nearly the same as in person. However, Rubin quickly learned that desktop videoconferencing changes communication guidelines. Says Rubin, "You have to say to the cop when he gets on, could you position yourself so I can get the best view of you?"

One Assistant DA learned muting the audio during the videoconference was sometimes necessary if he wanted to have a side conversation with a colleague that the police officer on the remote end had no need to hear. Rubin and the DA's office also discovered that the size of the video window at the outset of a videoconference makes a difference. "If you start off with the little box image, that can set the tone for the whole interview. The experience then seems less real," Rubin explains. For the DA's office, adjusting to desktop videoconferencing communication practices is significantly easier for new classes of Assistant DAs. "It's much less of an adjustment for people who have never done it as an in-person interview," according to Rubin.

Etiquette

Organizations that use personal videoconferencing are learning as they go about best practices, including etiquette. Because etiquette is evolving, it is dangerous to tack up a list comparable to table manners. Technology advances will continue to drive the evolution of etiquette. As video and audio quality increase and as network functions become more available, some etiquette will change. However, certain practices will likely have a longer shelf life. One of those practices is the hand wave. Waving has evolved almost universally as the proper way to begin and end videoconferences.

When we wave, we smile almost automatically. Try it. We have to struggle to avoid smiling when waving. This reaction likely dates back to early childhood. When we waved to a parent or a playmate, we were happy to see them. In desktop videoconferencing, the wave and smile combination helps us connect with our videoconferencing partner on a more human level. It has become the videoconferencing equivalent of the handshake we use before and after face-to-face meetings. Waving helps everybody feel more comfortable with everybody else. It is possible that waving will disappear as personal videoconferencing becomes second nature to us, but it is at least as likely that this welcome gesture will remain as a symbol of videoconferencing etiquette.

In the Sun Microsystems Laboratory study described in the Isaacs and Tang paper, researchers found that personal videoconferencing etiquette regarding interruptions differed significantly from face-to-face communication. In meetings, it is usually considered impolite to take long phone calls or read e-mail. However, the subjects in the Sun study talked on the phone and read e-mail during desktop videoconferences. The researchers concluded that a major reason for the shift in etiquette between face-to-face and personal videoconferencing interactions is that the technology allows all participants an equal opportunity to engage in other activities during a conference.

Many other forms of etiquette will evolve as the technology advances. Eliminating or reducing audio delays through higher bandwidth and better audio compression, for example, will diminish the need to wait until the other party has finished his or her last word before we start talking. Many users have complained that the audio some personal videoconferencing systems provide is still like radio transmissions in that it is almost necessary to say "over" after one participant is finished talking. However, Tom Manley of INET Marketing and Lockheed Martin says, "Our brains adjust quickly to that delay, and you learn how to read the cues of a video conversation." One school of thought says it is high time that we wait until the other person is finished talking before we start. "We are a culture of constantly interrupting people. We have to change," says Toni Alonso, Video Services Manager for Pfizer. "Americans are out of line with the European and the Asian cultures. If we realize we are part of a global arena and become a bit more formal in our discussions and presentations, we will communicate more effectively."

Another etiquette issue comes up when the phone rings during a desktop videoconference. Bigley of Credit Suisse says he and other users have dealt with the phone issue. "It's part of the evolving protocol. It's something that has to be learned." The solution, according to Bigley, is tied to available technology. If the user has Caller ID, for example, he or she can check to see if the call is urgent and then decide whether to answer or let voice mail take the call. As phone functions become embedded in personal videoconferencing or become available through the network, we can choose to put a video call on hold rather than allow our videoconferencing partner to see and hear one end of our phone conversation. Similarly, the hold function becomes important when somebody walks into one's office or work space.

Network service providers have taken their time incorporating phone functions into their service offerings for personal videoconferencing. This is because they are waiting for a major market growth spurt, so they can gauge customer needs before the next round of investment. In the meantime, Senior Partner Jim Elacqua of the law firm Arnold, White & Durkee says he has worked out a call management system that gives personal videoconferencing priority. "If I'm on a ProShare call, I'll ignore the phone," says Elacqua. "If I'm on the phone and expect a ProShare call, I'll let the caller know that I'm about to do a desktop videoconference, and that I'll have to go when the call comes in."

Whether it is acceptable etiquette to make a surprise video call is questionable. The answer depends heavily on the relationship between the caller and recipient. It seems acceptable to *video* somebody who is a collaborator on a project or somebody with whom you share a close working relationship. However, making a video call to a person you have never met is far more intrusive than calling the person on the telephone. "It can be like walking into somebody's office without being introduced," says Christine Traut of Andersen Worldwide. "I use it to leverage contacts with people I've already met."

Traut says she uses desktop videoconferencing to drop in on people with whom she shares a close business relationship, but that she first uses the phone to arrange video calls with others she knows less well.

Since the camera displays only a portion of the room, it is possible that somebody else is out of the camera's eye. Therefore, etiquette suggests that all parties in a videoconference should reveal the names of all others at their respective sites, regardless of whether they can be seen in the camera shot. This avoids the awkward situation of talking about somebody who is viewing and listening to the videoconference or exchanging confidential information without knowing others are present.

Accountability through video

Communicating through video screen-to-screen adds a dimension that holds people more accountable. Rather than being simply a voice at the end of the phone or an e-mail address, our video image offers far more information about who we are. This impacts everything from customer service to organizational communication. The snapshot capability that many desktop videoconferencing systems provide lets us take a picture of the other party and store the image instantaneously. The unresponsive customer service representative or rude clerk may shape up, if they know their picture is attached to their words. If a customer has a problem with the service they received, they can show a supervisor the picture of the person who gave them poor service.

This notion extends to interdepartmental communications within companies. Video makes it far more difficult to brush off responsibility. When the marketing department calls accounts payable to run down some paperwork, a clerk is more likely to respond to the request if the caller knows what they look like. It is much easier to hide behind the partial anonymity of a faceless phone call than a desktop videoconference. Video forces people to sign their work. When people sign their work, they often do their jobs better.

What works and what doesn't

The San Francisco-based architectural firm of Stone Marraccini Patterson has had mixed results with desktop videoconferencing, because of the firm's communication approach. Stone Marraccini Patterson has used ProShare primarily for linking groups of people in San Francisco and Santa Monica. Around ten people would sit along a rectangular conference table, with the ProShare at the end of the table. Essentially the application was a low-cost alternative to a room videoconferencing system with the occasional use of document conferencing.

"It turns out to be a bare bones way of interacting for what our objective is," says Architect Marc Arnold. Because the image of the remote end was ten feet away from many of the participants in San Francisco, communication suffered. "There's camaraderie when they're here in the flesh. But through desktop videoconferencing, there are some nuances that don't translate well," explains Arnold. "These include jokes, facial expressions. ProShare is designed for one-on-one. It's not too great for group communications. We realize we're stretching it." The result was that the group responded to the far end by looking at the speakerphone that was generating the remote audio. Since the speakerphone was at the center of the table, the effect was that the group mostly ignored the camera and monitor. Stone Marraccini learned from its ProShare experience that desktop videoconferencing works best on the desktop, rather than in a conference room. The firm has since had many productive experiences using desktop videoconferencing as a one-to-one collabication medium.

Another company that has used desktop videoconferencing for groups in a conference room is Chromatic Research. Sometimes a telecommuting worker will join the conference. However, the group-to-one communication with desktop videoconferencing at both ends can fall short. "To get a word in edgewise is very difficult," says Jon Loeliger, a software designer for Chromatic who often joins videoconferences from home. "You have to break in. It's hard to see who's about to speak or who wants to speak." In general, personal videoconferencing works best for one person. (See Figure 3–1.)

Distractions: The enemy of personal videoconferencing

Whether personal videoconferencing requires preparation and production planning depends on the purpose of the video meeting. If the objective is to get to know somebody better and perhaps share a virtual beer, minimal preparation is necessary. However, delivering a training seminar or giving a project status briefing through the technology may require more preparation than a face-to-face class or meeting. Because participants have more potential distractions at their own desks than in the more controlled environment of a classroom or meeting room, taking steps to hold the attention of participants is even more important.

Unlike traditional television, personal videoconferencing is a two-way medium. However, what both media have in common is that they require holding the attention of an audience. Television news professionals know that

Courtesy of CLI

Figure 3–1: Desktop to group videoconferencing connectivity using CLI Desktop Video System and CLI Eclipse Gold roll-about system

the typical viewer is constantly distracted. Dinner is burning, the kids are crying, and the telephone is ringing. The video must be compelling enough and the writing seductive enough to compete with all of those distractions and hoist the viewer out of his or her easy chair or yank them in from the next room. Likewise, the person delivering a presentation through personal videoconferencing competes with distractions. E-mail is arriving, the telephone is ringing, a fax comes in, a colleague walks in the office. One manager at a leading software company says he answers e-mail and does other computer tasks during desktop videoconferences, and his remote colleagues believe he is simply taking notes on the video meeting.

With all of these distractions at several desktops during a multipoint link competing with the presenter, production and planning are critical. The key is to plan a training seminar or a project status briefing as a producer would organize a newscast. Use video clips, simple and colorful graphics, sound effects, exciting presentation software, varied camera angles, props, and anything else that will pace the presentation and keep the personal videoconferencing participants at the edge of their seats. Keep each element as short as possible. If you can make the point with a one-minute video clip, there is no reason to use a three-minute clip. Make sure the presentation is easy to understand. "Confuse 'em, and you lose 'em," a veteran television news executive is fond of saying. Remember that the attention span of the videoconferencing participant may be one e-mail away. Lt. Richard Stakelum of the US Navy believes successful desktop videoconferences are like MTV. "At MTV, they don't tell you about things. They show them to you. They blast you with images. MTV is mesmerizing. We can learn from that, and make desktop videoconferencing better."

Producing compelling presentations through desktop videoconferencing requires creating and choosing visual aids that reinforce a message. Run through the presentation several times. Make sure you can easily call up graphics and other files. If the other participants must wait ten or twenty seconds while you hunt for a chart, they will be reading the memos on their desk.

Active listening is also important to holding the attention of one or more other video meeting participants. Be sensitive to facial expressions and voice tones. Do the other participants look or sound bored or confused? If you are starting to lose them, you may have to pick up the pace or ask them a question to bring them back.

Turn that thing off

Research has shown that comfort level on camera varies considerably from one person to the next. Some people enjoy having their pictures taken, while others feel uncomfortable. Common concerns about desktop videoconferencing include, "What if I'm having a bad hair day?" and "Suppose I want to scratch myself." However, many of these same concerns could apply to face-to-face meetings. Some users grow weary of the medium after an initial honeymoon communicating through desktop videoconferencing. "After the newness wears off, the frustration sets in. The phone is easier to use," says Dennis Riley, who runs Microsoft's desktop videoconferencing lab. "Now you're required to establish eye contact and give the person the attention you didn't have to give them on the phone," insists Riley. Riley says despite collaborative tools that personal videoconferencing provides, multitasking can be more difficult when using the technology compared with the telephone. In Riley's view, it is easier to get away with reading a memo or writing a note if the other person is unable to see you. "I don't have to give 100% to the phone."

Clothes: Turn-ons and turn-offs

Just like in a face-to-face meeting, clothing can either enhance or detract from a personal videoconference. (See Figure 3–2.) There are some videoconferencing clothing guidelines, however, that differ from that of in-person meetings. Shirts and ties are the most critical consideration, because these items are most obvious in a head and shoulders shot. Normally, we sit at our desks in shirt sleeves or blouses even if we wear a suit. Since personal videoconferencing is a collaborative medium, it is rarely necessary to put on a suit jacket. The exceptions would be if you are giving a presentation, attending an important video meeting, or you are wearing a white shirt that you wish to tone down. The most important videoconferencing dress guideline is that white shirts or blouses are the worst choice. They wash out the picture, and are so bright that they are actually a bit hard on the eyes of the person who must look at one on video.

READY ON YOUR PICTUREPHONE® CALL... IF YOU ARE, MR. JONES!

Courtesy of AT&T Archives

Figure 3–2: This cartoon, released by AT&T in 1969, made light of concerns that Picturephone might turn business people into television personalities

The best shirt or blouse for videoconferencing is solid blue. Blue is a rich color that enhances the presentation. Studies show that blue gives the wearer credibility and authority. Blue and white striped, red and white striped, lavender, and yellow shirts can be acceptable second choices depending on your skin tone and preferences. However, be careful of narrow striped shirts that tend to electrify or wiggle on video. Also, cameras tend to read light pink shirts as white, so they are best avoided as well. The best approach here is to test a shirt on camera before you wear it for an important video meeting.

A good rule of thumb is to keep a blue shirt on hand in case the shirt you are wearing looks poor on video or in case a last-minute video meeting is scheduled. Tie guidelines are that complicated patterns are best avoided. "When I know I have a ProShare meeting, I make sure I don't wear a shirt with lots of busy stripes," says Jim Elacqua, Senior Partner of the law firm Arnold, White & Durkee. "But I'm not going out and buying a whole new wardrobe." It is best to avoid red outfits, because they tend to bleed on camera. However, red ties are fine. Large prints and plaids appear busy, and therefore can distract the other person and interfere with communication. Shiny jewelry often reflects light, and is therefore best avoided.

Casual dress is becoming the norm for many professionals, because research has convinced many human resources departments that a more relaxed work environment contributes to greater productivity. Also, the increase in telecommuting has contributed to the decline of suits and dresses, because the home environment encourages people to dress comfortably. Considering these trends, it is often acceptable to wear casual clothes for desktop videoconferences. If the climate permits, sweaters look better than open shirts. Subtle patterns do better on camera than loud ones. Unless the corporate culture is extremely relaxed, tee shirts and sweat shirts are usually far too casual even when telecommuting. And since the other person is usually unable to see below your waste, you could wear your underpants while holding a desktop videoconference from your home office. Just don't jump up to answer the doorbell.

4

Personal Videoconferencing in Action: So What's the Killer App?

Saving time and saving money drive the implementation of almost any technology. Is there a more fundamental killer application, however, for desktop videoconferencing? Katherine Hirzel of Impact Video Communication, a San Francisco-based videoconferencing and communications consulting and training firm, says she believes that problem-solving is the "killer app". "Personal videoconferencing lets everybody who can contribute to a solution come together all at once and work out the problem," says Hirzel. "This synergy allows for more immediate solutions that can be 'make-or-break' for an organization." Dennis Riley, who runs Microsoft's desktop videoconferencing lab, views the "killer app" as customer support. Riley says a trial with Microsoft's Fortune 500 clients revealed that the technology went far in satisfying customers who had problems using products. "The better you support the product, the more people will come to your product," says Riley. "Video seems to be the likely way."

Despite notions of the "killer app", many personal videoconferencing users are finding industry-specific applications for desktop videoconferencing. Product designers, teachers, doctors, engineers, lawyers, customer service representatives, military professionals, recruiters, consultants, financial traders, real estate agents, architects, trainers, and telecommuters are using personal videoconferencing as a communication and collaboration tool. These professionals are slashing time-to-market, speeding decision making, reducing commute time, gaining access to experts, reducing long-distance travel costs, and improving their quality of life.

Not only did AT&T's Picturephone team contribute broadly to the development of later personal videoconferencing technology, but the team also developed applications that many organizations are now applying. In the 1970s, the Phoenix court system used Picturephone so that public defenders could remotely interview their clients in jail. In a high-profile organized crime case, attorneys took depositions through Picturephone. Nurse practitioners used Picturephone to remotely consult with doctors and share X-rays. "We tried to find those segments of the market that would really benefit from visual content," according to Joe Horzepa of Horizon Consultants, a former member of the Picturephone team at AT&T Bell Laboratories and later a marketing director for Picturephone at AT&T headquarters.

This chapter offers a sampling of how corporations, organizations, and individuals are using desktop videoconferencing to make a difference both in business and in life. The first section of this chapter focuses on applications relevant to many corporations. The second section focuses on specialized applications.

Corporate Applications

Product development/manufacturing

In many industries, decreasing time-to-market can translate into millions of dollars a month. Desktop videoconferencing can allow people who are critical to the product process examine and change manufacturing plans in real time. Previously, delays resulted as engineers and managers exchanged numerous phone calls. They would then change the blueprints individually, follow up with faxes or overnight packets, review the changes, and then talk again. Now it takes a one-hour desktop videoconference to accomplish what previously took several days.

Funrise Toy

Funrise Toy in Woodland Hills, California is chalking up major successes through Mega-Conference, a POTS videoconferencing system by Alpha Systems Lab. Funrise designers use desktop videoconferencing to examine toy colors and to approve new samples and artwork while collaborating with their suppliers and partners in Hong Kong. Funrise Toy is using what might be called a "product conferencing" application of the technology. There is no face-to-face communication. Nevertheless, product conferencing can slash time-to-market by two months. This time savings is particularly important as Funrise approaches the November deadline, when toy chains make decisions for their Spring line.

Says Information Systems Manager John Meyer, "We can immediately approve the designs. The clarity is just phenomenal." Funrise is also refining an application in which the toy prototype images can be downloaded to lap tops. The sales force could then use the pictures while on the road. Then Funrise can get immediate customer feedback on designs from salespeople. "They'll know better than we will sitting in the office whether it will fly with the customer or not," says Meyer.

Caterpillar

Peoria, Illinois-based Caterpillar has deployed AT&T Vistium and Intel ProShare at offices and manufacturing plants in the US, England, and Belgium. Caterpillar has boosted manufacturing efficiency by using desktop videoconferencing so that engineers at headquarters can check quality control at plants. In its Greenville, South Carolina and Mossville, Illinois engine plants, for example, Caterpillar has installed Vistium on a cart. Fifty feet of cord connects the Vistium to a camcorder. A quality control person at the assembly line videotapes the engine. At the other end, the Peoria-based engineer can evaluate the product and make changes in the manufacturing process through desktop videoconferencing. "In the past if there were any problems, we've had to fly people down there," says Kristi Moushon, Caterpillar's Video Product Manager. "We're trying to eliminate that day of travel, day of effort, and day back of travel."

Ford Motor Company

Ford Motor Company's design group is reducing time-to-market through the Silicon Graphics InPerson system and other desktop technology. (See Figure 4–1.) InPerson is part of the Ford Global Studio, the company's approach to design through computers. Ford deployed desktop videoconferencing to enhance design efficiency worldwide. Now Ford designers, engineers, and suppliers in Germany, England, Italy, the US and Japan collaborate on drawings and animation in real time while communicating through video face-to-face.

Courtesy of Ford Motor Company

Figure 4–1: A Ford Motor Company Design engineer uses the Silicon Graphics InPerson system to collaborate with colleagues on car designs

Giuseppe Delena, Ford's chief engineer for computer aided industrial design, explains that the real value of desktop videoconferencing is the ability to tackle issues immediately, regardless of distance. Previously, Ford designers either traveled abroad or sent faxes and attempted to walk other designers through changes by describing circles and marks on the page. Says Delena, "The major difference is that rather than having to describe what you're seeing on a fax, everybody can actually see the document together in real time." Delena says desktop videoconferencing has a far different application from that of room videoconferencing, which is used for scheduled group video meetings. "The function of the desktop is an interactive way of solving problems as you go along. You see something and you give somebody a call right away. It's a way of virtually being in the same place as somebody."

Midwest Information Systems

Midwest Information Systems has customized Intel's ProShare in a quality assurance application. (See Figure 4–2.) The software package lets users capture microscope images, digitize, and store them. Users include car companies, chip companies, and medical equipments firms and laboratories. ProShare lets users view and collaborate on the microscope images while communicating through video. For example, the engineering manager of a circuit board manufacturer can work with a technician on the factory floor to correct cracks and other defects. That same manager can remotely evaluate a part coming off the line. A doctor can review tissue samples with a lab technician. "A remote user can actually see what's on a microscope thousands of miles away," says Marketing Director Randy Schnack. Schnack says usually users of Midwest's customized ProShare will begin their collaborative sessions with video interaction. Then they will switch from face-to-face video to the microscope camera and get down to business.

Before Midwest enhanced its software with ProShare, Midwest's customers faxed images among team members. This was inefficient, however, because collaborators were never sure whether they were holding the image the right way. The upper left corner, for example, changes depending on how one holds the image. Also, the additional time spent faxing, phoning, changing, and making follow-up calls required slowed production. "Time is a crucial issue. If I've got a production line sitting idle because we need modifications made, and engineering has to review and sign off, there's a big dollar value attached to that," explains Schnack. Schnack says the customized ProShare application has saved some of Midwest's customers millions of dollars.

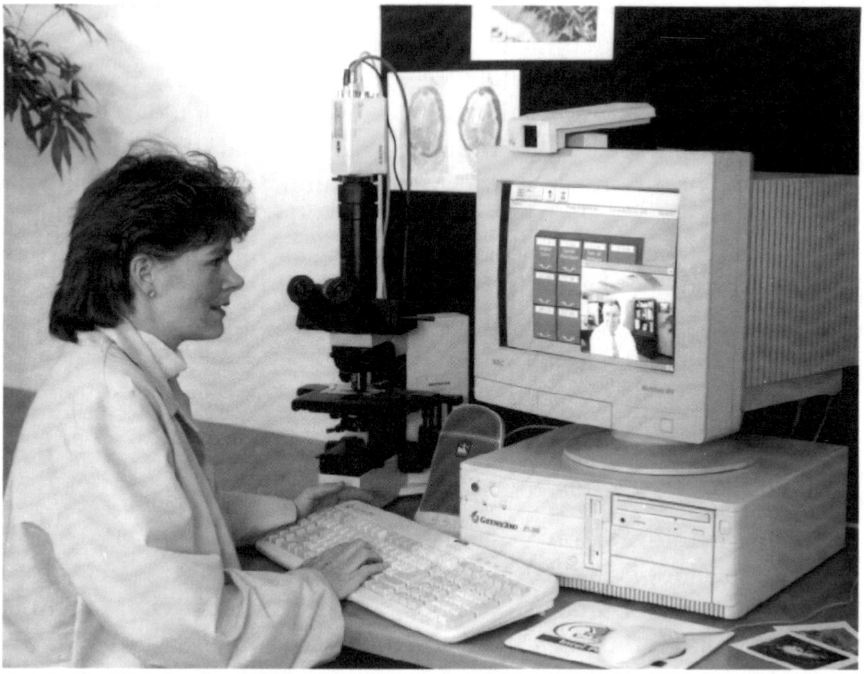

Photo by John Schnack

Figure 4–2: A lab technician uses Intel ProShare in a customized application from Midwest Information Systems to share microscope images with a colleague

NASA

NASA Ames Research Center in Mountain View, California uses a customized InPerson system from Silicon Graphics to link its corporate customers with its remote-access wind tunnel. Defense contractors and aerospace companies like Boeing and McDonnell Douglas contract with NASA to test product models in the wind tunnel. "What we're trying to do is reduce the design cycle time, reduce cost overruns, and keep a tighter reign on the budget," says NASA Engineering Technician Bruce Gilbaugh. "By making the testing dynamic through desktop videoconferencing, we can accomplish that." Previously, a team from a corporate client would visit the wind tunnel periodically. However, desktop videoconferencing allows NASA to involve the client whenever questions or problems arise. NASA has found that numerous phone calls and faxes are tedious and less effective for product testing than face-to-face collabication.

Smith Micro Software

Smith Micro Software in Aliso Viejo, California has deployed C-Phone from Target Technologies to speed time-to-market. Smith Micro develops 65% of data/fax communication software bundled with modems. C-Phone links the company's engineering satellite offices in Boulder, Colorado and Plano, Texas with headquarters and with customers. The key to Smith Micro's business is customizing software to the customer's needs, and doing it quickly.

While desktop videoconferences have replaced travel much of the time for engineers, company management explains that the savings go well beyond the price of plane tickets. "Our window of opportunity is often very small," explains Director of Marketing Bruce Quigley. "And when we have a customer on the East Coast, we'd lose 48 hours of time flying there." Quigley says the 48 hours includes travel time, jet lag, and regrouping. Also, transporting software development tools is difficult. Through desktop videoconferencing, the engineers can conduct product development sessions with all their tools at their fingertips. The result is savings of days—or sometimes weeks—in time-to-market.

Mead Corporation

Mead Corporation in Dayton, Ohio is using desktop videoconferencing to boost manufacturing efficiency in its forest products division. The operations extend from managing forests, through paper mills, to finished paper products, packaging, and distribution. Mead uses desktop videoconferencing to link engineers with contractors and consultants. They use document sharing to collaborate on technical drawings and exchange data files in real time. This approach has substantially increased productivity at manufacturing meetings.

SEMCO

SEMCO, a contractor for the US Air Force, uses document conferencing without video to help design airplanes. SEMCO's district office at Wright-Patterson Air Force Base in Dayton provides logistics and maintenance support, as well as design analysis. Through DataBeam's FarSite system, SEMCO professionals collaborate on design plans with airforce bases across the US and with McDonnell Douglas, which builds the airplanes. SEMCO conducts document conferencing primarily over the Internet through modems. If project parameters change and McDonell Douglas must redesign part of the plane, the company will "put it up on the FarSite" so that all the team members can collaborate on the change.

Previously, changes required people from six air force bases to fly to McDonell Douglas in Long Beach, California. Alternatively, collaborators exchanged countless faxes and phone calls. "It was a nightmare," says Henry Musard, logistics database manager for SEMCO. "Bringing in FarSite, everybody's got it on screen at the same time. It's instantaneous. It's been a tremendous asset to us." Musard says document conferencing has reduced the time it takes to implement design changes from several days to less than an hour. Musard estimates that use of document conferencing by SEMCO, McDonell Douglas and the Air Force for aircraft design has saved taxpayers up to $600,000 per year in travel expenses. This figure excludes savings in labor costs.

3M

PictureTel's Live 100 is linking 3M Corporation's manufacturing directors with supervisors in plants. The technology lets the manufacturing directors give constant input into product quality and design. 3M also uses Live 100 in a remote maintenance application. Says Keith DeStasio, video services product manager for 3M,"If you have a sophisticated piece of manufacturing equipment and limited expertise to repair it, the technology gives you immediate access to that expert." DeStasio says the remote maintenance application can save 3M two weeks of down time on a manufacturing line.

Boeing

Boeing uses Intel ProShare to troubleshoot problems while building airplanes. Because of desktop videoconferencing, the company was able to slash nearly $7 million in door maintenance costs during the 777 project. That represented an 80% savings. "What people have forgotten is the revenue part of it," says Ray Sollars, Boeing's operations manager for network applications. "Not only do we get increased turn-around and reduction in cycle time, we also generate revenue." Desktop videoconferencing has helped Boeing shave two months off of a one-year airplane product cycle schedule.

Recruitment

Viewnet

Corporate recruiters, who often travel to campuses, are saying goodbye to long weeks on the road. Madison, Wisconsin-based Viewnet has customized a

ProShare application for corporate recruiting. Among other changes, Viewnet has modified ProShare's *notebook* to accommodate a full resume. Citibank and Procter & Gamble are among the companies that have implemented Viewnet's InterVIEW product for college recruiting. In some cases, the campuses themselves are providing the technology to corporate recruiters to get their students jobs. However, the opposite is true with Citibank. The company is paying to install desktop videoconferencing at college recruitment offices in the US and Europe. Some are big-name schools, but many are smaller colleges, physically distant from the headquarters of most major corporations.

Citibank

"A big thing desktop videoconferencing can do is allow people who are off the beaten track to get into the process," says Peter Thorp, Citibank Vice President for Corporate University Relations and Educational Programs. "You can be a superb person, but if you go to a school not on a company's list, it's hard to overcome that." Thorp says the technology has proved valuable in recruiting African-Americans and other minorities attending smaller colleges.

Typically Citibank uses InterVIEW, the customized ProShare application, for initial interviews and closing interviews. Usually, the company flies in a candidate for an in-person meeting in between. Without videoconferencing, however, Citibank would never gain initial access to some candidates, and those people would never have the opportunity to interview with Citibank. "You've all of a sudden made the world that much smaller without an airplane ticket," Thorp says.

Citibank's initiative to buy desktop videoconferencing systems for colleges stems from a similar effort when fax machines first became standard business technology. When the bank discovered that many schools—including one Ivy League college—were without fax machines, Citibank bought 23 machines and distributed them to the schools.

Desktop Videoconferencing Consortium

More than twenty colleges in the southeast US have formed the Desktop Videoconferencing Consortium. The Consortium has installed Intel Proshare on each of the campuses. As recruiters make their rounds of the Consortium colleges, they can use desktop videoconferencing to interview candidates at any participating campus. "It certainly helps employers who only get a few students they want to talk to at a school," says Bob Greenberg, Career Services Director for the University of Tennessee. "They can reach out to more schools at a reasonable cost." Kimberly Raddee, a University of Tennessee student, was among the early users of InterVIEW. During a promotional video for the product she commented, "At first it seemed a little bit awkward because of the camera, but once you got going you forgot all about that you were talking to a computer."

Telecommuting

Companies worldwide are deploying desktop videoconferencing to make telecommuting more viable. The technology can reduce isolation that home-based workers sometimes feel, while cutting real estate and travel costs for employers. Desktop videoconferencing also makes rural living more practical for professionals, because they can do their jobs without being cut off from meetings and other face-to-face interaction with clients and coworkers.

Jack Nillis, author of *Making Telecommuting Happen* and a corporate consultant, believes desktop videoconferencing is important in reducing feelings of isolation while working from home. "It's useful as a psychological aid. People seem to feel better about decisions if they can see people's reactions." Nillis says desktop videoconferencing is more valuable for some kinds of meetings than others. He says a key use is last-minute or emergency meetings that require professionals to stop work and commute to the office. In this case, desktop videoconferencing saves time. Nillis believes, though, that prescheduled monthly meetings are more effective in person, so that telecommuters keep plugged in to the corporate culture.

Aside from his desktop videoconferencing model for emergency meetings, Nillis emphasizes the value of document conferencing and application sharing over talking-head video for most telecommuting applications. Nillis also cautions companies who are tempted to use the technology for keeping tabs on home-based workers. "Using videoconferencing as a monitoring technique is very destructive," Nillis says. "If employees feel that someone's watching them all the time, they will behave like prisoners, doing just the minimum work."

Gil Gordon, editor of *Telecommuting Review* and a Monmouth Junction, New Jersey based consultant, says there is a need to understand what desktop videoconferencing can and can't do for telecommuting. Gordon agrees with Nillis that "techno-pseudo supervision" is an ineffective application for desktop videoconferencing. Gordon insists that if managers are that concerned about workers staying at their desks at home, the solution requires more than technology.

Gordon advises against mandated telecommuting, and also believes working from home is less effective for single professionals who desire social interaction. Desktop videoconferencing, according to Gordon, allows some professionals to telecommute who previously had to work from a company office. He says the technology is most valuable for telecommuters whose jobs have a visual element. "If I'm a manufacturing manager with product coming off the line and I've got to show it to my design engineer at home, then it's great," says Gordon. "But these types of jobs do not constitute most telecommuting jobs."

British Telecom

In 1993, British Telecom (BT) conducted a telecommuting trial in which 11 directory assistance operators in Inverness, Scotland participated. (See Figures 4–3 and 4–4.) BT based the study in Inverness, because northern Scotland

Courtesy of British Telecommunications

Figure 4–3: A British Telecom directory assistance operator in Inverness, Scotland works from home

Courtesy of British Telecommunications

Figure 4–4: A supervisor at the British Telecom Inverness Directory Assistance Center

had an early roll-out of ISDN. The objective of the study was to develop support systems and products so that BT's customers could implement telecommuting. In the trial, BT provided the operators with BT's VC8000 PC desktop videoconferencing system, which was developed with IBM. The ISDN-based system included a shared whiteboard. Other capabilities BT provided the operators included emergency alert for notifying a supervisor of a domestic emergency, Newsflash to distribute urgent information to the telecommuters, electronic forms to replace paper forms, e-mail, and electronic bulletin boards.

The primary application of desktop videoconferencing for the Inverness operators was to reduce isolation by linking them with the break room at the office. This way, they could enjoy a virtual tea break with coworkers. Mike Gray, Teleworking Systems Project Manager for BT, presented a paper on the study at the Telecommute '93 Conference in Washington, D.C. In the paper, Gray reported that isolation never materialized for most of the study participants. During the study, the directory assistance operators ranked six technological capabilities considering criteria including importance and usefulness. (See Table 4–1.) They ranked desktop videoconferencing as the most important utility. More information on BT teleworking projects is available on the Web at

`http://www.labs.bt.com/innovate/telework/index.html`

	SOS	News Flash	Video phone	E-mail	Docket	White Board	Comfort Break
Importance	2.73	3.09	6.45	4.73	4.36	4.36	2.27
Usefulness	2.55	3.91	5.41	4.77	4.32	4.27	1.95
Ease of Use	3.73	3.91	5.36	2.27	4.91	4.18	3.64
Enjoy	1.27	2.73	6.64	4.64	4.82	3.45	4.45
Learnability	2.95	4.41	4.91	1.27	4.82	4.64	4.09

Courtesy of British Telecommunications

Table 4–1: Six technological factors plus comfort break ranked by British Telecom directory assistance operators.

Ernst & Young

Ernst & Young LLP has implemented AT&T's Vistium and other desktop videoconferencing solutions for applications that include telecommuting. "You can extend your workforce to get the best people, not just those who are locally available to you—and that makes you more competitive," says Bill Muller, Visual Communications Manager for Ernst & Young LLP. Ernst & Young uses desktop videoconferencing in its consulting business to link full-time, home-based software consultants with coworkers in company offices, as well as clients. Previously, the company had to fly its consultants to company offices once a week and also pay hotel bills. Desktop videoconferencing allows Ernst & Young LLP to hold meetings without necessarily scheduling them. Now for many of the consulting firm's professionals, Muller says "Work is something I do rather than someplace I go."

Bank of Boston

The Bank of Boston uses InSoft's (now Netscape's) Communique! to link home-based programmers with the bank's headquarters. Stephen Scullen, Director of Treasury Systems for the bank, says the bank has found Communique! particularly valuable for programmers who are sick or on maternity leave. "It keeps them in the loop on things that are happening," says Scullen. There is also an advantage to managers at headquarters in that there is immediate, video face-to-face access to telecommuters. "Desktop videoconferencing makes it feel like they're at work and you can get at them more quickly," says Scullen. The Bank of Boston has found that personal videoconferencing has reduced isolation for telecommuters. A problem the bank encountered before implementing the technology was that telecommuting interfered with informal face-to-face communication that helps preserve the company's culture. Desktop videoconferencing has partially bridged the gap, according to Scullen.

Novacor

Calgary-based Novacor uses PictureTel Live 100 systems to link its Switzerland-based sales managers with headquarters. Because of the time difference between Canada and Switzerland, Novacor has installed Live 100 in the managers' homes. This allows them to talk with sales people using PictureTel room systems in Canada. Novacor says desktop videoconferencing serves the Switzerland-based sales managers better than the phone, because the managers often need access to information in their computers while they are talking with headquarters. Video is also a major factor, says Senior Telecommunications Specialist Peter Lee. "They find it a lot more effective to be able to see people at the other end and be able to share information with them than simply talking on the telephone," Lee explains. "They feel like they've met the person. People feel like they have something at stake with the person. It's as if something more personal happens than with a phone conversation."

Chromatic Research

Chromatic Research, a multimedia software and chip company in Mountain View, California, hires engineers around the country because of desktop videoconferencing. Engineers in Texas and Massachusetts, for example, collaborate from their homes with their counterparts in California through VIVO Software's Telework-5 system. While data and application sharing are more important than video for many engineering applications, Chromatic Research relies heavily on face-to-face exchanges. "Communication isn't just words. It's also facial expressions. When you're doing development work, it's important for people to see each other on a fairly regular basis." says Dave Holt, Vice President of Software. For Chromatic Research, there is also a recruitment value in desktop videoconferencing. "In some areas, it's been very difficult for us to find quality people, and this has really helped," according to Holt. "We've been able to use the entire US as a recruiting base." Desktop videoconferencing has also allowed engineers to avoid typically higher living costs in California.

Help desk

SAP Software

SAP Software technical support professionals are using Intel ProShare to walk customers through programs. Waldorf, Germany-based SAP is the fifth largest software manufacturer in the world with a rapidly growing base of over 4600 customers in over 40 countries. The software, which is used for everything from human resources to sales, involves moving through up to ten screens to reach the section the user needs. Therefore, providing help desk services is critical to SAP's business. Previously, SAP technical support people would spend half an hour on the phone walking customers through software. With desktop videoconferencing, however, the help desk operator and the customer can simultaneously view the application on screen while communicating face-to-face through video.

"It's a more powerful or complete form of communication," says Remote Services Manager Bob Leader. "Sometimes the telephone is not enough and going to the customer site is too much. So, it's almost like being there, looking over their shoulder."

Training

NYNEX

C-Phone from Target Technologies is letting NYNEX remotely train accounts receivable professionals. NYNEX is deploying desktop videoconferencing to reduce in-person instructor training by half and curb rising education costs.

Amoco

Amoco is slashing time and expense by using Intel ProShare for remote training. The company's technology division has used desktop videoconferencing to remotely train professionals in using basic software. It takes 15 minutes for people to learn a client/server calendar application, for example. That's down from three hours before the division implemented the remote approach. "It's just-in-time training, which is what you want," says Amoco Staff Consultant Joe Jesson. "All you miss is the coffee and rolls and B.S.ing around."

Project management

3M

3M Corporation uses PictureTel's Liveshare document conferencing software to manage projects. In one example, managers and others in a supply chain project collaborate from home, the office, hotels, and manufacturing plants to get the job done. 3M uses Liveshare document conferencing, which works over analog phone lines, because it is difficult to support video in all of the environments that the project team uses.

Eisys

Houston-based Eisys uses desktop conferencing without video to manage projects for its clients in the environmental field. (See Figure 4–5.) Eisys is an information resource company for natural resources exploration. Clients include oil companies, mineral companies and railroads. Eisys uses

Courtesy of Mark Price

Figure 4–5: Peter Price of Eisys uses DataBeam FarSite document conferencing software to share satellite images with clients

DataBeam's FarSite to share satellite images, maps, and diagrams with its clients as part of environmental evaluations. In one project, Eisys collaborates with Marathon Oil through FarSite. The project includes an environmental evaluation of an oil pipeline site on Sakhalin Island in the Sea of Okhotsk. Desktop conferencing has eliminated the cycle of overnight mail, faxing, delivery by messenger, and follow-up phone calls.

Eisys Director of Exploration Peter Price says his use of FarSite has saved the hour commute to Marathon and has also reduced stress. Instead of making a formal presentation in a foreign environment like a board room, Price can dress casually and remain in his environment. "This gives me the opportunity to make presentations from my own computer where I have all of my resources around me." Eisys is also using FarSite to conference through voice and data with engineers using laptops in the field.

Lockheed Martin

Lockheed Martin has deployed Apple Computer's QuickTime Conferencing in the offices of its President and other senior executives. Project management is one of several applications the company has found for desktop videoconferencing. Tom Manley is a Senior Systems Analyst for Lockheed Martin as well as President of an Internet marketing firm called INET Marketing. Manley has used both CU-SeeMe and QuickTime Conferencing both at Lockheed and at INET. "At Lockheed, projects seem to drive the need for desktop videoconferencing," says Manley. "I've gotten several requests from project managers whose work could benefit from desktop videoconferencing. Engineers and others need to be able to see each other and show each other projects." Manley says the technology has allowed project team members in different cities to collaborate. He says the technology has also provided the ability to make faster financial decisions for projects by letting professionals collaborate on spreadsheets in real time.

Laidlaw Environmental Services

Columbia, South Carolina-based Laidlaw Environmental Services uses AT&T Vistium to manage corporate reengineering projects. The company is using desktop videoconferencing to link internal software developers in Tampa with business process professionals in Columbia. Laidlaw originally implemented desktop videoconferencing to save travel costs between Columbia and Tampa, but the company has discovered far more valuable benefits. "The increased efficiency is more of an issue than the reduced travel cost," says

Louis Belt, Regional Network Administrator for Laidlaw. "You end up with a company that can respond much more quickly, especially for emergencies." Laidlaw software developers and reengineering professionals also maximize collaborative capabilities. Explains Belt, "We can diagram out what we're talking about so people at the other end can see."

Remote expert/consulting

SAP Software

Besides manufacturing software, SAP also provides consulting to modify the software for the customer environment. Consulting projects can last from two months to two years. Through ProShare, SAP boosts efficiency and saves its customers money. Instead of charging by the day for on-premise consulting, SAP can charge by the hour by delivering services through desktop videoconferencing. There are other benefits as well. Bob Leader, remote services manager, says "It no longer becomes a matter of who's available in the area, but rather who has the expertise." An expert in Germany, for example, may consult with a client in the US. Previously, SAP might have assigned a consultant who was geographically closer. SAP uses remote consulting for database reorganization, upgrades, pricing, costing, some customizing, and answering questions. However, SAP finds on-site consulting works better for developing strategy and concepts.

Andersen Worldwide

Andersen Worldwide has implemented ProShare across its organization. The consulting firm has pockets of experts who rely on teams of support people who are geographically distributed. "The biggest potential is changing the way people work," according to Christine Traut, Application Strategies Manager. Traut says that uniting the experts with support people creates more of a cohesive team. Before using desktop videoconferencing, Traut says that it was difficult getting the support professionals to feel involved in the experts' projects. However, the technology has gone far to accomplish Andersen's objectives of bridging the physical distance gap and providing more effective consulting to clients. "Video causes enough of an emotional relationship that people are willing to sit and interact with each other."

Telemaintenance

US Navy

Corporations and the military have deployed desktop videoconferencing to slash the cost of maintaining equipment. The US Navy uses C-Phone from Target Technologies to maintain ships remotely. C-Phone is aboard the USS Rentz, USS Mt. Whitney, USS Princeton, USS John Paul Jones, and the USS Lincoln. Instead of flying a repair person to a ship, the remote expert can view the equipment, diagnose the problem, and instruct the crew how to perform maintenance. The Navy uses telemaintenance to fix radar, other communication systems, and engines, among other applications. The customized system includes a wireless camera transmitting to the C-Phone unit.

Previously, it took as long as seven days to fly the repair person to a ship. The Navy estimates it saves 300-thousand dollars a year in technical assistance costs through the use of desktop videoconferencing. The Navy is constantly expanding telemaintenance applications for desktop videoconferencing. "It's really effective in training technicians," according to Lt. Richard Stakelum, electronic materials officer in San Diego. "Instead of training them on shore, we can train them in the use of their equipment while they are standing at their equipment." Lt. Stakelum says C-Phone saves the Navy the cost of building mock-up equipment for on-shore classrooms.

Emergency management

Consolidated Edison

Consolidated Edison in New York has deployed Datapoint's Minx system to manage emergencies and improve communications during major repair jobs. During power outages, for example, Con Ed uses a camera connected to a wireless link to a truck. The truck microwaves video to a transmitter atop New York's Empire State Building. From there, a combination of fiber and coaxial cable transmits the video to desktops at headquarters. Previously, Con Ed relied on television news reports of disasters. Desktop videoconferencing has allowed the utility to gather more useful visual information. "We have control of our destiny," explains Hussein ElBadaly, a research and development section manager. "We're watching everything rather than watching censored clips from the news media and trying to make sense of it by phone." The Minx system also lets Con Ed field professionals share

Computer Aided Design (CAD) drawings and taped video clips with managers at headquarters.

Duke Power Company

Duke Power Company is managing emergencies via Incite's Conversational Media system. The desktop videoconferencing system links nuclear power plant personnel with the company's emergency operations center. During emergencies, on-site engineers share vital information including response checklists with the operations center while communicating through video face-to-face. The utility says that deploying desktop videoconferencing has enhanced communication and has therefore improved crisis management.

Relocation alternative

Amoco

When Amoco moved its human resources managers from the Chicago area to Tulsa, the support people balked. Many told the company they would quit rather than move. When Amoco officials began tabulating the new hire training costs, they realized they needed an alternative. Amoco Staff Consultant Joe Jesson presented the desktop videoconferencing solution. The company implemented Eris from RSI Systems, Intel ProShare and other systems, creating a work environment that is "location independent." Support people around Chicago can communicate and collaborate with human resources managers now based in Tulsa. They can work together to eliminate bugs from human resources system software. "This is an extremely powerful alternative," explains Jesson. "It's expensive to rehire people. If someone leaves the company and they have a skill in their head, you lose that. It takes six months before someone is up to speed, plus you have to pay recruiting costs."

Document production

Amoco

Amoco is using RealTime Notes, which is a combination of ProShare and Lotus Notes, so that teams can collaborate on technical position papers. These papers are used to brief internal users on the merits and pitfalls of many technologies. Also, the papers set internal standards for office suite software, operating systems, networking and other technologies. Typically, team members work asynchronously through groupware in the earlier stages and then "glue it all together" through desktop videoconferencing. Previously, professionals based in different cities had to cut a week or two out of their schedules. They would spend the time in a conference room working on the document. Besides slashing project time by about 30% and saving travel costs, using desktop videoconferencing has created a more effective process. "This way you have more time for research and to build a case. You're not locked up in a room cut off from new developments and information," says Joe Jesson of Amoco.

Specialized Applications

Distance education

Distance education promises to transform the way people learn. No longer does a school require bricks and mortar. What is more important is effective teachers and eager students. Those students may attend classes from the convenience of their livingrooms, home offices, or even company offices through personal videoconferencing. Children are now at less of a disadvantage based on their geographical location. Rural students, for example, can get access to better teachers through personal videoconferencing in their classrooms. There is always a flip side to the benefits an application offers. Sometimes real-time distance education falls short, because busy people are unable to attend classes at the scheduled time. In these cases, store-and-forward distance education is more effective.

The School of Visual Arts

The School of Visual Arts in New York City uses CLI's Cameo to link its Institute for Computers in the Arts with students and teachers in other cities. SVA is the largest independent school of the arts in the United States, drawing more than 2,200 full-time students and 4,000 continuing education students. SVA was the first site in New York to receive ISDN, and began using desktop videoconferencing in late 1992.

Through distance learning, SVA teachers David Biedny and Bert Monroy have remained on the faculty even though they now live in California. Biedny and Monroy are authors of the computer image-processing book called the

Official Adobe Photoshop Handbook. Biedny and Monroy have taught classes by remotely controlling a computer in a New York classroom and by evaluating students' work remotely. The school now offers a graduate course devoted to developing curricula for teaching interactive multimedia and art history remotely. Students in other countries who would otherwise have to travel thousands of miles can now remotely see and talk with other students in New York. They can also team up on projects by working on each other's computers.

SVA has also used Cameo in a unique desktop videoconferencing experiment called Rest Rooms. The purpose of the study was to examine changes in concepts of privacy and equality, and the experiment was designed to stimulate political and social debate. SVA customized Cameo in a kiosk and installed the systems just inside both men's and women's restrooms but outside the stalls. Each screen was divided into four sections. One section displayed the video image from the other sex's restroom while another smaller section showed the local image. Another section displayed a common "graffiti" space so that people from both locations could write comments or draw on a shared whiteboard. The final section showed Quicktime movies that were clips of gender-related television advertising. The project provoked debate about how privacy and gender guidelines are evolving.

Clarendon College

Clarendon College in Nottingham, England is using GPT desktop videoconferencing systems to make college courses available to more people. Transmission is over a 2-Mbit fiber optic cable, and the college can vary the bandwidth based on the quality of video required. Desktop videoconferencing links the campus with the African Caribbean National Association Centre, a language business centre, and a community center. Courses include training in basic business skills, language training, and sign language.

Northwestern University

The School of Education and Social Policy at Northwestern University is using Apple's QuickTime Conferencing and CU-SeeMe to teach grade 6–12 students. The project is called Learning Through Collaborative Visualization (CoVis), and the objective is for students to "learn science by doing science." The approach involves encouraging students to ask diverse, open-ended questions of teachers and experts. CoVis has used desktop videoconferencing to let students sit in on real-time weather briefings by atmospheric scientists at the University of Illinois. Also, the technology has allowed students to take virtual field trips to the Exploratorium, a hands-on science museum in San Francisco.

The Exploratorium

The Exploratorium has used both Apple's QuickTime Conferencing and CU-SeeMe over the Internet to teach science students. The museum got interested in desktop videoconferencing as a way to expand its influence beyond the 600-thousand visitors a year that it can accommodate. "It's definitely a way of extending our reach," says Technical Curator Larry Shaw. Through desktop videoconferencing, the Exploratorium demonstrates everything from reinforcing buildings for earthquake protection, to the phenomenon of light and shadows. The special desktop videoconferencing system includes a backpack with a video transmitter worn by a cameraperson who takes students through the exhibits while a teacher talks. Presentations also include photo CD stills of the outside and inside of the museum. During the videoconference, the students are free to ask questions. The Exploratorium has also used desktop videoconferencing to link elementary school students with the museum's biologists and physicists, so that the students can pick the brains of the experts.

The Exploratorium's desktop videoconferencing program received worldwide attention in September of 1995 when President Bill Clinton and Vice President Al Gore visited the museum and helped teach a class through the technology. The President's mission was to promote computers in the classroom. He engaged fifth-graders from Ross School, north of San Francisco, in a videoconference discussion of hurricanes and other storms. One student asked the President if he had ever been caught in a tornado, and the President described the many twisters that tore threw Arkansas while he was Governor.

Oregon Museum of Science and Industry

The Oregon Museum of Science and Industry is incorporating CU-SeeMe into exhibits, allowing visitors to explore Internet-based videoconferencing. Also, the Museum is using desktop videoconferencing to link its experts with elementary school classes. The technology helps experts teach technology, geography, socialization skills and communication. The museum also uses CU-SeeMe to train staff.

Strathclyde Regional School District

A regional school district in Scotland is linking rural classrooms through BT VC8000 desktop videoconferencing systems over ISDN. (See Figure 4–6.) The network includes classrooms from the inner Hebridean islands and the Argyll and Bute. Some of the schools are so remote that one or two teachers instruct students whose ages range from five to twelve years old. Officials of the Strathclyde Regional Council says desktop videoconferencing is helping keep rural communities alive by bringing higher quality education to students.

Courtesy of British Telecommunications, Enigma Publishing

Figure 4–6: In the remote islands and highlands, Scottish schoolchildren use a British Telecom VC8000 system to communicate and collaborate with their teachers and children in other rural areas

Astrophysical Research Consortium

The Astrophysical Research Consortium (ARC) uses CU-SeeMe to monitor the atmosphere. ARC has built a 3.5-meter remotely controlled telescope that sends images over the Internet through a Macintosh computer with a graphical interface. A related project called the Center for Astrophysical Research in Antarctica (CARA) is also applying the ARC model to monitoring the South Pole. Besides letting high school students observe the South Pole, CARA uses CU-SeeMe for face-to-face communication between researchers at the University of Chicago and the ground staff at the South Pole.

The Open University

The Open University in England uses CU-SeeMe so that students around the world can attend a Virtual Summer School. Students take classes from home, communicating with other students in other continents and also interacting with guest lecturers.

Telemedicine

RDS America

Desktop videoconferencing is changing medicine by containing costs and linking patients with specialists who might otherwise be beyond reach. RDS America Corporation's core business is interpreting medical images, including X-rays, MRI, CAT scans, and ultrasound. RDS uses Intel's ProShare with Radiology Telenetwork International software to let doctors, radiologists, and patients examine a CAT Scan, for example, that may hold the key to treating the patient. Particularly in rural areas, many specialists are in short supply. Their ability to review a medical report and consult with a patient through desktop videoconferencing is far more efficient than traveling or mailing documents and following up by phone.

"We were able to generate a report on a patient literally before they got dressed," says Dr. Roger Stronell, former President of RDS. Stronell now heads RTI, the software company that implemented the specialized videoconferencing systems for RDS. He says desktop videoconferencing also produced some surprise benefits for RDS. RDS now uses the PC platform to store X-rays and reports. Instead of paying roughly $5 per X-ray film and taking up shelf space to store a file, RDS pays $10 for a CD-ROM disc that stores up to 600 patient records on video. "This allowed us to be able to pay for the technology out of savings," says Stronell.

Bassett Healthcare

Cooperstown, New York-based Bassett Healthcare is using AT&T Vistium to link 17 rural hospitals or outreach centers throughout upstate New York. A primary reason Bassett deployed the videoconferencing systems is the unpredictable weather the region experiences between November and May. Snow frequently caused cancellations of continuing medical education classes and administrative meetings for doctors and staff that commuted from remote hospitals to Cooperstown. Desktop videoconferencing allows Bassett to schedule classes and meetings with more confidence that they will take place.

Bassett Healthcare says it has discovered other benefits to the technology. In the past, the network has lost professionals to bigger towns, because of the isolation they have experienced at outreach centers. Desktop videoconferencing is providing a sense of community for Bassett, and is a major plus in recruiting and keeping doctors and other health care providers. "Some people would say why not pick up the phone," says Martha Gorman, Bassett Healthcare's Research Institute Manager. "But if I can see you, I can see what you're wearing. You can see my body language and the whites of my eyes. I think that adds a dimension that a simple phone call doesn't give you." Bassett is also working on other telemedicine applications, including patient consultations with nutritionists, nurses, and physical therapists. In these applications, Bassett can videotape the consultations to give the patient a take-home treatment guide.

Maritime Health Services

Maritime Health Services in Seattle has used desktop videoconferencing for remote medical consultations with medical professionals aboard ships. Typically, commercial ships have a medical officer aboard with basic training. Therefore, MHS contracts with shipping companies to provide doctors remotely. MHS has used desktop videoconferencing boards from Workstation Technologies to conduct medical consultations via satellite. Dr. Raymond Jarris, President of MHS, says he sees a particular value for desktop videoconferencing in cases where doctors must view wounds. "A burn, eye injury, laceration, rash, something with a real visual component could make the technology very important," Jarris says.

Thomas Jefferson University Cancer Center

Thomas Jefferson University Cancer Center in Philadelphia uses ProShare to link cancer specialists with primary care physicians. The primary care doctors treat patients at eight affiliated hospitals in the Jefferson Cancer Network. Desktop videoconferencing allows a specialist and a primary care doctor to review medical images including X-rays, CAT scans, and MRI's on screen while using video to communicate. "It just makes consulting much more efficient," says Jack London, Director of the Laboratory for Applied Computing at Jefferson. "This is a whole added dimension. The main value is being able to share images. The video is an added bonus." Besides lowering treatment costs, desktop videoconferencing lets patients throughout Pennsylvania receive treatment near their homes rather than driving to center city Philadelphia.

The Bowman Gray School of Medicine

The Bowman Gray School of Medicine at the University of North Carolina is reducing diagnosis time through the Silicon Graphics InPerson system. InPerson links a general pathologist at Wilkes Regional Medical Center, which is a hundred miles away, with specialized pathologists at Bowman Gray via a T1. The doctor at Wilkes uses a microscope connected to a video camera to show the specialized pathologists tissue samples. The images can be frozen and displayed on a white board.

The doctors also communicate video face-to-face through InPerson during the diagnosis session. Previously, Wilkes used Federal Express to send still pictures of tissue samples. In cancer diagnosis and treatment, however, an extra day of waiting can make a difference. "The time factor here is what's important," says Dr. Robert Rainer, Director of Telemedicine for Bowman Gray. "Typically, people are waiting to find out what they have and treatment doesn't begin until then."

Financial trading

Bank of Boston

When the Bank of Boston built its treasury trading floor, the bank searched for ways to eliminate the overhead video monitors that provide essential information but that also block views. Foreign exchange, emerging markets, and derivative traders, for example, needed to see and yell at other traders across the room. To achieve the objective, the bank deployed InSoft's (now Netscape's) Communique! cross-platform and cross-network desktop videoconferencing and INTV! multicast products.

The bank gave each trader access to both video news broadcasts and desktop videoconferencing from their Sun Microsystems workstations. Desktop videoconferencing lets over a hundred traders at various stations around the 30-thousand square foot trading floor collaborate on documents and communicate through video without having to leave their seats. For example, a derivatives trader could collaborate with a fixed income trader while structuring a deal for a customer. Also, "A head trader in Boston can have a videoconference from his position with a head trader in Brazil," says Stephen Scullen III, Director of Treasury Systems for the Bank of Boston. "We can actually have them look at each other, which breeds familiarity. They can also share applications."

Legal/judicial

Law firms are deploying desktop videoconferencing to give clients more one-on-one encounters with attorneys and to slash travel expenses. The technology can also increase billable hours for the firms. Law firms also use desktop videoconferencing internally, so that attorneys in remote offices can collaborate on cases. Courts are using desktop videoconferencing to arraign defendants remotely.

Arnold, White & Durkee

Arnold, White & Durkee uses the Intel ProShare to link clients with 120 lawyers in six US cities. ProShare lets the firm and its clients interactively draft legal briefs while holding face-to-face meetings.

"The greatest value for me," says Senior Partner Jim Elacqua, "is it helps me be face-to-face with clients, giving them the service they want and saving travel and expense." Arnold, White & Durkee says the technology especially pays off for its patent practice. An inventor and an attorney can create a draft of the patent application together by pulling a WordPerfect or Microsoft Word document into a shared on-screen notebook. After two more videoconferences, the application is ready for filing with the US Patent and Trademark Office.

Using desktop videoconferencing saves the law firm travel time and saves the inventor the billed-through travel expenses. Desktop videoconferencing is also essential for tapping the expertise of an attorney in a remote office, and linking that expertise with clients and other attorneys. Growing numbers of the firm's clients are investing in the technology. However, Arnold, White & Durkee has found that in many cases it pays off for the firm to buy clients desktop videoconferencing systems.

Arnold, White & Durkee says desktop videoconferencing is also an effective selling point during interviews with prospective clients. The clients realize that if they invest in desktop videoconferencing, they can collabicate with their lawyers far more often. Desktop videoconferencing also involves clients more in their cases rather than turning their legal plights over to a distant firm.

For internal meetings, Arnold, White & Durkee has found many uses for desktop videoconferencing, among them, management board meetings that can last more than six hours. When the board meets in the firm's Palo Alto office, Elacqua says he has joined the discussion from his desk in Houston via a ProShare to room system video call. Elacqua says desktop videoconferencing "has already had an impact on my firm, and it will have a serious impact on the practice of law in general."

Parnon & Pratt

Parnon & Pratt, LLP in New York has created a virtual law firm through InSoft's (now Netscape's) Communique!. Parnon & Pratt uses Communique! running on Sun Microsystems workstations and PCs to connect its offices in Rockefeller Center with Huntington, Long Island and Houston. The firm provides high-level strategic legal consulting, which includes assembling customized legal teams for complex commercial litigation projects. Fred Parnon, the partner who started the firm, attracted Judge George Pratt to leave the federal bench. Parnon says a selling point for Pratt was his ability to work from Huntington, rather than commute to Manhattan. A T1 connects Rockefeller Center with Huntington. "All day long we watch each other work," says Parnon. "In the old days, partner desks were touching. It's like our desktops are touching."

Parnon & Pratt also uses a 10-foot screen in the Rockefeller Center office, so that clients can meet and share documents with Pratt, who remains in Huntington. Desktop videoconferencing is critical to the firm's business of bringing together ad-hoc legal teams. "I'm trying to have complete locational independence," Parnon says. "Anybody we decide to work with can live anywhere they want to. They can live in Nepal if they want as long as there's a high-speed digital phone line available."

3M

Corporate legal departments are also deploying desktop videoconferencing so that in-house lawyers can collaborate with outside law firms. 3M Corporation's legal department works with fifty outside legal firms. The legal department is using both PictureTel Live 100 and Intel ProShare in its legal collaboration application. While some lawyers have systems in their offices, 3M has also equipped a legal "work room" with desktop videoconferencing systems. Desktop videoconferencing has allowed 3M and its outside law firms to interview expert witnesses before trials. The witnesses have either participated from the outside law firm or another location. Says Keith DeStasio, video services product manager, "They were able to easily screen potential experts. Timewise, they had easy access to the individuals."

Manhattan District Attorney's Office

The Manhattan DA's office in New York has cut in half the time it takes a police officer to conduct post-arrest procedures. It used to take up to fourteen hours for an officer to complete the charging document, called the *complaint*. The process used to require the officer to visit Central Booking and do some paperwork there, then travel to the DA's office for a meeting and more paperwork. Desktop videoconferencing, however, has reduced the time to six hours, and curbed overtime costs considerably. The DA's office uses VTEL 117S video systems which include ProShare data collaboration software. The systems link the assistant district attorneys with each of Manhattan's twenty police precincts.

After an officer makes an arrest, the officer and the assistant DA collaborate on the complaint on screen in real time. The desktop videoconference also gives the DA an opportunity to interview the officer and assess the case. The face-to-face interaction through video is vital, because the assistant DA may decide whether to make a plea bargain based on the interview. Because crisp video is essential to this application, the DA's office is using 1/4 T1 running at 384 kpbs.

MIS Director Leonard Rubin says the telephone falls short compared to desktop videoconferencing. "You want to get a sense of that person, how they're relating to you, whether they make a good witness, things you can't get just from a phone conversation." Rubin says while video may not be essential for every desktop conferencing application, television-quality video would be ideal for the DA's office. "You want to be able to pick up on cues. If a person's giving you an account of something that happened, the video helps make an assessment of the completeness of that account."

Fulton County, Georgia Courts

The Fulton County Courts in Atlanta uses the Datapoint Minx system for video arraignments and other hearings. Dedicated fiber optic cable connects the corrections center with the Superior Court building. The arrangement, which GPTV Cable installed in 1988, was one of the first fiber optic applications in Atlanta. There is one Minx system on the judge's bench, another in front for witnesses and attorneys, and one system in a hearing room inside the jail. Before deploying desktop videoconferencing, the Fulton County Courts had to transport prisoners 3-1/2 miles to the courthouse. This involved gathering prisoners in holding areas, boarding them into buses, unloading them, gathering them in more holding areas in the court building, unshackling them, and then repeating the process after the hearing.

"You essentially had a man who had to have a five or ten minute court appearance and you had personnel who had been moving him from five in the morning to six o'clock at night," explains Bill Smalley, assistant Superior Court administrator. Desktop videoconferencing is reducing the number of days the Fulton County Courts must hold and maintain prisoners before their arraignments. This saves the taxpayers thousands of dollars a year. "It's more efficient justice. Bottom line is what we're about," Smalley says. "It's part of a best use of judicial resources."

Banking and retail kiosks

US Bank

US Bank in Portland, Oregon features UBANK ON-Sight, a ProShare customized as a video banking kiosk. (See Figure 4–7.) Through the system, customers can meet face-to-face with a personal banker at the touch of a video screen. The bank uses the system to sell CDs, checking accounts, overdraft protection, and to process credit card applications. US bank also plans to expand video kiosk services to include consumer lending, mortgage loans and investment services. The technology allows US bank to conduct business in shopping malls and office buildings without having to build and staff branches. "It also allows us to get experience with selling through video. Consumers will be making investment decisions and purchasing decisions through video from their homes," says Mike Cebula, Assistant VP and Product Manager. "By US Bank having this in place, it will give us experience to prepare for that."

Courtesy of Intel Corporation, US Bank

Figure 4–7: A customer uses US Bank's UBANK On-Sight video banking kiosk, a customized Intel ProShare system

Best Buy

Beneficial Corporation has customized Intel's ProShare as a kiosk that lets shoppers apply for credit. Customers of Best Buy stores in Richfield, Minnesota and Hawthorne, California can use the kiosk to collaborate on the application with a credit analyst. The analyst appears screen-to-screen through the ProShare kiosk and can approve the application on the spot. If the customer gets the okay, the kiosk generates a temporary credit card that includes a computer freeze frame picture of the customer. The customer benefit is immediate credit, while the store can free up sales associates so they can move merchandise rather than process paperwork.

Consolidated Edison

Consolidated Edison in New York is using a customized Minx system from Datapoint in a video kiosk application. (See Figure 4–8.) The kiosks let the utility's customers pay their bills, initiate service, or close an account while communicating screen-to-screen with a customer service representative. Because Con Ed requires identification for most services beyond paying bills, a document camera provides an important solution. The customer uses the document camera to show the representative a driver's license. The technology is allowing Con Ed to streamline operations while enhancing customer service. Rather than keeping an army of customer service representatives on standby in case a rush comes, Con Ed can use video kiosks to keep a smaller staff of agents busier as they connect with customers at many locations.

Courtesy of Consolidated Edison

Figure 4–8: A customer uses Consolidated Edison's video kiosk, a customized Datapoint Minx system. The system can be used to start service or pay bills while communicating screen-to-screen with a customer service representative

Huntington Bancshares

Cleveland-based Huntington Bancshares has rolled out The Personal Touch Machine, a video banking kiosk originally based on the AT&T Vistium and now being updated with newer technology. (See Figure 4–9.) Customers can open accounts, apply for an instant loan and get assistance through a video link with a "personal banker." At the customer's touch of a screen, the representative pops up and the video interaction begins. The kiosks also allow customers to locate bank branches and offices by viewing maps, and to calculate loan and investment options. The Huntington video kiosks are available 24 hours a day, 7 days a week.

Huntington's approach is based on consumer demographics. According to a statement from Huntington Bancshares Chairman Frank Wobst, "People are working longer hours, enjoying less leisure time, and struggling to keep up with the pace of their daily lives." Wobst's statement says, "Consumers demand—in fact, will not accept less than—total customer service, anytime, anywhere." Says Bill Randle, Huntington's Marketing and Strategic Planning Director, 80% of customers are delighted with what Huntington calls its "Access Branch," which features the video banking kiosks. "The customer who uses debit cards, credit cards, and has mutual fund accounts tends to be disposed towards video banking," says Randle. Randle, an early believer in customized desktop videoconferencing applications, says the decision to adopt video banking came from the gut. "It was fairly intuitive. I'm trying to complete the cycle of customer self-service."

Courtesy of Huntington National Bank

Figure 4–9: A Huntington National Bank Customer in Columbus, Ohio uses a video banking kiosk in an "Access Branch"

Citibank

Citibank has implemented video banking kiosks based on technology developed by Incite and National Semiconductor. The implementation comes after a trial in Australia. What surprised Citibank were the demographics of the customers who warmed up to the video kiosks the fastest. Customers over 40 were more at ease using the technology than younger people. According to National Semiconductor, the average deposit at six sites in New South Whales was $1 million and the average age of the person making the deposit was over 50. "It was people looking for sophisticated experts. They did not want to open a $1 million account with an 18-year-old teller," Mike Sodergren of National Semiconductor told an audience at the DVC '96 West conference. "It completely violated all of our market research."

Real estate

Virtual Realty

Real estate firms are slashing the closing time on buying houses by more than half through desktop videoconferencing. Virtual Realty of Newport Beach, California uses Intel's ProShare to bring consumers screen-to-screen with lenders at the point of sale. The company has developed loan origination software to customize ProShare for its business. The real estate agent meets with the buyer in a conference room. After the agent qualifies the buyer's purchasing power, the agent begins a desktop videoconference that brings in the Virtual Realty representative. The representative prepares the loan application online, while the borrower and real estate agent provide input. The representative also gathers title information, lot descriptions, and credit information by accessing public records online. The representative then searches a loan database and displays the results, so that the buyer can review the options.

Buyers can circle items on screen and work through all the options with the representative. After the borrower selects a loan, the agent and borrower initiate a second videoconference with the right lender. The lender's representative appears on screen to finalize the deal, using forms that Virtual Realty has transferred electronically. The videoconferencing approach can save consumers 50% on loan origination fees and can also save on mortgage costs by eliminating the middle person. Besides an easier process for home buyers, desktop videoconferencing substantially increases the market penetration for lenders. They can enter and exit any market without needing to open an office in every city where they do business.

Virtual Realty President Michael Barron says the company's customized ProShare product has prompted business from the major real estate companies. Also, Barron says, consumers are rapidly warming up to the technology. "It's incredible. The public goes crazy for this, "Barron says. "They can shop efficiently and effectively. We can speed the process and compress things from weeks down to days, and the consumer really appreciates this."

Contempo Realty

Another company that has customized ProShare for a real estate application is Contempo Realty of San Jose, California. Contempo's Virtual Loan Officer product lets a buyer in a real estate office get loan preapproval on the spot. (See Figures 4–10 through 4–12.) The system connects an underwriter from Contempo's mortgage company subsidiary with the real estate agent and buyer. The group can share the loan application on screen while communicating through video face-to-face.

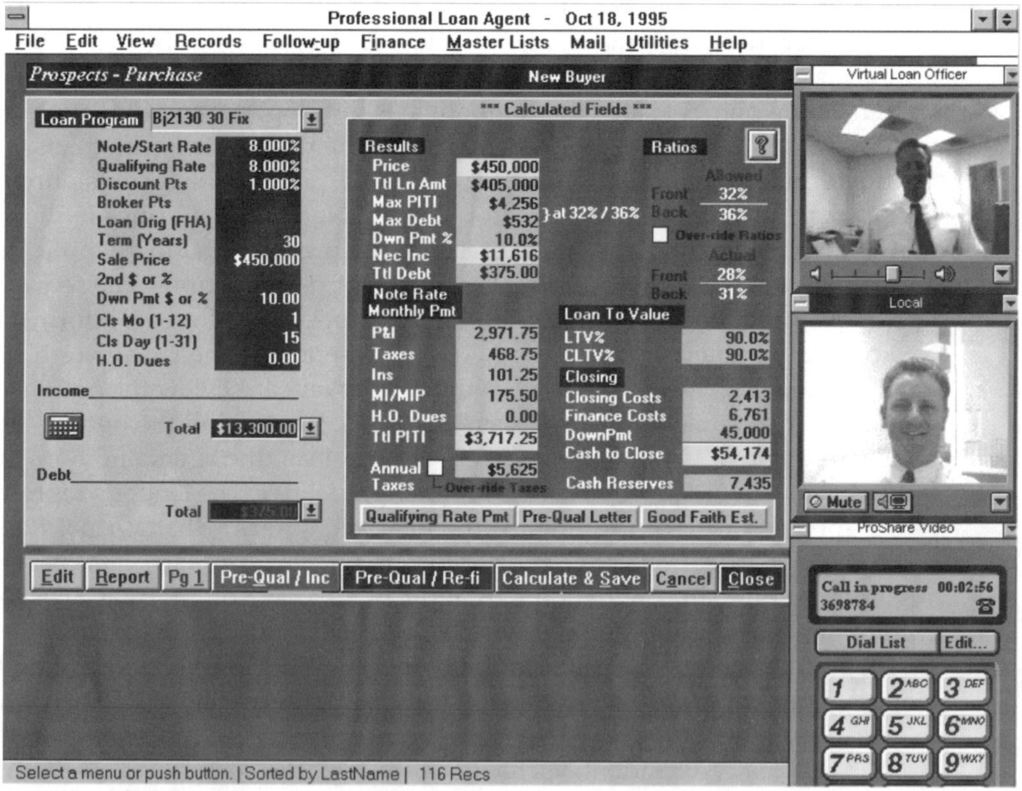

Courtesy of Princeton Capital

Figure 4–10: Contempo Realty's Virtual Loan Officer, a customized Intel ProShare application

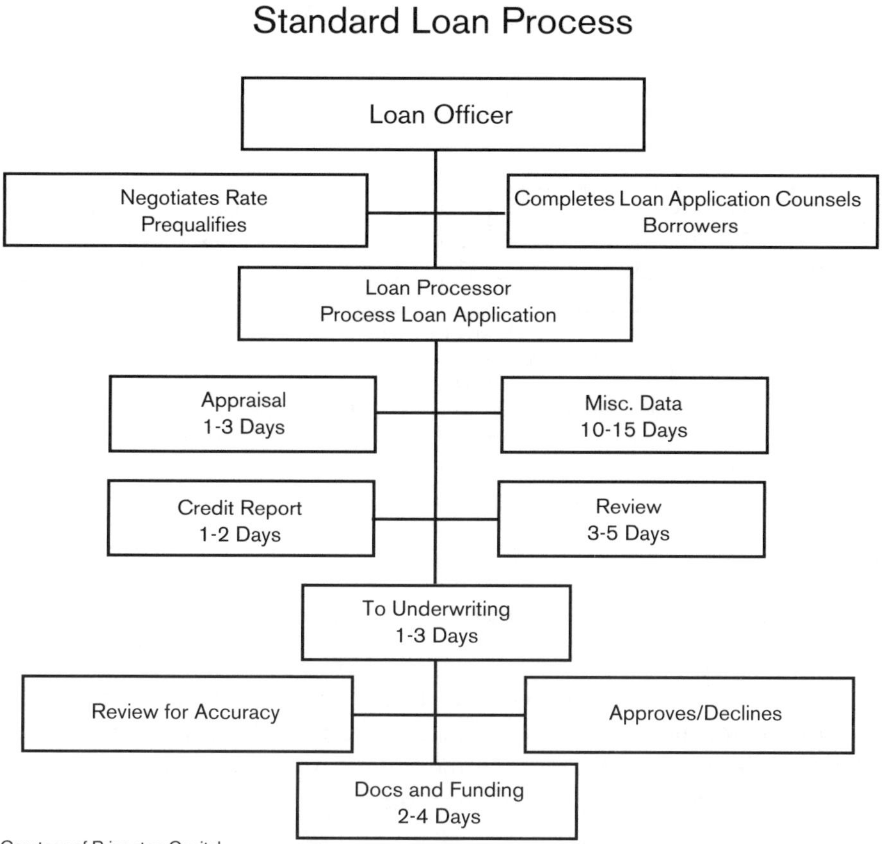

Courtesy of Princeton Capital

Figure 4–11: The traditional home loan process

"From a marketing point of view, it's a great tool. There's also the convenience aspect for the real estate agent who is trying to sell a house and doesn't know how much the buyer is worth," says Marketing Director Kyle Krajewski of Contempo Realty. "For the buyer, it's absolute convenience." Virtual Loan Officer can cut the pre-approval process from 4–10 days to under an hour. However, the borrower must still follow up with tax returns and check stubs before the loan is final. Contempo says companies developing new tracts of land are also using Virtual Loan Officer to presell houses.

Informedia Interactive

Informedia Interactive in Louisville, Kentucky has customized ProShare for a different kind of real estate application. The company's Relocation Station

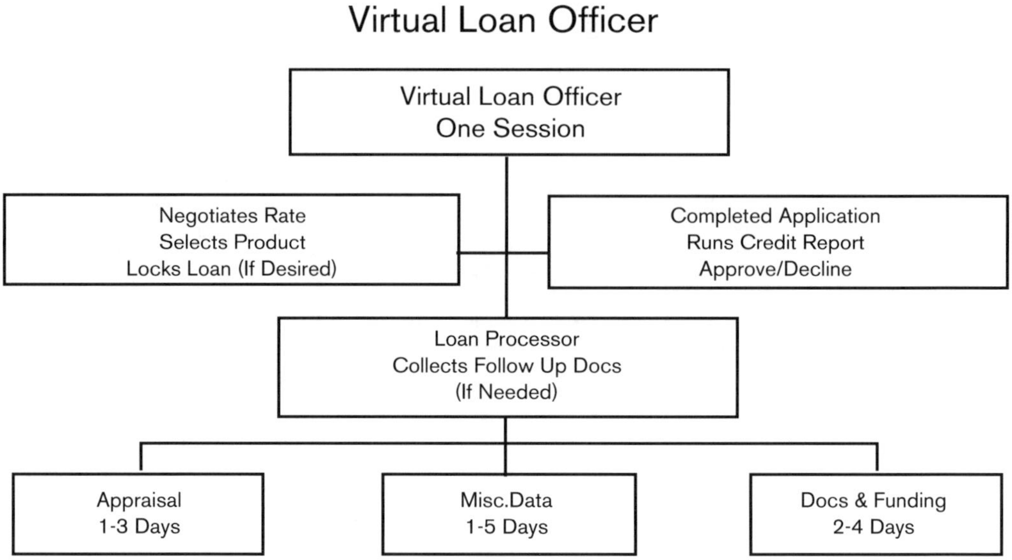

Courtesy of Princeton Capital

Figure 4–12: The home loan process using Virtual Loan Officer

product lets professionals who are relocating review still pictures of houses while collabicating with a realtor through desktop videoconferencing. Through Relocation Station, a home buyer can view up to fifteen interior and exterior pictures of a home. Companies that transfer people frequently are installing Relocation Station, and so are franchise real estate offices. Typically, a professional can visit a real estate franchise in one city and work with a realtor in another city. The realtor can help target a neighborhood based on price range, school district, and other selection criteria. Informedia Interactive says its Relocation Station saves time for both realtors and buyers. "It takes a lot of stress away from relocating, which is one of the top five stress factors in people's lives, ranking with divorce and death," says Chief Operating Officer Chuck Morrison. "It's the whole aspect of using your time more effectively, and minimizing wear and tear from the relocating process."

Film and video production

Mott 4 Productions

Mott 4 Productions in Los Angeles uses Apple's QuickTime Conferencing in its broadcast and interactive design business. Specific jobs require Mott 4 to assemble ad-hoc teams, with many participants working from their homes. Project teams use Apple's QuickTime Conferencing to collaborate on motion graphics, for example, while communicating face-to-face through the technology. Clients include television stations, advertising firms and film production companies. Owner Harry Mott is the former education director of the American Film Institute. Mott says the major advantage of using desktop videoconferencing is time savings. "Instead of having to travel from 10 to 40 minutes in Los Angeles, I can continue to work...especially when I'm on deadline," Mott says. Apple's QuickTime Conferencing also eliminates the hassles involved in ripping out a video production set-up and hooking up drives and reconfiguring the set-up in another location, so that another project participant can view motion graphics.

R/GA Digital Studios

R/GA Digital Studios is using the Silicon Graphics InPerson system to send animation and other produced video between the production company's New York and Los Angeles offices. Producers in both cities then collaborate on the product and make changes in real time almost immediately. R/GA transmits the video over the DRUMS fiber optic, high-speed network developed by Sprint and Silicon Graphics. R/GA has used the DRUMS and InPerson combination to produce television commercials for both Chrysler and NEC. Because even one extra day can break a budget in the time-sensitive entertainment industry, desktop videoconferencing has significantly boosted efficiency for R/GA Digital Studios.

Architecture

Stone Marraccini Patterson

Architecture firms are deploying desktop videoconferencing to collaborate on building plans with clients. San Francisco-based Stone Marraccini Patterson (SMP) focuses on corporate buildings, medical buildings and high technology research facilities. The 125-employee firm has satellite offices in Santa Monica, California and St. Louis, Missouri. Almost every day, at least one architect was shuttling back and forth from San Francisco to Santa Monica, or vice versa, to review drawings with other architects. However, the firm is now using Intel's ProShare, so that architects in different offices can easily collaborate on building plans and make notes on an on-screen whiteboard. For Stone Marraccini Patterson, desktop videoconferencing has substantially reduced the time lost from using overnight mail or wasting a day traveling for a one-hour meeting.

"We're able to get more response and work more closely with a client, and our approval process can be speeded up, "says Projects Administrator Steven Friedland. "We believe it improves the communication both with the client and other members of the team, and therefore desktop videoconferencing improves the product." The Veterans Administration (VA), one of the firm's clients, has also deployed desktop videoconferencing. The technology has not only reduced travel from Washington to San Francisco for the VA, but also has allowed a larger group to participate in reviewing drawings and plans. Also, more frequent client involvement means the firm is able to meet the client's needs more effectively. SMP says desktop videoconferencing has also become an important marketing tool. During presentations to prospective clients, architects join in through ProShare.

Advertising

Netsurf

Netsurf uses Apple's QuickTime Conferencing for its World Wide Web advertising and design business. The Milpitas, California-based firm uses desktop videoconferencing over the Internet so that Web site designers can collaborate with clients. President Rich Herndon says besides communicating screen-to-screen through Apple's QuickTime Conferencing, he shares Macdraw documents with his customers. This gives them an opportunity to provide feedback. For Netsurf, the value of desktop videoconferencing is basic. "They know you. It's human to human. Voice is okay, but it's just not everything."

Media

CNN's "TalkBack Live"

CNN is broadening the studio audience for its "TalkBack Live" show by linking participants through personal videoconferencing. (See Figure 4–13.) MCI and PictureTel are collaborating on the project which features a PictureTel Live 100 system, also marketed as a dvMCI 2000 system. The show's approach is to leverage communication technologies including e-mail, fax, 800 phone lines, and desktop videoconferencing in creating an interactive town meeting. MCI Senior Sales Engineer Patricia Garriga says desktop videoconferencing gives the program special appeal. "It allows people from all over the US to participate in the show," according to Garriga.

CNN has placed the MCI/PictureTel systems at technology trade shows including TeleCon, Interop, and COMDEX. Mostly, the systems run at a bandwidth of 128 kbps. However, CNN has installed one system running at 384 kbps for greater video quality at the Lemelson Learning Center at the Smithsonian Institution. MCI's Cyber-Rig, a semitruck promoting communications technology, also provided a personal videoconferencing link to "TalkBack Live," when the truck rolled across the United States.

Courtesy of CNN "TalkBack Live"

Figure 4–13: The set of CNN's "TalkBack Live. The show uses many communication technologies, including personal videoconferencing, to involve guests remotely

Community service

Education First program

Students at Jedediah Smith Elementary School in Sacramento have taken virtual field trips through desktop videoconferencing. The students, for example, have journeyed to Marine World Africa USA in Vallejo, California without leaving Sacramento. The students have used AT&T Vistium for a link from the Sacramento Public Library to Marine World. Conducting desktop videoconferencing over ISDN, the children have learned about how animals survive both in the wild and in captivity. The park's animal trainers have introduced the students to baby Bengal tigers Gombi and Dakota, and the students have been able to ask the trainers questions screen-to-screen through video.

The virtual field trips are part of the Education First program, sponsored by Pacific Bell and the California Superintendent of Public Instruction. Pacific Bell has installed Intel ProShare and AT&T Vistium in libraries, schools, and community colleges. Objectives of the Education First program are to bring digital bandwidth to communities, develop community-based applications for videoconferencing, and to integrate technology into curricula. At libraries, desktop videoconferencing users have been able to interact with health care professionals through an application called "Doc in a Box." Users have also communicated video face-to-face with Internal Revenue Service agents. This application links taxpayers in California with IRS help desk professionals in Washington, DC Taxpayers share tax forms on screen with an agent who helps them do the paperwork. Also, IRS technology specialists have used application sharing to guide taxpayers through the IRS World Wide Web site while communicating face-to-face through desktop videoconferencing. "It's a win, win, win situation for everybody, including the general public," says Kevin Acoveno, treasury department telecommunications specialist.

Project DIANE

Federal, state and corporate funds are paying for Project DIANE, coordinated by Tennessee State University. DIANE stands for Diversified Information and Assistance Network, which uses desktop videoconferencing as a community outreach and economic development tool. The network links more than thirty schools, community service organizations, and economic development agencies in the Nashville area. DIANE uses PictureTel Live 100 and other systems to keep people plugged into technology, regardless of their economic status. As part of DIANE, desktop videoconferencing is deployed at Cumberland

Science Museum, Grassmere Wildlife Park, the Nashville Zoo, the Elephant Sanctuary, and Looby Metro Public Library.

The network allows students to take virtual field trips and interact with scientists, animal specialists, and other experts. DIANE has also allowed senior citizens at a community center to remotely "adopt" grandchildren at a central-city center for preschoolers. DIANE is also stimulating business development through desktop videoconferencing. The program links small business incubation and resource centers with the Nashville Area Chamber of Commerce and NationsBank. The bank provides courses through desktop videoconferencing in accounting, marketing, management and planning. Also, entrepreneurs share loan applications and business plans in real time with bank officials through conferencing software.

Navajo Outreach Program

Lawrence Livermore Laboratory in California runs a Navajo Outreach Program that links the Native Americans with scientists in the lab. The Navajo reservation is in the four corners area where Utah, Colorado, New Mexico, and Arizona join. Many parts of the reservation are without electricity and phones. Lawrence Livermore is using PictureTel Live 100 to link its liaison at Navajo Community College in Shiprock, New Mexico with professionals at the lab. Lawrence Livermore will expand the program, so that the community gains broader access to lab experts. "The impact is when children have questions about science and engineering, they can carry on a dialogue," explains David Dirks, Videoconferencing Project Manager. "Not only is information transferred, but the experience raises the students' self-esteem. Suddenly, they're not disconnected from society." Dirks says that connection is essential for Navajo children to compete.

Specialized military

US Navy

The US Navy is improving the quality of life for sailors through the use of C-Phone from Target Technologies. The Navy allows families, chaplains, and counselors to communicate with sailors screen-to-screen through ship-to-shore desktop videoconferencing via satellite. During a 6-month stretch at sea, problems at home often arise for sailors. Lt. Richard Stakelum, electronic materials officer in San Diego, offers an example of a sailor opening a letter from his wife. The letter might say his wife needs an operation or a child has been in an accident. However, it is difficult to tell from a letter how serious the situation is. Desktop videoconferencing bridges that gap for the Navy. "A picture's worth a thousand words," says Lt. Stakelum. "You can tell right away the extent of the impact on your family." The Navy also uses desktop videoconferencing to link sailors with their families regardless of whether there is trouble back home. Being able to see and talk with a spouse and children tremendously boosts the morale aboard ships. Because the sailors are less preoccupied wondering about their families, their productivity can rise. The Navy also uses C-Phone to link its bases with hospitals. This allows remote diagnosis and treatment. (See Figure 4–14.)

Photo by K.R. Hirzel

Figure 4–14: Lt. Richard Stakelum of the US Navy demonstrated C-Phone from Target Technologies and a remote diagnosis application

Government

NASA

On September 8, 1995, astronaut Jim Newman made history by conducting the first PC-based "personal conference" from space. Newman, aboard the

Space Shuttle Endeavour, used Intel ProShare conferencing software without video to collaborate with flight ground controller Marsha Ivins at the Johnson Space Center in Houston. During the session, Newman and Ivins shared photographic images and annotated documents with words and drawings. Before deploying personal conferencing, sharing computer information between the shuttle and Houston required time-consuming file transfers.

Department of Trade and Industry

Great Britain's Department of Trade and Industry is deploying desktop videoconferencing to reduce bureaucracy for businesses. The project called ACCEPT uses systems from British Telecom and document sharing software from Olivetti. ACCEPT links six sites across England, allowing businesses to submit required forms electronically while communicating video face-to-face with government workers through the technology. The project is also increasing exports for British companies by linking British embassies and consulates around Europe. Businesspeople in England can use desktop videoconferencing to gain insight into future markets for their products in other countries.

PART II

THE NUTS AND BOLTS

5

The Technology that Makes Personal Videoconferencing Happen

Personal videoconferencing has developed because of an evolution of technology and a revolution in demand. Enabling factors include progress in the design of computer microprocessors, the advent of multimedia PCs, advances allowing viable video compression, the availability of ISDN service, and an explosion in the use of the Internet. Other enabling factors include the ability of PC operating system software to handle real-time video and audio, the development of small and inexpensive cameras, and the emergence of international standards for videoconferencing.

Merged Applications on the Collaborative Desktop

Desktop videoconferencing is part of a larger trend that brings to the desktop many activities that previously required larger facilities and a much bigger investment. These functions include desktop publishing and desktop video production. Some activities, though, were born on the desktop, including collaborative computing.

The merging of collaborative applications has revolutionized the desktop. Several technologies have joined together to turn the desktop into a collaborative computing and communications environment. A useful way to view the collaborative desktop is to divide it into live-interactive applications and stored applications, as is Figure 5–1. The collaborative desktop can also be divided into video applications and information sharing. Visual communica-

	Live/Interactive	**Stored**
Video Applications	Personal Videoconferencing	Video Mail
Information Sharing	Document Conferencing/ Screen Sharing	Groupware E-mail

Figure 5–1: The collaborative desktop

tions include both live, interactive applications like videoconferencing, and stored applications, like video mail. Information sharing includes both screen-sharing, which is live and interactive, as well as stored groupware.

How Desktop Videoconferencing Works

Before we can discuss how video gets from desktop to desktop, it is essential to understand video itself. What is video? Well, we know what it looks like, but a more technical explanation helps us understand desktop videoconferencing. Video is a stream of data made up of frames that include pictures and sound. Shows we watch on television are usually video that is broadcasted. Television networks and stations in North America and Japan broadcast video at 30 frames per second, while European stations broadcast at 25 frames per second. Video signals are analog, which means the signal is continuous. An analog signal when drawn looks like a curvy wave. Computers, however, are digital, and therefore process information as a precise value, which is represented as 0s and 1s. To send and receive video on today's digital telephone networks, it is necessary to convert the signal from analog to digital. Not only is it necessary to digitize video, but it is also essential to compress it.

Compression: Understanding the technology

Video compression is the technique that makes personal videoconferencing feasible over digital networks. Compression would be unnecessary, if plenty of cheap bandwidth were available. Bandwidth is the amount of information or data that can flow through a telephone channel per unit of time. We will discuss bandwidth in more depth in Chapter 6. Since bandwidth availability is currently limited, and technology advances have reduced the cost of compressing video, compression and decompression comprise the most practical desktop videoconferencing solution. Compression reduces the amount of data required to describe a video picture and allows the video signal to be transmitted at a faster and cheaper data rate.

The guts of group videoconferencing systems is called the *codec*. The name is derived from the coding/decoding or compression/decompression functions that the codec performs. Because uncompressed video requires an incredibly fast network transmission speed of about 90 million bits per second, compression is critical to make videoconferencing viable using today's slower networks.

Mission impossible

Think of compression as achieving the nearly impossible. Compression involves squeezing the video signal so that it can be sent over a transport such as ISDN Basic Rate Interface (BRI), which provides base-level transmission speeds of 128 thousand bits per second. For desktop videoconferencing, however, putting a codec—an expensive piece of hardware—on every desk is costly. Therefore, compression and decompression are usually achieved another way. Most desktop videoconferencing systems perform the codec's tasks in software. Some systems use special hardware for compression and perform decompression in software. The hardware normally consists of one or more chips implemented on a single electronic board. This is called hardware-assisted compression. Software-only technologies usually offer lower resolutions and maximum frame rates of 15 frames per second, or about half the rate of television in North America. However, technology advances are constantly increasing the performance of software-only compression.

Compression calculation processes called *algorithms* determine the performance, interoperability and network operations of a desktop videoconferencing system. The compression ratio has a major impact on the performance aspect of the algorithm. The ratio is a fraction that compares the size of data after compression with its precompression size. For example, if a compression algorithm uses data that is 800 bytes and returns 400 bytes of data, the compression ratio is 2:1. The fraction is actually an average compression ratio for data that the algorithm would typically process. In the late 1970s, codecs could compress a video signal by a ratio of 15:1. Important advances came throughout the 1980s, until several codec manufacturers achieved compression ratios high enough to send and receive video over Integrated Services Digital Network (ISDN).

Something lossy is something gained

There are two main types of video compression algorithms or techniques—lossless and lossy. In lossless compression, when an algorithm compresses data and later decompresses it, the algorithm delivers the same information it originally accepted. Lossless techniques provide typical compression ratios of 2:1. Lossless techniques work fine for compressing spreadsheet files or other text. The amount of information contained in video, however, requires a higher ratio than lossless methods alone offer. That's where lossy compression applies. In the lossy methods that videoconferencing systems use, the algorithm discards parts of the signal. Lossy approaches produce higher compression ratios, often in the range of 100:1 to 200:1.

It is also important to understand two major categories of lossy compression which are relevant to videoconferencing. These are *interframe*, or between frames, and *intraframe*, or within a frame. Both interframe and intraframe compression eliminate redundancy in visual information. Intraframe compression is based on the idea that there is redundancy in the parts of a picture that are close together. Interframe compression involves the notion that there is redundancy between frames of video, or that there is little change between successive frames. A "talking head" or a person's head-and-shoulder image, for example, has a high degree of redundancy because the picture changes only a little frame-to-frame. If there is a lot of action, or a big change between frames, there is less redundancy between frames, and this can produce a bigger drop in the quality of the picture on the receiving end. "No compression algorithm looks good for basketball, but they're almost all good for meetings," says Saul Rozinsky, Telecommunications Engineer for Bankers Trust and a 20-year veteran engineer for public television. Interframe and Intraframe techniques reduce the amount of information that is compressed.

Four basic kinds of compression algorithms achieve the compression ratios necessary for videoconferencing. They are Discrete Cosine Transform (DCT), Vector Quantization (VQ), Fractal Compression, and Discrete Wavelet Transform (DWT). DCT algorithms are the most prevalent and form the foundation of international videoconferencing standards. DCT techniques work by preparing data for compression. DCT essentially converts picture parts or pixels into numbers, and video information becomes frequencies and amplitudes. The receiving codec then reads the numerical code and reconverts it to pixels.

Less than picture perfect

Compression algorithms can employ an approach that is kind of like predicting the future of video frames. This approach is called *motion estimation*, which is based on the interframe compression concept of redundancy between frames of video. Motion estimation means the coder uses the information in one video frame to anticipate the next frame. When the coder processes the second frame, it actually codes the difference between the two frames. The ability to predict the next frame makes the algorithm several times more efficient than one that fails to anticipate what the next frame will look like.

DCT-based algorithms use a lossy technique, which means the picture at the receiving end lacks some visual information that is considered nonessential. Eliminating the redundancy in visual information produces a less than picture perfect image. This contributes to why videoconferencing looks less crisp than broadcast television.

Iterated Systems, a company formed by a team from Georgia Tech, has advanced fractal compression. In this approach, the fractally compressed image is stored as a set of equations with instructions about how to *reiterate* the image. The equations describe the image in terms of internal relationships between its components. This differs from pixel-by-pixel descriptions of the image. Tighter compression is possible, because there is no need to store a pixel representation of the image. No matter how large the picture, the formula that describes the image stays the same. This kind of fractal compression relies solely on interframe coding. In contrast, standard implementations of DCT require occasional intraframe coding. "The biggest difference is the quality of the image for a given bit rate and the latency," according to Iterated Engineering Manager Michael Zeug.

At the Houston Advanced Research Center (HARC), scientists have refined other compression techniques based on digital wavelet theory that could improve picture quality. Their approach involves using wavelets to compress pictures smaller and faster, losing less visual information. In mid 1995, the research center unveiled software called HARC-C. The software disproves assumptions that high compression ratios reduce picture quality. The technology may have the potential to create smooth, television-quality desktop videoconferences.

Compression is power

Because many general microprocessors fall short of meeting the demands that video applications place on computers, several companies have developed special video processors. Some only decode, while others also encode. One company that has developed a single chip that encodes and decodes is 8×8 (formerly Integrated Information Technology). Stanford physicist Chi-Shin Wang founded the company in 1987, after he realized that multimedia computing called for a different approach to designing microprocessors. 8×8's chip is called the Video Communications Processor (VCP), which the company introduced in 1993.

The primary feature of the VCP is that it is programmable, which means it can implement any standard algorithm as well as future and custom algorithms. Other pre- and post-processing features include scaling between

National Television Standards Committee (NTSC) video or Phase Alternate Line (PAL) video and FCIF or QCIF (see page 133). Special video chips like the VCP power everything from high end room videoconferencing systems to desktop videoconferencing. 8×8 is also working on integrating video compression technology inside CCD cameras. "If you add something into the camera head to support compression, that's very attractive," says Kevin Deierling, 8×8's Director of Marketing. "The connectivity is there." Additional information on 8×8 is available on the web at

`http://www.8x8.com`

Lucent Technologies Microelectronics (formerly AT&T Microelectronics) also offers a single chip called the AVP Processor that performs the function of a codec. One feature of the chip is that it provides built-in pan and zoom capability that can serve as a lower cost substitute for local or far-end camera control features on desktop videoconferencing systems. More information on Lucent Technologies Microelectronics can be found on the Web at

`http://www.lucent.com`

Another company that provides a codec microprocessor product is C-Cube Microsystems. The company offers a two-chip VideoRISC 2 set. Additional information on C-Cube is available on the Web at

`http://www.c-cube.com`

By using a special video chip instead of a more expensive general processor, manufacturers of some consumer video products like non-PC-based video telephones can keep prices lower.

Chromatic Research offers the Mpact media engine, which combines seven multimedia functions on a single chip. Besides desktop videoconferencing, additional functions include 3D graphics acceleration, fax/modem, Dolby Surround AC-3 sound, and video playback, among others. More information on Chromatic Research can be found on the Web at

`http://www.chromatic.com`

Native signal processing

It is possible to achieve video compression without the help of special chips. Intel Corporation's approach to compression has revolved around Native Signal Processing. NSP uses the computing power of host or general microprocessors to perform multimedia and communications functions. The host microprocessors of the mid to late 1990s are capable of driving software that achieves video compression. In 1996, Intel enhanced its approach to NSP by incorporating the multimedia extensions (MMX) instruction set in some host microprocessors.

The power of MMX

MMX optimizes the Intel architecture to handle multimedia applications like personal videoconferencing. MMX can as much as quadruple the speed at which processors handle multimedia applications, with power left to accomplish other tasks. The enhancement includes 57 new instructions, yet MMX processors are compatible with previous generations of the Intel architecture. MMX allows more simultaneous real-time activities, with multiple channels of audio and high-quality video.

Intel worked closely with software developers in creating MMX. Teams identified and analyzed the most compute-intensive activities, including videoconferencing, and discovered fundamental similarities among different applications. Based on these similarities, Intel designed MMX as a set of basic, general purpose integer instructions that can be easily applied to a broad range of multimedia and communications applications. A technique called *Single Instruction Multiple Data* (SIMD) is the foundation for MMX. SIMD allows a single instruction to process many pieces of information. Fred Pollack, Intel Fellow and director of measurement, architecture and planning, was quoted in *Computer Reseller News* as calling MMX "the most significant announcement from Intel since the introduction of the 386 chip," which extended the architecture to 32 bits. Additional information on MMX is available on the Web at

`http://www.intel.com`

The little camera that could

Another technological advance that has fueled desktop videoconferencing is the development of small, inexpensive charge-coupled device (CCD) cameras. These are mostly single-chip cameras that sit atop the computer monitor for videoconferencing. CCD cameras have made the image capture function viable for desktop videoconferencing. In 1970, Willard Boyle and George Smith of AT&T Bell Laboratories introduced the CCD. The advance challenged the prevailing technology of silicon-diode tube video cameras. Tube cameras required a scanning electronic beam, which was a complex set-up that hogged power. Because CCD technology was simpler, it could produce products that were smaller, faster and less costly to build. Though CCD technology had many potential applications including television, Bell Labs developed it because of the need for a small and cheap camera for the Picturephone. Throughout the 1990s, work continued at Bell Labs on advancing CCD technology. In 1996, Bell Labs introduced the first panoramic viewer for use with CCD cameras. The viewer provides 360-degree views from a single vantage point. Applications include desktop videoconferencing, video surveillance, and television. Bell Labs inventor Vic Nalwa completed the product in time for the 1996 Olympics in Atlanta.

Riding the express bus

A major improvement in the PC infrastructure has made desktop videoconferencing more efficient. The Peripheral Component Interconnect (PCI) coupled with constantly increasing computing power can support more demanding compression/decompression requirements. PCI is an Intel-developed *bus*. A bus is a common path that links peripherals and the host CPU within a computer system. PCI is specifically a local bus, because it connects directly with the host CPU.

Older buses, including the Industry Standard Architecture (ISA) bus, often required clumsy connections between graphics boards and codec boards, which slowed data delivery. Immediately predating PCI was the Video Electronics Standards Association (VESA) local bus. Rather than replace ISA, VESA added local bus capability to the existing bus standard. However, unlike PCI, VESA failed to off-load processing duties from the host CPU.

PCI is like the autobahn, compared with the dirt road of the past PC infrastructure. PCI can move 64 or 32 bits of data at 33 MHz, many times faster than old buses like ISA, which could deliver 16 bits of data at 8 MHz. PCI also serves as a bus coprocessor, performing file transfers and other routine duties. This frees up the host CPU to decompress video faster.

On a practical level, PCI allows for easier implementation of some important features of desktop videoconferencing. One of these is "picture-in-picture," or the ability to view the image of the near-end camera in a window while simultaneously viewing the larger image of the far-end camera. Because PCI simplifies the PC infrastructure, PCI permits plug-and-play desktop videoconferencing systems, which are easier to install. More information on PCI is available on the Web at

`http://www.ti.com/sc/docs/asic/srga013`

Universal Serial Bus (USB) and Fire Wire (IEEE 1394)

Two other bus technologies that impact personal videoconferencing performance are the Universal Serial Bus (USB) and the Institute of Electrical and Electronics Engineers (IEEE) 1394 interface, commonly known as *Fire Wire.* These technologies compliment the PCI bus by providing efficient systems for connecting peripheral devices outside the PC box. USB provides a 12-megabit per second data rate, and is designed to make PCs easier to configure and use. Also, USB expands Input/Output (I/O) capabilities and provides an easier way to integrate computers with telephony. An objective of USB is to make low- and medium-speed peripherals plug-and-play and hot-pluggable into a standard external connector port, eliminating the need to open the PC case and install boards. In the case of desktop videoconferencing cameras, these devices would be USB-tethered rather than plugging into a specialized port. USB expands computer-telephony integration (CTI) by letting users access functions such as voice mail with a graphical user interface. Also, USB can connect a PC with higher-bandwidth digital lines such as ISDN. More information of USB can be found on the Web at

`http://www.intel.com/pc-supp/platform.html`

While USB improves personal videoconferencing performance, Fire Wire (IEEE 1394) goes much farther. Apple Computer developed Fire Wire, which was later endorsed by the IEEE standards group. A trade association including Apple, Compaq, Intel, Matsushita, Microsoft, Seagate, Sony, Texas Instruments, Yamaha, Adaptec, and others has endorsed the standard. Fire Wire supports isochronous or time-dependent data rates at up to 400-megabits per second, and the interface provides guaranteed bandwidth to such devices as video cameras via simple, low-cost cables. This allows multiple simultaneous channels of full-motion, 30-frames-per-second video and Digital Audio Tape (DAT)-grade audio. 1394 uses a peer-to-peer communication protocol that allows any two peripherals to communicate without the host CPU getting involved. Also, Fire Wire uses a daisy-chain topology, connecting one device to another on the chain.

Personal videoconferencing, desktop video editing and desktop publishing are major applications for Fire Wire. Fire Wire can more efficiently carry compressed or uncompressed digital video from the camera to the PC or to other peripherals. Also, Fire Wire will eventually allow the connection of digital VCRs and digital video-disk players to TVs and digital set-top boxes. Additional information on FIre Wire (IEEE 1394) can be found on the Web at

```
http://www.adaptec.com/firewire/1394main.html
```

and at

```
http://firewire.org/
```

Multipurpose video capture cards

Multipurpose capture cards are boosting personal videoconferencing functionality and flexibility. An example of this technology is Winnov's Videum video and audio capture board which works with any software codec, transport, or application (Figure 5–2). This gives the user the flexibility of choosing among several personal videoconferencing codecs, all loaded on the PC. Videum allows the user to assemble video, audio, and still images from multiple sources. Also, the card supports POTS, ISDN, Internet, and other trans-

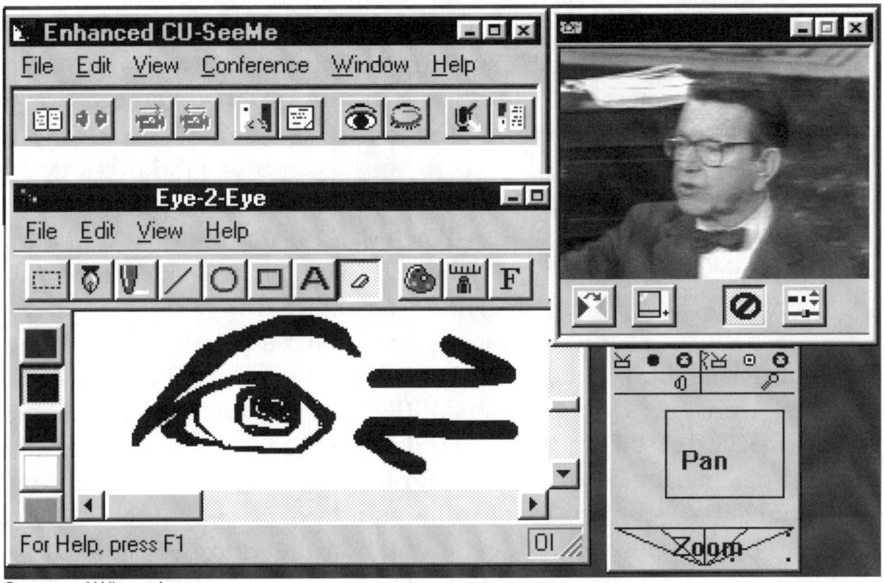

Courtesy of Winnov, Inc.

Figure 5–2: The Winnov Videum audio-video capture board lets users conduct personal videoconferences using a variety of codecs and transports

ports (transport options are discussed in chapter 6). Videum adds functionality to personal videoconferencing by supporting up to three cameras at each end and allowing remote pan, tilt, zoom, contrast, and brightness controls for any camera. A significant benefit of the technology involves audio. Videum provides full-duplex, low-noise audio with low latency. Also, the board supports both telephony-based (in multiples of 8 kHz) and multimedia-based (in multiples of 11.025 kHz) audio standards up to 48-kHz studio quality, and synchronizes audio with video at capture time. The board also allows video, audio, and still image editing, and lets low-cost cameras serve as scanners. The technology can be used to create multimedia Web pages. Additional information on Winnov can be found on the Web at

`http://www.winnov.com`

Standards: A Green Light to Worldwide Deployment

Many standards govern desktop videoconferencing. The major objective for standards groups, many vendors, and users is making all of the standards talk with each other. This ensures that systems based on different technologies can interoperate. The ability to join an ISDN conference from a POTS terminal, for example, is critical. Standards determine how telecommunications products talk to each other. Three groups ratify standards that impact desktop videoconferencing: the International Telecommunications Union (ITU), the Internet Engineering Task Force (IETF), and the Institute of Electrical and Electronics Engineer (IEEE). The IEEE standards include IEEE 802.3 (10Base-T) and IEEE 802.9a (isoEthernet), which are different types of local area networks (LAN). The IETF standards ensure cross-platform interoperability over the Internet, and include the Real-Time Transport Protocol (RTP), the Real-Time Transport Control Protocol (RTCP), and the Resource Reservation Protocol (RSVP). IEEE and IETF standards are covered in detail in Chapter 9.

The International Telecommunications Union is the body of the United Nations that develops and ratifies standards. (See Figure 5–3.) One branch of the ITU, the Telecommunication Standardization Sector (ITU-T), focuses on telephony standards. Within the ITU-T, there are fifteen study groups. Within the study groups, work parties concentrate on more specific areas. If a work party accepts a proposal, the standard is considered "determined." Then a voting body must approve the standard.

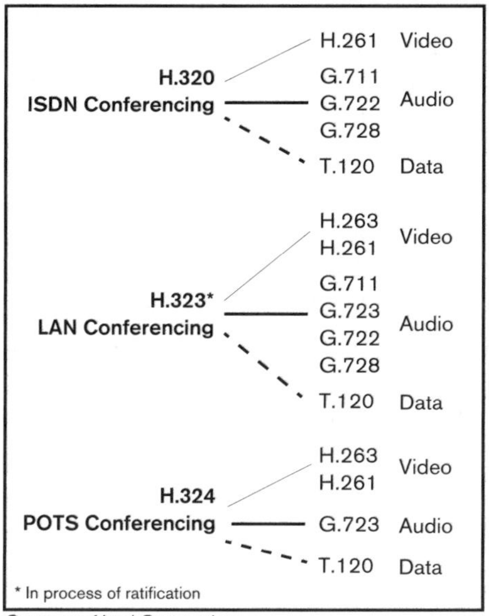

Courtesy of Intel Corporation

Figure 5–3: ITU Conferencing Standards

Typically, companies generate the standards, and the process is open to any firm that wants to participate. However, countries —not companies—vote on the standards. A company can produce a compliant product before a standard is ratified, assuming the standard is firm or determined. This can give a company an edge in the marketplace, but the company also risks that the specification will change before being ratified.

Before the CCITT (the former name of the ITU-T) established the Group 3 fax standard, universal deployment was impractical. Fax machines were slow, and expensive, and could interoperate only with machines made by the same company. Users of fax machines yearned for the ability to send documents without worrying about which brand of machine would receive the fax. The standard provided the solution. Similarly, desktop videoconferencing users demanded interoperability.

Internet videoconferencing got a big boost when Microsoft, Intel, and more than a hundred other telecommunications, computer, and Internet companies endorsed an open platform in March of 1996. The platform includes T.120, H.323 standards as well as the RTP/RTCP and RSVP specifications. Broad industry support for the platform allows a Macintosh user, for example, to more easily and reliably establish a video and collaboration link with a Windows PC user over the Internet.

The H.320 family

In late 1990, the ITU-T approved the H.320 family of standards (also called px64) that impact videoconferencing. Of that family, H.261 leads the pack. H.261 is the standard for video codecs, with the compressed video signal operating over one or more 64-kbps ISDN B-channels. H.261 defines two picture or resolution structures that are compatible with all three worldwide television display formats. The picture structures are the Common Intermediate Format (CIF) and the Quarter Common Intermediate Format (QCIF). CIF is also referred to as "full CIF" (FCIF). A CIF display paints 352 pixels per line and 288 lines per picture, normally displayed full-screen. QCIF, with 176 pixels per line and 144 lines per picture, looks best squeezed to quarter-screen. H.261 requires codecs to operate using QCIF, but CIF is optional in the standard. Some US vendors, however, have used a CIF-like de facto standard for some videoconferencing systems that includes 256 pixels per line and 240 lines per picture.

As a compromise, the CIF and QCIF use the 30-frame per second rate of North American TV and a resolution technique that works better with European television. Under the standard, though, an H.261 compliant codec can code fewer than 30 frames per second. While H.261 ensures interoperability, the picture quality from different manufacturers will vary based on nonstandardized encoder design factors, including the degree of picture filtering and the accuracy of motion compensation.

T.120 for document conferencing

Another important family of standards for desktop videoconferencing is the one that governs document conferencing, whiteboarding, binary file transfer, and application sharing. The ITU-T approved T.120 in mid 1995, after companies worldwide pooled their expertise to develop the standard. Neil Starkey, Chief Technology Officer of DataBeam, calls T.120 "the most widely supported communications technology ever." Starkey says the industry is making the standard work, because there are so many vested interests in T.120. Microsoft, Apple and Sun are all embedding T.120 in their operating systems. Unlike the H-series standards, T.120 was designed to be multipoint first. "When you start with a multipoint design, you can do things right," explains Starkey. T.120 supports many network options, including POTS, ISDN, Packet Switched Digital Networks (PSDN), Circuit Switched Digital Networks (CSDN), and popular LAN protocols. Also, these different transports can connect with one another in the same multipoint conference. T.120 is cross-platform, meaning it can work with Windows, several versions of UNIX, Macintosh, and other proprietary operating systems. "It's the brand unification standard," says PictureTel Chief Scientist Rich Baker.

An important aspect of T.120 is Generic Conference Control (T.124). GCC provides structures for managing electronic meetings. Included is a hierarchy of nodes that connect to conferences, ensuring that a conductor controls each conference. GCC allows users to reserve the same time next week or reserve another half hour off the bridge with a mouse click. T.120 also lets users collaborate on documents running on completely different platforms. One important capability the standard provides is vote tallying at an electronic gathering. Multipoint control units, which link parties for multipoint videoconferences, simultaneously support both the H.320 family and T.120 standards.

Also part of the T.120 family is T.130-T.133, which the ITU-T was working on in late 1996 and into 1997. These standards extend audio and video controls, providing the ability to remotely operate VCRs. They also provide real-time link management, to make calls involving more than one long distance carrier seamless. "If we get to the point where your cable box needs to be involved in a conference," says Neil Starkey, "We'll be able to download T.120 into your cable box."

H.323 for the LAN and Internet

Over the Wide Area Network (WAN), the H.320 standard working over ISDN-BRI is the primary solution for desktop videoconferencing. However, most corporations link their desktops through a Local Area Network (LAN). On the LAN, video is just one of many kinds of information using the transmission resources. Therefore, desktop videoconferencing on the LAN must adjust to the constantly-changing available bandwidth. This means LAN-based videoconferencing requires special compression technology. H.320 falls short here, because the standard's architecture is ISDN-oriented. Throughout 1996, the ITU-T was working on adopting the H.323 standard that provides a gateway for LAN/WAN videoconferencing. H.323 also covers Internet videoconferencing. Early in 1996, Intel and Microsoft, along with more than 70 other companies, announced support for the standard. Intel and Microsoft also collaborated on the H.323 stack that would become part of Microsoft's operating system.

H.323 makes PBX-like functions such as call transfer easier. According to PictureTel Chief Scientist Rich Baker, "Transferring a call is just like shipping a packet somewhere else." Baker adds, "the quality one can attain on the LAN in this standard is identical to that of the ISDN/POTS world."

H.324 for POTS

Another family of standards covers desktop videoconferencing over POTS. This family is called H.324, which the ITU-T ratified in early 1996. H.324 covers low-bit-rate videoconferencing between multimedia telephones. These telephones include stand-alone video phones, PC-based video phones, and TV-based video phones that resemble cable boxes with built-in cameras that sit atop televisions. This standard improves on H.320 in its flexibility. H.324 calls for transmission of real-time video, audio, and data over V.34 modems, which have a maximum bit rate of 28,800 to 33,600 kbps. For V.34 modems to be video phone ready, they must support a protocol called V.80. Part of H.324 is a newer video codec standard called H.263. H.263 defines and requires a new low-end SQCIF picture format of 128 × 96 pixels. QCIF is also required in H.263, and FCIF is optional. H.263 is a major breakthrough in video compression, and is substantially better than H.261 at low data rates. However, at 384 kbps and above, the difference is less apparent. Work is underway in the ITU-T to migrate H.263 into the H.320 family. However, it is mandatory that the H.324 terminal support H.261 as well as H.263. The H.324/M series covers videoconferencing over mobile or wireless radio networks. H.324 is critical in delivering desktop videoconferencing products to the home and small office/home office (SOHO) market.

MPEG and JPEG

Another standard that indirectly impacts desktop videoconferencing is MPEG. MPEG stands for the Moving Picture Experts Group, which is part of the International Organization for Standards (ISO). ISO, like ITU is part of the United Nations, and the two standards organizations often overlap. MPEG-1 can provide VHS picture quality, and allows for compressed audio and video to fit on a compact disk. The compressed video can then be played back on a PC. The most successful MPEG-1 application to date is VideoCD 2.0, which is backed by Sony, Matsushita, and Phillips, and which is used for playing back music videos and movies primarily on a TV platform in China and India. In the US and other countries that use the NTSC television format, MPEG-1 provides a standard image format (SIF) of 352 × 240 at 30 frames per second, as well as CD-quality audio. MPEG-1 has become important in the evolution of the advanced desktop.

MPEG-2 covers high-speed coding for set-top boxes, video-on-demand, direct-broadcast satellite, cable television and video recording and storage. The ITU approved both the MPEG-1 and MPEG-2 standards in 1993. MPEG-3, which addresses HDTV, has become part of MPEG-2. MPEG-4 is aimed at low bit rate videophone applications, and will be finalized in 1997 and 1998. Currently, MPEG has greater implications for playing back stored video than for real-time applications. MPEG could be used to compress and store a

CEO's company-wide broadcast and corporate training videos, so that employees can view the videos later on their PCs.

A standard called JPEG is also relevant to desktop videoconferencing. *JPEG* stands for the *Joint Photographic Expert Group*, which began as a joint effort of the ISO and the ITU. JPEG covers still image compression. M-JPEG or Motion-JPEG establishes a method to produce movement by compressing sequential images.

The IMTC

The International Multimedia Teleconferencing Consortium (IMTC) based in San Ramon, California promotes standards compliance to insure growth of multimedia telecommunications. The Consortium is the result of a merger by the Consortium for Audiographics Teleconferencing Standards (CATS), the Multimedia Communications Community of Interest (MCCOI), and the Personal Conferencing Work Group (PCWG). Besides benefiting the companies that support IMTC, the consortium also educates desktop videoconferencing users about standards, and helps protect their investment. Microsoft and Intel are active members of the IMTC. Both companies worked with the IMTC to host Event 120 in early 1996. The event was the first round of T.120 interoperability trials. The IMTC also serves as a US coordination point for communicating with the ITU, which is based in Geneva, Switzerland. More information on standards and the IMTC is available on the Web at

`http://www.imtc.org/imtc`

Additional information on the ITU can be found on the Web at

`http://www.itu.ch`

Breaking barriers to interoperability

By early 1995, desktop videoconferencing was familiar technology to readers of computer and telecommunications magazines. Also, some articles in *The Wall Street Journal* and other mass media publications gave the industry some marketing momentum. However, a major barrier still prevented large-scale acceptance and deployment. Two rival standards were competing for dominance. This discouraged investment in systems, because corporations wanted a guarantee that their desktop systems could easily talk to any other videoconferencing system.

The ITU had set international standards for personal conferencing, which included both the H.320 family of video standards and the T.120 data standard. Meantime, an Intel-led body called the Personal Conferencing Work Group (PCWG), which would ultimately merge into IMTC, was introducing its own standard, called the Personal Conferencing Specification (PCS). The standard was based on Intel's proprietary Indeo compression algorithm. One objective in developing PCS was to reduce the required processing power in running desktop videoconferencing applications. The PCWG originally comprised twelve core members and grew to 19, including Intel, AT&T, CLI, VTEL, Novell, VideoServer, Compaq, Software Publishing, Northern Telecom, Ericsson, Lotus, Deutsche Telekom, Digital Equipment, France Telecom, Hewlett-Packard, Netscape, NEC, Olivetti, and Sun Microsystems. Besides the core members, the PCWG included more than 170 consulting members.

As the PCWG worked on refining its personal conferencing standard based on Indeo, large buyers of systems grew increasingly wary of investing in desktop conferencing units that could not talk H.320. Many of these corporate buyers had invested millions of dollars in group videoconferencing systems that work with H.320. The sentiment led one industry-watcher to proclaim, "Multiple standards are symptomatic of an industry in its infancy." That kind of talk stood as a barrier to widespread deployment of desktop videoconferencing. The PCWG responded to the climate and the demands of large customers.

When the core members met in Denver in February of 1995, they unanimously voted to support H.320. This meant that PCS-compliant hardware and software conferencing products would automatically set up connections to H.320 systems without any special instructions by the user. What still needed to be addressed was interoperability between ISDN, POTS, LAN, and Internet standards. Nevertheless, the PCWG move cleared major hurdles.

The standards war was over. Universal interoperability had begun, and the destiny for desktop videoconferencing as standard business technology was apparent. However, barriers to deployment would persist. For businesses hungry for high-quality real-time video, cost would remain an issue. Even as prices for software and hardware drop, they multiply quickly when desktop videoconferencing is deployed enterprise-wide. As we will discuss in Chapter 9, companies must still resolve network infrastructure issues as they implement desktop videoconferencing on the local area network (LAN). Finally, conceptual problem-solvers and software developers must invent more business-specific applications for desktop videoconferencing. Then, what began as laboratory technology can provide a real-world pay off.

6

Getting from Here to There: Bandwidth and Personal Videoconferencing

Gaining Access

Personal videoconferencing requires access to wide area or long distance networks. The primary exception would be videoconferencing within a company's building or campus over the local area network (LAN). Long distance networks and options for access are evolving, and many business interests are struggling to ensure that the infrastructure develops to fit their business models. Primary players include telecommunications carriers and cable television companies.

Before the 1960s, the long distance telephone systems in the United States used analog technology. By 1980, though, AT&T had upgraded to a mostly digital network, and other telecommunications companies, including Sprint, provided an exclusively digital backbone. Digital technology offered better voice transmission quality and also made high-speed data transfers possible. Today's primarily digital long distance network backbone is ideal for video compression, because compression requires digital communication channels. The increasing availability of digital bandwidth drove down prices throughout the 1980s. By the 1990s, lower priced bandwidth made personal videoconferencing far more viable than Picturephone was in the 1960s.

Even with the existence of a digital network backbone, users of personal videoconferencing have a variety of choices to access that backbone. These choices include analog lines via V.34 modems with bandwidth up to 33,600 kbps, older digital services including Switched 56 and leased T1, newer digital services including ISDN Basic Rate Interface (BRI), ISDN Primary Rate Interface (PRI), and Broadband ISDN. Other options include Internet services, cable modems, wireless services including Personal Communications Services (PCS), local area networks (LAN) with gateways to long distance networks, and asynchronous transfer mode (ATM).

Sorting out access options

The wide area network (WAN) transport option that works best for personal videoconferencing depends entirely on the application. Companies of all sizes have successfully used ISDN, POTS, Switched 56, T1, and the Internet for desktop videoconferencing. Also, desktop videoconferences can travel over many types of physical media, including copper, coaxial cable, fiber optic, or a hybrid.

Ernie DeNigris, Vice President of AT&T in charge of the WorldWorx business unit, conducted "shuttle diplomacy" in the mid 1990s getting videoconferencing industry players to agree on international standards. His view has been, "we need to bake the cake before we can cut it." As decision-makers sort out which transmission methods will prevail, DeNigris advises that many kinds of services can successfully co-exist. "Like everything else, this market is not one-size-fits-all," says DeNigris. "Some applications fit ISDN, particularly business applications in which security is an issue. Others will require the Internet."

John Walsh, former Senior Vice President of CLI and an industry pioneer, believes POTS is viable for many business applications. "I like POTS. I do think video is an additive element with POTS. I like it because of the simplicity of the execution. You're not stuck with LAN issues. The video is not bad, if you can get 28.8 kbps effectively."

Bandwidth and why it matters

All access options deliver bandwidth to the buyer. The bottom line about bandwidth is the more that is available for personal videoconferencing transmission, the better the picture becomes. However, the greater the bandwidth the higher the transmission charges. Bandwidth is the speed at which information or data can flow through a communications channel. Think of the channel as a highway and the information as the vehicles moving along. Using this analogy, bandwidth refers to the amount of traffic that can drive down the highway. The highway, like a communications channel, has a capacity. If traffic is too heavy for the number of lanes, a bottleneck forms. Then the vehicles—or in this case information—back up onto the entrance ramps. The wider the highway, the greater the capacity to handle traffic. The bigger the communications channel or *pipe*, the more information can move along and the greater the bandwidth. While highway speeds are measured in miles or kilometers per hour, digital bandwidth is measured in bits per second.

The amount of bandwidth necessary for desktop videoconferencing depends on the application. The more important video quality is, the more bandwidth is needed. For an executive presentation to a company's major customer, for example, 128 kbps most likely falls short. However, 128 kbps is probably plenty of bandwidth for an application in which two marketing professionals are collaborating on a newsletter or two technical professionals are sharing data and documents. In these types of applications, video is necessary, but near television quality is less than critical.

Bandwidth availability may depend on several factors. These include the type of transport, the kind of access to long distance networks, the switch in the local exchange carrier's central office, and the physical medium or type of line through which access is gained.

The Evolution of ISDN

In the broadest sense, Integrated Services Digital Network (ISDN) is about rebuilding all national telephone systems to international guidelines. National ISDN standards (NI1, NI2, and NI3) govern implementation of ISDN within the United States. The deployment of ISDN Basic Rate Interface (BRI) has made desktop videoconferencing possible for many users. Because videoconferencing hogs bandwidth and does best with digital transmission, ISDN fits the bill better than POTS for many applications. Compared to POTS, ISDN BRI allows higher frame rates for desktop videoconferencing and greater picture clarity. When ISDN BRI became more available in the US in 1994, there was a far greater gap in video quality between POTS and ISDN-oriented compression algorithms. This gap has since closed somewhat. Before ISDN, leased access was the primary option for digital communication. Because leasing a T1 is economically viable only for major telecommunications customers, only medium and larger-sized companies could use videoconferencing systems.

ISDN BRI has provided digital communications access to small businesses, engineers, doctors, students, entrepreneurs, lawyers, real estate agents, telecommuters, and millions of others. ISDN has also become a bandwidth solution for major corporations, and works with many emerging telecommunications technologies that we will discuss in Chapter 9.

Some ISDN background

The concept of ISDN dates back to the early 1970s. The CCITT officially recognized the technology in 1976, and adopted the current definition in 1986. After a decade of planning and developing ISDN, the service became available in the mid 1980s in the US and is now widely available. ISDN has been widely available in France, Germany, and Japan since the 1980s.

In mid 1988, AT&T became the first interexchange (IXC) or long-distance carrier to tariff ISDN. That means AT&T received FCC approval to offer ISDN service at specific rates. In 1990, Sprint and MCI started offering ISDN. Soon after, equipment vendors began announcing ISDN-ready equipment, including LAN bridges, switches, gateways, multiplexers, terminals, PC boards, and terminal adapters. The local exchange carriers (LEC) offer ISDN service that varies considerably region-to-region. Prices and service options run the gamut, and are available for both homes and businesses.

ISDN Basic Rate Interface (BRI)

ISDN is a standard that allows anybody in the world to communicate through the worldwide digital network. ISDN BRI was designed to run from the central office (CO) into the home or office. (See Figure 6–1.) ISDN BRI is actually

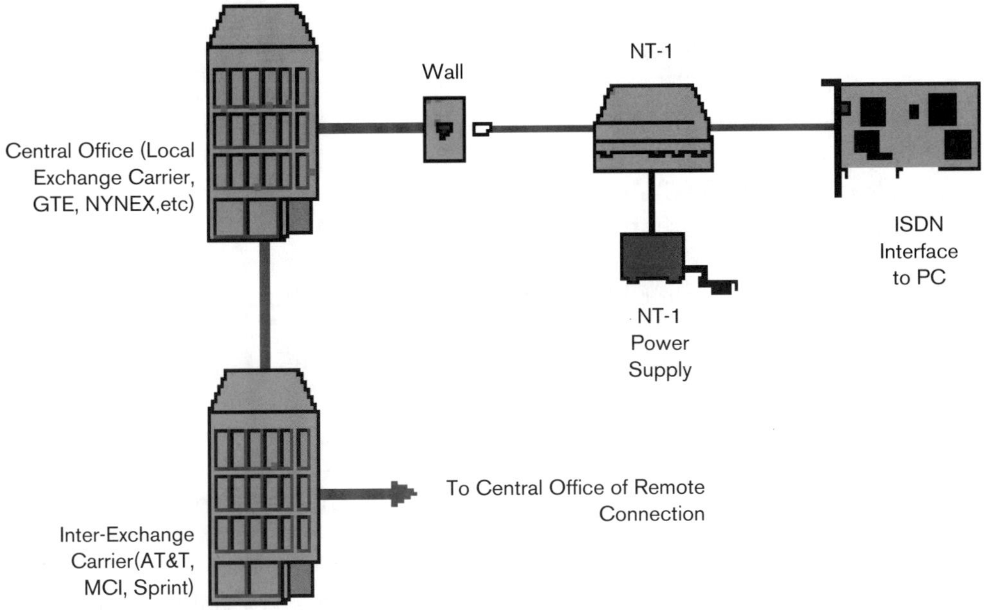

Courtesy of Intel Corporation

Figure 6–1: ISDN from local carriers

a *middleband* digital enhancement to the twisted copper pair. The CO connects the line to digital switching equipment. Since ISDN is out-of-band, the signaling information travels separately from the video, voice, and data that the user is sending. There are two kinds of ISDN service: ISDN Basic Rate Interface (BRI) and ISDN Primary Rate Interface (PRI). ISDN BRI is the more economical choice for most small businesses and individuals. The service requires two standard phone lines. In the ISDN BRI set-up, one 16-kbps D channel carries the housekeeping messages and other signaling. Two 64-kbps B channels transmit whatever information the user sends. The ISDN BRI configuration is often called 2B+D. The two channels can be bundled to gain a total bandwidth of 128 kbps. Using a multiplexer, greater bandwidth can be achieved by combining multiple ISDN BRI B channels.

ISDN Primary Rate Interface (PRI), ISDN Multirate, and B-ISDN

Primary Rate Interface (PRI) links medium and large companies to a central office (CO) ISDN switch. The ISDN PRI service provides 23 64-kbps B channels for transmission and one 64-kbps D channel for signaling and synchronization. This is essentially a switched T1. Some long distance providers, particularly in Europe, use E1 standards. In this arrangement, ISDN PRI service includes up to 31 B channels and one D channel. PRI allows a telecom manager the flexibility to adjust bandwidth needs based on usage patterns and time-of-day requirements. For example, 2 or more B channels can be combined through the use of an inverse multiplexer or I-mux. Since each B channel provides up to 64 kbps of bandwidth, holding a desktop videoconference at 384 kbps would require bonding 6 B channels. The standard that governs I-muxes is the Bandwidth-on-Demand Interoperability Group (BONDING) standard.

ISDN multirate, also known as switched fractional T1 service, is a network service tariffed by carriers that lets users combine up to 24 B channels on demand. ISDN allows greater flexibility than older bandwidth-on-demand services like H0 and H11 in North America. H0 delivers 384 kbps, and H11 provides an aggregate bandwidth of 1.536 Mbps.

The ITU is currently finalizing a standard for Broadband ISDN. B-ISDN will provide greater bandwidth to big customers. SONET, which we will address later in this chapter and in Chapter 9, provides the traffic-directing or physical layer interface between B-ISDN and the transmission wire or cable.

In early 1996, Microsoft announced a broad alliance to promote the acceptance and use of ISDN. As part of the alliance, Microsoft said the company would coordinate with almost all of North America's major telephone companies, more than two dozen communications hardware manufacturers, and several Internet access providers. The plan was to simplify ISDN service for use with Windows 95. Additional information on ISDN is available on the Web at

```
http://www.alumni.caltech.edu/~dank/isdn
```

Signaling

Signaling is the part of a call that controls how video, voice, and data are delivered. For example, signaling includes supervision, or establishing and breaking down a call. Signaling also includes addressing the call. In short, signaling defines the network-to-network interface. There are two primary methods associated with setting up video, voice, and data calls over a network. One is called *in-band* signaling and the other is called *out-of-band* signaling. In-band signaling means each 64-kbps channel loses 8 kbps to call control, leaving 56 kbps of bandwidth for transmission of the user's information. Out-of-band reserves 23 64-kbps channels for transmitting the user's information and employs the 24th channel to do all of the signaling for the other 23 channels, thus preserving a full 64 kbps of bandwidth per channel for the user's information. Because videoconferencing requires the largest bandwidth available, in-band signaling is less desirable in that it removes some of the transmission bandwidth. The better approach for videoconferencing is out-of-band signaling.

Until the mid-1970s, signaling was mostly done on a country-by-country basis. This caused problems as companies increasingly conducted business internationally. Much signaling translation was necessary between one country's long distance carrier and that of another, and this kept transmission costs high. Therefore, countries worked together within the CCITT (now the ITU-T) to pound out specifications for common signaling.

The SS7 signaling approach

Common Channel Signaling System 7 (SS7), the most recent international signaling protocol, is out-of-band, and therefore transmits information more efficiently than previous signaling protocols. Advantages of SS7 include reduced signaling cost, improved reliability, and compatibility with ISDN. SS7 differs substantially from many older signaling methods. When we make a traditional phone call, we push buttons and send a series of tones to the network. The network then interprets these tones as a request to reach the person we called. ISDN networks handle this process differently. SS7 is a message-oriented signaling protocol, which means that the network sets up calls by sending a message in precise digital bits rather than tones. This is similar to how data networks achieve signaling. More information on SS7 is available on the Web at

`http://www.dts.harris.com/pages`

Some ISDN snags

ISDN can stop short of providing *64 clear*, or the full 64 kbps per B channel bandwidth. This is because some local exchange carriers have been slow to implement SS7, the out-of-band signaling standard. The hold-up involves delays in finalizing the standard, and resulting delays by companies that make switching equipment used by local exchange carriers (LECs) in their central offices. Without SS7, some bandwidth bites the dust for transmission, as it is used for in-band signaling. Therefore, some LECs can provide only 56 kbps per ISDN B channel in some parts of their service areas. However, a National ISDN initiative that involves all the Regional Bell Operating Companies (RBOC) has ironed out specifications that should eliminate SS7 implementation problems.

In early 1996, Pacific Telesis and US West petitioned regulatory agencies for ISDN rate increases that would more than double prices. The costs of providing service were apparently higher than these regional bell operating companies (RBOC) had anticipated. In its tariff filing, Pacific Telesis indicated it had expected only 12 percent of customers to be more than 12,000 feet from Central Offices (CO). However, that percentage turned out to be double the anticipated figure, according to the tariff filing. The closer the customers are to the COs, the lower the cost for the LEC. The proposed rate increase was a blow to companies delivering ISDN-oriented desktop videoconferencing products.

In an article by John Markoff in the January 6, 1996 edition of the *New York Times*, Intel CEO Andy Grove reacted to the proposed ISDN rate boost. "I can't begin to understand their perspective," Grove was quoted as saying,. "When these people were kids did they ever try to sell lemonade at the lemonade stand?" ISDN has its limitations, including higher toll charges than a phone call and the lack of universal availability. "From a pervasiveness standpoint, ISDN has a long way to go," according to Blake Irving, Group Manager of Microsoft's Personal Systems Division. "We're going to see a lot of POTS and LAN." Huntington Bancshare's Marketing and Strategic Planning Director Bill Randle also has reservations about ISDN. "ISDN is something whose time has come and gone before it was ever here," insists Randle. "I don't see it being deployed widely in many areas of the country. ISDN is probably not going to be cost effective."

In Europe and Asia, ISDN was available earlier and became more prevalent faster than in the United States. Does widely available ISDN mean that ordering service is easy? "Everything is more difficult with telecommunications in Germany versus the US," says Stephan Wenger, assistant professor of communication systems at the Technical University of Berlin. "But it's as easy to get ISDN as it is to get POTS. An NT1 is included."

ISDN ordering codes

Configuring ISDN can get confusing, so service providers and desktop videoconferencing vendors have devised a more simple solution. Ordering codes represent a set of network services associated with specific equipment for a specific application. The codes allow an ISDN customer to avoid understanding line provisioning and other complexities. Intel ProShare, for example, uses the ordering code *Intel Blue*. Telling the service provider you want Intel Blue provisioning circumvents potentially confusing questions.

ISDN shopping list

Using ISDN for desktop videoconferencing requires some special hardware. A Network Termination 1 (NT1) provides the network interface for each BRI connection. In the US, the Federal Communications Commission (FCC) has mandated that the customer rather than the telecommunications carrier provide the NT1. In Europe, the NT1 is considered network equipment and is therefore provided by the telecommunications carrier. Besides an NT1, a power supply is needed. However, some power supplies are integrated into NT1 units. Telecommuters who want to connect their PC to an office LAN via ISDN will also need a remote access adapter card or an ISDN bridge device with a LAN adapter in the PC.

The Analog Nature of the Local Loop

Even though telecommunications carriers use digital networks almost exclusively, the *local loop* remains primarily analog. The local loop, comprised of a pair of twisted copper wires, connects the subscriber's premise with the central office (CO), the building that houses switching equipment and provides dial tone. The technical term for the local telephone company is the *local exchange carrier* (LEC), and the somewhat less technical term for the analog lines they provide for the local loop is *Plain Old Telephone Service* (POTS).

Converting analog to digital

Because the local loop is still almost entirely POTS, long distance carriers must convert the analog signal to digital. The primary analog-to-digital conversion technique is called pulse code modulation (PCM). Sending voice encoded with PCM requires a transmission line with a channel speed of 64 kilobits per second. In North America, Japan, and Europe, digital hierarchies of PCM systems have evolved. In the North American Digital Hierarchy, one PCM-encoded 64-kbps channel is called a DS-0, indicating it is the lowest bandwidth or *baseband* digital signal. The next step up is a DS-1, also called a T1.5, because it has a bandwidth of 1.544 million bits per second (megabits/second). A T1.5 channel is commonly referred to as a T1.

A process called time division multiplexing (TDM) subdivides the T1 into 24 DS-0 channels. TDM allows the single line to carry multiple signals of voice, video, and data. On each channel, frames carry the information. Each frame contains 193 bits—192 encoded signal bits, plus one bit that synchronizes the transmitting and receiving terminals. Each channel processes 8,000 frames per second. Multiply 1 synchronization bit by 8,000 frames and you get 8,000 bits of synchronization and signaling bandwidth. The 1.544 Mbps bandwidth of a T1 is derived from multiplying 64 kbps by 24 channels. That equals 1.536 Mbps. Add the 8 kbps synchronization signal, and that totals the 1.544-Mbps bandwidth of a T1. In North America, a T3 includes 28 T1s.

Migrating to newer digital networks: T1 versus E1

T1-based digital networks were primarily designed to handle digitized voice. Because of this, there were design constraints that result in a reduction of bandwidth for transmission. Namely, only 56 kbps of digital transmission bandwidth is available, even though 64 kbps is sent. E1 is the newer generation, ISDN PRI-oriented digital network designed to provide the most efficient bandwidth for many kinds of services, including videoconferencing. E1 is more prevalent in Europe, while networks in the US are still T1-oriented. E1 is a 32-channel pipe with two channels reserved for signaling and synchronization. Each channel has a bandwidth of 64 kbps, and therefore the bandwidth of an E1 is 2.048 Mbps. Increasingly, the US will migrate from T1 network connections to E1. This will happen as the network evolves to one that more closely follows international recommendations. When there is a choice, E1 is preferable to the older T1 network arrangement.

The LECs realize they must upgrade not only their analog loops to digital, but also their T1 trunks to newer digital network standards. The dilemma for these companies is that it is clear that the future is going to require far higher bandwidth than the 2.048 Mbps of E1. Because of applications like videoconferencing, at least 45-Mbps communication channels are likely needed. As long as the LECs are going to invest heavily in infrastructure, they want to make sure that they can recover that investment. Remaining questions include how the LECs will fund infrastructure improvements, and which areas and subscribers will receive upgraded services.

Leased versus switched access

Making a video or voice-only call beyond the local loop normally requires access to a long distance provider's network. The choice here is leased access or switched access. Switched circuits have the advantage that the customer pays only for the time connected, and the customer can use the same line to call many different people or places. In a leased circuit arrangement, the customer has the advantage of paying once a month for unlimited time connected. The disadvantage of a leased circuit is that the connection is only point-to-point, meaning the customer can only call one place. ISDN is circuit-switched in its network configuration. However ISDN tariffs contain pricing for leased access. In this arrangement, the customer pays for a dedicated point-to-point connection. In reality, however, the network appears to provide a dedicated connection, but achieves this through a switched set-up.

Switched 56: An older method

Switched 56 was just an appetizer for customers hungry for bandwidth in the 1980s. With the advent of ISDN, the popularity of Switched 56 is declining. The service gets its name from the 56 kbps of bandwidth per channel. A Switched 56 set-up for desktop videoconferencing usually combines two lines for a total of 112 kbps. The equivalent of an NT1 for Switched 56 is a data service unit (DSU). The DSU interfaces between the desktop videoconferencing system and the network.

POTS via V.34 modems

Depending on the application, personal videoconferencing is viable over analog Plain Old Telephone Service (POTS) using V.34 modems. However, the H.324 standard for POTS video phones requires that the modem support a protocol called V.80 to be video phone ready. In this scenario, the maximum data rate is 28,800 to 33,600 kbps. The advantage of POTS is that it is a nearly universal method of access to the long distance backbone. The disadvantage is the limited bandwidth of POTS compared to other choices.

Circuit-Switched versus Packet-Switched

Unlike ISDN, which is circuit-switched, some communication channels are packet-switched. Packet-switched networks are optimal for sending data, rather than voice or video. An example of a packet-switched network is the Internet. Packet-switched communication channels distribute bandwidth to all the users who need it. Users send their information in packets over a shared channel. If the channel is heavily loaded, a user gets less bandwidth and sends data—including video— more slowly. However, if the channel is lightly loaded, a packet-switched scenario may send data—including video—faster than a circuit-switched channel would. The Internet, for example, includes a group of service providers using packet-switched channels. If you send e-mail over the Internet, the speed at which the mail is received depends on traffic.

Users of circuit-switched channels are charged based on connection time, while users of packet-switched channels often pay by the quantity of data sent. Normally, packet-switched channels are used for sending less time-sensitive data over networks. E-mail and other printed information can often be delayed seconds or even minutes without causing problems. Video and voice, however, would break up if the information arrived at varying intervals. Therefore, packet-switched channels work for video and voice only if there is available channel capacity.

ATM

Asynchronous Transfer Mode (ATM) is an emerging network infrastructure that merges packet-switched and circuit-switched channels. Benefits of ATM include faster networks, bandwidth-on-demand, and more efficient transmission. Picture ATM as a kind of freight delivery service. Everything that is shipped has a tag that describes both the contents and the level of priority. Perishables like medical specimens, for example, must arrive quickly and so they are tagged with the highest priority, and therefore travel by air. Books bound for another continent which reach their destination in weeks travel by ship.

ATM works similarly, by sorting out high-priority from low-priority data. Video and voice must reach their destination immediately so that a desktop videoconference, for example, appears in real time. Therefore, ATM sends video and voice over a channel that resembles a circuit-switched delivery. ATM sends most printed data such as e-mail over a lower-priority, packet-switched channel. The packets of e-mail arrive at their destination after higher-priority information like voice and video are transmitted.

ATM provides fast-packet service with bandwidth up to 2.5 Gbps. The ATM standard indicates that all data travels in cells, often called *packets*, each of which are 53 bytes. David Ginsburg, consulting engineer with Cisco Systems Europe, points out in the *Newsletter of the European Teleconferencing Federation* that as videoconferencing and ATM evolve, conferencing software will make use of the Quality of Service (QOS) capabilities of ATM. A conferencing application that is *QOS aware* will request the needed bandwidth and other requirements from the network. A router using a protocol called Resource Reservation Protocol (RSVP) will then map the requirements.

In California, Pacific Bell has funded a $27-million dollar trust called the Bay Area Gigabit user group. The group's mission is to develop applications for ATM and other emerging communications services. The consortium includes technology companies, government research institutions, and universities. Among the applications the group is developing are telemedicine, distributed multimedia libraries, and remote collaborative software development. Pacific Bell is also sponsoring an ATM trial that links over 30 companies primarily in California's film and video industry. The project, called Media Park, lets the companies exchange film and collaborate face-to-face through video at a bandwidth of 45 Mbps. More information on ATM can be found on the Web at

`http://www.atmforum.com`

Goodbye copper, hello fiber

Long distance networks are already digital and primarily fiber optic. However, replacing the twisted copper of the local loop means tackling the job one home or office at a time. Replacement lines will be made of fiber optic cable. In 1970, Corning Glass announced the development of glass transmission wires that could provide broad bandwidth. Also, the wires used low-cost materials and were light weight. They are also immune to electromagnetic interference and crosstalk. The glass fibers are encased in a sheath, and a laser-generated light is transmitted through the core of the fiber. While it will be well beyond the turn of the century before all service areas in the US are wired with broadband (up to 1.7 gigabytes) fiber optics, some local exchange carriers have already made progress.

Pacific Bell had said it would spend 16 billion dollars by the year 2000 to rewire half of California with a combination of fiber optic trunk lines to neighborhoods and coaxial cable to homes. Though Pacific Bell appeared to scale back the effort in late 1995, the company still announced plans to wire 3 million homes by the end of the decade. The company's new focus would be to target more strategic markets for fiber/coaxial upgrades. "We're going to change our deployment plan substantially and go after the San Francisco and Bay Area and build out really quickly," Michael Fitzpatrick, president of PacTel's Enterprise Group was quoted as saying in the *Wall Street Journal*. Bell Atlantic originally committed 11 billion dollars to rewire the mid Atlantic region. Across the board, the LECs are investing their rewiring dollars in the areas where their dollars will bring the largest return. This means in urban and technology centers, where use will be the greatest.

The broad bandwidth that fiber optics can provide is generally defined as exceeding 45 Mbps. This is easily enough bandwidth to support high-resolution, full-motion desktop videoconferencing. In late 1993, the California Public Utilities Commission recommended to the Governor that the state adopt policies that would encourage overhauling its telecommunications infrastructure. The report indicated that revamping telecommunications was essential if California was to enhance its competitive strength. However, the recommendations stopped short of pushing for mandatory widespread deployment of broadband capabilities. Nevertheless, the report indicated that such a mandate may "be desirable" in the future. A broad coalition of telecommunications carriers, universities, hospitals, neighborhood groups, and major corporations wrote the recommendations. They indicated growing support in America's most populated state for broad bandwidth, enough to revolutionize the quality of desktop videoconferencing.

SONET

Synchronous Optical Network (SONET) is an interface standard for sending data over fiber optic-based networks. SONET specifies line speeds, transmission encoding and multiplexing techniques, and also creates a standard for equipment used with fiber optic lines. SONET essentially updates the North American Digital Hierarchy, which was developed for copper lines. A similar European standard is called Synchronous Digital Hierarchy (SDH).

Competing with cable TV

The stage is set for competition between telephone companies and cable television companies to deliver video services. Cable television companies already have networks of coaxial cable in nearly every neighborhood in their service areas. However, cable television networks face a different upgrade challenge. Unlike telephone networks, cable television networks are one-way. Cable companies like TCI, Cox Cable, and Comcast are committing billions of dollars to add switches, amplifiers, and fiber optics that will convert their networks for two-way communication. Other potential players in the broadband video game are electric utilities, which maintain thousands of miles of fiber optic cable for internal communication, and wireless service providers.

Cable modems

Cable modems are yet another means of gaining access to the long distance backbone. There are several broad categories of cable modems. One kind routes Internet protocol (IP) messages exclusively. Other types of cable modems support network protocols other than IP. Some cable modems support ATM. Cable modems provide bandwidth at speeds from 3 Mbps to 37 Mbps from the network to the personal computer or set-top box. In the other direction, however, the speed often ranges from 200 kbps to 2 Mbps. This is because common applications for cable modems including Web navigation require more data downstream than upstream. Also, more limited bandwidth out of the home helps prevent people from distributing content and protects intellectual property. Cable modems are an emerging option for personal videoconferencing. A key issue, however, is the bandwidth cable companies and cable modem makers choose to provide in the send direction.

Turning copper to gold: ADSL, HDSL, and SDSL

Because replacing the local loop's copper wire with fiber optic cable costs billions of dollars, many local exchange carriers are embracing technologies to further enhance the current infrastructure while providing broad bandwidth to the home. Pulling fiber to neighborhoods is far more viable economically than running fiber into every home. Therefore, LECs are considering a range of technologies that will link the subscriber's bedroom, livingroom, or home office with the fiber that will run to the telephone pole. The various technologies favor different business models. The primary options are asymmetric digital subscriber line (ADSL), high bit rate digital subscriber line (HDSL), and symmetrical digital subscriber line (SDSL).

ADSL allows copper wire and other media—even wireless signals—to carry up to seven channels of compressed video, providing TV-quality. (See Figures 6–2 and 6–3.) Bell Communications Research (Bellcore), which is

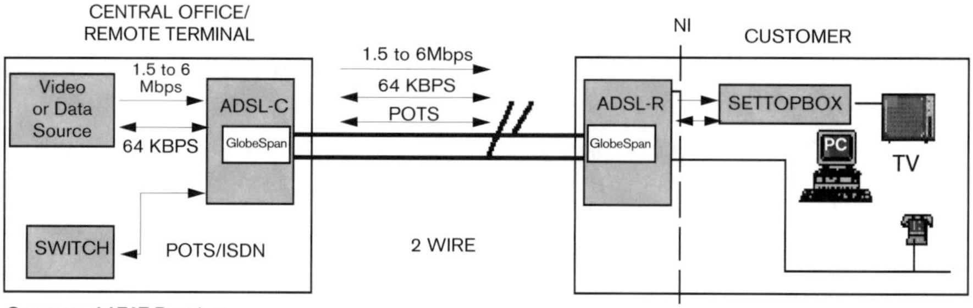

Courtesy of AT&T Paradyne

Figure 6–2: ADSL interactive video/data application

owned by participating local telephone companies including the seven Regional Bell Operating Companies (RBOC), developed the technology. Early trials were used for video-on-demand and were designed to let local exchange carriers compete with cable television companies. In early 1995, AT&T Paradyne announced a suped-up VideoSpan, its ADSL product, which was for sale to phone companies worldwide. Paradyne's offering was based on the Carrierless Amplitude Phase Modulation approach (CAP), in contrast to a competing ADSL approach called Discrete Multitone (DMT) developed later by Amati Communications.

Paradyne's VideoSpan-Plus allowed existing copper and fiber phone networks to support both video and data services and provided bandwidth up to 2.048 Mbps. The product also allowed end users to pause, rewind, and fast-forward video stored on networks, as well as enabling live broadcasts. AT&T billed VideoSpan-Plus as a boon to telecommuting, because of lightning-speed Internet access capability.

By mid 1995, AT&T Paradyne had expanded VideoSpan to support ADSL, HDSL, and SDSL. The new product called GlobeSpan was the first fully integrated transmit and receive chipset supporting all of these technologies. Paradyne developed the product with Bell Laboratories. Besides Paradyne, other companies providing products include Amati Communications, Westell, and PairGain Technologies which makes HDSL modems.

ADSL is closely related to the cable modem business model in that the technology provides typically 1.5 or 2.048 Mbps and up to 6 Mbps to the subscriber site. However, the bandwidth from the customer premise to the network is a maximum 64 kbps. For this reason, ADSL is ideal for delivering video-on-demand and other "content" to the home. The limited bandwidth for sending video protects intellectual property and therefore benefits content

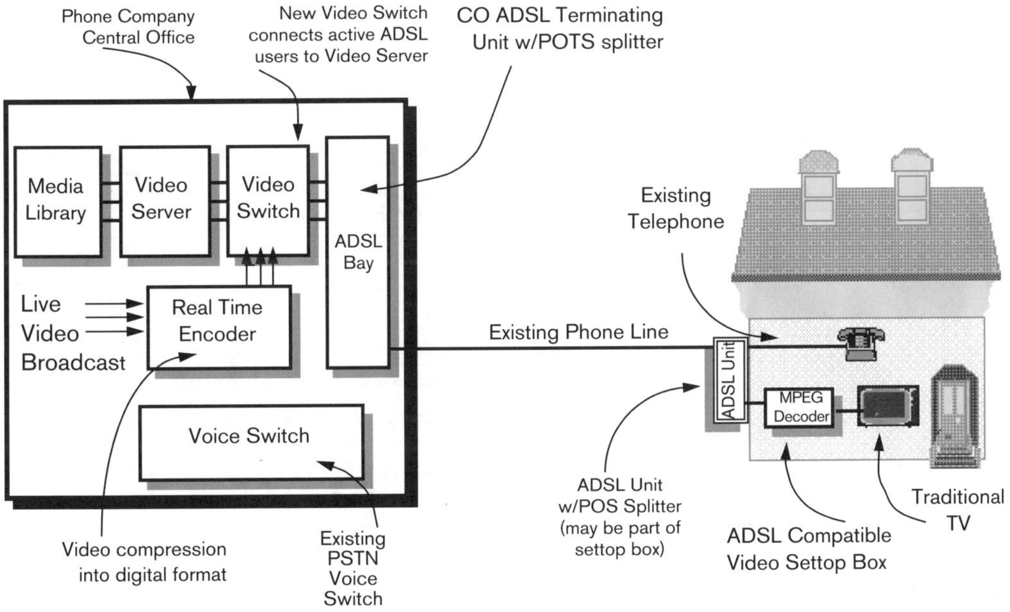

Courtesy of AT&T Paradyne

Figure 6–3: Video dial tone market trial using ADSL

providers, because subscribers are less able to distribute content to others. This same limited bandwidth is enough for voice traffic and credit card transactions, so that subscribers can easily pay for content. However, the limited bandwidth out of the home means that ADSL falls short for videoconferencing. This is because bidirectional, real-time communication favors broad bandwidth in both directions.

In contrast to ADSL, HDSL is ideal for videoconferencing, because the technology provides equally fast video to and from the customer's premises. (See Figure 6–4.) HDSL provides a full 2.048 Mbps in both directions, and is essentially ISDN PRI to the home. This means content can be easily distributed once it arrives at the customer's premise, and therefore the potential exists for abusing intellectual property. The HDSL business model favors companies that sell time on the network rather than those that provide content. HDSL requires two twisted-pair copper wire lines, while ADSL needs one.

SDSL is billed as the first single twisted-pair solution to transmit simultaneous voice and data at speeds from 160 kbps to 2.048 Mbps in both directions, and therefore also to meet videoconferencing criteria. (See Figures 6–5

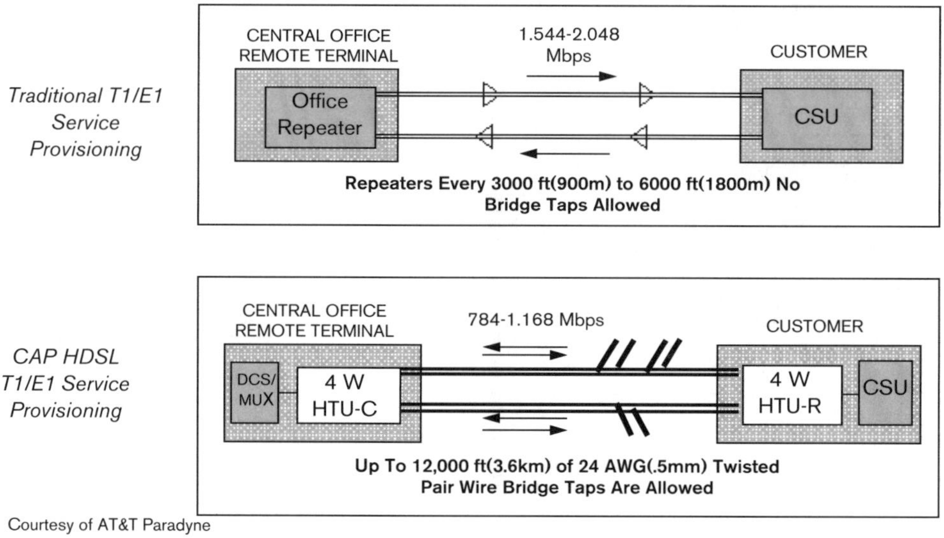

Courtesy of AT&T Paradyne

Figure 6–4: CAP HDSL versus traditional T1/E1 provisioning

and 6–6.) SDSL allows the simultaneous use of POTS or ISDN BRI on the same loop. Several telecommunications companies conducted trials of ADSL and HDSL throughout 1996. NetworkMCI Services was conducting its ADSL trial in Sioux City, Iowa while US West was beta testing both ADSL and HDSL in Boulder, Colorado. Meantime, GTE was conducting an ADSL trial in the Dallas-Fort Worth, Texas area.

Internet Videoconferencing: Democracy in Action?

Founders and proponents of the Internet believe it is the ultimate democratic communication medium. Low access fees mean that anybody with a personal computer can surf the World Wide Web, the graphical portion of the Internet, or send e-mail practically for free. Now users can conduct real-time voice and video calls over the Internet. Some advocates believe that the Internet is the best vehicle for freedom and democracy. However, the ability of companies to make a profit through Internet-delivered services may determine whether the Internet achieves democratic ideals and provides nearly free access, or ulti-

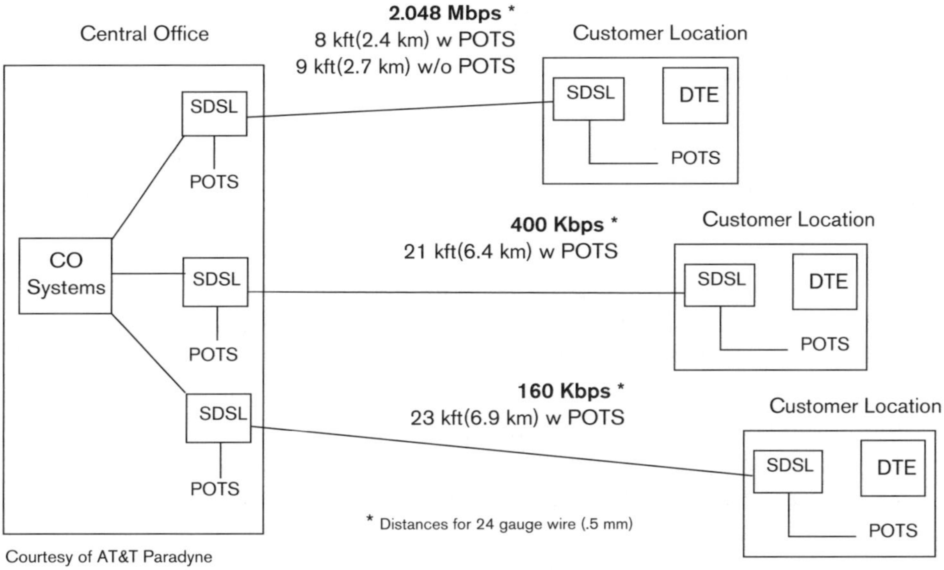

Courtesy of AT&T Paradyne

Figure 6–5: SDSL data rate and service reach range

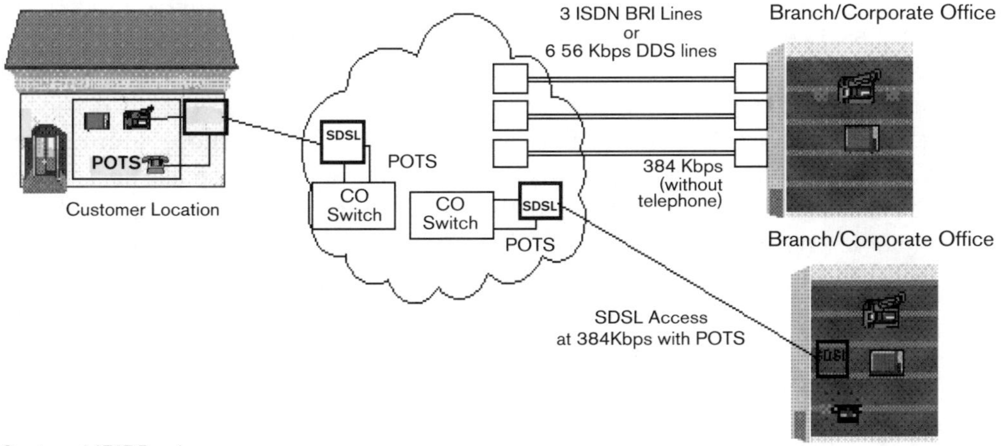

Courtesy of AT&T Paradyne

Figure 6–6: Switched 384 (H0 + D) service application

mately costs more to use. Accessing Web sites, for example, may ultimately require paying a fee in return for a service or information.

Internet videoconferencing is rolling forward as Microsoft, Intel, and more than a hundred other companies jump on the Internet standards bandwagon. The endorsement of standards, as described in Chapter 5, clears the way for cross-platform video, voice, and data collaboration over the Internet to become commonplace. Microsoft is including Internet communications capabilities in its operating system, and Intel is introducing an Internet Video Phone product that will comply with the H.323 standard.

The Internet provides an exciting, and perhaps the most accessible opportunity to conduct desktop videoconferencing. Desktops are already linked globally, and e-mail addresses and Web sites can become video phone numbers. Adding video and audio enhances the virtual community that the Internet provides. Unlike circuit-switched connections, the Internet allows video and audio signals to be inexpensively broadcast to many users. All this takes is addressing signals to multiple people, instead of establishing connections for each recipient, as ISDN and POTS calls require. Many kinds of products allow personal videoconferencing over the Internet. These include Apple's QuickTime Conferencing, InPerson from Silicon Graphics, Netscape's Communique!, VDOphone from VDOnet Corporation, White Pine Software's CU-SeeMe, and the Intel Internet Video Phone.

The VDOphone approach

VDOphone provides color videoconferencing over Internet connections as slow as 14.4 kbps. (See Figure 6–7.) VDOnet Corporation is providing both freeware and commercial versions of the software. The company insists that its VDOphone compression technology, related to wavelet compression, has advanced the quality of both video and audio for Internet communication. VDOnet's technology is optimized for the Internet, because it adjusts to available bandwidth. To accomplish this bandwidth scalability, VDOnet uses a scalable compression algorithm. This algorithm not only compresses video small enough to run over the limited bandwidth parts of the Internet, but also it allows the quality of the video to increase with the size and quality of the connection at the other end. Over a 28.8-kbps connection with average Internet throughput, VDOphone provides 3 to 8 frames per second. The technology also provides full-duplex audio. "What we're doing is enabling the mass market to have access to video telephony," says Tony Zuccarino, VDOnet Corporation's marketing director for telephony.

Courtesy of VDOnet Corporation

Figure 6–7: Internet videoconferencing using VDOphone

A major agreement between VDOnet and America Online has created a video-enhanced chat space in Global Network Navigator's Virtual Places section of AOL, which can be accessed via keyword `GNN`. This is significant because of AOL's reach and popularity. However, direct access to GNN is available on the Web at

`http://www.gnn.com`

Specifically, AOL has licensed the audio-only version of VDOphone and is working with VDOnet to make video capabilities available to users. This means that all AOL subscribers with audio-capable PCs can hold voice conversations on-line. They can also communicate through video face-to-face with additional enhancements available from VDOnet. Virtual Places is a portable client that allows users to chat on any Web site. This is accomplished through the use of a graphical avatar or thumbnail image that represents each user on screen. Virtual Places includes gestures to enhance communication with expressions. Its interface guides the user to locations on the Web where other Virtual Places users are located. In short, Virtual Places lets people meet and find one another on the Web. VDOphone enhances that exchange with real-time video and audio. More information on VDOphone can also be found on the Web at

`http://www.vdophone.com`

The evolution of CU-SeeMe

CU-SeeMe was one of the earliest Internet videoconferencing projects. Cornell University developed the software with funding from the National Science Foundation and others. CU-SeeMe is available for free on the Internet, and provides black and white video. It requires no proprietary hardware, and is designed to perform over low-bandwidth connections.

Cornell has selected White Pine Software as the master licensee of CU-SeeMe, and White Pine has released Enhanced CU-SeeMe commercial versions of the software (Figure 6–8). When Cornell and White Pine announced their agreement in mid 1995, they broadcasted the news conference live over the Internet from the Desktop Videoconferencing Conference (DVC) in San Francisco. Cornell researchers participated through a videoconference link from Ithaca, New York. White Pine set up a worldwide reflector network, so

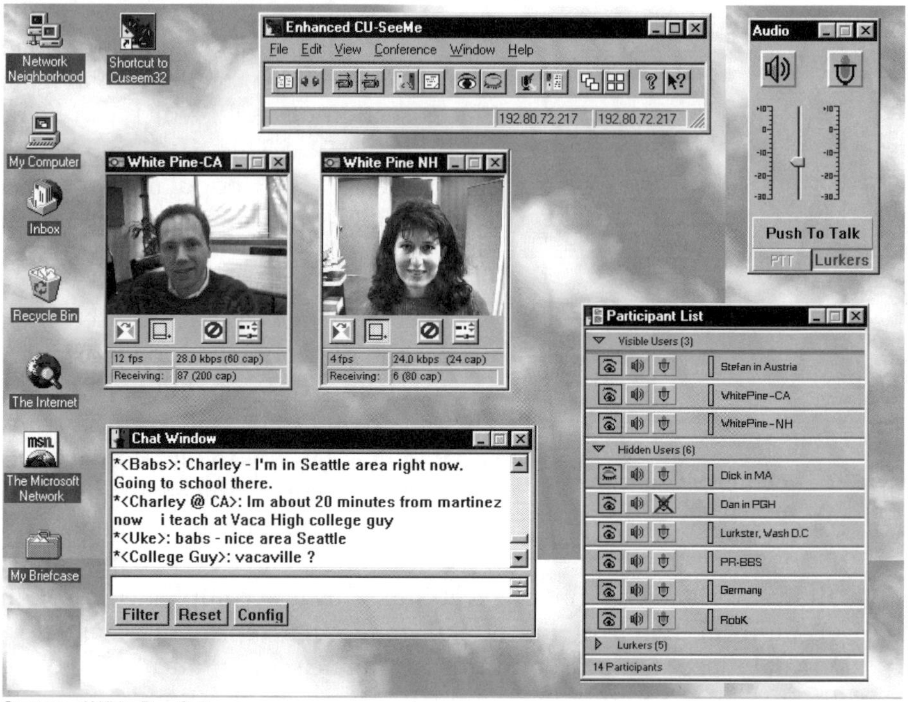

Courtesy of White Pine Software

Figure 6–8: The Enhanced CU-SeeMe user interface

that reporters who could not attend and ask questions in person could listen and view from their desktops. At Net Day '96, President Clinton and Vice President Gore used Enhanced CU-SeeMe to communicate with students. (See Figure 6–9.) The event showcased the objective of wiring all schools in California for Internet access.

Enhanced CU-SeeMe for Windows and Macintosh include color video, whiteboarding, Web browser support, and Caller ID for security. White Pine's version supports connections over 28.8-kbps modems and ISDN networks with TCP/IP network support. (TCP/IP stands for Transmission Control Protocol and Internet Protocol, a group of global networking standards that let different types of computers communicate over the Internet.) CU-SeeMe also includes Reflector technology, a UNIX-based application, which accomplishes "server-like" functions in software. Reflector allows multiple CU-SeeMe users to hold videoconferences and share documents. Linking multiple reflectors enables broadcasting to large audiences. The primary advantage of the reflector is that it unifies lower and higher bandwidth networks. CU-SeeMe's reflector works over the existing Local Area Network

Courtesy of Winnov, Inc.

Figure 6–9: Net Day '96: President Clinton and Vice President Gore using White Pine Enhanced CU-SeeMe software and Winnov Videum videoconferencing hardware

(LAN), Wide Area Network (WAN), and Internet infrastructure. Conducting CU-SeeMe videoconferencing with a 28.8-kbps modem, the video achieves a few frames per second. In contrast, ISDN BRI-based videoconferencing produces at least 10 frames per second. More information on Enhanced CU-SeeMe is available on the Web at

`http://www.cu-seeme.com`

Intel Internet Video Phone

Intel's H.323-compliant Video Phone is part of a suite of Internet technologies that the company is introducing. These capabilities help make communicating and collaborating over the Internet easy. PhotoNet, which Intel developed with a company called Storm, lets people share photographs over the Internet as they conduct videoconferences. The Intel Connection Advisor describes the quality of the connection, providing such information as the connection speed and processor type at both ends. This capability helps set the expectation of video quality.

A capability code-named the Intel PC TUNEUP tells the user what the PC needs. For instance, the user learns whether applications are overloading the CPU or whether the video drivers are out of date. Then, Intel PC TUNEUP can automatically download new drivers. "I call it grandmother-ready," says James Johnson, Marketing Vice President of Intel's Internet and Communications Group. If the Intel PC TUNEUP recommends a faster CPU, the Intel Web Tour gives the user a multimedia walk-through of information throughout the Internet on the latest CPUs.

Issues in Internet videoconferencing

The advantage of Internet videoconferencing over other solutions is the lower cost. Besides a PC and monitor, all that is needed is an Internet connection, a camera, the sound and video boards that ship with multimedia-ready PCs, and inexpensive software. There is also a transmission cost advantage to Internet videoconferencing, which is especially apparent in making transatlantic and transpacific video calls. Instead of paying premium continent-to-continent rates, an Internet videoconferencing user pays little or no toll cost to access the Internet provider's point of presence.

Current drawbacks to Internet videoconferencing involve questionable security and unpredictable video quality. Protocols used for Internet desktop videoconferencing are packet-based, which means the information travels in chunks. In comparison, H.320 information over ISDN flows in a stream. Packets can get lost, because of unpredictable routing, among other reasons. When this happens, Internet applications typically retransmit the packets until they are received. The time the network takes for retransmission can cause jumpy video and broken sound. Beyond its packet-based structure, the Internet may suffer in other ways as traffic increases. Insufficient bandwidth on backbones, local access problems, and servers with insufficient capacity are all potential problems.

Intel is addressing the drawbacks with a suite of diagnostic capabilities. However, video quality problems are likely to persist. "Codecs will get better, but you're always going to be at the mercy of the Internet. For a lot of applications, the quality is good enough," says James Johnson, Marketing Vice President of Intel's Internet and Communications Group. "If it's me talking to my kid, I'll take less video quality and be grateful for what I get."

Web videoconferencing

Videoconferencing has many potential applications as companies integrate the technology into the World Wide Web, the graphical portion of the Internet. As real-time video and audio make their way into Web sites, consumers can point and click their way to a customer service representative. In January of 1996, Netscape announced its LiveMedia framework. LiveMedia enhances Netscape Navigator, the company's popular World Wide Web browser, with videoconferencing, desktop broadcasting, video on-demand, and Internet telephony. The framework also brings real-time video applications to corporate intranets. The product was the result of Netscape's deal to acquire InSoft in a stock swap valued at $161 million. Netscape gained the video and audio networking standards of the desktop videoconferencing software company. Audio capabilities work over 14.4-kbps modems, and video features require 28.8-kbps modems. More than twenty hardware and software companies, including IBM and Apple Computer, announced their support of LiveMedia.

Just days after the Netscape/Insoft deal, industry analyst Sarah Dickinson insisted the arrangement could have a major impact. "It brings Netscape into the WAN world. What you really want to do is go between these two environments to give videoconferencing a computer telephony feel, so that you can have telephony features," according to Dickinson. Bridging between the environments would let other users join an H.320 ISDN videconference through an Internet—or intranet—link.

Van Romine, Director of the Institute for Telework, also hailed the Netscape announcement as significant. "The Web provides an unlimited directory of places to call and it's so much easier to navigate. Businesspeople get that," says Romine. "If it's an H.320 solution where lots of coordination is involved—the machine must be on, you must arrange to call on a certain day— that's too much of a hassle for business people." However, Netscape's move also raised questions about the Internet's ability to handle videoconferencing. George Michaelson, a participant in an Internet mailing list about videoconferencing, wrote, "I fear the lack of bandwidth-management control is going to become very visible, Internet-wide as people find 'batfones' are as simple as a web-click, 3 questions and go... ."

The Netscape announcement set the stage for widely-adopted Internet and intranet Web videoconferencing. Tom Manley, President of INET Marketing, is developing Web strategies for a Florida entertainment complex called Church Street Station. Manley envisions putting cameras in ballrooms, conference centers, and other attractions, and making real-time video available through Church Street Station's Web site. If visitors to the site are interested in making reservations or other services, they could establish a videoconference with a Church Street Station representative with a mouse click.

Them bones, them bones, the MBONE

The MBONE is the Internet's multicast backbone, and is a network functioning as a subset of the Internet. The MBONE is a network of *mrouters* which efficiently distribute packets without congesting any single Internet node. Similar to Multicast TCP/IP, the MBONE reduces network traffic and bandwidth. Using the MBONE often requires a powerful workstation, but PC and Power Macintosh users are rapidly gaining access. The MBONE provides one-to-one and multipoint connections, allowing videoconferences to be one-to-many and few-to-few. However, the MBONE is primarily a one-to-many distribution system. It is best suited for a speech, special event, or training session that requires little interaction. Companies and individuals have used the MBONE for broadcasting everything from space shuttle activities to a Rolling Stones concert. More information on the MBONE can be found on the Web at

```
http://www.best.com/~prince/techinfo/mbone.html
```

As networks evolve

There are many options for access to the long distance backbone and wide area networks for personal videoconferencing. These options will continue to increase as networks evolve. However, network upgrades and available bandwidth are directly related to the business models of telephone companies and cable systems. Since the Telecommunications Reform Act of 1996 has opened the gates to competition, the consumer may face more choices for access. However, realizing the promise of "free" bandwidth over the Internet and cheap broad bandwidth to and from the home depends largely on politics, regulation, and corporate decisions about business models. Ultimately, the struggle is over finding the killer application that upgrades the network—or finding the killer application that works over the existing infrastructure and prevents the network from being upgraded. Ubiquitous quality personal videoconferencing is an application that depends on how emerging networks take shape. As networks evolve, they will likely reflect corporate profit, consumer demand, and the public good—and probably in that order.

7

An Insider's History of Personal Videoconferencing

AT&T and the Roots of Personal Videoconferencing

Courtesy of ATT Archives

Figure 7–1: April, 1930: Walter Gifford, President of American Telephone & Telegraph Company, prepares for his first "television-telephone" conversation as Herbert Ives of Bell Laboratories looks on

The roots of personal videoconferencing date back long before the personal computer. In April 1930, the Great Depression was underway in the US. Radio kept people's spirits up, and regular television broadcasting was still more than ten years away. The same month, though, reporters gathered at AT&T corporate headquarters on Broadway in New York City. They were there to witness and participate in the first public demonstration of 2-way video telephony. The event linked the headquarters building with a Bell Laboratories building on West Street. (See Figure 7–1.)

At each location, participants sat in sound-proof and light-proof booths containing the picture telephones. A neon lamp displayed the image of the person at the other end on a receiving disk. A blue light illuminated their faces while they looked into photo-electric cells, which captured their image for transmission. They spoke through a mounted microphone and listened though a loudspeaker. Herbert E. Ives, the Electro-optical Research Director for AT&T Bell Laboratories, wrote in the May, 1930 *Bell Laboratories Record* that engineers designed a hands-free audio system "because the ordinary telephone instrument conceals part of the face and would thus prevent the system from approximating to the conditions of ordinary face to face conversation."

The New York *Daily Mirror* participated in the demonstration by assigning a reporter at each location. An article in the April 10, 1930 edition compares one-way commercial television to the laboratory-stage picture telephone. While television was considered more advanced, the article insisted that the picture telephone seemed more user-friendly. The article described the speech as clear, the blue light as inoffensive, and the picture telephone as "more highly developed" than television. Telephones could be made to see, but it would be more than thirty years before AT&T would release a product.

Enter the space age with Picturephone

Fast forward to 1964. The economy was thriving in the United States, and unemployment was low. The space program was making history, and within five years a human would walk on the moon. The future was in and so was anyone or anything that looked futuristic. That's why the crowd at the World's Fair in New York City was hungry for new gadgets that might bring them personally into the Space Age. It was there that AT&T introduced *Picturephone*, the world's first digital video telephone (Figure 7–2). Like the "con-

Courtesy of AT&T Archives

Figure 7–2: The 1964 World's Fair: At the AT&T pavilion, the public tried Picturephone for the first time

cept" cars of auto shows, Picturephone was not ready for prime time. Digital bandwidth was barely available and Picturephone required 1 MHz, so the product was nearly impossible to use. Some members of the Picturephone team worked on positioning the product as an exclusive tool for senior executives. Ken Pickar, now Senior Vice President for Engineering and Technology at Allied Signal Aerospace, was part of the Picturephone team. "The demand was zilch," says Pickar. He says part of the reason was that the exclusive toy concept never caught on, and executives had little desire to communicate through the technology. Americans talked about Picturephone, but hardly anybody bought one.

Courtesy of AT&T Archives

Figure 7–3: L.H. Meacham and A.D. Hall, two AT&T Laboratories engineers, use Picturephone in April, 1964. Meacham uses the hands-free speakerphone while Hall uses a handset

In the 1960s, Picturephone was heralded as an incredible example of modern engineering. (See Figure 7–3.) The device included a Touchtone telephone, the Picturephone set or display unit, a control unit, and a service unit containing the power supply. The Picturephone set contained a screen, camera, and loudspeaker, with the lens just above the screen. The control unit included a microphone and the audio and picture adjustment knobs. To make a Picturephone call, a user would press the # button, followed by the phone number. The answering party could prevent the caller from seeing his or her picture by choosing to push a *privacy selector* button. Also, a *Vu-self* option let the user adjust his or her own picture. Picturephone provided a maximum 30 frames per second. A special issue of the *Bell System Technical Journal* in February, 1971 suggests that the Picturephone user sit about three feet away from the screen for optimum communication. (See Figure 7–4.)

Picturephone was a forerunner not only of "talking head" desktop videoconferencing, but also of data sharing. (See Figures 7–5 and 7–6.) Picture-

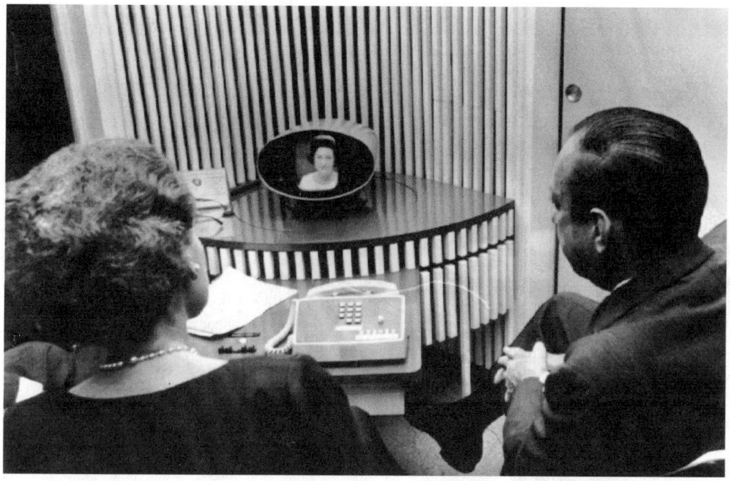

Courtesy of AT&T Archives

Figure 7–4: In June of 1964, AT&T began limited commercial Picturephone service between public rooms in New York, Chicago, and Washington, D.C. Ladybird Johnson, First Lady of the United States (on screen), inaugurated the service with a call to Bell Laboratories Scientist Elizabeth Wood. Robert Wagner, Mayor of New York, is seated at right

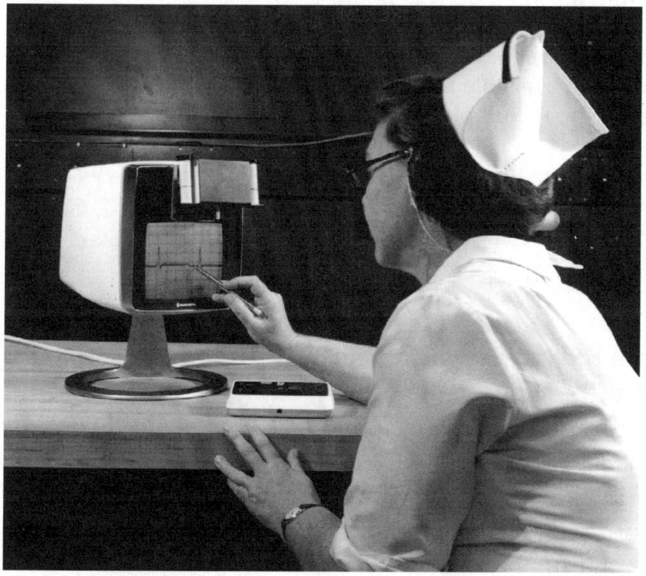

Courtesy of AT&T Archives

Figure 7–5: Picturephone could be used for viewing everything from engineering drawings to microfilm. Here a nurse views an electrocardiogram in 1973

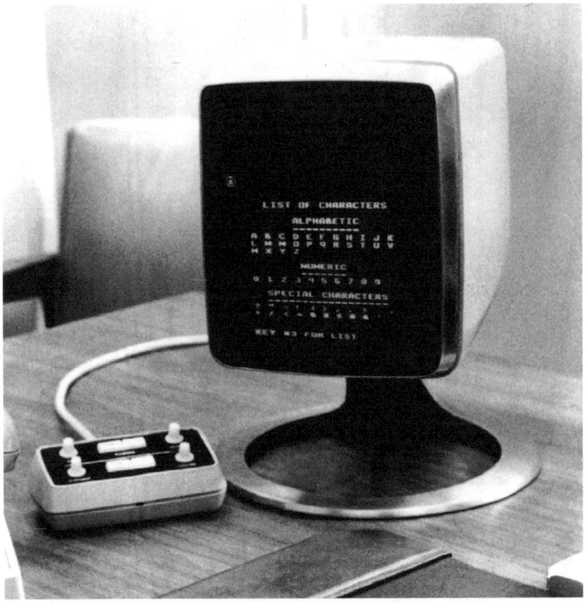

Courtesy of AT&T Archives

Figure 7–6: Besides linking people through video, Picturephone also let the user communicate with a computer. This photograph displays the second-generation "Mod 2" Picturephone and the variety of characters available to display information on the Picturephone screen

phone could display data through a computer link. The user would use a Touchtone phone pad in choosing the type of information to display. An AT&T data set would translate the computer output, and the data would then appear on the screen. AT&T Bell Laboratories tested this capability with an IBM 360/50 computer and Picturephone software written in Basic Telcommunication Access Method and Basic Assembly Languages. Westinghouse Electric Corporation later tried data sharing using a Picturephone and a Univac 494 computer with the company's own software. AT&T planned to offer high-speed data transmission through Picturephone lines. However, Picturephone stopped short of allowing simultaneous face-to-face communication and data sharing, so a user had to choose one function or the other.

Pick your video telephone

Throughout the late 1960s and early 1970s, other companies rolled out 2-way video products. One of them boasted better resolution than the somewhat blurry Picturephone picture. The L M Ericsson Company of Sweden called its product the *LME*. In late 1971, Ericsson used the LME at both ends for the first transatlantic video telephone demonstration. For connecting to AT&T's lines, Ericsson offered a converter. Stromberg-Carlson, a subsidiary of General Dynamics, manufactured the *Vistaphone*. GTE tested the *Pictel*. Three French companies—CIT-Alcatel, Thomson-Brandt, and Matra—demonstrated the *Visiophone*. In Japan, NEC, Fujitsu, Hitachi, and Toshiba also developed video telephones.

The Japanese telecommunications giant NTT was slow to recognize value in face-to-face video communications. One managing director of NTT was quoted in *Electronics* in November of 1971 as saying that people would use video phones more for transmitting drawings, documents, and pictures of products. However, Julius P. Molnar, Executive Vice President of AT&T Bell Laboratories, had a different view. He wrote in the May/June, 1969 issue of the *Bell Laboratories Record* that Picturephone's "chief value is the face-to-face mode of communication it makes possible." Despite the many international development efforts, it would be more than twenty years before desktop video communication products would become viable.

Bell Labs after Picturephone

Courtesy of AT&T Archives

Figure 7–7: The home videophone. A woman uses the AT&T Videophone 2500 in 1992

Many parallel efforts to bring video communications to the desktop continued at Bell Labs after Picturephone. Ultimately, AT&T introduced five product lines in the early 1990s: VideoPhone 2500, Vistium, the AVP processor, a Multipoint Control Unit, and the WorldWorx service. VideoPhone 2500 was a low-bit-rate device designed to run on ordinary POTS phone lines. (See Figure 7–7.) AT&T joined with CLI to develop the technology for the VideoPhone 2500. In March 1993, AT&T Global Information Solutions (now NCR) released the Telemedia product line, and then renamed it Vistium. Vistium was AT&T's desktop videoconferencing system designed to work over ISDN or Switched 56. AT&T discontinued Vistium in late 1995. AT&T Microelectronics (now part of Lucent Technologies) provided the AVP processor, a video compression chip. Multipoint Control Units (MCU) from AT&T Global Business Communication Systems (now Lucent Technologies) provided the capability to link three or more desktop videoconferencing users. The WorldWorx service was AT&T's video network service offering.

Before AT&T announced the WorldWorx service, Bell Labs engineers were busy designing and testing desktop videoconferencing prototypes so that AT&T could configure its network to support the hardware. Between 1991 and 1993, a Bell Labs team led by Fred Haisch designed two prototypes. The first desktop system was based on a room codec, with much of the technology contained in two external boxes. A second prototype integrated the codec into chips on boards inside the PC.

When AT&T announced the WorldWorx service in mid 1994, the company placed Ernest G. "Ernie" DeNigris at the helm of the business unit. Besides having a top-notch sales and marketing track record, DeNigris is an MIT-trained engineer who holds five Bell Labs patents. DeNigris was instrumental in getting separate standards groups to unite behind the H.320 and T.120 families of international standards. In early 1995, DeNigris and his team searched for partners to build desktop videoconferencing systems that would complement AT&T's network services. The WorldWorx team formed alliances with Intel, Apple, IBM, and Sun Microsystems to provide compatible products. This assured that customers using different platforms could communicate and collaborate. By July 1995, DeNigris and company had made history by announcing the world's first service to make real-time voice, video, and data communications possible for multiple participants on one call. A former member of the Picturephone team, DeNigris is still proud of the Picturephone that sits on his desk in Bridgewater, New Jersey. Alongside the Picturephone are a Vistium and an Intel ProShare. (See Figure 7–8.)

Intel's early involvement

Intel jumped into desktop videoconferencing primarily to create a demand for more powerful microprocessors. However, many industry analysts view Intel's involvement as the single biggest development that has fueled the desktop videoconferencing industry. "Intel created a viable market and brought desktop videoconferencing into mass market proportions," according to industry analyst Sarah Dickinson. "That made it easier for other players to join this market."

Intel began to chalk up successes in driving the market for personal videoconferencing in late 1995, but these triumphs were the culmination of a strategy that had begun five years earlier. There had been concern at Intel that the computer industry at large was falling short in advancing the PC architecture. Therefore, Intel realized it should develop applicationsthat would allow

Photo by K.R. Hirzel

Figure 7–8: Ernest G. "Ernie" DeNigris, Vice President of the AT&T WorldWorx service, with his lineup of personal videoconferencing systems. From right to left: Picturephone, Intel ProShare, AT&T Vistium

the PC to perform more functions. In late 1990, Intel President and CEO Andy Grove decided the company needed to enable the PC architecture with rich media types, including voice and other kinds of audio. These media would also require greater computing power, and would drive sales of the company's microprocessors. In early 1991, Intel assigned a two-person team to develop ways of enabling the PC with audio. The team included Sudhir Bhagwan, who focused on business relationships and market research, and Don Dennis, whose expertise was technical.

The team's early efforts were in speech recognition and audio annotation. After concluding that these technologies had limited appeal, the focus shifted towards marrying the PC with telephony. The team worked on acquiring technologies that would allow the PC to communicate using telephone lines, but in a more effective way than through modems.

In November 1991, Bhagwan and Dennis presented their findings to an executive group that included Grove. They detailed the potential of the PC as an audio and document conferencing tool. Meantime, Grove had been thinking about video. Intel had invested in Digital Video Interactive (DVI) technology that was later renamed Indeo. This technology focused on compressing and playing back CD-ROMs. DVI had stalled, however, mostly because the technology was limited by the talent of people creating content, and the cost of CD-ROM drives. Bhagwan and Dennis indicated during their presentation that marrying the PC and telephony could support voice, text, audio, and video. For Grove, "Suddenly the light bulb flashed," according to Bhagwan. It became obvious to Grove that desktop videoconferencing was a video technology that could thrive without waiting for content. Grove then gave the group an additional assignment of deciding how to integrate video into the foundation of PC telephony.

Bhagwan and Dennis continued their work, looking at both videoconferencing and integrated messaging that could include voice and video mail. Intel executives ultimately decided that because other companies including Lotus and IBM were working on integrated messaging and there was less progress in desktop videoconferencing, Intel should focus on videoconferencing over messaging.

Bhagwan reviewed other company's efforts in developing and marketing video phones. He realized that market acceptance was minimal, partly because standard phone lines provided bandwidth too slow for acceptable video quality. "We had to bite the bullet and accept that we had to go with higher speed digital lines of which ISDN was the publicly available standard, even though the installed base was much smaller than that of regular phone lines," says Bhagwan, now Director of International Marketing for ProShare. In May 1992, Intel formally began a videoconferencing project.

Throughout 1992, three Intel teams worked to enable the architecture with rich media types. One team focused on data conferencing, another on PC telephony, and another on adding videoconferencing to the PC telephony foundation. In late 1992, Intel combined the teams into the Business Communications Division, which was later renamed the Personal Conferencing Division. Running the new division was Pat Gelsinger, who had previously managed projects within Intel's Microprocessor Group. There was considerable internal debate about whether to emphasize videoconferencing or audio/data conferencing. Some at Intel felt that many business PC users were far more interested in sharing applications and documents than in seeing each other through video. Intel ultimately decided to push video as well as audio/data conferencing, because video consumes many more millions of instruction sets (MIPS) in the microprocessor. This would increase the demand for future generations of Intel processors.

During 1993, Intel hired outside firms to help name its personal conferencing product. Many names were proposed. InTouch was a favorite, but AT&T had the rights to that name. Intel executives eventually narrowed the field to a short list that included CommCenter, Mergent, Comnos, and GeoComm. In the Fall of 1993, Grove himself made the final pick and named the product ProShare. Video was a particular interest of Grove's, and he continued to be far more involved with ProShare than almost any other product Intel had developed.

By early 1994, Intel was shipping ProShare. Engineers in the company's architecture labs continued refining their video compression work. In early 1996, Intel released a more refined version of ProShare that included multipoint capability and toll-quality audio as well as a suite of enhanced collaboration capabilities. The ISDN version of ProShare allowed up to 24 people to simultaneously participate in a personal videoconference.

In mid 1996, Intel introduced the Intel Video Phone with ProShare technology, a product running over POTS. The product, was geared towards the home PC market and required a 133-MHz Pentium processor-based system as well as a V.34 modem supporting the V.80 "video phone-ready" protocol. At least a dozen PC manufacturers would bundle the Intel Video Phone into their products, sowing the seeds for a mass market. James Johnson, Marketing Vice President with Intel's Internet and Communications Group, insisted that his company's POTS product would drive PC sales. "People that previously had decided not to buy a PC are starting to inch in," according to Johnson. Also in 1996, Intel was planning to release its Internet Video Phone. This product would support the H.323 standard. More information on Intel ProShare is available on the Web at

`http://www.intel.com`

PictureTel's desktop moves

PictureTel, which had chalked up group system video compression advances, moved towards desktop videoconferencing in the early 1990s. MIT Professor David Staelin and two of his students founded the company in 1984. Early in 1996, PictureTel's board hired Staelin's school mate Dr. Norman Gaut to run the company. Before PictureTel developed a PC-based desktop videoconferencing product line, AT&T approached PictureTel about forming a partnership to develop AT&T's videophone. However, PictureTel was less than convinced that a free-standing POTS product was a viable investment at the time. AT&T ultimately cut a videophone deal with CLI, another leader in group videoconferencing systems. Meantime, PictureTel focused its desktop videoconferencing development efforts on the personal computer. "Historically, we looked out there and asked ourselves why did IBM and DEC almost fail and why did Wang fail?" according to Dr. Norman Gaut, Chairman and CEO of PictureTel. "Every one of those companies misjudged the importance of the PC. We weren't going to make the mistakes that those other folks had made." PictureTel concluded that because the PC platform was pervasive, it would become a powerful platform for video communication.

In 1991, PictureTel and Intel agreed to work together on developing a chip that would perform most videoconferencing functions. "It was clearly a solution that could have gotten down to a two-board set, if not one," says Gaut, who holds a PhD in planetary physics. PictureTel developed the chip's fundamental architecture, but Gaut says Intel suddenly abandoned the project in 1992. So, PictureTel tackled PC-based videoconferencing on its own. In many ways, the company faced unchartered waters. "We were going from a proprietary architecture to one that was open and not proprietary," explains Gaut. "It was pretty clear that the PC was not just another room system. You had to have software that would allow you to share information and data." PictureTel's development efforts culminated in 1994 with the PCS product line, later renamed PictureTel Live.

PictureTel and Microsoft forged a development agreement in 1995 that focused on data conferencing. That agreement helped produce NetMeeting, a Microsoft product that allows real-time collaboration over the Internet. The product is fully interoperable with PictureTel's LiveShare Plus data conferencing software.

In mid 1996, PictureTel broadened its potential market by acquiring the rights to VIVO Software's POTS videoconferencing technology based on the H.324 standard. PictureTel took an equity interest in VIVO and received a seat on VIVO's board. In announcing the agreement, PictureTel revealed plans to form alliances with PC and modem manufacturers who would bundle the POTS videoconferencing offering with their products. Additional information on PictureTel is available on the Web at

`http://www.picturetel.com`

VTEL and personal videoconferencing

Austin, Texas-based VTEL Corporation delivered the Personal Collaborator desktop videoconferencing product in 1995 after forging an alliance with Intel. The Personal Collaborator includes ProShare collaboration software along with VTEL's compression technology. VTEL, a manufacturer of room videoconferencing systems since the mid 1980s, began desktop development efforts in 1992. The company first publicly demonstrated a prototype called the DeskMax in early 1993. The DeskMax became the S-Max 115S and 117S, which the Personal Collaborator replaced in 1995.

Despite delivering the product, there was debate within VTEL whether to compete in the desktop arena. VTEL's room videoconferencing systems are PC-based and provide the same user interface as the desktop systems. Therefore, there was concern that VTEL desktop products would compete with the company's room and roll-about products. Some executives also believed the eventual commodity nature of personal videoconferencing would inhibit profits. However, VTEL's room system customers were asking for a desktop solution that would compliment the group videoconferencing approach.

The customers and the desktop advocates won the debate, and VTEL headed down the personal videoconferencing path. However, the company would continue to revisit the viability of desktop videoconferencing as a business strategy. In May of 1995, Vice President of Marketing Tom Stevenson made a presentation to VTEL's Board of Directors that included all the reasons to bypass competing in the desktop videoconferencing market. One of the concerns Stevenson described was that "We don't have the compelling, killer application identified." Also, many customers had returned desktop videoconferencing products because of ISDN questions that went unanswered, because resellers and PC dealers lacked the knowledge.

VTEL weighed the negatives with positive reports from industry analysts that desktop videoconferencing boosted demand for room systems. After a group gathers around a computer to conduct a videoconference, a corporate user may realize desktop videoconferencing falls short for that kind of application. Instead, the corporate user may turn to room systems as a more effective approach for that kind of application. Considering this phenomenon, VTEL decided to stay on track with desktop videoconferencing, as long as they could market the Personal Collaborator as an extension of the company's room videoconferencing product line. In fact, the company drew major media attention in early 1995 when NBC's Tom Brokaw and Microsoft CEO Bill Gates conducted an interview using VTEL's S-Max desktop systems.

Throughout the Summer of 1993, VTEL and Intel were negotiating a deal that would turn both companies into partners, as well as competitors. In October of 1993, the companies announced an agreement which included cross-licensing, joint development, an equity investment by Intel in VTEL, standards work, and cross-distribution. Through the VTEL deal, Intel was ultimately able to leverage the Texas company's expertise in the H.320 family of international standards. More information on VTEL is available on the Web at

`http://www.vtel.com`

CLI and desktop videoconferencing

CLI, a major player in room videoconferencing, developed an early desktop strategy. In 1990, CLI cut deals with AT&T and PaineWebber that would help deliver a desktop product. AT&T would get exclusive rights to CLI's algorithm and hardware for use in a consumer videophone and CLI would have "free reign" in the desktop computer arena. PaineWebber would provide roughly $13 million in financing to cover both videophone/desktop videoconferencing and high definition television (HDTV) development work. In January of 1992, AT&T introduced its videophone. A week later CLI released the Macintosh-based Cameo, which ran over ISDN. CLI chose the Mac platform, because at the time Apple's operating system was far more video-friendly. At the 1992 Macworld Expo, CLI was the only non-Apple partner to display a product at the Apple booth. Since Cameo used CLI's proprietary algorithm, a Cameo could talk only with another Cameo. CLI priced Cameo at under $5,000.

"It was a major breakthrough," says John Walsh, former CLI Senior Vice President who led the project. "There was nothing at the time under $20,000." Walsh was a former AT&T executive who managed both UNIX minicomputer and microprocessor products for the telecommunications giant. He had also held management and sales positions at IBM. Cameo broke new ground in the desktop videoconferencing arena, and Walsh describes it as the "first desktop videoconferencing system truly on the desktop." Customer acceptance, however, was minimal. "It became blatantly clear that we could not get volume either on the videophone or Cameo," according to Walsh. One problem was that the cost of group videoconferencing systems plunged from over $70,000 to less than $25,000.

CLI introduced an H.320 based desktop videoconferencing product family in January of 1996. CLI's new desktop strategy would give users a choice of collaboration software, either Intel ProShare Premier or DataBeam FarSite. The release of CLI Desktop Video 1000 and 2000 was a culmination of CLI's development efforts, industry alliances and contribution to the Personal Conferencing Work Group (PCWG). Intel and CLI signed a memorandum of understanding in early 1994. CLI would resell ProShare and the companies would work together to develop a market for desktop videoconferencing. Also, Intel would invest in CLI. Additional information on CLI is available on the Web at

`http://www.clix.com`

VIVO's software compression approach

Former PictureTel executive, Dr. Staffan Ericsson, founded VIVO Software in 1993 with a vision of developing software-only video codecs. Ericsson led PictureTel's research group, then coordinated international sales and marketing, and then became PictureTel's director of videophone programs. Ericsson's desktop videoconferencing efforts at PictureTel were focused on dedicated videophone terminals, rather than PC-based videoconferencing. VIVO's origins grew out of a mass e-mail within PictureTel. The e-mail raised the question of whether PictureTel would ever become a software company. Most people responded no. "That made me think, and it became clear to me that videoconferencing would become a software application just like a spreadsheet or an e-mail package," says Ericsson. Ericsson then began evangelizing internally to get PictureTel people excited about a software codec approach. "It became pretty clear that that's not where the company was going. I thought it would be a better approach to build a company from the ground up," explains Ericsson.

Ericsson left PictureTel in mid 1992 and launched VIVO Software roughly a year later. VIVO ultimately developed a software-only codec, licensed its technology to PC vendors, and delivered its own product called VIVO Telework-5. Telework-5 is geared towards telecommuters. Ericsson's PhD thesis at the Royal Institute of Technology in Stockholm entitled "Adaptive Methods for Interframe Picture Coding" is considered the foundation for the H.261 video coding standard, which is part of the H.320 standards family.

VIVO continued its development work and produced technology for POTS-based videoconferencing. In mid 1996, VIVO licensed that technology based on the H.324 POTS standard to PictureTel. The alliance would put PictureTel's marketing muscle behind the VIVO technology. Staffan Ericsson had come full circle, making a major deal with the company he had left four years earlier. More information on VIVO is available on the Web at

`http://www.vivo.com`

Apple's videoconferencing initiative

Apple Computer developed its own desktop videoconferencing system, releasing QuickTime Conferencing in 1995. Apple's efforts in videoconferencing date back to 1989, when an engineer named Eric Hoffert left AT&T Bell Laboratories for Apple. Hoffert had focused on 3-D graphics at Bell Labs, but he was fascinated with the potential of multimedia.

When Hoffert arrived at Apple, multimedia was in its infancy. Multimedia development required a laser disc player and an expensive video digitizer card. Hoffert was committed to finding a better way, and he spearheaded a project to create software-based digital video playback. Hoffert's compression algorithm was code-named "Road Pizza," his view of how animals look after they are compressed on highways. Road Pizza evolved into a project code-named "Warhol." Warhol referred to Andy Warhol, the late artist who is famous for saying that "Everybody is famous for 15 minutes." Warhol might bring fame to those who made QuickTime movies. The project culminated in bringing to market the Apple Video Compressor for use with CD-Rom technology.

By 1992, Hoffert and another Apple engineer, Dean Blackketter, had turned their attention to desktop videoconferencing. In Hoffert's view, visual collaboration and communication needed to become a layer of Apple's operating system, rather than simply a niche application. "At the time the computer was still an island," says Hoffert. "It was really the vision of being able to interact with other people and share information with them in real time that was very exciting."

Apple code-named the desktop videoconferencing project "Movie Talk." It turned out, though, that another team in another Apple division was developing a videoconferencing application for the Quadra 840 Macintosh. That project was code-named *Elroy*, after the character in the Jetsons TV show. The Elroy team, lead by engineer Ramiro Calvo, was pushing towards a fast implementation. When both teams discovered their efforts were overlapping, friction developed. After some tense relations, the two groups joined forces, with Eric Hoffert and Ramiro Calvo as coproject leaders. The synergy produced a prototype of QuickTime Conferencing.

The next hurdle for the unified QuickTime Conferencing team was to persuade the rest of the company and Apple's upper management that desktop videoconferencing would do well in the marketplace. Internal Apple-style evangelism prevailed, and Apple brought its platform into the world of real-time collaborating and communicating. By late 1995, the company was shipping Apple Media Conference, a kit including the system extension, software and camera. Additional information on Apple QuickTime Conferencing is available on the Web at

```
http://www.apple.com
```

A different approach from Target Technologies

While larger companies were spending bigger dollars on personal videoconferencing research and development, Target Technologies was looking for its next home run. In early 1992, the small modem company had chalked up big successes with sales of 14,400 modems. However, the company had fewer market share prospects for succeeding generations of modems. One of Target's Ohio resellers was experimenting with desktop videoconferencing by combining several modems. That's when Target's CEO Daniel Flohr first saw PC-based videoconferencing. The former architect and his wife Tina, COO of Target, began strategizing. "I said who's best at delivering video. Hands down it was the cable TV companies."

So, Flohr used cable TV as a model for designing Target's C-Phone product. C-Phone links networked PCs via a CODEC server. The C-Phone units and the server use dedicated shielded-pair or coaxial cable wiring, instead of the local area network's (LAN) existing twisted-pair wiring. Also, the C-Phone provides PBX-like features such as call-waiting, call forwarding, Caller ID, and voice mail functions. The option of a wide area network (WAN) server provides a gateway for H.320 ISDN standards-based communication.

As Flohr sought financing for his fledgling company, the first response from the company's investment banker was cool. Flohr's company had half a million dollars in the bank. He and his wife took a calculated risk by investing $300,000 on a booth at COMDEX. C-Phone was a major hit. The second night of the show, the investment banker committed to taking the company public. "I wasn't sure about God before. I was sure after COMDEX," says Flohr. Early contracts came from the US Army and US Navy. Additional information on Target Technologies is available on the Web at

`http://www.cphone.com`

Sprint's conference connections

Sprint introduced personal conferencing services in 1995, after a rich history of providing innovations in the room videoconferencing network arena. Sprint Meeting Channel's Conference Connections provides dial-up multipoint video and audio network services. The company's involvement in videoconferencing traces back to 1982, when the former United Telecom bought ISACOMM, a satellite communications company. The company's early association with CLI helped drive the room videoconferencing industry. In 1986, Sprint introduced a codec conversion gateway so that sites having different equipment could connect. Throughout the late 1980s, Sprint migrated from a satellite-based to a fiber optic videoconferencing network. Sprint has initiated a comprehensive certification program to ensure that vendor equipment meets international standards. More information on Sprint Meeting Channel's Conference Connections is available on the Web at

```
http://www.sprint.com
```

MCI gets in the game

In September of 1994, MCI launched networkMCI BUSINESS, a package of desktop communication and collaboration services. Part of the package was conferenceMCI, a point-to-point collaborative software tool. As a networkMCI BUSINESS option, the company offered "desktop video from MCI." The ISDN-oriented application was compatible with MCI's multipoint videoconferencing network service, called VideoNet that the company introduced in 1991. In June 1995, MCI bought Darome Teleconferencing and formed the networkMCI Conferencing business unit. MCI then upgraded its product to support multipoint document sharing. This allowed participants in up to 23 locations to collaborate screen-to-screen. As part of the service, the networkMCI Conferencing Scheduler books reservations electronically and sends an e-mail confirmation to all participants. Early in 1996, MCI agreed to invest in Multimedia Medical Systems, which provides PC-based telemedicine products. As part of the deal, MCI's network would carry Multimedia Medical System's telemedicine traffic. MCI has also partnered with other companies to develop personal video communications hardware. Products include the set-top box-based MCI Video Phone and video call center and kiosk offerings. Additional information on networkMCI Conferencing is available on the Web at

```
http://www.mci.com
```

Groupware meets Videoconferencing

While video telephones and group videoconferencing were the most important precursors to desktop videoconferencing, groupware was a universal forerunner to document conferencing and application sharing. Groupware got people accustomed to working together through personal computers. The importance of groupware led IBM in June of 1995 to pay $3.5 billion for Lotus Development Corporation, the most paid to date for a software company. The acquisition gave IBM the most innovative product Lotus had developed. The product, called Notes, allowed distant computer users to collaborate. The client-server application let users share information stored in a server. Users could customize the information to suit their individual needs. Notes boosted productivity for organizations ranging from Union Pacific Railroad to a Dallas drug treatment program.

Nearly a year before IBM bought Lotus, Intel and Lotus announced a deal to market and develop their products together. The agreement was designed to deliver data and videoconferencing products for Lotus Notes software. The products were based on Intel's ProShare conferencing technology. However, the deal was far from exclusive for Lotus. The company had already cut a deal with PictureTel to integrate that company's desktop videoconferencing products into Notes software. In April 1995, two months before IBM's acquisition of Lotus, came another important development. AT&T, Intel, and Lotus announced plans to jointly develop their products. This would speed interoperability of AT&T's WorldWorx network, Intel's ProShare, and Lotus Notes.

"We think of this as a marriage made in heaven," Pat Gelsinger, the Intel Vice President running the Personal Conferencing Division, told industry analysts and media during a conference call in September, 1995. Intel, Lotus, and IBM were announcing RealTime Notes, the product resulting from the comarketing and development agreement. Notes users could now share computer files and applications with other users in real time. RealTime Notes would ship with Intel's ProShare Premier Edition, which includes audio and data conferencing capability, along with whiteboarding. RealTime also would support an upgrade to provide video. Responding to a reporter's question, an IBM executive said the company had reevaluated its own desktop videoconferencing product called Person-to-Person and would be emphasizing Intel's product instead.

During the same conference call, IBM's Consumer Division announced it would preload ProShare on selected models of its Aptiva personal computer line, leading Intel's Gelsinger to proclaim, "We've moved from the 'what is personal conferencing' to the 'how can I start using it' phase." About a month later, Compaq Computer announced plans to include ProShare in several PC models. The die was cast for desktop videoconferencing as mainstream consumer technology.

The computer meets the telephone

Video, data, and document conferencing using the personal computer have similar roots to e-mail and the Internet. In 1971, the Federal Office of Emergency Preparedness developed the first computer-mediated communication system. The purpose was to enforce the wage and price freeze that President Richard Nixon had ordered. Two years later, the Institute for the Future developed *Forum*, the first computer teleconferencing system available over networks. Forum used the Advanced Research Projects Agency Network (ARPANET), the forerunner of the Internet. In 1974, the Institute developed a more advanced system called *Planet*. Planet evolved into *Notepad*, which was operated by Informedia. Notepad provided users with real-time text conferencing, keyword searching, some graphics, and e-mail. Notepad was a hierarchical system in that the system operator could impose tight controls on the exchange of information.

By the late 1970s, researchers at the New Jersey Institute of Technology were experimenting with a less formal and more complex system called the Electronic Information Exchange System (EIES), pronounced *eyes*. The objective of EIES was to provide the user group of scientists with computer functions that would facilitate the greatest amount of open communication. The system provided shared access to comprehensive databases and emphasized structured interaction far less than did Notepad.

In their 1979 book *Electronic Meetings*, Robert Johansen, Jacques Vallee, and Kathleen Spangler of the Institute for the Future noted that computer-based conferencing is least like the face-to-face meeting. Further, the social interaction involved in computer conferencing is a radical departure from videoconferencing. This is because all communication is text-based without voice or video. Emotion, for example, is easily concealed. Users can delay responses until they have thought them through. Because of the distinct differences between these two media, it is perhaps ironic that videoconferencing has emerged on the same platform as computer conferencing. Not only do both media now share the same platform, but also they have merged into a hybrid form of desktop-based communication.

PART III

TAKING THE PLUNGE

8

Integrating Desktop Videoconferencing into Organizations

Planning for Success

Some might think that Peter Knight has risked his twenty-year career as a division chief and economist with the World Bank to pioneer desktop videoconferencing and other forms of electronic media within the organization. "I left a division where I was responsible for forty people to a position where I don't have full-time bank staff, with no assurance of anything down the road," says Knight, who runs the bank's electronic media center. He accepted the challenge, because "The convergence is the most powerful wave of technological change and set of tools to promote development around the world that I can think of." Knight insists, however, that his pioneering work is no risk to his career. He believes the desktop videoconferencing and electronic media project will help the bank disseminate its analytical work, support its operations, conduct training, and enhance its external relations.

Knight has encountered plenty of roadblocks. "Obstacles run from how much bandwidth is available to the culture. People have to get used to it. There's a logistics curve. A few pioneers get it going. People see it, and it takes off." The stakes can be high for Knight and others who believe in desktop videoconferencing, as they develop deployment plans, negotiate bureaucratic obstacles, promote the technology, and counter resistance.

The key to deploying personal videoconferencing—or any strategic technology—in an organization is getting professionals to use it, and use it properly. This helps deliver a return on investment. Beyond the dollars and cents for systems, however, leveraging personal videoconferencing is increasingly becoming critical to maintaining and gaining a strategic advantage in the marketplace. In some industries, a successful deployment of personal videoconferencing may become fundamental to maintaining market share in the late 1990s and into the 21st Century.

A successful deployment is by no means automatic. This is because of the significant change in work habits and communication approach that make this technology stand out from others. "If all I had to do was pick a product, my job would be much easier," insists Fred Campo, who runs the technology integration lab for Northrop Grumman. Campo provides technology solutions to Northrop's internal customers. "The hardest part is understanding, educating, training, and demonstrating how desktop videoconferencing can make the department a more effective organization, and Northrop a more effective company."

The deployment plan

Writing a deployment plan has made a difference for many companies that have integrated desktop videoconferencing across their organizations. The plan should address objectives, department-specific applications or uses, the network, the capability of existing computer systems, and end-user support. Objectives include the bottom line and soft benefits of implementing the technology. Department-specific applications might include recruitment for human resources and collaborating with an outside firm for the legal department. The plan should review the current network arrangement and include upgrade options. Also, it is important to include the capability of the installed PC base and necessary upgrades. Finally, the plan should include internal marketing and education strategy, as well as training and support of end users.

Fred Campo of Northrop Grumman says his company included everything from hardware requirements to standard call procedures in the deployment plan. "We even wrote down procedures like California initiates the call and New York answers," says Campo. Tom Manley of INET Marketing and Lockheed Martin believes having an implementation plan is critical. "You want to decide what you're going to do with it before you deploy," says Manley. Ellen Grace Henson, Ambassador of Visual Communications for Silicon Graphics, believes that "You need an initial framework, but you need to remain flexible." She explains that it is important for end users to understand how desktop videoconferencing can be applied and to begin with some initial uses, but that people will discover other ways to apply the technology.

Steven Bennett, Videoconferencing Project and LAN manager for Reuters America, says the implementation plan should identify all initial deployment locations and a "responsible party" who will insure success at each location. Bennett says the plan should also insure that each end user receives technical information and instruction booklets. "A lack of information is your worst enemy," says Bennett. Bennett says the plan should spell out how the capital is to be raised for the project and cost justification. He says the plan should also indicate the ordering process for desktop videoconferencing systems. "You place orders from a central location. Also, a great deal of coordination from the central point with the telephone companies is necessary."

Bill Muller of Ernst & Young says an "infrastructure plan" is important. He says that an important element of the plan is determining whether an ISDN BRI server is cost-effective. Muller says that a good rule of thumb is that eight or more desktop videoconferencing units requires a BRI server or upgraded PBX.

The implementation plan should identify strategic initial deployment spots for desktop videoconferencing. Putting the technology in the wrong department or area early on can encourage naysayers, create negative feedback, and damage the technology's potential within a company. "An organization needs to make a decision about where the initial high value place is to put this," says Henson. She says the best approach is to implement desktop videoconferencing with a group that is already anxious to collaborate better with one another. As the early adopters within an organization start chalking up successes, the reluctant people will look over their shoulders and eventually adopt the technology themselves. Fred Campo of Northrop Grumman agrees. "I like to target people who are more progressive and willing to jump into the technology. Then they become proponents and help spread the word." Michael Black, Vice President for Sales and Marketing of Datapoint Corporation, suggests another approach in a Datapoint white paper. "Target those areas where there is a critical need to improve the business situation," according to the white paper. The white paper says this approach is likely to produce immediate results and will help in determining how to use desktop videoconferencing throughout an organization.

The first end users of desktop videoconferencing in corporations are frequently senior executives anxious to be the "first on the block" with the new technology. The problem with this approach is that these early-adopter executives are often scattered throughout an organization, and have little need to work directly with one another. Therefore, the systems can end up gathering dust, and the notion that the technology is rarely used can become pervasive. To head off this potential problem, it is often advisable to encourage receptive executives to include their direct reports in the implementation pilot. "An organization has to have a community of interest, rather than 100 people who never work together using desktop videoconferencing" says Bill Muller.

The deployment plan should also identify the type of desktop videoconferencing systems that an organization will use. Arriving at this decision requires establishing evaluation criteria. Travis Kringlen, a video engineer with the Williams Companies, faced a challenge that originated with Williams Companies CEO Keith Bailey. Bailey's directive was to select a desktop videoconferencing system for him and for other senior executives. Kringlen says he began the process by listing the system capabilities that his organization required. "You must format what you're looking for so that the solution meets your objectives," according to Kringlen. Kringlen wanted to integrate the desktop solution into the company's DS3 system for use over a T3. Therefore, Kringlen needed an analog output and input to the WAN. "We didn't want to be limited to the LAN, in case the CEO wanted to address everybody in all of our locations out over the WAN," says Kringlen. Kringlen wanted an auxiliary video input so that users could attach a VCR or an additional camera. He also wanted to steer clear of systems that drain the resources of the PCs host microprocessor. "I gave my boss a list of the three that I thought were best suited. I told him which of the three I thought should be implemented," explains Kringlen. "We have to be accountable for which one we choose." Some companies use a similar evaluation process, and certify all three final choices for desktop videoconferencing use, while other companies narrow the list to one system.

Deployment strategy

Establishing success stories is critical to a successful desktop videoconferencing deployment. Managers are more likely to implement the technology if they see concrete internal examples of how desktop videoconferencing has boosted the bottom line. These success stories are far more valuable than more general application examples provided by vendors. The deployment team must create success stories and then document them through video, still photographs, and written profiles. These can then be used in an internal marketing campaign. Success stories also breed champions. The department head that saves time and money can then become an evangelist.

It is a common notion that younger people accept technology advances more readily than older people. Battling this notion will do wonders for deployment. The answer is to involve an older professional as a champion. Martha Gorman of Bassett Healthcare tells the story of the 66-year-old doctor who still used a rotary phone at home. During a telemedicine deployment, Gorman and her colleagues figured that getting this doctor involved would make many others feel they too could easily use the technology. First came the touch tone phone, and then the desktop videoconferencing. "We dragged him kicking and screaming into the 20th Century, and now he's made a quantum leap into the 21st Century," says Gorman. Gorman's strategy of developing an older technology champion worked. "They can say to their peers this isn't difficult."

Many companies view desktop videoconferencing as a product that a project management group can internally market to business units. The product can be bundled with support services such as training and application consulting. Wells Fargo has taken the product approach. "If you're going to be successful, you must think of it as a business," says Allen Helvajian, Senior Project Manager. "You must determine what your customers want and be able to deliver that product reliably and cost effectively." However, Wells Fargo's technology group stops short of dictating policies or controlling desktop videoconferencing deployments in business units. "Our approach to desktop videoconferencing network management matches our culture, which emphasizes decentralized decision-making," explains Helvajian. "We're here to provide all the consulting services and system support that the business units require. But we never try to control the process, because that would be counterproductive."

For Wells Fargo, the benefits of implementing desktop videoconferencing go beyond internal productivity. The technology is also having a major impact on how banks deliver products and services to retail customers. Helvajian's strategy is to keep tabs on technology while keeping a finger on the pulse of the banking industry. "When you become more comfortable with something yourself, you can find more uses elsewhere," Helvajian explains. "Our internal deployment could be the basis of rolling out video environments to our customer base, including videoconferencing for customer service and video kiosks."

Peter Knight of the World Bank has walked a tightrope while balancing the need to promote desktop videoconferencing internally with the need to avoid too much attention, which can bring with it bullets and arrows. "If you make a lot of noise, everybody's going to kill it," explains Knight. "Instead, crow when you have a success." Knight's strategy has been to chalk up concrete case studies proving that the technology has delivered results. Only then has he let his project become higher profile. So far, Knight's approach has worked. "Now we're actually being challenged. If you want to keep doing this, you have to go sell it to divisions within the bank," Knight says.

An important part of desktop videoconferencing strategy for many companies is preventing rogue users from conducting parallel implementations. Johnson & Johnson anticipated this potential problem, and therefore eliminated it. Anticipating the growth of desktop videoconferencing in 1994, two executives issued a directive to J&J's worldwide information technology organization. According to Videoconferencing Manager Scarlett Moore, the directive was essentially "Please don't go buy a desktop videoconferencing unit on your own." A few months later, another directive went out indicating a deployment team would conduct official pilots. A few months later, the executives issued another directive with the pilot results. The approach worked in part because the purchasing department stayed in the loop. "In Asia, somebody tried to buy a DVC (desktop videoconferencing) unit. The purchasing director flagged the order and sent it to us," says Moore.

The implementation team

Selecting the right implementation team can be a critical success factor. It is also important that the team establish criteria for success at the outset, so that there is a means of evaluating whether the deployment worked. The implementation team should include a project manager who can keep the deployment on schedule and coordinate the gameplan. Critical to the project manager's success is that he or she have enough time. When a project manager must juggle several projects at once, this can substantially slow the deployment schedule. Because personal videoconferencing involves a major shift in the way people work, the project manager should be somebody who has a keen sense of how to motivate people and who also knows the organization well.

Bruce Gilbaugh, NASA engineering technician and desktop videoconferencing coordinator, calls an implementation plan "extremely important." He says a team approach is essential and so is the right mix of expertise. "You need visionary people and people who have a technical background in what the job entails," says Gilbaugh.

Steven Bennett of Reuters America says it is critical that the implementation team include representatives from departments that will use the technology. He says dictating from a central point builds resentment, which can be avoided by getting input and encouraging participation. "If you get the departments involved, you've got automatic buy-in," says Bennett.

At Boeing, a "change board" presides over desktop videoconferencing implementation. The board includes a representative of each of the company's three major divisions, operations people, and maintenance professionals. The board has developed "vision mission goals," according to Ray Sollars, operations manager for network applications. One of those goals is to establish guidelines for evaluating and standardizing desktop videoconferencing approaches companywide. The board meets biweekly, and a smaller group gathers weekly to solve problems that users present. One issue the board has addressed is whether to move beyond one brand of system for use companywide. When international standards were embryonic, Boeing chose to stick with one system. Now, however, the company is looking towards a variety of solutions. "As the standards become more focused, we can go pick and choose," says Ray Sollars.

Another responsibility of the Boeing change board or implementation team is clearing up misconceptions that others in the company may have about the technology. For instance, "Some higher-up has read something in a magazine that has piqued his interest," explains Sollars. "We always have to address a VP or some higher-up on why something will or won't work." Sollars says the two biggest issues facing the board are upgrading the network and storage capability for stored videoconferences and video mail. "We're always upgrading voice mail storage capability. If we're talking about FCIF video, we have to determine where to put it," according to Sollars.

Johnson & Johnson approached desktop videoconferencing in much the same way the company tackled room videoconferencing implementation. J&J assembled a task force that included members from more than 20 of J&J's operating companies plus a consultant and the videoconferencing manager. The team evaluated carriers, vendors, and systems integrators. The task force then conducted trials to determine, among other things, the "true" minimum PC requirements to handle desktop videoconferencing. Then the task force certified systems for several vendors for deployment for different applications worldwide. Unlike its approach to group system deployment, the J&J task force bundled the network and equipment offerings and offered them to its operating companies or divisions, creating "one-stop end-to-end" for its internal customers worldwide.

CEO buy-in

There are two basic approaches to deployment: top-down and bottom-up. Either can work, but the latter is a slower, bumpier ride. Sarkis Zartarian, who leads a software development lab and also runs a consulting firm called Applied Communication Concepts, believes the top-down approach is essential to success. "The top executive has to be a proponent," insists Zartarian. "Then you need a person at the executive operational level who will say the CEO wants this." In Zartarian's implementation model, a "champion" at the next lower rung of management is also needed. This champion is an active, aggressive communicator who can easily operate the technology. Zartarian, who used to run an advanced technology lab for IBM, says the importance of CEO buy-in involves long-range planning. "This must be part of a long-term strategy, one of the bricks in a broader vision." Then, desktop videoconferencing becomes a tool to make the CEO's vision real.

So, how does a champion make the case to the CEO? Cost justification analysis is essential, but hard numbers alone may fall short. "It must be acceptable to the CEO on soft reasons. This way he is less likely to stop you if you don't do a good job on hard benefits," says Zartarian. The soft benefits case is all about intuition. "Typically the top executive will have a gut feeling that he will be left behind," explains Zartarian. "The CEO will feel that the time cycle for information flow must be reduced."

Approaching the CEO, however, requires laying the groundwork with other key executives. It is important to make separate kinds of cost/benefits analyses for marketing, technology, human resources, telecommunications, and key division heads. Getting these buy-ins gives the proponent a pedigree or list of advocates to help make the case with the CEO. "All executives are insecure," insists Zartarian. "They want to know who saw your pitch and who thinks it's good." Once the CEO has blessed the effort, operations management is implementing the CEO's directive, and a champion is demonstrating the technology, the troops warm up to the technology. Zartarian says the implementation spreads like fire once directors and managers start giving directions through desktop videoconferencing. "Once you know the bosses are telling you what to do through the technology, you sign on," according to Zartarian.

Developing department-specific applications

People need a compelling reason to change their behavior, and using any new technology involves a behavioral change. Compelling reasons to use desktop videoconferencing vary considerably from department to department, and from job function to job function. Therefore, the one-size-fits-all approach falls flat when implementing desktop videoconferencing in organizations. The answer is to involve departments in the deployment process.

At the DVC '96 West conference, Ann Earon of Telemanagement Resources stood before an audience filled with desktop videoconferencing vendors. "Shame on you vendors," thundered Earon. "Most of you have done a lousy job." Earon's point was that corporate users were tired of the vendors simply shipping boxes of equipment with little or no application development support. Earon also reported the results of a survey of over 500 personal videoconferencing users. When asked what was missing from product offerings, the overwhelming response was "applications." According to Earon, "They might have one specific application in mind. They use it for that, and then the unit gathers dust." Other popular responses to the "what's missing?" question included implementation expertise, better multipoint capability, and better audio/video quality.

Bill Muller of Ernst & Young says he always insists that a potential user complete a questionnaire about objectives for desktop videoconferencing. "That way we know they have thought it through, so when they get it they begin using it right away," says Muller. "Otherwise, desktop videoconferencing might end up as an executive paper weight."

Steven Bennett of Reuters America says most people have no idea about uses for desktop videoconferencing. He believes both input and direction in determining applications is important. "Usually one or two visionaries have an idea what to do with it," explains Bennett. "People in the field usually subscribe to it and catch up later on. Then more ideas start to develop as use increases.

"You've got to define when you use it, how you use it, and when you don't use it," according to Ralph Ungermann of First Virtual Corporation. "Finding applications is the most important thing." Keith DeStasio of 3M agrees. "You can't just say here's this tool, figure out how to use it. You need a real business need, a real application," insists DeStasio. "Fixing one outage faster can pay for the technology."

Allen Helvajian of Wells Fargo says it is critical to develop department-specific applications for desktop videoconferencing before, during, and after deployment. "It's where the business requirement makes sense," says Helvajian. "We match the installation to a business need. We don't just go out and implement across the board."

Ernie DeNigris, Vice President of AT&T WorldWorx services, believes developing applications early and often is the key to personal videoconferencing success. "You've got to do it at the front end. Our experience is that if you just drop this technology onto someone's desk, they are not going to know what to do with it in an intuitive fashion." DeNigris says that unless the applications are in place, use levels remain low because people fail to substitute desktop videoconferencing for other communication methods. He says, however, that the growth of Internet videoconferencing could change this equation in that universal acceptance of the technology—in all of its forms—could follow.

John Walsh, former Senior Vice President of CLI, says deployment success depends on developing applications with two fundamental elements: perceived value in video and perceived value in data collaboration. Walsh believes that applications that involve only one of these elements will fall short in driving use of the technology. He insists that developing department-specific applications before deployment works best. "The notion of put it out there and they'll use it probably won't work," Walsh explains. "You probably need something for each set of folks that spells out the benefits for them."

Ray Sollars of Boeing believes developing applications before deployment complicates the process. "We'd never get from *A* to *B*," Sollars explains. Instead, he believes the deploy and follow-up method works best. "Slap it on their desks. There's training classes if they have any desire," Says Sollars. "To me, desktop videoconferencing is just another application." Sollars says he believes Boeing's extensive experience with room videoconferencing has made the transition to desktop easier.

The Corporate Culture Shift

Desktop videoconferencing helps reinforce new approaches to corporate culture. These approaches include a more open information flow, a less pronounced hierarchy, and more decentralized decision-making. Companies have adopted these approaches, because studies have indicated that professionals are more motivated and productive when they gain more access to information and they feel that their input is valued. Corporate cultures of days past required that professionals receive information on a need-to-know basis. However, the advent of the World Wide Web and the increasing availability of immediate information mean that professionals have grown to expect that their organizations will encourage an open exchange. "Organizations who don't anticipate and encourage this shift are effectively obsoleting themselves," says Ellen Grace Henson of Silicon Graphics.

Desktop videoconferencing moves corporate *perastroika* several steps forward by allowing instantaneous collaboration and real-time video interaction between professionals of all levels in an organization. As collaboration and communication increase, professionals gain more opportunities to meet video face-to-face with senior executives. In this way, desktop videoconferencing can break down some barriers between executive suites and departments. When questions arise during an important meeting, an executive may make a video call to a specialist. This gives the executive unfiltered access to the professional's expertise as well as to pertinent spreadsheets and other documents. Executives can then learn more about the specifics of business decisions made at other levels. Despite the corporate culture shift that desktop videoconferencing can advance, the technology may do little to accomplish the shift in an organization that resists the change. "Technology is a facilitator," says Henson of Silicon Graphics. "It might accelerate social trends. But if the tendency is not already there, the technology is not going to create it."

Fred Campo of Northrop Grumman compares deploying desktop videoconferencing to introducing the PC in organizations. A major shift occurred when the PC moved beyond the "propeller heads," according to Campo, and on to the desks of administrative people. "We literally had secretaries crying when the computer landed on their desks. They would take sick leave."

Campo concedes that while deploying desktop videoconferencing may prove less drastic, the technology nevertheless has an impact on organizations comparable to the power of the PC. "This is a major revolution in the culture," says Campo. "It's changing the way we do business, and changing our lives."

Travis Kringlen of the Williams Companies believes that a widespread deployment of desktop videoconferencing changes the expectations of users, and that the corporate culture must adjust. Kringlen compares the shift to a longer-than-expected wait in a fast food restaurant. He says such a wait upsets people. "The same thing will happen with desktop videoconferencing," according to Kringlen. "We'll get used to immediate results. When someone doesn't have this on their desks, and you have to leave an e-mail or voice mail, we'll get frustrated, because you won't be able to resolve a problem as fast."

Another major cultural shift worthy of consideration during deployment is that desktop videoconferences are for keeps. Real-time video communications and collaborative sessions can be stored for future reference and forwarded to others. This capability raises such issues as who can access these electronic files, how they gain access, and how participants can keep their communication and collaboration private. In June of 1995, *The Wall Street Journal* ran a story describing "The Message," which was a voice mail message that bounced around Wall Street, then made it to Washington DC and Hollywood. The message was a woman's 2-minute, graphic review of her date that climaxed in "some cheesy motel, mirrors on the ceiling, red light." The story by Dennis Kneale points out, "Therein lies the digital moral: Your private gossip can belong to everyone, anyone, when it can be digitized and diced, and copied and forwarded."

Add video to the equation, along with a media server and upgraded data network, and there is the potential for organizational embarrassment. Suppose, for example, a manager conducts a performance evaluation through desktop videoconferencing, one of the participants stores the session, and others gain access to the electronic file. Like television archives, stored desktop videoconferences can potentially provide a legacy of our meetings, presentations, and collaborations. These video anthologies may follow us through our careers and personal lives.

Senior management: Setting the right tone

Desktop videoconferencing helps flatten organizational hierarchies, because the technology lets senior managers collaborate easily with professionals at all levels. However, there is a danger that senior managers will have trouble resisting the temptation to micromanage through the technology. Bruce Gilbaugh of NASA believes that the way senior managers approach desktop videoconferencing is critical to successful implementation. Gilbaugh says that senior managers must avoid using the technology to check up on the troops. "This is an enhancement tool, not a control tool," says Gilbaugh. Gilbaugh says he has seen senior managers insist on "1 to 3 hour show-and-tells every morning" in which a technician must walk the brass through the latest wrinkle in a production process. "The show-and-tell has a cost. It impacts the work load," says Gilbaugh. Part of the reason that executives may ask for "show-and-tells" is that the technology is novel and exciting, or as Gilbaugh puts it "the new toy on the block." Gilbaugh suggests that a solution may be to set up two demonstration units that will allow professionals throughout an organization to "go play without interrupting" productivity.

Multicompany study of collaborative computing

A multicompany deployment study has produced significant findings regarding the benefits of implementing desktop videoconferencing and other tools in organizations. The study also provides insight into deployment success factors. Silicon Graphics and a high-technology management consulting firm called Stratiquest conducted the study during 1995 and 1996. Three companies participated, including 3M, Varian Associates Oncology Systems Division, and an unnamed high-technology manufacturing firm. The study involved implementing several collaborative computing tools, including desktop videoconferencing, e-mail, video mail, creation and transfer of movies and 3D models, Web publishing, and Web navigation. The study found that collaborative computing could slash time-to-market and reduce operating costs. Within five months of deploying collaborative computing at the high-tech manufacturing company, complex assembly redesign time dropped from three or four months to less than a month. The time it takes to rework simple parts dropped from two weeks to one day.

The study also showed that immediate access to experts through collaborative computing sped up problem resolution at all three participating companies. The companies often used the technology to replace travel, and this approach boosted efficiency. Previously, problem resolution caused delays because experts were often unavailable to travel immediately.

A report on the study identified the value of training. "Training is a critical investment if companies are to accrue the benefits of collaborative computing as quickly as possible," according to the report. The report recommends a three-tier approach that includes a formal training class with "adequate" lab time, development of "experts" in each group who can provide on-the-job help, and regular user group meetings so that experiences can be shared.

Among other important results of the study were that deployment of collaborative computing tools requires "unique organizational considerations." Companies must make sure, for example, that individuals and groups have a clear sense of how to begin applying collaborative tools to their jobs. Also, management must ensure that individual and group deployment goals match. The study also found that training should bring all participants along at about the same pace, regardless of varying computer skills. More information on the study and a document entitled "Deployment of Collaborative Computing: Best Practices" is available on the Web at

`http://www.sgi.com/Products/collaborate/`

Revisiting the Andersen Worldwide study

The Andersen Worldwide desktop conferencing comprehensive study described in Chapter 2 also provides significant information about deploying the technology in organizations. The study identified potential barriers to use, including availability and cost of the technology, the need for training, and the lack of comfort with the camera and "sharing the mouse." The study divided 54 participants into a video group and a non-video desktop conferencing group. 40% of video users expressed some discomfort appearing on camera. Only the video group cited "ability to share workspace" and "inappropriate use of the technology" as barriers. A report on the study quotes one participant as saying, "When sharing a workspace, known control parameters will be critical to maintain productivity."

Internal marketing and education

An implementation plan should include an internal marketing approach. The approach may involve communicating key messages about the technology through many communication channels. Those channels can include an intranet Web site, electronic billboards, electronic and hard-copy newsletters, and demonstrations. Impact Video Communication, a San Francisco-based videoconferencing consulting and training firm, has advised corporations to name their videoconferencing networks. The name can cover both desktop and room videoconferencing systems. Naming the program lets companies use systems from different vendors while still preserving internal brand identity. Kathherine Hirzel of Impact Video Communication has worked with many corporations in creating, naming, and internally marketing videoconferencing networks. "The best approaches that work within different corporate cultures come from brainstorming. Internal marketing campaigns can get pretty creative," explains Hirzel. "One major bank we've worked with has even considered covering the manufacturer's brand name with nameplates promoting the internal videoconferencing network." This approach gives departments greater flexibility in choosing a variety of systems while maintaining an interoperable, unified network with a common identity.

Northrop Grumman leverages its investment in a technology integration lab to introduce professionals to desktop videoconferencing. At the lab, specialists demonstrate the technology. "The demonstrations show our internal customers examples of how to improve their processes and communication through the technology," says Fred Campo of Northrop Grumman. Pilot programs give end users at least a month to test desktop videoconferencing in their own environments.

Reuters America has found that "person-to-person" marketing is the most effective approach. Steven Bennett, Videoconferencing Project and LAN manager, says starting at the manager level and working your way down works best. "Get the managers involved and their people will follow. Get the training department involved, and sooner or later everybody will follow." The Williams Companies has also had success with face-to-face marketing. One technique the company uses to introduce new technologies and approaches is organization-wide lunch meetings. During the meetings, internal experts conduct presentations and demonstrations.

Ralph Ungermann, CEO of First Virtual Corporation, insists that a top-down internal marketing approach is most effective. "The top of the company is the easiest place to sell, because they are desperate to have more frequent high-impact meetings with peers and reports, and avoid travel as much as possible," says Ungermann.

An intranet or internal Web site can be a powerful internal marketing and information tool. The site should bear the name of the videoconferencing program with a link to desktop videoconferencing resources. Those resources may include internal success stories, applications, white papers on desktop videoconferencing, descriptions and hardware requirements of available systems, and support options. Ultimately, the intranet Web site can also provide a point-and-click videoconferencing link to a videoconferencing coordinator. An internal marketing program should encourage champions to include additional desktop videoconferencing information on their personal home pages. Then the videoconferencing site can provide links to these personal pages.

One organization that has successfully used an intranet site to internally market desktop videoconferencing and other technologies is the World Bank. The site includes a videoconferencing guide that reviews the differences between group and desktop systems. The guide also presents photos and descriptions of successes. Those examples include a multipoint link as part of an international conference on distance learning. The desktop videoconferencing session connected the World Bank with the Russian Academy of Sciences in Moscow and the University of Tennessee. The guide includes quotes from champions of the technology. The intranet Web site, is also available on the World Wide Web at

`http://www.worldbank.org/html/emc/documents/vcguide.html`

The site fit into Electronic Media Center Chief Peter Knight's strategy of low-key marketing for starters, then a bigger push after developing concrete success stories. "We were told not to do a lot of marketing at first. We did it passively through the Web site, and word gets around," Knight says. Other marketing approaches Knight has used include talking to groups in different divisions about the benefits of desktop videoconferencing. The message, says Knight, is simple: "The death of distance."

Allen Helvajian of Wells Fargo says an effective internal marketing approach underscores the ideals that a company embraces. For Wells Fargo, those ideals include quick decision-making, providing service, and creating value for both internal and external customers. "Value is however you want to define monetary gain," says Helvajian. "If desktop videoconferencing helps you get something to market faster, that's value. If it helps you provide a better product than your competition, that's value. If it enhances communication, that's value."

Helvajian believes that a successful internal marketing approach keeps users' expectations in line with what the technology can deliver. "It is important that people understand that nothing can replace two people meeting in person and talking, except for maybe real-time holographic projection. But desktop videoconferencing can be much better than the phone and certainly better than e-mail for many interactions." Helvajian points out that internally marketing desktop videoconferencing differs from room system marketing approaches. The key is that most desktop systems are PC-based. "Now that the PC is as common as the typewriter was, it's important that people understand that desktop videoconferencing has recast the PC as a unique productivity tool." Once they understand how desktop videoconferencing unleashes the PCs power, Helvajian says "There's a great deal of excitement associated with desktop videoconferencing."

Anticipating and countering resistance

The most frequent objection to desktop videoconferencing—and many other technologies—is "Why do we need it? We've done without it before." Bruce Gilbaugh of NASA responds that desktop videoconferencing for problem solving is like a tool in a toolbox. "If all you have is a hammer, everything will be done with a hammer. If you have a wrench and a screwdriver, you have a choice. Desktop videoconferencing just adds to the toolbox."

Gilbaugh identifies the Big Brother syndrome as another major form of resistance that must be countered. Some professionals worry that videoconferencing on their desktops or work areas gives managers and others the opportunity to spy on them. Particularly in an era of corporate downsizing, professionals fear somebody may decide they are doing their jobs wrong. "I try to reassure people that that's not our intent," says Gilbaugh. "One guy threatened to put a pair of dirty shorts over the camera." Countering this kind of resistance may involve educating managers that sensitivity to privacy concerns is important.

Steven Bennett of Reuters America says being prepared to counter resistance is important to the success of desktop videoconferencing. He says resistance includes a preference for in-person meetings and travel. "They'll say nothing beats face-to-face communications. But that's what desktop videoconferencing is," says Bennett. "A lot of people would rather take the trip. That's often not necessary except for a very high level." Bennett says in countering resistance, the bottom line usually prevails. "If you can achieve the same goal with a few hundred dollars worth of time instead of thousands of dollars in travel, it's obvious."

Bennett says another hurdle is that many professionals still believe desktop videoconferencing requires a technologist to set up video calls. He says the solution is for informed technologists to educate end users. "There's a small technology core and forward-thinking managers trying to implement this and their goal is to drag everybody else kicking and screaming into the 21st Century," insists Bennett.

Resistance can sometimes come from proponents of room videoconferencing, particularly if separate teams are promoting desktop and room solutions. Peter Knight of the World Bank says resistance from room videoconferencing advocates often gets down to dollars. "The entrenched people who think that videoconferencing is a videoconferencing room have to recover the money they invested in an older technology," according to Knight. One way to avoid this scenario is to merge desktop and room efforts, and to develop guidelines that distinguish when each of the technologies does the trick. Scarlett Moore of Johnson & Johnson says the perception that desktop videoconferencing means death to group systems misses the mark. "Just because we can rent movies at Blockbuster doesn't mean we don't like to go to the movie theater and hear the roar of the crowd," Moore insists.

While the proliferation of video has helped people warm up to being on camera, it is nevertheless realistic to anticipate resistance to the video medium itself. Dennis Riley, who runs Microsoft's desktop videoconferencing lab, believes the biggest challenge is that many people aren't ready for videoconferencing. "It's kind of like the PC in the 80s. It wasn't an easy sell to businesses or individuals," says Riley. "With desktop videoconferencing, it's like 'I'm not accustomed to this. I don't know if I like seeing them and them seeing me.' "

Other potential resistance may involve dashed expectations of television-quality video. Ken Pickar was on the original Picturephone team. Now he is Senior Vice President for Engineering and technology of Allied Signal Aerospace. Pickar is an experienced room videoconferencing user, and he says that desktop videoconferencing falls short for him. "It's been very disappointing. I see not a lot of value added for holding management meetings and performance evaluations. It has not added much to voice," says Pickar.

John Walsh, former Senior Vice President of CLI, says "positive publicity" is the best way to overcome resistance to desktop videoconferencing. "People want to see evidence that others have embraced the technology and have gotten results," explains Walsh. Walsh says that because desktop videoconferencing is fundamentally different from group conferencing, a different strategy is necessary to encourage use. He says peer pressure frequently works in driving group videoconferencing. If several people plan to participate in a group videoconference, a reluctant participant will often give in to the group. "Desktop videoconferencing is such an individual choice that it will never work on a push basis," says Walsh. "You have to have people perceive the value." Walsh also says that an implementation team can overcome naysayers by developing "real business applications" for potential resisters. "That way they can get experiential data on their own."

At its Center for Strategic Technology in Palo Alto, Andersen Consulting has introduced the Davinci program. Through Davinci, Andersen demonstrates to clients the benefits of the virtual corporation. The day-long program shows participants how technology can change traditional business approaches to demand chain management, relationship management, joint venture management, and strategic information management. Desktop videoconferencing is one of several technologies included in the program.

During one Davinci session, several representatives of a relatively low-tech hospitality industry company attended. The Andersen facilitator wanted these professionals to understand how they could lead their company and their industry into the 21st Century by adopting new technology and approaches. The senior representative was skeptical at first. "If you are the first one, you are going to get all of the arrows in your back," he told the facilitator. "You're the pioneer and your competition's going to learn from your mistakes."

The Andersen facilitator ultimately persuaded the executive and his team that changing their traditional approach to the hospitality business could boost the bottom line. However, the executive's reaction is typical of the resistance that proponents of the technology can encounter during deployment. Getting doubters to verbalize their concerns as the Andersen facilitator did is the first step towards countering resistance. This is because once objections are out in the open, it is easier to explain the specific points raised. In this fashion, it is sometimes possible to turn a resister into a proponent of the technology.

Corporate managers in many countries—including Germany— have been slower to use PCs than managers in the US. While some believe that desktop videoconferencing will encourage more professionals to implement and fire up PCs, Stephan Wenger of Technical University of Berlin disagrees. "Desktop videoconferencing only works for people who are using PCs every day. If a manager sets videoconferencing on his desk simply as a telephone substitute, it will not work."

Training

Many studies have indicated that training is a critical success factor in implementing personal videoconferencing. Bruce Gilbaugh of NASA conducts initial training during two half-day sessions. Those sessions include an overview of the system, physical recognition of each component of the system, an introduction to the collaboration software, and some conceptual guidance of how the technology can be used. Advanced training might include learning to organize utilities better and instruction in how to organize utilities on different electronic desktops using the Silicon Graphics InPerson system. Steven Bennett of Reuters America insists that hands-on training works best. "There's nothing that beats on-site training," says Bennett. "I can teach someone in a day. Within a few days, they may come back with a couple of questions. Then they're set."

Training should also include configuration options for desktop videoconferencing systems. The options often include whether the local or remote video window stays on top, and also whether video calls are answered automatically or manually. Those who choose auto answer should proceed with caution. This option allows callers to virtually visit a work area without an invitation. Bill Muller of Ernst & Young believes manual answer is usually a better choice "so that nobody interrupts a private meeting." Bennett of Reuters America agrees. "For security reasons, I would never recommend anything but coordinated system operation. No system should be left on."

Training professionals in how to communicate and collaborate effectively can be at least as important as teaching the mechanics of using desktop videoconferencing. "Training is important, because if you throw all of these products at people without showing them what to do with them, you're not going to have much success," according to Campo of Northrop. Campo says that his lab provides initial training through interactive demonstrations. However, the lab also trains corporate training professionals in the effective use of desktop videoconferencing. As the deployment expands and the need for training grows, the professional trainers can then design and deliver a program.

US Bank in Portland has trained telemarketers to use personal videoconferencing for a customized application. The bank has introduced video banking kiosks called UBANK ON-Sight. When a customer activates the videoconferencing function on the kiosk, the telemarketer must spring into action. Moving from simply phone telemarketing to real-time video has required that the bank sharpen the communication skills of its "outbound" team. However, "It's a very fast learn," says Mike Cebula, Assistant Vice President and product manager. "The biggest challenge is remembering that there's a camera on them and being aware of quick movements and eye contact."

"There's an element of retraining people how to work on their PCs, so they can effectively use this technology," explains Ernie DeNigris of AT&T WorldWorx. DeNigris says training must include protocol, etiquette, and the mechanics of real-time collaboration. "It's different from face-to-face, in which everything is spontaneous," says DeNigris. However, DeNigris believes most users warm up quickly to appearing on camera, and he says few people display inhibition. DeNigris also says training should include how and when to use personal videoconferencing on the road. For instance, a business traveler should learn to use the technology to handle "short fuse" projects. Instead of waiting until he or she returns to the office, the traveler can move a project forward by holding a personal videoconference from a remote sales office, according to DeNigris.

Dale Harris, the Executive Director of Stanford University's Center for Telecommunications, believes personal videoconferencing should be viewed as one element in a suite of new tools that also include store-and-forward video and corporate intranets. He believes these new capabilities will force people to have different skills. "In organizations we have developed skills for face-to-face collaboration primarily and for working in groups," says Harris. "It's not as simple as just putting the technology in there and saying just continue on. The skills you learn for running meetings get different when you put the technology in."

The Silicon Graphics study points out that it is important that end users have an opportunity to begin using collaborative computing immediately following training. Because a lag time can inhibit training success, it is necessary that hardware, software, network installations and upgrades be complete before training begins.

Establishing a user group

An end-user group within an organization helps deployment of personal videoconferencing succeed. The user group provides an opportunity for sharing successes and resolving problems. Because user groups cut across many departments and divisions, an added benefit is that participants learn more about their organization. Companies such as Varian and 3M have established user groups. The frequency of meetings may depend on corporate culture and deployment schedule. Varian has held meetings every two weeks, while 3M has held meetings every three weeks. An option is to schedule user group meetings more frequently early on, and then switch to once a month as users become more comfortable with the technology.

Put it in writing

Written guidelines for desktop videoconferencing can help encourage smooth implementation. The guidelines should give users hints about when to use desktop videoconferencing and when another collaboration or communication medium may accomplish the objective more effectively. Bruce Gilbaugh of NASA points out that short clarifications such as "Did you turn in your time sheet today?" fail to lend themselves to desktop videoconferencing. E-mail would work much better for that kind of communication.

However, Bill Muller of Ernst & Young believes written guidelines including when to use the technology are superfluous. Muller says, "People want to make their own decisions. No one would follow guidelines anyway. The main issue is: Does the other person have video?"

Security issues

Holding detailed strategy meetings that include confidential documents and applications through desktop videoconferencing can raise security concerns.

Boeing's big communications pipes between plants make up one of the largest private networks in the United States. The company is confident that using the network for desktop videoconferencing poses almost no potential for security breaches. However, the company has increasingly been using the technology for external meetings and collaborative sessions. "We don't feel comfortable with security when we talk to our customers through desktop videoconferencing," according to Ray Sollars of Boeing. The company is exploring encryption options. Scarlett Moore of Johnson & Johnson says vendors and carriers should provide better security. "Encryption–encryption–encryption. Please help us protect our data that we're sending all over the world," Moore pleaded with vendors at the DVC '96 West conference.

Personal Videoconferencing with Partners and Suppliers

An organization can successfully use personal videoconferencing to collaborate and communicate more closely with business partners. The benefits of the technology can be substantial when partner companies work closely to develop products and deliver them to market on schedule. The Silicon Graphics study determined that personal videoconferencing and other collaborative computing tools can produce lower-cost components and better manufactured products. However, the study also revealed that this shift in approach gives partners and suppliers greater input into product design decisions. Sometimes companies perceive this as a loss of power or control, and corporate cultures may need to adjust. It is important to anticipate this shift when implementing personal videoconferencing.

Multipoint: Coping with the carriers

Managing and arranging multipoint calls is getting easier, but not fast enough for many corporations implementing desktop videoconferencing. Some of these companies are leveraging their experience with group videoconferencing systems, as they tackle multipoint. The choice is to buy a multipoint control unit (MCU) or let the long distance carriers or bridging service bureaus handle linking three or more sites. (See Figure 8–1.) The T.120 standard includes reservation protocols that define how long distance carriers' reservation systems and MCUs talk with each other. This is critical to many companies that have had nightmares arranging and connecting videoconferences that involve several carriers. "If we're building a spontaneous capability and still require people to reserve days in advance, it isn't going to fly," says Andy Moorwood of National Semiconductor. "The carriers have to interoperate. As users, we have to bludgeon them."

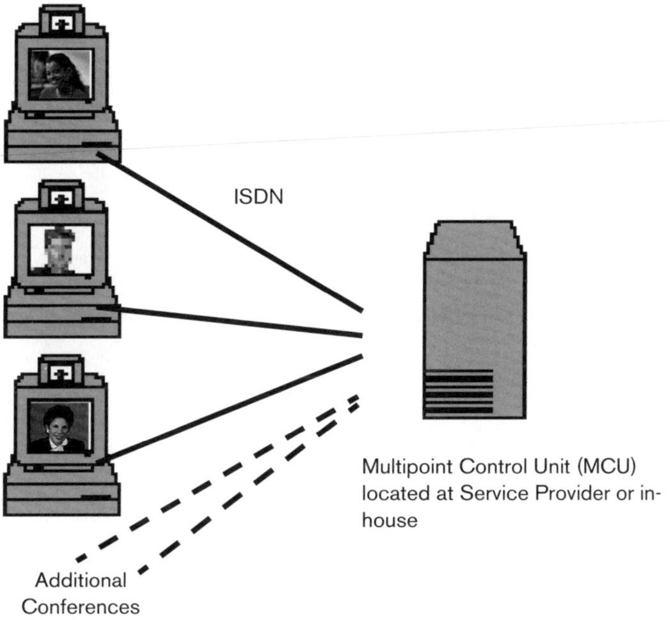

Courtesy of Intel Corporation

Figure 8–1: Multipoint Conferencing over ISDN Lines

The Zen of Implementation

An organization must struggle with the dilemma of how soon and how comprehensively it should deploy desktop videoconferencing. Dale Harris of Stanford University's Center for Telecommunications suggests "appropriate flexibility" in introducing and reacting to desktop videoconferencing, store-

and-forward video, and other emerging technologies. "The one who does it most quickly won't necessarily win. If you move too fast, you can have problems," insists Harris. "If you don't move fast enough, you can get left behind. It's a tradeoff."

9

Personal Videoconferencing over the LAN

Desktop videoconferencing pushes the limits of most current corporate networks. This is because these networks were designed to handle data, rather than desktop video. "Saturating 10 Mbps Ethernet with video makes MIS nervous," says Blake Irving, Group Manager of Microsoft's Personal Systems Division. "That is the number one barrier to making desktop videoconferencing fly in business." Conventional LANs lack the bandwidth, class of service, and scalability to carry time-sensitive multimedia traffic along with bursty data traffic. Most corporations use several independent networks to transmit specific kinds of traffic. These networks handle voice, transaction-based data, and room videoconferencing. Desktop videoconferencing systems for Wide Area Network (WAN) environments have evolved from room videoconferencing approaches, and therefore they are designed to work with telecommunications protocols. Establishing a connection with one of these products over ISDN or POTS, for example, is similar to making a phone call. In contrast, desktop videoconferencing on the local area network (LAN) works with data protocols.

Because personal videoconferencing includes voice, video, and other kinds of data for real-time collaboration, the technology has blurred the distinction between types of traffic. Deploying several parallel networks in a multimedia age is becoming less practical. Therefore, the need has arisen for a single infrastructure that can carry all kinds of traffic. Ultimately, the solution is Asynchronous Transfer Mode (ATM), which will require replacing the network infrastructure. This is an expensive proposition, however, and impractical for many organizations. The alternative is enhancing existing networks, and there are several types of solutions that provide greater bandwidth and manage the flow of different traffic. This chapter focuses on solutions that make desktop videoconferencing practical over the LAN.

Ethernet and Token Ring

Most corporations use Ethernet and some use Token Ring LANs to link personal computers on desktops. Because personal videoconferencing is usually PC-based, using the LAN to transmit the video within a building or campus is a natural solution. However, both the nature and the speed of these networks fall short as demand for desktop videoconferencing and other multimedia applications increases.

The nature of LANs is that they are packet-switched and bursty. This means that all the data that travel over the network are assembled into separate containers that are addressed to different recipients. These containers move on the network whenever and wherever space exists. When the network is heavily loaded, packets must wait for space and the network slows down. This type of packet-switched scenario usually works fine for quarterly reports or other transaction-based data that can wait a little longer for transmission. However, desktop videoconferencing requires that the video and audio information arrive immediately. This is because we have little tolerance for jerky motion or poor lip synch. Therefore, the packet-switched nature of LANs is less than ideal for desktop videoconferencing.

An Apple QuickTime Conferencing white paper by Christine Perey and Eric Hoffert points out that after years of using the telephone, which provides the same speed of voice delivery as face-to-face, people have little tolerance for audio delays. According to the white paper, "Studies have shown that the variation in delivery time should not exceed 50 milliseconds to avoid audible clicks, and the end-to-end latency should not exceed 250 milliseconds in order to maintain reasonable lip synchronization between voice and video." The white paper can be found under the QuickTime Conferencing section of the Apple Web site at

`http://www.apple.com`

The Ethernet standard

The speed of most LANs ranges from 4 to 16 Mbps. Ethernet is the leading LAN, with a 70% market share in the US. (See Figure 9–1.) Ethernet dates back to 1972, when recent MIT graduate Robert Metcalfe joined Xerox PARC. Xerox PARC had invented the first PC with a graphical user interface, called ALTO, and the first laser printer, called EARS. Metcalfe and another early networking specialist named David Boggs designed a network to link ALTO computers with the EARS laser printer. This Ethernet prototype ran at 2.94 Mbps. In the late 1970s and early 1980s Xerox, Digital Equipment Corporation and Intel worked on standardizing Ethernet. In December 1982, nineteen companies announced support for the IEEE 802.3 standard. Meantime, Metcalfe and four other entrepreneurs had founded the Computer, Communication and Compatibility Corporation. 3Com was the first company to turn Ethernet into a product.

Ethernet runs at 10 Mbps and mostly uses 10Base-T wiring, which is unshielded twisted pairs arranged in a star hub. This speed is too slow to handle desktop videoconferencing and other multimedia applications in bulk. A study conducted by Apple Computer in association with Purdue University and several other public and private institutions revealed the impact of desk-

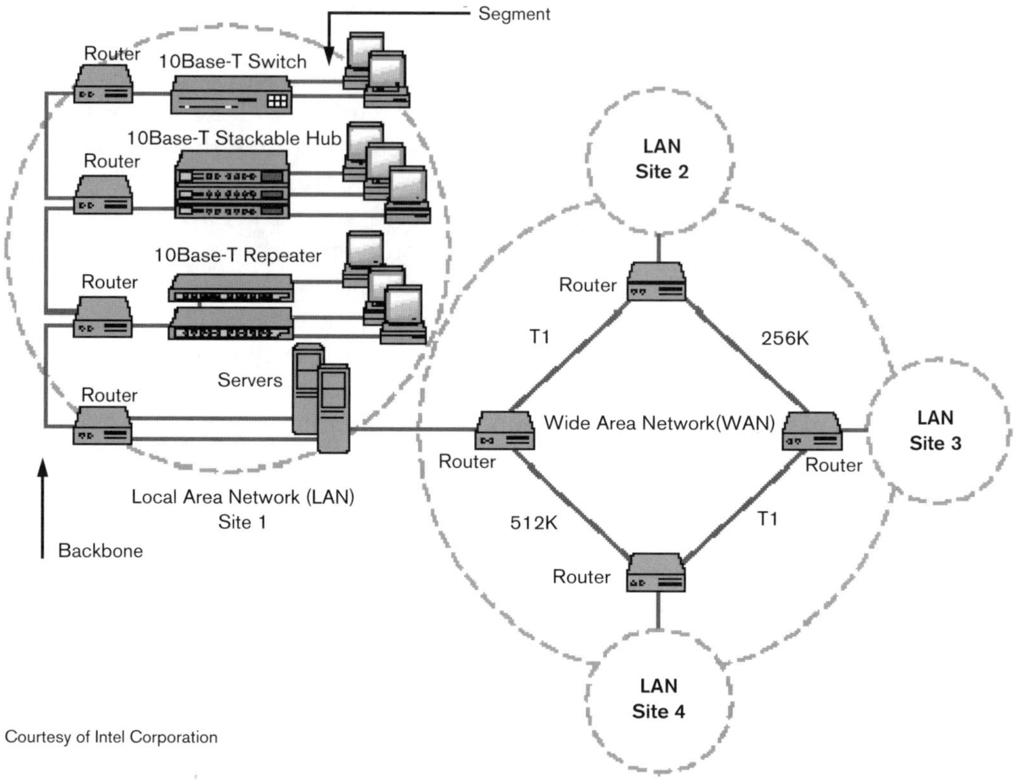

Figure 9–1: The Enterprise Network

top videoconferencing on traditional 10-Mbps Ethernet. The study indicated that LAN users begin to experience "slight effects" with three full-duplex desktop videoconferences in progress, consuming 1200 kbps of available bandwidth. However, the study found that the impact was minimized when using a lower bit rate codec such as H.261, which is part of the H.320 family of international standards instead of Apple's proprietary codec. Additional information on the Ethernet standard can be found on the Web at

`http://ee.wpi.edu:8080/EE535/hwk3cd95/jhp.html`

Fast Ethernet

A newer standard that has been dubbed Fast Ethernet speeds up Ethernet LANs to 100 Mbps. IEEE officially adopted the 802.3u standard in early 1995.

The Fast Ethernet Alliance, which includes more than a dozen technology companies, developed the standard with the goal of providing LAN users ten times the speed of 10Base-T at less than double the cost. Wiring is a critical factor when pushing Ethernet speeds up to 100 Mbps. Level 5 cable is highly recommended, but the standard also supports levels 3 and 4 wiring. 100Base-TX is the basic standard that specifies two-pair unshielded twisted-pair (UTP) Category 5 wiring with RJ-45 connectors. This configuration requires a hub, and the maximum cable length is 100 meters. 100Base-FX is an enhanced set-up that calls for fiber optic cable. This version supports greater distances between the desktop or node and the hub. 100Base-T4 is a version that specifies a four-pair implementation and that will run on Category 3 wiring.

Fast Ethernet leverages much of existing technology and infrastructure. Therefore, upgrading a network to Fast Ethernet has many price advantages over other LAN enhancement or replacement approaches. Both Ethernet and Fast Ethernet use an access method called Carrier Sense Multiple Access with Collision Detection (CSMA/CD). In CSMA/CD, the PC or workstation sends information when the channel is clear. If two PCs transmit simultaneously, the signals collide and delays happen. Because Fast Ethernet employs CSMA/CD, the enhanced technology may fall short for desktop videoconferencing. This is because delays are intolerable for real-time video traffic.

By 1996, Sun Microsystems was shipping SPARC motherboards with embedded Fast Ethernet. Intel was also planning to ship its motherboards with the faster LAN technology included. The advantage of Fast Ethernet on the motherboard is that it is more cost effective than add-in adapters. The disadvantage is that without using adapter cards for Fast Ethernet, switching to another networking technology is more difficult. More information on Fast Ethernet is available on the Web at

```
http://www.iol.unh.edu/consortiums/fe/
fast_ethernet_consortium.html
```

100VG-AnyLAN

100VG-AnyLAN is a 100 Mbps Ethernet standard that is designed to employ voice-grade Level 3 wiring. Hewlett-Packard and AT&T Microelectronics (now Lucent Technologies) developed the technology. The standard uses four pairs of wires, instead of two. The 100VG hub used in this kind of network provides for prioritizing packets through a protocol called *demand priority*. This allows time-sensitive data like videoconferencing to go first. Migrating to a 100VG network requires replacing all hubs. Unlike Fast Ethernet, 100VG stops short of providing full duplex operation. Pat Thaler, 100VG developing engineer for Hewlett-Packard, says her team was looking to speed up corporate networks while keeping costs down. "We wanted to find something that would not require new wire for most users," says Thaler. Additional information on 100VG-AnyLAN is available on the Web through a key word search at

`http://www.hp.com`

Isochronous Ethernet

Isochronous Ethernet is a standard that separates video/voice applications from data/image applications while maintaining the existing LAN infrastructure. *Iso* means equal, and *chronous* means time; IsoEthernet gives equal time to desktop videoconferencing applications. National Semiconductor and IBM developed the IsoEthernet standard which became the 802.9a recommendation of the Institute of Electrical and Electronic Engineers (IEEE).

The advantage of IsoEthernet is that it prevents bandwidth-devouring applications like videoconferencing from blocking other network traffic. In the IsoEthernet standard, the 10-Mbps Ethernet data channel remains. However, IsoEthernet adds another 6 Mbps for isochronous or time-sensitive data traffic like desktop videoconferencing. The 6 Mbps consists of 96 ISDN B-channels of 64 kbps each. The PC or workstation transmits a signal through IsoEthernet requesting a number of B channels for an undetermined length of time. Switches provide the required bandwidth, the call proceeds, and the allocated bandwidth and path remain dedicated to the call until the user breaks the connection. With IsoEthernet, the user can request bandwidth from 128kb up to 2Mb. Leading computer and telecommunications companies have formed a group called incAlliance, which focuses on driving implementation of IsoEthernet. Companies including Ascom Nexion and Incite offer IsoEthernet products. More information on IsoEthernet can be found on the Web at

`http://www.nsc.com/isoethernet/index.html`

FDDI, CDDI, FDDI-II

Fiber Distributed Data Interface (FDDI) is a LAN standard that provides 100 Mbps over fiber optic cable. FDDI works similarly to a Token Ring network, with tokens counter-rotating around rings. The main difference is that FDDI uses dual rings. The dual-ring approach helps protect data when the system fails. If a ring breaks, the network loops back the packets. Copper Distributed Data Interface (CDDI) is identical to FDDI, except the physical medium is Category 5 copper cable. The advantage to CDDI over FDDI is that it costs less. However, CDDI can be less reliable. Just like FDDI, FDDI-II runs at 100 Mbps over fiber. However, FDDI-II provides a structure that supports isochronous traffic. FDDI-II's hybrid mode was designed with an eye towards videoconferencing. This mode allows part of the available bandwidth to carry such time-sensitive data as videoconferencing and voice with little delay. More information on FDDI and CDDI is available on the Web through a keyword search at

```
http://www.cisco.com
```

Switched Ethernet

Using routers to segment the LAN is the traditional method of resolving bandwidth deficits. As bandwidth demands soar because of more powerful computers and more information-rich applications like desktop videoconferencing, however, LAN segmentation no longer fits the bill. Also, LAN segmentation delivers a complicated architecture that can become miserable to manage.

Ethernet switches and switching hubs maximize available bandwidth and decrease packet collisions. Switches function similarly to bridges, but provide higher performance. Ethernet switches directly link the sending and receiving device, creating a 10-Mbps path. As a packet enters the hub, its destination determines which port it will exit. Other ports never see the packet, and therefore network efficiency increases. Switched Ethernet supports multiple 10-Mbps connections over the LAN. It runs on Category 3 UTP wiring, fiber, and coaxial cable. This approach allows users to conduct videoconferences without zapping all of the available bandwidth across the network. The drawback of switched Ethernet is that it still only delivers a maximum of 10 Mbps. However, some networking companies are now providing a solution that combines switched and Fast Ethernet.

SONET and LANs

As we discussed in Chapter 6, Synchronous Optical Network (SONET) essentially updates the North American Digital Hierarchy, which was developed for copper lines. SONET and the similar European standard called Synchronous Digital Hierarchy (SDH) are interface standards for sending data over fiber optic-based networks. SONET defines high-speed, fiber-based techniques for transmitting video, voice, and data. SONET's base-level bandwidth is 51.84 Mbps, and higher speeds are multiples of this rate. Corporations including Citibank are deploying SONET, achieving data transfer speeds up to 2.4 gigabits per second. This is far greater than the 45 Mbps of a T3. SONET's dual-ring architecture allows data flow both ways. SONET also anticipates and corrects transmission problems and is therefore considered self-healing. When a service interruption such as a fiber cut occurs, the network instantaneously reroutes data traffic.

LAN Solutions for Personal Videoconferencing

"There are MIS managers who say videoconferencing over the LAN...over my dead body!," concedes Shykeh Gordon, President of RADVision's US subsidiary. "We are trying not to push our way through dead bodies. If you have a good enough LAN, it's viable." RADVision manufactures gateways that link the telephony and data networks. Gordon insists that ISDN to the desktop is cumbersome and expensive. "We don't believe there is a need to create a third network for videoconferencing," explains Gordon. RADVision's OnLAN product lets a manager limit the number of desktop videoconferencing packets per second. If the network begins to get clogged, an automatic backoff kicks in and lowers the number of packets that can be sent.

Despite the reservations of many MIS managers to deploying desktop videoconferencing over traditional LANs, Gordon and other networking experts insist success is possible within parameters. The guidelines are that there must be available bandwidth, proper segmentation, and a reasonable number of users. If hundreds of users will participate in conferencing, however, the LAN will likely give out. RadVision's solutions often involve switched Ethernet and 100-Mbps Ethernet. The H.323 LAN standard allows different videoconferencing products to communicate over local area networks. "Sooner or later, desktop videoconferencing will reside on the LAN," says Gordon. "There's no doubt about it. That's the reason for H.323."

Steve Bennett of Reuters America is one LAN manager with reservations about deploying desktop videoconferencing on the LAN. "Videoconferencing on the LAN works. However, the impact on the network is still unacceptable as far as I'm concerned, so we still don't use it." Bennett uses a unique ISDN configuration that avoids running ISDN to every desktop. "Anyone worth their salt who is a good networking manager would never wire one connection to one station," insists Bennett. "We put in a Category 5 patch panel and roll a DVC unit on a cart to a desktop anywhere in the building. Desktop videoconferencing doesn't mean it's dedicated to the desktop of one owner." Bennett says the major exception at Reuters is desktop videoconferencing for senior executives. Because these users want the technology on demand, Bennett runs ISDN to their desktops. Even as data networks evolve to handle desktop videoconferencing, Bennett believes the bandwidth required for building-to-building connections on the WAN may be a cost issue.

Tom Hall, a contractor managing videoconferencing for Hughes Aircraft, wrestles with the issue of deploying desktop videoconferencing over the 10-Mbps LAN. "The interest in running desktop videoconferencing over the LAN is there," says Hall. "The bandwidth management today would be so untenable that it wouldn't make sense." However, Hall says as the number of users grows, Hughes will test desktop videoconferencing over the LAN. He says for Hughes the short-term solution may be 100-Mbps Ethernet, with an eventual move to ATM.

"Some of our IS planners shriek with horror when they think of what we could do to their bandwidth requirements," says Andy Moorwood who is part of National Semiconductor's desktop videoconferencing deployment team. As a major player in incAlliance, National Semiconductor looks towards IsoEthernet as a solution to conducting videoconferences on the LAN.

Keith DeStasio, Video Services Product Manager of 3M, says his company is moving towards a LAN environment for desktop videoconferencing. *LAN Times* has quoted DeStasio as saying, "The future of our LAN is going to be switched Ethernet to the workstations, with an ATM backbone." 3M is working on a five-year implementation schedule for the network upgrade.

Williams Pipeline in Tulsa has deployed desktop videoconferencing over traditional Ethernet, but in a limited fashion. The company has three InVision systems and conducts videoconferences about twice a week at 6 frames per second. Senior Network Analyst David Down says that level of use puts a noticeable load on the network. "When the available bandwidth increases, we see it on peoples' desks," says Down. "If we were running 20 frames per second with four or five links, it would really impact it."

Fred Campo of Northrop Grumman says that the biggest roadblock to desktop videoconferencing for his company is getting money to upgrade the network infrastructure. "We're not going to install ISDN on everyone's desktop," explains Campo. "We have 50 thousand employees. We will use this technology as another piece of the justification to upgrade our networks." Campo says the quick fix and his short-term recommendation is Fast Ethernet or switched Ethernet.

ATM and the LAN

Picture multiple video windows on the PC, and you get a snapshot of what ATM can offer. One window allows a videoconference with a colleague. Another window displays a clip of a training video, commercial, or television news story that becomes part of the collaborative session. Another window shows Web content. High-speed performance is guaranteed for multiple video streams. This is the end-user desktop world that ATM can facilitate. "It's a tool for power collaborators," says Doug Tsui of First Virtual Corporation.

ATM is transforming corporate telecommunications, and is the ideal solution for LAN bandwidth and management concerns. ATM, as we discussed in Chapter 6, is a data transfer infrastructure that combines packet-switched and circuit-switched channels. ATM sorts out time-sensitive data, including videoconferencing, and delivers those packets to their destination immediately. Therefore, ATM provides isochronous service. This simplifies information exchange and can eliminate bottlenecks that challenge networks. ATM offers "free bandwidth" that can be "wasted" to maximize application quality. Another major advantage of ATM is that it lets the LAN, WAN, and MAN use the same switching and routing solutions.

Global standardization will eventually let information move between countries at least as fast as it moves between offices. ATM is designed to carry voice, data, images, and video over Broadband ISDN at gigabit speeds. Unlike Ethernet, which handles variable sized packets, ATM uses cells with a fixed length of 53 bytes. The fixed size maintains the high-speed data flow, because hubs can process the cells without evaluating the size.

Implementing ATM for private enterprise networks is the first deployment stage for most organizations. A later stage will let ATM interface with public networks. ATM can be implemented using either fiber optic cable or level 5 unshielded twisted-pair (UTP) copper wiring. The speed and flexibility of ATM make the technology the most effective choice for handling video. Also, the technology allows organizations to manage costs through more efficient bandwidth allocation. However, ATM comes with a higher implementation price tag than other LAN solutions.

As corporate networks evolve to ATM, the challenge is to protect investments while preparing for future demands. LAN Emulation (LANE) lets organizations migrate to ATM without replacing the current network. This is accomplished by using bridges to connect LANs to an ATM backbone. An ELAN is a group of LAN Emulation clients. For a device on a Token Ring ELAN to talk to a device on an Ethernet ELAN, a router is required. LANE stops short of providing key advantages of ATM, including guaranteed bandwidth and Quality of Service.

David Beering, senior staff telecommunications analyst at Amoco Corporation, is Chairman of the Enterprise Network Roundtable (ENR). The global business group's mission is to make sure ATM meets user requirements. Beering was quoted in the September, 1995 issue of *Fortune* magazine as saying, "For any company that does not have access to ATM capability within five years, the game is over."

Bay Networks, which makes ATM networking products, believes educating corporate decision-makers about the value of video is critical to speeding ATM deployment. "The issue is building a business case for video," according to James Slaby, Banking/Finance Industry Manager for Bay Networks. "For most people, it's glitzy but stupid" in that there is a lack of understanding of how desktop video can produce business results. Slaby insists that the most significant ATM costs that turn off potential customers are prices of ATM adapter and interface cards, as well as the cost of laying Category 5 wire.

Tom Manley of INET Marketing and Lockheed Martin says Lockheed has been using an ATM network in its advanced technologies labs. "ATM may well be the real technology that provides full motion video over a network, if the technology can provide a guaranteed link and guaranteed bandwidth," says Manley. In the short run, there are some who believe that ATM may not be ready for prime time. Says Dennis Riley, who runs Microsoft's desktop videoconferencing lab, "I do not believe that at current cost rates ATM would be a solution for an MIS director, because there has not been a lot of history with the products that are on the market today." Northrop Grumman has delivered ATM to the desktops of some engineers. However, Fred Campo of Northrop Grumman says, "ATM appears to be the end-all solution for everything, but it's not the immediate solution for anything." Ray Sollars of Boeing agrees. "We want to make sure ATM is tested and proven before we deploy it," says Sollars. More information on ATM can be found on the Web at

`http://www.atmforum.com`

First Virtual Corporation and ATM

First Virtual Corporation was one of the first companies to bring viable ATM products to market. The company's approach was to move beyond LAN emulation, while protecting investments in traditional LANs. FVC is the creation of Ralph Ungermann, the former CEO and founder of networking company Ungermann-Bass. The company provides a desktop video networking solution that can run on Level 3, 4 or 5 UTP wiring. The product line includes a 25-Mbps ATM switch, adapter and a gateway server that eliminates having to run ISDN to each desktop. (See Figures 9–2 and 9–3.) FVC also delivers a layer of middleware called the Multimedia Operating System (MOS), which ensures that older LAN applications can run. The MOS lets Windows applications interface with ATM. Because different kinds of files must be handled differently, the MOS optimizes the flow of the multimedia between the ATM network and the application.

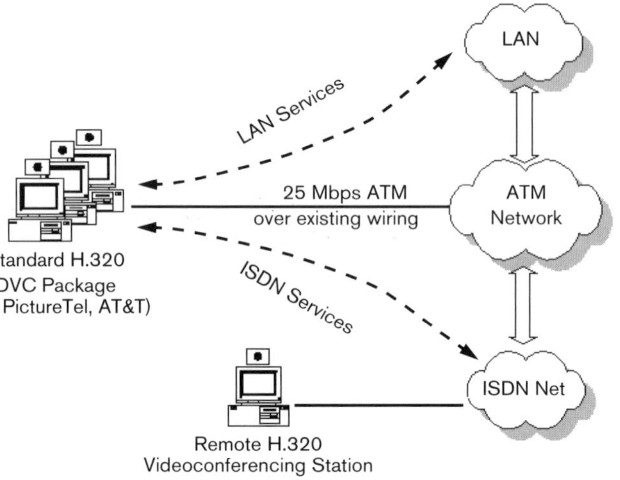

Courtesy of First Virtual Corporation

Figure 9–2: A workgroup ATM solution

When Ungermann launched FVC, he looked hard at the obstacles preventing ATM from making it to the desktop. The three problems he repeatedly encountered were cost, ease of use, and the need to address standards. Because FVC's hardware architecture is software-based, the company can easily update its installed base with ATM Forum standards as they evolve. Using a business model that involved outsourcing everything from engineering to human resources, FVC established early leadership. One analyst described FVC in a December, 1995 issue of *Communications Week*. "They are the only ones who have been able to put all the pieces together and sell ATM as a desktop video solution," said the analyst.

In January 1996, FVC and Bay Networks formed a partnership allowing Bay to resell and support a private-label version of FVC's ATM switch and product package. This gave FVC access to Bay's extensive reseller channel.

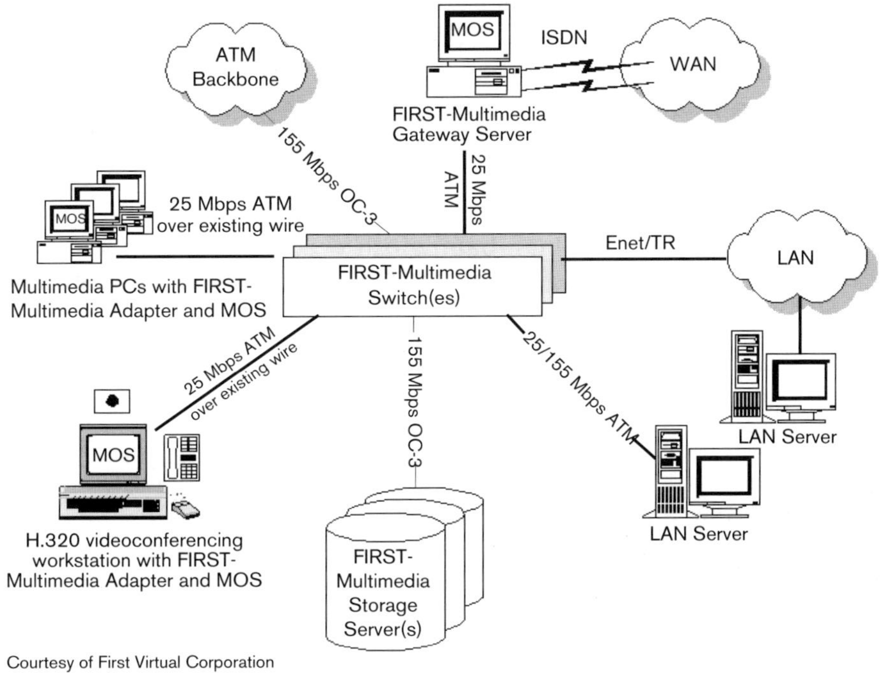

Figure 9–3: An ATM network

Reseller Jeff Leffingwell, owner of Virtual Northwest, according to *Computer Reseller News*, said the Bay Networks/FVC solution would enable his company to install ATM at the desktop, regardless of whether an organization has upgraded its network backbone to ATM. No replacement of network wires would be necessary. Resellers would simply replace Ethernet adapter cards from each PC with ATM adapters. More information on First Virtual Corporation can be found on the Web at

`http://www.fvc.com`

Other ATM efforts

In early 1996, 3Com and IBM both announced roll outs of ATM products. IBM released a 25-Mbps ATM switch and adapter that delivers ATM to the desktop. 3COM announced Ethernet/ATM and Token Ring/ATM, switches and a workgroup ATM switch with a 25-Mbps concentrator, bridges, modules and interface cards. According to an article in the February 12, 1996 *Infoworld*,

"Both rollouts are attempts to counter the conventional wisdom, which suggests widespread adoption of ATM is still years away." The article mentioned that several recent studies have predicted that ATM deployment by 2010 will reach a maximum of 55 percent and that some studies estimate closer to 30 percent. However, the *Infoworld* article also quoted Trudy Barker, an analyst with Dataquest, as saying that sales of 25-Mbps ATM are coming into their own. "A lot of Token Ring users are migrating to it, and it appeals to people with video and other high-bandwidth needs," Barker was quoted as saying. Other major ATM vendors include Fore Systems and Cisco Systems.

Intranets and videoconferencing

As corporations deploy intranets with internal Web sites, the next step is to enhance those intranets with richer media types. Netscape's LiveMedia framework is an important mile marker on that road. The human resources department, for example, can design a home page displaying detailed information about medical plans and vacation policies. If employees want a benefits administrator to walk them through their options, they can establish a real-time video link with a mouse click. This might prove more efficient than the employee leaving a voice mail, waiting for a call back, taking time for a phone conversation, then waiting for human resources to deliver brochures through internal mail or fax. Some desktop videoconferencing pioneers are licking their chops over the intranet prospects. However, video can make network administrators nervous because of the required bandwidth. "Whenever I say 'how about video,' they say 'not now Scarlett,' " says Scarlett Moore, Johnson & Johnson's videoconferencing manager.

Eric Hughes, Vice President and intranet infrastructure manager at Wells Fargo, believes LiveMedia will allow more efficient corporate training via intranets. However, Hughes feels that company-wide, real-time video communication through intranets will take time, planning and a cultural shift. "Until everyone is media-savvy enough to be able to take advantage of the medium, it will have just niche impact on corporate nets," explains Hughes. "Just because you have the technology, that does not mean you can use it effectively." Hughes adds that a poorly crafted message is in many cases worse than no message at all.

Media Servers and Multicasting

Video and media servers manage networked video. They are the key emerging technology for central control of desktop videoconferences over the LAN. Media server tools may include bandwidth allocation and accounting or charge-back capability. This feature is essential for desktop videoconferencing within large organizations that bill departments for use of networks. Video and media servers also store and forward video, which enables video mail. Video mail enhances e-mail with voice and video. An Apple white paper by Christine Perey and Eric Hoffert entitled "Understanding and Optimizing QuickTime Conferencing for Use on Shared Networks" describes the benefits of store-and-forward video. "Sometimes stakeholders cannot be present for a meeting, but their review and approval warrant retrieval at a later date," according to the white paper. "The ability to record conversations and archive interaction during meetings is another way to mix the benefits of real-time information transfer with store-and-forward information retrieval."

Video and media servers are also used for interactive television and broadband cable networks, allowing subscribers to access video on demand. Companies that make video and media servers include Oracle, IBM, Novell, Starlight Networks, Silicon Graphics, and Digital Equipment Corporation. In June 1994, Silicon Graphics and AT&T Network Systems announced a joint venture called Integrated Digital Solutions to develop and deliver media servers. Oracle and Intel inked a deal in June 1995 that will integrate the Oracle Media Server with Intel's ProShare. The resulting product will let users record, store and forward desktop videoconferences.

Media servers let CEOs communicate to the troops via store-and-forward video. Because of the flexibility of this arrangement, professionals in an organization can access a speech or a message from their PCs when their schedule permits.

Multicasting or desktop broadcasting lets executives and others communicate in real time with staff members. In early 1996, Intel introduced ProShare Presenter. The software product would allow a person to broadcast a live speech or training class with spreadsheets and graphics to many participants watching from their PCs. ProShare Presenter is interactive in that participants can submit written questions or request to speak (audio only) to all participants. The presenter has the option of granting or declining a participant's request for the floor. Participants can also use ProShare Presenter to record the presentation and play it back later. Recording a broadcast requires 2MB of hard disk space per minute. The product allows presenters to password-protect private broadcasts. ProShare Presenter uses Internet multicast technology, with each presentation requiring five percent of a 10-Mb LAN no matter how many PCs are receiving the video.

IP multicasting versus MAC-layer multicasting

ProShare Presenter supports both MAC-layer multicasting and IP multicasting. Of these two types, IP multicasting is more flexible. Benefits include greater network control and increased network efficiency. MAC-layer multicasting requires a network administrator to manually configure each of the routers located between the originator and the destinations. This allows bridging of MAC-layer packets for multicast traffic to flow from one subnet to another subnet. IP multicasting lets an administrator avoid manually configuring routers, because routers supporting IP multicasting are self-configuring. In this scenario, the multicast traffic flows automatically from one network node to another. Another benefit of IP is that the multicast goes to the subnet only if users on that segment request the multicast. This is more efficient than MAC-layer multicasting, which routes packets to the subnet regardless of whether any users have requested the multicast. An Intel white paper entitled "IP Multicasting: A Strategic Tool for Rich, Efficient Business Communications" points out that "media independence" is also a significant benefit of IP. "This can be a key benefit in light of today's heterogeneous network environments," according to the white paper. "For instance, if a company operates with multiple Ethernet subnets and a Token ring subnet, IP multicast traffic can flow among them freely." The white paper also indicates that Intel will eventually standardize all of its multicast products to support only IP multicasting.

Deploying IP multicasting requires upgrading routers with software or hardware plus network stack client software installed on the workstation of every multicast recipient. Microsoft has included a basic TCP/IP stack with Windows 95. More information on IP Multicasting is available on the Web at

`http://ganges.cs.tcd.ie/4ba2/multicast`

RTP/RTCP

Unlike bursty data such as text file transfers, audio and video data is described as *streaming* and is therefore time sensitive. TCP, the data transport mechanism for the Internet and most other packet-switched networks, is designed primarily for bursty data delivery. Therefore, TCP falls short for delivering multimedia data. The Internet Engineering Task Force (IETF) has approved a newer transport protocol to support real-time audio and video delivery. The Real-Time Transport Protocol (RTP) works alongside TCP to transmit streaming data over the network. RTP uses packet headers to describe the packet's payload and ensure that multimedia data arrives on time and in the proper sequence. RTP supports multiple compression algorithms.

Because network traffic conditions constantly change, multimedia applications must be able to adapt. The IETF-approved Real-Time Transport Control Protocol (RTCP), which works alongside RTP and TCP, provides feedback on network conditions and reception quality. RTCP sends feedback to the sender and all recipients of a multicast stream, letting all users diagnose network problems. RTCP also informs multicast participants who has subscribed or is participating. In a distance training application, for example, RTCP would indicate who is attending.

Precept Software has based its FlashWare Multimedia Networking Software on the RTP and RTCP protocols. This means that FlashWare multicasts real-time audio and video across LANs, WANs and the Internet. Like RTP, the software supports multiple compression schemes. FlashWare runs over IP, the routing layer of the TCP/IP protocol suite. When used with a multicast-enabled TCP/IP stack, FlashWare allows audio and video to be sent once to all addressees instead of having to send the same stream repeatedly to each recipient. More information on RTP and RTCP can be found on the Web at

`http://www.ietf.org`

RSVP

Resource Reservation Protocol (RSVP) helps organizations implement LAN-based desktop videoconferencing, multicasting, and other multimedia applications without disrupting other traffic. RSVP is a standard approved by the Internet Engineering Task Force. Building networks that support voice, data, and videoconferencing requires RSVP to ensure that each traffic type receives the QOS that it demands. RSVP is a kind of reservation agent. In much the same way that a travel agent checks the availability of flights and train schedules, RSVP books the bandwidth necessary for a desktop videoconference or other application. This traffic management is necessary, because real-time video must arrive at its destination almost immediately. Users have no tolerance for poor lip synch, for example. Before the application sends traffic, it uses RSVP to confirm with the networking device that QOS requirements can be met. Network managers can set RSVP parameters, allowing for changes in traffic flow during different times of day. RSVP works with any network protocol, including TCP/IP. Additional information on RSVP can be found on the Web at

`http://www.ietf.org`

The impact of desktop broadcasting and multicasting

Some technology industry insiders believe that desktop broadcasting is more significant in business than desktop videoconferencing. "For one-to-one conferencing, I don't think video will be a huge success in business," says Blake Irving, Group Manager of the Personal Systems Division for Microsoft. "For training purposes or seeing the CEO talk or a shareholder meeting through a desktop broadcast...video has value." In fact, Irving describes one-to-many communication as one of the "key scenarios" that will drive real-time desktop video. Irving says he believes one-to-one desktop videoconferencing is most valuable in enhancing existing close interpersonal relationships, such as "grandmother-to-grandchild" or "husband-to-wife separated by continents."

Ellen Grace Henson, Ambassador of Visual Communications for Silicon Graphics, believes one-to-many video communication is valuable only if it is interactive. "It needs to include a minimum of audio both ways, so that if you're giving a lecture, I can raise my hand," says Henson. "Passive receipt of information is not that interesting to me." This notion points up a problem with traditional distance education or "instructional television," which has tended towards one-to-many communication with limited interaction. In this scenario, the teacher gets the lion's share of the bandwidth and students often get a voice-only return path. Personal videoconferencing has shaken up what David Connolly of Andersen Consulting has termed the "hierarchical educational delivery model." This model collapses as personal videoconferencing provides a symmetrical communication path in which students get the same bandwidth as teachers.

Mary Lindsay, a consultant to Starlight Networks, believes that desktop video, coupled with the Internet, bypasses traditional middlemen both within and outside an organization. This phenomenon could change the nature of business. "For a company to use the Internet to conduct transactions with customers or to use the intranet to deliver a CEO address to employees, you're bypassing human resources people and retailers and others who are middlemen. Those people may take on new roles," explains Lindsay. "Multimedia is becoming the new middleman."

PART IV

New Lives in a New Universe

10

Telecommuting and Killer Apps at Home

When Allen Helvajian was recovering from emergency back surgery, commuting daily to his job as a Senior Project Manager for Wells Fargo was nearly impossible. Sitting in his car for an hour and a half each direction would jeopardize his recuperation; besides, Helvajian required physical therapy near his home. The solution was telecommuting. To avoid isolation and to stay in closer contact with his colleagues, Helvajian turned to desktop videoconferencing. The technology was familiar to Allen, because the project he manages for Wells Fargo is videoconferencing. So, Helvajian navigated his way through some difficulties in configuring his ISDN service to support both desktop videoconferencing and access to his company's WAN. He began using desktop videoconferencing from home to participate in staff meetings and conferences with his internal customers.

Telecommuters like Helvajian are part of the home market that network service providers, desktop videoconferencing system providers, Internet browser companies, and others are after. The telephone companies, the cable systems, and the electric utilities are scrambling to edge each other out for the business of delivering video network services to consumers. POTS reaches all but a few homes in the US. Besides being nearly ubiquitous, POTS has another important advantage in that it is two-way. The problem with POTS is that the bandwidth falls short for many applications. Cable television companies provide service to more than 60% of the country's households. The problem is that most cable service is one-way, although the increasing availability of cable modems is providing limited bandwidth in the upstream direction. The advantage of cable service is that it delivers broad bandwidth, which lends itself to video, in at least one direction.

Electric utility communication lines run to nearly all homes, providing the companies with meter-reading capability. However, the lines can also carry video and audio. The Glasgow Electric Plant Board, a city-owned utility in Kentucky, is delivering ultrahigh-speed data services. One of those services is Internet access at T1 speed. "If you could overlay videoconferencing at that speed, the products we're delivering would support that," says General Manager William Ray. Ray says hundreds of electric companies have evaluated Glasgow's system and that a dozen are building similar systems. The problem for the utilities is that the Public Utilities Holding Company Act of 1935 prevents most companies from providing telecommunications services. So, the utilities must overcome regulatory hurdles while the phone companies and cable operators must upgrade their networks.

Despite the race for the home video services market, the bottom line for most consumers is:

- How much will it cost?
- How easy is it?

As PCs ship with videoconferencing as a standard feature, the cost becomes difficult to distinguish from the overall cost of a PC. Both the H.324 standard for personal videoconferencing over POTS and Web videoconferencing promise to make the technology more practical at home, despite less than picture-perfect images. Greater availability of ISDN is also providing a home transmission solution. However, ISDN is still far from universally available, and the increased transmission costs of ISDN compared with POTS is less appealing to many consumers. Lucent Technologies Microelectronics (formerly AT&T Microelectronics) makes a codec chip that supports both the H.320 ISDN standard and the H.324 POTS standard. However, Product Line Director Mort Herman believes POTS makes the most sense for home videoconferencing. "You need a network that's ubiquitous, ISDN is not—POTS is," says Herman. For desktop videoconferencing to catch on at home, Herman believes there are also some other requirements. "You need a level of quality that's usable. That's very subjective, of course. Then you need some good applications."

When *MacWorld* conducted a survey in mid 1994 about the on-line capabilities of interest to consumers, videoconferencing ranked low. Only 16% of the 600 randomly selected adults expressed a high level of interest in videoconferencing; 15% expressed moderate interest, and 66% responded they had little or no interest. The ability to vote topped the survey results, with 50% expressing high interest, while video dating came in last, with only 4% responding they had high interest. The *San Jose Mercury News* ran the results of the survey to show a gap between consumer demand for services and the supply of services that companies were planning to offer. However, the survey predated the rush to the Web and the ratification of the H.324 POTS standard as well as the shipping of videoconferencing-equipped PCs.

A study by Bellcore provides insight into the primary applications for home videoconferencing. Keeping in touch with family and friends tops the list, with 80% of respondents indicating they would use videoconferencing for that application. Monitoring children came in second, with 46% saying yes. Shopping and making inquiries weighed in at 31%. Telecommuting and viewing birthdays and special events tied with 27%. Lagging the home applications choices were distance education at 24% and security monitoring at 21%.

Video Quality and Home Videoconferencing

There are two schools of thought on the importance of video quality to the home user. One school says that people are used to watching television and therefore expect television-quality video. Anything that falls short of that expectation is a consumer turn-off. The other view is that personal videoconferencing is a gee-whiz technology that people will embrace, regardless of video quality. The low frame rates of POTS products aimed at the consumer market might sour anybody bent on getting television-quality video. Gil Gordon, editor of *Telecommuting Review* and a leading telecommuting consultant, believes video quality is important to consumer acceptance of videoconferencing. "We have become spoiled by broadcast TV. The bottom line is people want TV to look like TV, and I don't think this is a case where half a loaf is better than none," says Gordon. However, industry analyst Sarah Dickinson believes products that use POTS are fine for many home applications. "If I'm 6 years old and want to talk to my friend, quality's not going to matter as much as if I'm a CEO," says Dickinson.

Dickinson points out that video quality is less important than ease of use. "POTS is like a phone call, and POTS desktop videoconferencing has to be integrated well into a consumer environment." The POTS video quality issue is becoming less significant as compression algorithms improve. Engineers at many companies have worked practically round-the-clock to deliver POTS video that is acceptable to consumers. A team at 8×8 (formerly Integrated Information Technology) spent early 1996 perfecting the H.324 software that works with the company's programmable compression processor. Industry analyst Elliot Gold told an audience at the DVC '96 West conference they would be surprised by the quality of POTS video. "I can't see a difference in the quality between H.324 and the quality of ISDN I'm getting at my desktop right now," said Gold.

Driving a Mass Market

Intel's mid 1996 release of the Video Phone using ProShare technology gave home videoconferencing a major boost. More than a dozen PC manufacturers would begin bundling the POTS system with personal computers. The product was geared towards geographically dispersed family members who want to see and talk with one another. (See Figure 10–1.) "More and more of us are becoming more mobile, and it's becoming rare to have three or even two gen-

Courtesy of Intel Corporation

Figure 10–1: POTS (Plain Old Telephone Service) videoconferencing: A child shows her grandparents her art work using the Intel Video Phone with ProShare technology

erations in the same town," said James Johnson, Marketing Vice President of Intel's Internet and Communications Group. Many analysts and users compared the video quality of the Intel Video Phone with the earliest version of ProShare for ISDN.

On the heels of Intel's Video Phone move, PictureTel announced a deal that would give the company the rights to VIVO Software's POTS videophone technology. PictureTel would help drive the home videoconferencing market as the company forged alliances with PC manufacturers and modem makers to bundle the offering with products.

MCI is banking on POTS video as it markets its Video Phone, but its approach is different from that of Intel and PictureTel. MCI's Video Phone uses the home television as its platform via a set-top box. The product uses 8×8's VCP processor and the Apex-III algorithms developed at Comtech Labs. The VCP allows MCI Video Phone users to link with any other video phone by using the H.324 standard for POTS. The proprietary Apex-III algorithms let an MCI Video Phone achieve higher POTS video quality when connecting with other MCI Video Phones. Because the VCP chip is programmable, it can also process a variety of compression algorithms, including the MPEG series. This means MCI can expand the architecture of its Video Phone to handle interactive television.

"Pac Bell believes that 384-kbps data rate is the target to stimulate the mass market," Michael Ort, Pacific Bell's director of strategy and new opportunities told an audience in early 1996. "Transport will become very, very cheap." Just like PCs continue to pack in more power, carriers will provide more bandwidth. Higher bandwidth will come in many forms, including asymmetric digital subscriber line (ADSL) and cable modems. Pacific Bell was conducting broadband videotelephony trials throughout 1996 and 1997, with the goal of providing services to nearly 3 million homes before the turn of the century. Services include multipoint videoconferencing, video mail, ultrahigh speed Internet access, among others.

Whetting Consumer Appetites

While many view POTS as the primary medium for home videoconferencing, others believe that POTS will create a market for higher quality products and services. VIVO licenses its videoconferencing software to PC manufacturers. Anthony Antonuccio, VIVO's Vice President of Marketing, believes POTS-based videoconferencing drives ISDN deployment. "They'll get hooked with the concept and want better performance," says Antonuccio. In this scenario, vendors can sell upgrade kits that include an ISDN card and new software. Multimedia chip maker 8×8 is also counting on POTS products to stimulate the desire for personal videoconferencing upgrades. "POTS will whet people's appetites for better quality and better performance," says Kevin Deierling, 8×8's Director of Marketing.

In some countries, home ISDN is far more prevalent than in the US so that a POTS-to-ISDN migration is less necessary. Germany is one of those countries. "All of my students have ISDN at home," says Stephan Wenger, an assistant professor of communication systems at the Technical University of Berlin. Wenger says many of his students leave their families in rural areas so they can attend school in the city. They buy ISDN desktop videoconferencing systems for themselves and their parents to keep the family together.

An explosion in home videoconferencing may also bring businesses into the personal videoconferencing world. Dennis Riley of Microsoft says unlike the migration path of the PC, which began in business and then hit the home, videoconferencing will go the opposite way. "Videoconferencing will go into the home and people will use it in their own lives, and then use it in business." A major reason for this phenomenon is the relatively low-cost consumer-oriented videoconferencing products.

Home videoconferencing over cable

Cable companies have successfully provided ultrahigh speed Internet access through cable modems, but what about providing videoconferencing service? Some cable industry visionaries see videoconferencing as a potential gold mine for cable operators. "It would almost be an add-on service to Internet access that could become quickly profitable," says Amy Reiber, Business Development Manager in the wireless group at the Williams Companies. "Just think of all of the grandmothers who'd like to see their grandkids, more so than getting Internet access." Reiber believes that older people would flock to videoconferencing, if it were as simple as pushing a button.

Vyvx is a subsidiary of the Williams Companies that owns an 11-thousand mile fiber network. "Vyvx is constantly looking for a killer app that would lighten the dark fiber. Something like this is definitely a differentiator," insists Reiber. Reiber concedes, however, that there are plenty of potential stumbling blocks. Interoperability of set-top boxes would be essential, so that customers of different cable systems could communicate. Also, Reiber says many cable companies may find the thought of 2-way rather frightening, because they are unaccustomed to traffic management.

Daniel Flohr, CEO of Target Technologies, insists that cable will emerge as the primary solution for home videoconferencing. Flohr has used cable TV as a model in designing Target's C-Phone videoconferencing product. He says as his mother ages, he will increasingly need to check in with her through real-time video. "For my mother, forget about the 150-MHz Pentium. What does my mother have? A TV and a phone," says Flohr. Flohr's vision is that subscribers will pay a monthly fee plus usage charges for home videoconferencing. "NTSC (National Television Standards Committee) rules. The people who deliver the bandwidth will make the money—the cable companies," according to Flohr. "The 10-Mbps cable modem is a really big deal because it starts delivering Internet access plus possibly video phone service."

Industry analyst Sarah Dickinson views cable as a less viable solution than some others. "The problem is even though cable is a big business with a national footprint, it's still a local market," Dickinson explains. "When you're doing this kind of stuff, you need to be dealing with national carriers. Cable is a different economic model." Dickinson says videoconferencing over cable could present "billing nightmares." However, she believes that using cable modems to access Web videoconferencing makes sense.

In Fact, Motorola and Microsoft have cooperated in developing hardware and software for cable-based broadband networks. In early 1996, the two companies began collaborating on developing multimedia services, including personal videoconferencing. Motorola's CyberSURFR cable modem offers speeds of up to 30 Mbps downstream and up to 768 kbps upstream. Despite the broad bandwidth that cable modems can deliver in at least one direction, the available bandwidth declines as the number of users increases. Also, these devices are limiting in that they are transport-specific. Sarkis Zartarian of Applied Communication Concepts says a new kind of modem will emerge. This "compound modem" will provide a few different transport options, including cable, ISDN, and POTS.

SIPC and livingroom videoconferencing

When Microsoft Chairman Bill Gates announced the Simply Interactive PC (SIPC) hardware framework at the Windows Hardware Engineering Conference in 1996, he helped pave the way for livingroom videoconferencing. The initiative would bridge the gap between home entertainment and computing. The objective of SIPC was to give the PC the ease-of-use and the convenience of a consumer appliance. The framework would make PCs easier to connect to VCRs, stereos, camcorders, and TVs. "As the PC becomes a central device for entertainment and communications, it will be placed with these consumer devices in the family room," according to Gates. SIPC systems would support ISDN, cable modems, direct-broadcast satellite, and other high-speed data pipelines. The framework would also support videoconferencing, voice messaging, e-mail, and faxing, as well as 3-D graphics and multiple rich data streams.

A key element of the framework is its support of the Universal Serial Bus (USB) and the IEEE 1394 high-speed serial connector commonly called *Fire Wire*, which allows data transfers at up to 400 million bits per second. SIPC would allow people to simultaneously surf the Web, watch TV in a display window, and conduct a videoconference. They could do all this from the comfort and convenience of a livingroom couch. The same month that Microsoft announced SIPC, Sony Corporation also announced its strategy for the livingroom convergence. Sony President Nobuyuki Idei told reporters the company was developing a new software operating system to be used in products that combine computing with audio, video, and networking capabilities.

Enhancing Virtual Communities

The Internet revolution has created widespread virtual communities. Film buffs in France share opinions and information with movie goers in Boston. Parents in San Francisco share advice with other parents in Atlanta. The ability to exchange text in real-time through Internet relay chat (IRC) and in store-and-forward mode through Usenet has created villages without buildings. The Internet lets people with common interests who meet by chance share a cup of tea regardless of whether they are in the same city. Howard Rheingold balances the benefits and drawbacks of placeless villages in *The Virtual Community*. "Participating in a virtual community has not solved all of life's problems for me, but it has served as an aid, a comfort, and an inspiration at times: at other times, it has been like an endless ugly, long-simmering family brawl," Rheingold writes.

Enhancing IRC, Usenet, the Web, and other Internet features with video and audio undoubtedly produces mixed results. Usenet and IRC support groups could become grass-roots tabloid television. Harry Mott of Mott 4 Productions sees some other negatives to video-enhanced virtual communities. "When you're on e-mail, sometimes you want to go on as somebody you're not. Videoconferencing won't help that way." Mott points out, though, that in some science fiction stories people wear masks to go on screen. Video disguises would allow people to still pose as somebody other than themselves. Nevertheless, the power of a video Internet creates enormous potential for people with similar interests to connect. The added dimension of seeing and hearing a pen pal expands the definition of virtual communities. Says Christine Traut of Andersen Worldwide, "In a networked world, we'll be able to take our video selves, go into cyberspace, and be able to meet people we've never met before. That's profound."

The virtual community concept extends to POTS and ISDN desktop videoconferencing as well. Elementary and high school students, for example, can work together on projects regardless of where they live. Several students in the same class might collaborate on writing a play without the need for their parents to drive them someplace. Students in different countries can also collaborate on a project, with each submitting the results to their teachers. "It comes down to fun," says Anthony Antonuccio of VIVO. "It's the new definition of what a multimedia PC is."

Personal videoconferencing gives people greater access to experts. An amateur astronomer in Nebraska, for instance, might never get the opportunity to meet face-to-face with an astronomy expert in Norway. However, personal videoconferencing gives the amateur a chance to collaborate in real time and communicate with the expert through video face-to-face. The amateur might share a photograph of a star constellation with the expert. The view from Nebraska could be valuable to the expert, who might share some diagrams with the amateur. However, store-and-forward video will also play an important role in the video-enhanced virtual community. Dale Harris of Stanford University believes real-time video will take a back seat to store-and-forward in this kind of application because of time zone differences. "If my wife communicates with her virtual community in cross stitching, which is her hobby, many of those people around the world are not awake." Whether the video is real-time or store-and-forward, greater access to experts and information makes the world smaller and enhances global education.

Tom Manley of INET Marketing believes home videoconferencing will shrink the world. "It's a tremendous shift, considering the diverse cultures around the world. In the history of our species, fairly recently it would take days or weeks for information to travel across the world, and even then it was filtered by governments," Manley says. "Now with instant desktop videoconferencing, all of those barriers are broken down, and we can have one-on-one video communication with anybody in the world."

Manley points out that home videoconferencing will reshape institutions, including governments and the media. With instant live video of happenings and one-on-one visual communication, people may rely less on traditional filters. "There will still be a place for the media. It will change the way they do business. Maybe it'll keep them more honest," explains Manley. Manley also believes home videoconferencing will have a significant impact on repressive regimes. "If individuals in many countries can now obtain information themselves visually, it will be more difficult for countries with closed borders to keep a handle on people." Countries with poor human rights records, for example, would have a tougher time misleading the world if people there gain access to real-time video communications. Seeing and hearing human rights abuses in real time or through store-and-forward video could bring about social change.

Home videoconferencing may also encourage cultural exchange and understanding by forming virtual communities that span continents. "You can be out in the desert in Botswana, but you're dealing with the same problems as in inner city America," explains Kevin Pitts who directs the DVC lab for Link-VTC in Boulder, Colorado. "Those similar problems include how do you deliver quality education. We're all human. People will learn that we all have a lot in common. If I could see this in my lifetime, I'd feel that we made people's lives better." Pitts believes that home videoconferencing will enhance the "$22 a month" services that match pen pals from developing and developed countries. "You'd actually be able to see that child on video. People would be able to see where the rubber meets the road—where their money is going," says Pitts. Pitts envisions a nonprofit organization that would match people based on their common interests in third world and first world countries. First they could exchange e-mail and later begin communicating and collaborating through real-time video. If a water well breaks in an African desert village, people who know how to fix water wells could walk village people through the repairs. "There may be a way to do irrigation and farming more efficiently and feed the world population. They say there's enough food in the world to feed everybody," says Pitts. Home videoconferencing could also enable more basic cultural exchanges like cooking techniques, meditation, relaxation, approaches to health, and dress. "That would take the planet to the next level of understanding. If people understand issues and cultures, they're more willing to help out," insists Pitts.

David Dirks of Lawrence Livermore Laboratory believes that video-enhanced virtual communities will breed empathy. He believes text exchanges alone provide an intellectual connection, but lack a real emotional link. Similarly, Dirks believes that learning about other cultures from books and lectures seems distant and sterile compared to the personal connection that home videoconferencing could allow. "As long as they're a nameless, faceless nation of people, I don't get to that feeling level. For those unable to travel often, videoconferencing could provide a better understanding of people and their culture, which leads to a better understanding between nations. "It changes the perspective, broadens the heart, and brings a better world view," says Dirks.

Harry Mott of Mott 4 Productions agrees that the power of home videoconferencing can improve the world, but he tempers that optimism with realism. "Will it bring world peace? Hell no. Will it help in understanding a lot and bringing down some of the conflicts? I think so."

Impact on family and friends

Corporate transfers have spread families across regions, separating children from their grandparents—and even parents, in the case of divorce or separation. While so far technology falls short of an in-person encounter, desktop videoconferencing can fill the gap between holiday face-to-face visits with relatives. An estranged parent can form a closer relationship with a child, perhaps collaborating on a school assignment. These interactions could boost child support collections, because an estranged parent may be more likely to pay up if he or she had higher impact contact with their children. Grandparents no longer must wonder whether their grandchildren really liked the birthday gifts they sent. There is no substitute for a child's facial expressions when opening a gift, and personal videoconferencing provides the opportunity to enjoy gift-giving remotely. "Videoconferencing will change the way we live," says Dennis Riley, who runs the DVC lab at Microsoft. "It's an emotional connection or the third dimension now that I can see somebody. I can ship my folks a video phone. From a human standpoint, that has impact."

When a family relocates to a new city, personal videoconferencing can soften the blow for children. They can see, hear, and show things to their friends and former teachers in real time. Dropping a child off at day care causes mixed emotions for many parents. They may value a chance to work without interruption from a home office, but regret the lack of interaction with their child. Personal videoconferencing gives parents the opportunity to look in on their children at a participating day-care center without interfering with productivity.

Mort Herman, marketing director for Lucent Technologies Microelectronics, frequently plays chess and cards. He believes an application for home videoconferencing is remote game playing. This would require the right software, which players could share screen-to-screen. Beyond games, Herman insists the important aspect of home videoconferencing is the ability to maintain relationships from a distance. "If it's a person who's your friend and you haven't seen them for a long time, video makes a difference," says Herman.

Riley of Microsoft believes that the ability to see and hear family members in real time is videoconferencing's killer application at home. "It touches the heart. When it grabs somebody emotionally, you don't have to sell it—it sells itself." However, Riley also believes that collaborative capabilities are also important to the home videoconferencing user. "We can collaborate and share concepts and ideas. There's a limit to what talking heads can do even at home," according to Riley. "A lot of times people will say I want to look at this application, but I don't want to be bothered by someone I have to interact with through video."

Jon Loeliger, a software designer for Chromatic Research, uses desktop videoconferencing for telecommuting. However, he is rapidly discovering other home applications. One of these is uniting his family. Loeliger's parents and sister live in Madagascar. His family has had trouble getting a telephone line, and the only reliable communication method has been e-mail. Loeliger says the value of videoconferencing over e-mail so that his relationship with his relatives becomes richer than the written word. "We've resorted to sending video tapes back and forth. There is the need for that visual communication," Loeliger insists.

While increasing numbers of parents are using e-mail to communicate with their children, Lt. Richard Stakelum of the US Navy believes home videoconferencing will change that equation. "I hate to type. There are a lot of people who only type because they have to," insists Stakelum. Stakelum insists that communicating through video between family members makes more sense. "If I want my kid to do something, I don't send him an e-mail. I tell him. You can see if your kids are picking up their clothes. You're watching them do it, and you get immediate feedback," says Stakelum. "Videoconferencing allows the ability to make sure somebody does things right the first time."

Linking separated parent with children

Jim Malone, a California podiatrist, faced a custody battle in which he and his ex-wife would have "spent themselves to death." His wife had taken their 11-year-old and 6-year-old daughters and moved with her new husband to an island off eastern Canada. The first year, the children made the 24-hour trip to California four times. The trip was tiring for them, and Malone's ex-wife was seeking to reduce his visitation. Jim proposed personal videoconferencing as a way to avoid court. "I said if you'll let me install a videoconferencing system in your home and let me help the kids with homework a couple of times a week, we can reduce visitation." Malone chose a VIVO 320 system. He even retained a company to customize the system with an electronic pen, letting his children write their homework on their computer screen.

Malone says home videoconferencing has changed his life. "You get depressed when you can't see your own children. They're never going to be this age again," says Jim. "I can't believe something as cold as a computer with a few phone lines can help take that loss away." Malone says another benefit of videoconferencing is that it reduced the resentment he feels towards his ex-wife. Besides doing homework with his children, he has met their friends and played computer games with them. "People used to die before they had penicillin. I'm glad I was born at a time when people dream up these things. It allows you to come to terms with losses." Malone says his introduction to videoconferencing for home-based personal applications has made him realize the value the technology will have in his work. "Practicing medicine does not always require a physical examination. Videoconferencing will facilitate a lot of medical communication that never took place before."

Louis Belt of Laidlaw Environmental Services, based in South Carolina, uses home videoconferencing to stay close with and mentor his 16-year-old step son who lives in Tennessee. "I use it as a training aid. I put ISDN in my son's home. I'm constantly teaching him computer skills," says Belt. "We're able to see each other and able to work on projects together." Louis Belt's father, who lives in rural Missouri, has also installed videoconferencing at home. "Long distance relationships are much nicer when you can see people. It's a sense of closeness," explains Louis Belt. Belt says one year he was unable to physically join his family for Christmas. Home videoconferencing helped fill the void. "I could watch them open their gifts and they could watch me open my gifts," says Belt. "It will become a way of life for people. It's part of the evolutionary chain of technology." Belt says he is trying to talk his Arkansas-based grandfather into getting home videoconferencing.

Time for part-time

The demands of parenting and the increasing desire for time over money has fueled the trend away from stressful jobs. Particularly in the technology industry, many professionals have abandoned high-paying positions for more simple lives. These decisions are often tough, and produce mixed results. Companies lose their investment in those professionals, and that loss can impact the bottom line. Professionals lose the investment in their careers, and may later discover that their skills fall short in fulfilling their dreams of raising chickens or running a burrito restaurant. A compromise allowing professionals to work from home part-time may provide the right solution.

The enhanced communication and collaboration that personal videoconferencing can provide may help overcome corporate objections to part-time, home-based, and other alternative work arrangements. The technology may also allow people on maternity or paternity leave to balance new responsibilities as parents with continuing professional commitments. Some law firms now allow attorneys to choose a non-partner path that limits management expectations and work days. Other untraditional firms let lawyers work from home. Los Angeles-based Legal Research Network, for example, employs partners on maternity leave, retired judges, lawyers between jobs, and law professors. Each is an expert in his or her field and can therefore avoid the big-firm practice of starting many projects from scratch. These lawyers can put in hours that fit their schedules while balancing other responsibilities and activities. Desktop videoconferencing can reinforce trends like these in many industries, allowing part-time, home-based professionals to collaborate more effectively with colleagues and clients.

Telecommuting

Workplace experts have been predicting the rise of telecommuting since the 1970s, but the actual increase in home-based workers has lagged behind the predictions. Telecommuting proponents have often expected that such major events as natural disasters could boost telecommuting. The thinking has been that during a disaster companies would get used to letting professionals work from home, and that these companies would let those professionals continue to telecommute after the major event ended. When the Northridge earthquake hit southern California in 1994, the quake destroyed parts of Highway 14. This cut off people living in the high-desert areas. Getting to work would have required a several-hour commute. Instead, companies let these employees telecommute. However, as soon as the freeway reopened most companies insisted that their employees abandon telecommuting.

"Many employers still don't get it," says Van Romine, Director of the Institute for Telework. "As soon as the opportunity comes for them to go back to old habits, they do." Romine believes that desktop videoconferencing could fuel telecommuting. However, he believes Web videoconferencing may make the most sense assuming video quality is acceptable. "Web videoconferencing will give more credibility to all kinds of remote working scenarios, including the client's office, the car, the airport, hotels, supermarkets, and the home office."

A primary barrier to telecommuting is that corporate managers fear that professionals will goof off at home. "It's a manager's issue of trying to gauge performance and keep the corporate culture the same," according to Anthony Antonuccio of VIVO. However, VIVO has focused on the telecommuting market in marketing its Telework-5 product. "We've been successful in positioning desktop videoconferencing as a way to remove the out-of-sight, out-of-mind barriers," says Antonuccio. "Desktop videoconferencing can alleviate a manager's concern of 'how do I know they're working if I can't see them?' "

Antonuccio points out that the technology also reduces isolation, and makes telecommuting more appealing to workers. Steve Shao of Project DIANE agrees. They talk about the virtual corporation, the virtual office, and telecommuting. There are some real implementation issues. Your managers can't check up on you as easily. You feel isolated in the home office," Shao points out. Desktop videoconferencing compliments the technology portfolio and eases the management and isolation concerns. "You're still not in the office, but the two-way video gets you closer," says Shao.

Productivity statistics usually indicate that home-based workers accomplish more than their traditional office-based counterparts. One reason for this is the amount of time spent socializing at the traditional office. While moderate social interaction helps develop a corporate culture, often this practice degenerates into a productivity barrier. One manager with AT&T says he took the job because the company lets him telecommute. "I can hardly do anything in the office, because my colleagues are always interrupting me with questions and small talk. Also, the office politics gets in the way," he says. "When I work from home, I save the commute time plus the non-productive social time, and the company actually gets far more out of me, and I can spend more time with my family."

Many social factors may push companies toward telecommuting into the 21st Century. Car congestion is turning highways almost into parking lots in many metropolitan areas. People are growing weary of horrendous commutes and 12-hour days. As these professionals opt for more simple lives over demanding jobs, companies may accommodate telecommuting to keep a skilled workforce. Also, governments are applying greater pressure on industry to discourage commuting and reduce air pollution. The California Office of Traffic Safety reports that if 5% of Los Angeles County commuters worked from home one day a week, they would put 94 million fewer tons of pollution into the atmosphere each year. Beyond social factors, the business case for telecommuting will determine its future. Increased productivity is only one factor impacting the bottom line. The reduced need for office space can save many companies millions of dollars a year. Also, studies show that telecommuting reduces the number of sick days.

Before companies can embrace telecommuting, they must move away from a culture of controlling professionals. One leading technology company used to place professionals' names on late lists if they arrived for work after 8 AM. As 21st Century managers replace older-style, more traditional managers, telecommuting may become more prevalent. "The older-style ones will want to install telecommuting, because they want to be big brother," insists Anthony Antonuccio of VIVO. Companies must cut loose the control paradigm and buy in to the notion that freedom to telecommute benefits the bottom line because of a happier and more productive workforce. Desktop videoconferencing may encourage this shift, because many managers feel more secure knowing they can see their team members during the work day. However, telecommuting experts caution that using the technology to spy on workers backfires. That's because workers resent the control paradigm migrating to their homes, and consequently productivity can decline.

Jon Loeliger of Chromatic Research telecommutes from a Dallas suburb. His company is based in Silicon Valley. Loeliger says his company sees telecommuting as a trade-off. "On the one hand it's real high-tech and it's cool to brag that you have a role for telecommuters," says Loeliger. "But on the other hand, my boss prefers to have people be there. Videoconferencing bridges the gap." Loeliger says he uses desktop videoconferencing to interview prospective Chromatic employees. He used to hire people sight unseen, based on phone conversations. "Having the ability to see them and react with them and get that visual feedback of whether they're smiling or not is very helpful," says Loeliger. Loeliger says he also uses desktop videoconferencing to join group meetings at company headquarters from his home. He also uses the technology to collaborate with a coworker who lives down the street. In this case, he chooses desktop videoconferencing instead of a face-to-face meeting if the two collaborators need to exchange files or share documents. By doing this, the meeting is more productive because problems can be solved on the spot. There is no reason, for example, to delay sharing documents or other information because they are back at the office.

When Loeliger began using desktop videoconferencing as a telecommuting tool, he wanted his co-collaborators to know him better. When a person enters somebody's office or cubicle, the "stuff" around their desk and environment gives the professional some idea of his or her colleague's personality. This can help crystallize a business relationship. Loeliger sought to reproduce this result through the technology. "I literally picked up the camera and toured the room to give my coworkers insight into me. That was helpful to them in dealing with me," Loeliger explains. However, Loeliger worries that the technology could provide too much access to his home. He is debating whether to print his ISDN number on his business cards. "It's very intrusive. Unless you're prepared for that, it's very disconcerting. On a regular basis I don't necessarily want somebody calling me and getting a view of my house." He particularly wishes to avoid video calls from "random" business associates and cold callers. Jay Crookston, networkMCI Conferencing's VP for US Sales, recognizes the mixed blessing of using desktop videoconferencing to enhance telecommuting. "There could be a sinister side to this technology in that you'll never be able to escape," says Crookston.

A California developer has demonstrated desktop videoconferencing for telecommuting as a way to market homes. HCV Pacific Partners installed Intel ProShare at its "Information Highway House" at Madera del Presidio in Corte Madera, California. The model home featured ProShare in both a home office and a bedroom. Home-buyers had the option of ordering a house outfitted with desktop videoconferencing, fiber optic cable, and other information-age technology.

Alternative delivery of services

As bandwidth increases to homes and as increasing numbers of PCs become videoconferencing-enabled, real-time video and collaboration will change the delivery of services and products to consumers. Software developers are writing new sets of applications that exploit videoconferencing capabilities. Both general and specialized PC programs will increasingly include a videoconferencing element. Intel, for example, is reaching out to many industries—especially retail-oriented businesses like real estate and banking—through its ProShare Developer's Program. The idea is to give industries better contact with customers and speed transactions. Applications may incorporate both stored and real-time video. Increasingly, consumers can shop by watching stored videos of products. If they like what they see, they can buy it. If they need questions answered, they can connect to a sales representative for a real-time conference, ask questions and complete their transaction.

Lt. Richard Stakelum of the US Navy was an early adopter of desktop videoconferencing for ship-to-shore telemaintenance and dock-to-hospital telemedicine. "The exact same things we're doing on the ship relate to the home," says Stakelum. "Seeing the doctor, for example. It's not uncommon to think that you could plug right into a blood pressure monitor during a videoconference. Also, there's distance education and training. You could be taking an economics course from Harvard one minute and a physics class from Stanford the next." Stakelum's vision is that every home will have videoconferencing in almost every room, and that the technology will become as prevalent as the television set.

Dennis Riley of Microsoft says the home videoconferencing user will use Caller ID and other services to screen out some video sales pitches. If the sales pitch does get through, it will be either real-time or stored. "You may not see the video of the individual, but you may see a PowerPoint or a video tape, or a video caller may say 'hey look at this', " Riley says.

Personal video banking

US Bank in Portland, Huntington Bancshares in Columbus, and Citibank have already inaugurated video kiosks allowing customers to get loans and buy financial services products by communicating and collaborating with a customer service representative. As more personal videoconferencing finds its way into increasing numbers of homes, the next step is for banks to offer video banking to home-based users. Web videoconferencing may expedite that trend. A study released by the Bank Administration Institute surveyed 35,000 households, and found that half of the banking customers would prefer to stay away from branches.

Huntington Bancshares is considering the Web and ADSL technology as potential transports for home video banking. "Where we envision this going...we'll be able to do the videoconferencing directly into the home or business environment in addition to video kiosks," says Bill Randle, Director of Marketing and Strategic Planning for Huntington. "By the turn of the century, we will have very few banking branches." Randle believes that video banking is one part of a broader trend. "There's a lot of lifestyle changes that will occur. After the turn of the century, there will be a need for fewer strip shopping centers. The notion of going down to the supermarket or shopping mall will change for many people." Home video banking may also encourage more high-dollar transactions as investors gain access to bank professionals with specific expertise who are rarely found at bank branches.

Boon to rural living

Desktop videoconferencing is contributing to the economic rise of rural areas. After the decline of the family farm in the 1970s and 1980s, many rural areas fell on hard times. However, technology is bringing many of those areas back. No longer is it necessary for professionals to live in or near cities. The high cost of urban and suburban living and a desire to avoid pollution and other urban problems have fueled a rural resurgence. To encourage this trend, some state governments have worked with long distance carriers to enhance the telecommunications infrastructure. Nebraska now boasts roughly 7 thousand miles of fiber optic cable, which has allowed high-resolution telemedicine, distance learning and other videoconferencing applications.

911

Home videoconferencing coupled with video-enhanced 911 could save lives during emergencies. All 911 operators could use their eyes as well as their ears to evaluate and prioritize crimes and fires. This capability could become particularly useful in domestic disputes, which many police consider the most dangerous situations they face because of their unpredictable nature. If 911 operators pass on their observations to police, the additional information could help protect officers as they approach a domestic incident. If domestic abuse victims are scared that talking to a 911 operator would alert their attacker and jeopardize them further, home videoconferencing could be used to make a video-without-audio connection. Sign language could communicate a "help" message, and the 911 operator could dispatch police.

Surveillance

As police departments install video cameras in downtown business districts to prevent crime, governments can give citizens access to these camera views. If people could monitor public areas through home videoconferencing, they could use the information they gain to make their lives easier. For example, the ability to check traffic patterns before hitting the road could save time and reduce aggravation. "Videoconference locations of resource potential will be set up for special applications like police monitoring, and then they'll open it up to the public," says Steve Shao of Project DIANE. "Home videoconferencing will enhance that window on the world."

Video house calls

Yes, the doctor is in—but she or he may be on video. Not every symptom may require a trip to the doctor. Video quality is more of an issue, though, in a telemedicine application. Nevertheless, as the availability of cheap bandwidth increases, home telemedicine becomes more viable. Harry Mott of Mott 4 Productions is excited about pediatric telemedicine at home. "You've got a problem with your 3-year-old. Maybe it's a rash you don't understand. You call up the doctor and say take a look," says Mott.

Enhanced home schooling

Parents wishing to have greater input in educating their children no longer must choose between the traditional classroom and home schooling. Personal videoconferencing provides a compromise solution in which parents can school their children with help from educational professionals. Special education students, gifted students, and students with serious diseases can attend school through home videoconferencing. They might also attend after-school or weekend classes that are geared towards their special needs. No longer is a special student limited by mobility or geography.

Video sex

An application that could drive the use of home videoconferencing is video sex. An executive of one videoconferencing manufacturer compares his industry with the video rental business. "If you look at what drove video rental sales when it first came out, it was X-rated videos," says the executive. Consider as well the popularity of voice-only 1-900 sex lines. Some may argue that adding a video component to sex lines could reduce the popularity of red light districts. In fact, several companies advertise video sex on the World Wide Web. They offer free software and not-so-free video time with a staff member.

11

A New Way of Doing Business

The key word that may characterize business as a new century dawns is *mobility*. Productivity from anywhere is rapidly becoming the name of the game as people work from their homes, cars, airports, airplanes, hotel rooms, client offices—even street corners. Technology will let us access the Internet, send faxes, receive video mail, share documents, and conduct real-time video interactions from anyplace. "Smart networks" will find us. Wearable technology will allow us to communicate with colleagues and customers through video, text, and voice. *Wearable* may mean a camera-equipped palmtop device the size of a personal digital assistant or Apple Newton. The device may reside in a pouch on a belt. If this sounds overwhelming—even unnecessary— remember that we will control access to our wearable technology. We will instruct networks about which video calls to direct to us as we eat breakfast at a restaurant and which video calls to forward to video mail, or even to a colleague, for example. The trend towards portable videoconferencing is beginning with laptops.

Mobile Videoconferencing

As companies get accustomed to desktop videoconferencing, more professionals within those companies are demanding the ability to communicate through video while on the road. The H.324 family of standards for videoconferencing over POTS is making laptop videoconferencing more viable. H.324 includes H.324/M, which is the standard covering videoconferencing over mobile and wireless radio networks. POTS and wireless are important to laptop videoconferencing, because locating ISDN in an airport or hotel is far from easy. Laptop vendors and video card manufacturers are bundling videoconferencing capability into their products. Other companies, including RSI Systems, offer products that attach to laptops. The Eris product from RSI offers videoconferencing over either ISDN or POTS. The 5-pound portable box can connect to a laptop or desktop PC or Mac. An optional camera clips on to the laptop.

A major international oil company is using Eris so that its oil derivatives traders can collaborate on multimillion dollar deals. "We don't make trading plays without the consensus of the group, and it means money to us to be in touch all the time," says a Cleveland-based member of the trading team. The problem is that the traders are split among Singapore, London, and Cleveland, which means time zone hell. "We needed a system where we could have at least home and business settings without buying desktop videoconferencing for both locations. This avoids anybody having to come into the office at

4 am," according to the trader. The trader also says his team requires flexibility for traveling, which is why a laptop solution fits their needs. One trader says that ultimately he may install desktop videoconferencing at home, so that he can use laptop videoconferencing from the road for personal reasons as well as business. "When traveling it would be nice if the wife and kids could see me. I have three small kids who miss me when I'm away."

Laptop videoconferencing capability could make some business travelers warm up to portable computers. Christine Traut of Andersen Worldwide almost never brings a laptop on business trips. "I resent the fact that they're so easily stolen and I'm responsible," she explains. However, Traut is a frequent user of desktop videoconferencing, and finds it difficult to resist the prospect of real-time video on the road. "I'd be more likely to use a laptop if it had videoconferencing," says Traut. Tom Manley of INET Marketing says he envisions palm top videoconferencing. "It's sort of like the cellular phone. Instead of having phones pressed up to their ears, people will hold video communications devices," says Manley. The value of portable videoconferencing goes beyond novelty, according to Manley. "It's exciting. You're not restrained as much by time. Sales people won't have to come into the office as much for meetings." Dennis Riley, who runs the desktop videoconferencing lab at Microsoft, says the cellular phone could become the transport model for mobile videoconferencing. "Video cellular is going to be a hot market. I see it being impactual with the lap-top carrying executive," says Riley. Harry Mott of Mott 4 Productions believes portable videoconferencing will be as ubiquitous as the cellular phone. "Right now it's everyone from pizza delivery people to bank presidents using cellular phones. A few years ago, just people with a lot of money used them. The same thing will happen with portable videoconferencing," says Mott. (See Figure 11–1.)

Wireless technology could have widespread implications for doing business. Videoconferencing in cars could become viable, though potentially dangerous. David Dirks of Lawrence Livermore National Laboratory would like the ability to join a videoconference audio-only while driving. "I could be traveling down the highway and involved in a videoconference. I wouldn't be watching, but my laptop could be recording the conference." The CD-ROM that accompanies *The Road Ahead* by Bill Gates demonstrates videoconferencing in a police car. The detectives conference with their supervisor who is back at the police station. He gives them their next assignment while sharing an electronic map. The availability of mobile videoconferencing can also impact the expectation that companies have of their people. There is the potential that professionals enjoying their weekend or vacation could get roped into a meeting. "I could be in Lake Tahoe on vacation and still be par-

Courtesy of 8×8, Inc.

Figure 11–1: A prototype wireless videophone

ticipating in something that's very important," says David Dirks. "As I'm saying this, though, I don't like that." Dirks says rather than pollute his vacation with work, he would prefer to use mobile videoconferencing to work from an alternative location.

Dirks sees an important plant safety application for mobile videoconferencing. When emergency workers respond to a fire, for instance, they could use portable videoconferencing to view camera images inside the building. "What if you could even view where people were trapped? The emergency crew never has to endanger themselves to figure out what's going on," suggests Dirks.

Corporations are also achieving mobility through the use of docking stations, which are desktop compartments that convert laptops into desktop computers and can provide greater functionality. Boeing has installed Intel ProShare boards in docking stations throughout a factory. A camera-equipped monitor sits next to each docking station. As a quality control professional, for example, checks different aspects of production, he or she walks around the factory with a laptop. That laptop becomes a videoconferencing tool when the user docks it.

Personal videoconferencing as standard equipment

In the 21st Century corporation, desktop videoconferencing becomes standard business technology. For many businesses, there was a day sometime in 1989 when decision-makers realized that a fax machine was essential. Previously, they believed they could get by without one. Businesses needed the technology because their customers and suppliers had fax machines. Without the technology, businesses could not compete. They were effectively out of business. That day is coming for desktop videoconferencing. Certain kinds of businesses will reach that day sooner than others. "A key success factor for any business that is relationship-based and knowledge-based is: how many people do you know?" according to Christine Traut of Andersen Worldwide. "Desktop videoconferencing builds relationships. This is such a powerful networking tool. Using it directly with clients gives these businesses such a huge competitive advantage."

Vendors are pushing hard to ensure that professionals will demand desktop videoconferencing. "I want to eliminate distance between people in every sense of the word—psychologically, in terms of information flow, and emotionally," insists PictureTel Chairman and CEO Norman Gaut. Gaut points out that people often describe a lack of understanding as distance between two people. He believes that desktop videoconferencing helps fill that kind of gap. "A lot of information that you exchange in an office environment is visual. That richness as it becomes more pervasive will change the way we communicate over distance," says Gaut. Gaut intends to make desktop videoconferencing standard in the virtual office as well as in the traditional office. Videoconferencing in the virtual office "extends your reach to be able to do everything you'd normally do in an office to where distance has no effect."

The business-to-home bounce-back effect will turn desktop videoconferencing into standard equipment. Home videoconferencing will facilitate widespread deployment in business. As PC vendors bundle desktop videoconferencing with their products, home users will get used to video communication over POTS and the Internet. They will have the opportunity to learn how to communicate and collaborate effectively in lower impact situations. Users are more at ease making mistakes with friends and family than with colleagues at work. "They want to learn in an environment that is comfortable. There is less liability in the personal relationship than the business relationship," says Christine Perey of Perey Communications. "They will learn a great deal about the human interaction and relationship protocols."

This is similar to the business-to-home bounce-back effect that the telephone enjoyed. At first, the telephone fell flat in business because it provided no written record. Businesspeople were used to the telegraph. And, Perey points out, conceptually the phone was completely different from something else businesspeople were used to: the face-to-face meeting. After home users got used to the telephone as an entertainment and communication device, they became more comfortable using it for business.

The business-to-home bounce-back effect also applied to multimedia PCs. Businesspeople first got accustomed to using the technology for home entertainment. So, armed with video communication and the collaboration confidence their home experiences provide, desktop videoconferencing users will then apply those skills to their work. Meantime, the look and feel of business will change. "By then, business will be more distributed. The concepts of teaming, shared spaces and creative collaboration will take off," explains Perey. Those trends will solidify the necessity of desktop videoconferencing as standard business technology.

The Virtual Corporation

No longer is erecting buildings necessary to create companies and do business. The banking industry realizes this. That's why banks are creating virtual branches through video kiosks and on-line banking. The 21st Century corporation is increasingly virtual. A downtown location or headquarters may no longer be an asset. Professionals may work from home, telecommuting centers, hotels, or elsewhere. These workers may be consultants, business partners, or contractors. The virtual corporation may be ad hoc, coming together for a specific purpose and then disbanding afterwards. The virtual corporation may form by making strategic alliances with business partners to exploit a short-lived market opportunity.

The virtual corporation concept also extends to virtual work teams. Networks of individuals will form to provide services and products. People with complimentary core competencies will join forces for a project, disband, and come together again for future projects. Says Kevin Pitts who directs the DVC lab for Link-VTC, "In terms of opening up business to sole proprietors and consultants, this will give them opportunities to compete that they didn't have before." Traditionally, constraints of distance prevented small businesses from competing. "There's no reason why with desktop videoconferencing you can't establish intimate relationships and do business around the globe," says Steve Shao of Project DIANE. "Planet Earth becomes a small place." However, the flip side is that desktop videoconferencing allows fewer secrets than the phone. Says Harry Mott of Mott 4 Productions, "It's hard when you're a small company and you're juggling payments. Creditors are calling on video, and they're looking at your place saying why did we lend money to that person?"

The law firm of Parnon & Pratt is going full speed ahead with its original business plan of a virtual corporation. Founding partner Fred Parnon has used desktop videoconferencing to link partners dispersed across the US. Parnon is now getting requests from attorneys who wish to work for the firm while living in other countries. "I have no problem with this guy living in Italy," says Parnon. "You can assemble virtual workgroups within organizations. You can put together teams to solve problems. Physical meetings are extremely expensive and inefficient." Parnon believes that virtual approaches allow corporations to search the globe for the best talent. These power players who are geographically dispersed can boost the bottom line. "Corporations that won't work in this way lose out to the competitor who can get the smarter people," explains Parnon.

"In the old days, corporations built task forces out of people all working for the same boss," says Sarkis Zartarian of Applied Communication Concepts. "Before the task force leader had the power to define the tasks." Now team members come from different departments or may be contract professionals or consultants. They have more free rein to determine ways of solving problems. A desktop videoconferencing implementation team that includes members from different divisions, as well as operations people and contract professionals, is an example of that trend.

Desktop videoconferencing is part of the glue that holds virtual corporations together as well as a key enabling factor. Coordination, management, and communication issues are potential stumbling blocks for these kinds of enterprises. The technology helps alleviate these barriers by allowing partners in virtual corporations worldwide to collaborate and communicate as if they were occupying adjacent cubicles. "Desktop videoconferencing makes the virtual corporation or team concept really possible," says David Dirks, Videoconferencing Project Manager at Lawrence Livermore National Laboratory. "We're forming more diverse, synergistic teams. Desktop videoconferencing becomes an important tool to do this."

As the virtual corporation business model takes off, the traditional approach declines. Christine Traut of Andersen Worldwide believes that desktop videoconferencing may spark reorganizations of corporations. "This kind of technology will potentially break up large companies," says Traut. Many corporations are internally focused. The vast majority of professionals communicate with each other rather than with people at other companies, which has led to insular corporate cultures. Desktop videoconferencing lets professionals form strategic alliances, network, and chart paths that take them beyond the walls of their current employers. They can accomplish this from the comfort and convenience of their desks. Says Dennis Riley of Microsoft, "I can talk to people at other companies more efficiently. I can send you information on my research in real time."

Traut tells the story of the telecommunications researcher who was a colleague of somebody she had met briefly at a conference. A few days later the man dropped into Traut's office at Andersen Worldwide via desktop videoconferencing. He had some questions for Traut about the technology. "He was a total stranger. I chatted with him for 20 minutes. I would never have done that on the phone," says Traut. The episode helped build rapport between two professionals with common interests who work for different organizations.

This may sound like a raw deal for the corporation that implements desktop videoconferencing. After all, an employee is forging alliances and networking while on the clock. However, the external rapport building that the technology encourages may become good news for everybody as the objectives of corporations and their employees merge. As corporations seek higher profits, they will turn to outsourcing jobs and projects and downsizing the payroll. The potential for closer relationships across organizational boundaries also breeds joint ventures, which can deliver bottom-line results for companies. Likewise, the individual can benefit. As professionals seek higher paychecks, they will develop expertise that is worth more on the open market than it is to any one company. Employees become free agents, and employers operate leaner organizations. The virtual corporation becomes the business model of the 21st Century, and desktop videoconferencing helps make it possible.

Personal videoconferencing-enabled globalization

Corporations no longer do business only in their backyards. The world is the market. Globalization of business practices becomes essential to support this approach. For National Semiconductor, desktop videoconferencing enables globalization. Andy Moorwood, a member of National Semiconductor's deployment team, says globalization is the primary corporate-wide motivation for deploying the technology. "A picture is still worth a thousand words," Moorwood told an audience at the DVC '96 West conference. Phoning, faxing, and overnighting falls short for teams dispersed across multiple time zones. "We have so few hours where we can get valuable engineering interaction that we have to have desktop videoconferencing," according to Moorwood. "There's no other way to get over so few hours of overlap with the time difference." Moorwood says National Semiconductor had neglected communications with its plants in Asia before deploying desktop videoconferencing. However, he says that the plants, are key to the business process and working with them to speed problem resolution is essential.

Using the technology for telecommuting is increasingly becoming part of the globalization equation for National Semiconductor. Moorwood says desktop videoconferencing for telecommuting supports the objective of "the best access to the best brain power at the best price at the best time." Often, the company relies on home-based experts in a specific business process. Regular collaboration is essential, but traveling is unnecessary and unproductive. Many of National Semiconductor's sales engineers work from home. Moorwood says instant collaboration between a sales engineer in New England, for example, and a product manager in California is essential to delivering timely results for customers. Dennis Riley of Microsoft agrees. "Video support will be a critical element. It will be that bond between the customer and the company." Riley adds that people buy products from companies that have a track record of resolving problems quickly.

"Geography brings diversity," according to Louis Belt of Laidlaw Environmental Services. And diversity is good for business. "The ability of desktop videoconferencing is to bring that diversity into the corporate world. You'll have a broader perspective and be much better informed as an organization," insists Belt. The diversity that the technology brings can eliminate the skewed perspective that people from the same organization, same department, or even same country can develop. "The big edge is that you have better information and ideas. As long as you can market them, that makes a difference," says Belt.

Desktop videoconferencing also helps close the cultural gap and encourages business between people who live and work in continents that are miles apart both physically and ideologically. The benefit is that the fear and distrust among businesspeople of different cultures will decline. "What you're seeing is the ability to bring this very diverse, former xenophobic business environment into a much more homogeneous and culturally neutral business environment," says Norman Gaut of PictureTel. Gaut believes that the technology will also spark business between countries with political and economic differences. "If I can make a deal with anyone in the world on a moment's notice, you'll see more free trade zones," says Gaut. "Why are Cuba and North Korea still looked at as menaces? They're isolated."

The changing business landscape

Real-time video is transforming many industries. Many corporations are reaching beyond their boundaries, linking with customers and suppliers through personal videoconferencing. Traditionally, National Semiconductor purchased products and services via the phone and fax. "We would never see the supplier face-to-face," says Judith Hamilton, videoconferencing project manager. The purchasing approach, however, is rapidly changing. Increasing competition requires vendors to stay closer to the customer. Desktop videoconferencing helps customers and vendors build trust. "The trust level increases dramatically when people have face-to-face communication through video rather than just a faxed piece of paper or a voice at the end of a phone," explains Hamilton. Hamilton adds that these closer customer/vendor relationships blossom when people finally meet in person. "A simple handshake doesn't seem adequate. Often times, culture-permitting, people will embrace," says Hamilton.

Personal video communication is having a major impact on companies that deliver retail financial services. Huntington Bancshares was one of the first banks worldwide to implement video banking kiosks. In 1991, Marketing and Strategic Planning Director Bill Randle signed a contract with NCR to build the first kiosk based on what became the Vistium. Randle says he turned to video because banking customers were demanding faster, more convenient services. Also, Huntington was increasingly competing with "non-bank" mutual fund companies and brokerage houses for business. Randle rolled the dice in a major way in implementing video banking. Technologically, Randle says the Vistium (the name AT&T gave the product when it bought NCR) was designed for business communications, rather than video kiosks. Also, there were internal implementation hurdles. "They don't want to be the first to do it because video reduces the number of bankers going forward. That's threatening," explains Randle. In Fact, Huntington projects that by 2001 it will eliminate half of its 320 branches. "The branch is obsolete now," says Randle.

Huntington has been converting branches to "Access Branches" since late 1994. In opening the first Access branch, Huntington replaced its row of tellers with 3 video banking kiosks. This reduced the staff from 12 to 1. The remaining employee serves as a concierge who helps first-time customers with video banking and also manages the vault. The video banking approach gives Huntington better time-management control. "You've spread out the down time. Every physical branch has peaks at noon and at closing," according to Randle. "With video you can manage your key staff people and schedule them in a way that jives with customer habits." Randle believes that customized desktop videoconferencing applications will dramatically change business. "It will clearly impact any type of information-based commodity. Insurance, health care, entertainment, shopping will all be impacted by broadband capabilities delivering video and data," says Randle.

Video commerce may drastically change the way businesses approach the marketplace. Video-enabled transactions will occur on the Internet, through cable, and over other transports. "It will provide an opportunity without stress and commitment to browse. Once they decide they want to buy, they'll get a live body. It will be very practical," says Dennis Riley of Microsoft. VIVO Software President and CEO Staffan Ericsson believes desktop videoconferencing will redefine the meaning of mail order. "You want to be able to see the products that you're buying," says Ericsson. Ericsson also believes that the technology will change the travel industry. Instead of going to a store, travelers will use video kiosks and the Internet to work with a travel agent and view videos of destinations.

Commerce through video kiosks may impact a broad range of retail businesses in which customer service is paramount. The kiosk approach frees businesses from traditional requirements of maintaining real estate and larger staffs. Hussein ElBadaly, customer systems manager for Consolidated Edison in New York, pioneered the roll-out of video kiosks for utility transactions such as turning on electric service. ElBadaly points out that as businesses streamline operations, they are increasingly less able to keep staffs on standby in case there is a rush from customers. Keeping one window open falls short for the customer who would encounter a long line. For Consolidated Edison, video kiosks are a big part of the customer service answer. "This way a customer can do business with us at anytime. This is the first step. Later, this may be over the Internet," ElBadaly explains. "You can use the kiosk for advertising for other businesses, a movie next door for instance. Businesses will think beyond their boundaries."

Telecommunications carriers and hardware providers are scrambling to provide the infrastructure for kiosk commerce. MCI and Incite are working together to provide video call centers. These centers accept and process calls from video kiosks and other personal videoconferencing terminals. The MCI/Incite approach uses the IsoEthernet standard described in Chapter 9. Most calls between kiosks and call centers will run at a bandwidth of 384 kbps, using ISDN Primary Rate Interface. MCI and Incite enable the video call centers with PBX functionality, including call hold and transfer functions. Each kiosk includes a printer. For applications requiring a signature, the kiosk also features a signing pad. Each kiosk is equipped with Incite's Conversational Media, which includes a multimedia hub, a WAN hub, a video codec, and IsoEthernet network interface cards.

The markets that MCI is targeting for video call centers and kiosks include banking, real estate, retail sales, public safety, and printing. In the real estate application, a professional considering relocating from New York to Phoenix can walk up to a kiosk in an office building. He or she can use a keyboard to tell the computer all of the criteria for the move. Then the kiosk can find suitable homes and allow the prospective buyer to do a "video walk-through" of the properties. If the buyer wishes more information, he or she can push a button and connect with either the listing agent or a video call center that represents the agent. The call center representative will know the history of the buyer's activity on the kiosk. In the printing application, a professional arrives at an airport with a report or presentation on a disk. The kiosk would include a document camera, scanner, fax, and a credit card swipe or transaction device. The customer uses the video kiosk to link with a printing store. They consult with a service representative and then share the document that they want printed. Within two hours, the printing store delivers the printed copies of the document to the meeting site.

Not only are video call centers important to video kiosks, but also they are critical in providing services to home videoconferencing users. Consumers can connect with video call centers using regular phone lines or higher speed connections through their personal computers. "As videoconferencing becomes affordable and commonplace at home, there is something for people to access," says John Rushing, MCI senior consultant for call center systems. The video commerce approach will become increasingly critical to doing retail business.

The corporate culture fallout

Corporations that emphasize hierarchies and following orders above collaboration risk disintegrating. Some will change or die. Personal videoconferencing, intranets, the Internet, and other convergence technology can flop in a corporation where collaboration is a foreign concept. There is some evidence that collaborative technology can polarize organizations with noncollaborative cultures. An article by Michael Schrage in *Business Communications Review* describes field research by Wanda Orlikowski of MIT. According to the article, Orlikowski found that implementing Lotus Notes in a noncollaborative consulting firm increased internal tensions. "Notes actually exaggerated the chasm between the firm's professed idealism and its actual sharing of information," Schrage wrote.

Personal videoconferencing and other tools can help change a corporate culture, but the culture must want to change. Schrage has identified the bar or restaurant napkin as a collaborative space. According to Schrage, "collaboration is about managing interactions." However, Sarkis Zartarian of Applied Communication Concepts says that often "when you work on the napkin, you push the guy out of the way and write." That's the culture of dictating. It will never vanish, but it will evolve.

Dennis Riley of Microsoft believes that desktop videoconferencing coupled with intranets will force departments to communicate more openly with other departments within organizations. Also, these technologies will empower individuals to become more self sufficient, conducting their own research inside and outside of the corporation. Riley believes desktop videoconferencing and intranet tools will also give employees more direct access to human resources and technical development centers. Individuals at all levels will become more plugged in to corporate strategy. Stored videos of product release announcements will become readily available, and real-time video communication will let individuals gain a more complete understanding of a product line from an internal expert. "That gives you the impact of saying I can do now what I couldn't do before," says Riley. "People will feel like they are more part a part of the corporation, rather than just part of the process—and then go home." Riley views the shift as a recommitment to the corporation.

The success that 21st Century corporations achieve through desktop videoconferencing is directly tied to corporate culture, according to David Dirks of Lawrence Livermore National Laboratory. "It depends on how they deploy it and how they migrate desktop videoconferencing into their existing culture." Dirks compares the shift to the PC revolution. "It is the same kind of culture shock for those managers that didn't want to learn how to use a computer." Dirks insists that expectations that managers use the technology may force them into desktop videoconferences when other forms of communication may be more appropriate. Unnecessary use may offset the productivity gains that desktop videoconferencing offers. Bandwidth and network time, particularly for multipoint calls, may take a few years to become negligible. Better video quality and increased functionality may require greater and greater processing power. Dirks compares the potential negatives with those that PC use brought. "Computers were supposed to free us up, but my computer has also enslaved me. I keep having to buy the latest version of Word, which requires more memory. That broadens the technology gap."

Dale Harris, Executive Director of Stanford University's Center for Telecommunications, believes looking at personal videoconferencing in isolation misses the boat. Harris believes the business culture shift will reflect several complimentary technologies that also include corporate intranets and store-and-forward video. As virtual corporations take hold and people meet face-to-face less often, Harris believes organizations must cope with a "psychological barrier" that distance can create. "The way you motivate people may be different," says Harris. Barking orders and delivering ultimatums falls short in managing many people anyway, but when workers are geographically dispersed those approaches are even less effective. "These are very democratizing technologies. They would seem to flatten organizations," according to Harris.

Desktop videoconferencing flattens organizations by increasing the oversight capability of managers. Executives and managers can use the technology to stay in contact with a larger group than they could have otherwise. This eliminates the need for many levels of middle management. Traditionally, executives used middle managers to communicate their vision to lower levels and to find out about what the troops were doing. In many organizations, middle managers were the eyes and ears of executives. "When everyone has this technology, a CEO or senior manager no longer needs that middleman to send and receive information to the troops," says Steve Shao of Project DIANE. With the flattened hierarchies that the technology allows, companies can make strategic decisions more quickly. This reduces the possibility of as Shao puts it, "Getting steamrolled by leaner and meaner smaller companies that in the past they ate them for lunch." So, the technology delivers advantages to both the redefined large corporation and the small company. Size is less of a factor, and approach is almost everything.

Warming Up to Telecommuting

Corporate cultures will increasingly endorse telecommuting, because companies will increasingly discover that virtual work delivers bottom-line results. For this to happen, however, companies must embrace management by results, rather than management by control. "The companies that provide telecommuting ability to their employees will be able to retain their employees," says Louis Belt of Laidlaw Environmental Services. "Besides, virtual offices have much lower overhead, and people are more productive at home any way." Belt believes the move towards telecommuting will decrease business formality. "The days of a coat and tie are already gone. We don't care what they wear—pajamas or what—as long as they get their work done." However, Kevin Pitts who directs the DVC lab for Link-VTC views the impact of real-time video on telecommuters' attire another way. He believes that corporations can encourage better dress by implementing desktop videoconferencing for telecommuting. "The video will take some of the flexibility of working at home away," says Pitts. "You may have to shower and shave and put on a tie."

Belt says that telecommuting should be prevalent based on productivity statistics, but that the move towards virtual working is taking time because the shift is perceived as a dramatic change. "It's hard to export culture. That's the biggest thing. The virtual office would be more popular if it weren't for the trust factor," says Belt. There are many ways that companies can potentially police employees to make sure they are productive. Those include measuring "content on line"—essentially measuring packets—or time on line, according to Belt. These monitoring approaches can have mixed results both in delivering accurate information and in keeping employees happy. Even less effective, say telecommuting experts, would be to monitor professionals through desktop videoconferencing. "Those who micromanage and over police get a decrease in productivity," says Belt. "You just want to make sure that the overall workload at least maintains and hopefully increases." Companies get more than their money's worth from most telecommuters. "You don't have the commute, so people work longer hours," explains Belt. "If you think of something at 7 PM and you have to drive into the office, you're not likely to do it. If all you have to do is turn on the terminal, you're likely to do it."

The work habits of telecommuters have traditionally been obscure to their employers. A manager may see the result with little knowledge of how the employee achieved that result. Because monitoring the process is part of many corporate cultures, telecommuting has run against the grain for many organizations. Dale Harris of Stanford believes personal videoconferencing eliminates some of the mystery of telecommuter work habits for many managers. "They won't have to wait until an employee is done with a project to see if they're doing it," according to Harris. Harris also believes some organizations will ultimately refine telepresence among members of distributed workgroups. He believes more organizations will implement media spaces or constant links to preserve positive attributes of their old cultures. "If you're visionary enough to think that technology will help create virtual organizations, the ability to drop in and bring people together quickly is as important as it is in traditional organizations," insists Harris.

Because people will conduct business from home while refining their communication and collaboration skills in informal workgroups, the lines will blur between business and pleasure. People will conduct business globally well beyond the time constraints of the traditional work day. Also the distinction between business and personal relationships may become fuzzy. "You'll know more about people as human beings in the new business environment," says Christine Perey of Perey Communications.

A new type of speaking engagement

It was still nearly four years before the turn of the century, but PictureTel Chief Scientist Rich Baker was stealing the show at the DVC '96 West conference—and Baker was more than three thousand miles away. Alternating between his PictureTel office and his home office, Baker participated in several conference sessions. While other speakers seemed comparatively dwarfed at the podium, two screens at opposite ends of an auditorium-sized room projected Baker's likeness. He used desktop videoconferencing application sharing functions to display his visual presentation. There was no doubt about it—Baker had taken the power position at the conference. The clincher came when during somebody else's presentation, Baker's young daughter jumped up on her father's knee. "I'm putting my kids to bed tonight," Baker exclaimed as heads turned towards him. The speaker could say only this: "That's a cheap trick." Executives will increasingly fulfill speaking engagements remotely. Not only will this save time, but it will become the signature of the power player. To level the playing field, conference organizers may have to project in-person speakers on the screen as well.

Desktop videoconferencing will also transform the educational speaking engagement—the guest lecture. No longer will the constraints of physical space require specialists to show up in a classroom. Many educators feel something may be lost with the lack of a physical presence. However, many other educators believe that desktop videoconferencing will give students access to authorities worldwide with whom they previously had no contact. "You could have an expert join you and your class for five minutes from his or her desk," says Mark McLellan, Chair of Cornell's Food Science and Technology department. "Our universities of the future will rely more on these experts, and will become more specialized."

Building new networks

As the cost of bandwidth and the price of computing power plummet, new choices will emerge for decision-makers. Author Michael Schrage says the choices are easy when they are limited by economics. When the sky is the limit, however, values matter more. Organizations must decide what they wish to accomplish through building new networks. Rather than focusing on distributing information as the objective, Schrage says the goal of network architects should be creating collaborative relationships. He cites the airplane, the personal computer, and the transistor, among other examples of the results of collaboration. "It's not creative individuals at the core. It's collaborative relationships," says Schrage. Without focusing on the kinds of relationships we want to create, Schrage says we run the risk of designing dysfunctional networks. "The future organizational issue is going to be the creation and management of shared spaces," explains Schrage. His point is that organizational culture should determine network design. Should there be a standard home page for employees on the corporate intranet? Should employees be allowed to share some applications and not others through desktop conferencing?

Network architects can build restrictions into networks. These kinds of guidelines may go too far for some corporate cultures and not far enough for others. The technologies encourage an open exchange of information and increased collaboration. The corporation that implements desktop videoconferencing, video mail, intranets, and other technology may discover that the culture changes drastically. This may boost the bottom line, and propel the corporation to a new level of success. Blindly implementing technology without restrictions and then trying to eliminate access, dictate communication and collaboration guidelines, and rein people in could produce a disaster. It is critical to decide what networks should accomplish and how they should impact relationships before building them.

Competing for the new century

For centuries, companies have shaped and reshaped their business models around new technology. The automobile changed the restaurant industry, giving rise to fast food. The personal computer impacted the publishing business, eliminating the need for involved typesetting and drastically reducing turn-around time. The Internet has changed the marketing and communications businesses, forcing professionals to maximize a new medium. Smart companies have jumped on emerging technologies and incorporated them into their business models. Technology has dragged less innovative organizations kicking and screaming into the next growth phase. Companies that have failed to adapt have disappeared.

Some successful companies will restructure their businesses around desktop video communications, both real-time and stored. Tom Manley of INET Marketing says that businesses that make use of video will compete more effectively. "It's so much more effective to be able to face your business partner or customer," says Manley. "Businesses—even mom-and-pop shops—will be able to form partnerships more easily." However, Manley concedes that there are some hurdles even innovators must get over. "They have to get over their fears and the intimidation of this technology before they'll put money into it. But a company that does this gets a leg up on the competition," Manley insists.

Lingering issues

Dr. Paul Ekman of the University of California School of Medicine, a world-renowned facial expression expert, insists pervasive use of desktop videoconferencing raises many complex issues. Ekman points out that as using the visual medium becomes the standard, it will be harder for businesspeople to choose a less powerful medium that they may prefer. "You'll have to explain why you don't want to be seen," says Ekman. As bandwidth gets cheaper, Ekman wonders whether people will have to pay if they wish to avoid transmitting video in much the same way people pay phone companies to unlist their numbers.

Major legal issues also linger. If a doctor in New York is treating a patient in Pennsylvania through telemedicine, it is unclear which state's laws take precedence. If a company in England is doing business remotely with a company in Japan, it is fuzzy as to which country's laws govern the transactions. Another legal issue for organizations is whether a permanent record will remain of desktop videoconferences. It is safe to assume that many people will record videoconferences for review. However, it is less clear whether organizations would systematically record all videoconferences. According to Paul Ekman, the University of California has access to any e-mail that is sent via the University's system. Because of the legal ramifications of this loss of privacy, Ekman points out that some law firms forbid their attorneys and others from using e-mail either internally or externally. A related issue is whether indicating agreement by nodding one's head during a videoconference holds the same weight legally as an affirmative statement.

Increasing organizational use of personal videoconferencing will shine a spotlight on faces. Looks and grooming will become more important. Ekman believes the technology will make the role of corporate communications professionals more significant. "Organizations will use people who are trained to be able to present messages credibly," says Ekman. And because experts can analyze facial expressions to determine truthfulness, Ekman says "The best way to have someone present a message credibly is for them not to know whether they're lying or telling the truth." However, Ekman points out that his research indicates most people do "rather terribly" in determining whether someone is lying to them.

The potential for overemphasis on physical appearance concerns many in organizations about the role of video communications. Speaking well on the phone is an essential organizational skill. Speech impediments and bad accents do little to bolster a corporate image. Bad haircuts and poor complexions have never been building blocks for a successful corporate image, but video communications technology could make cosmetic issues paramount. "Will we require that only cosmetically-correct people do our communicating?" wonders Ekman.

12

The Competitive Advantage of Personal Videoconferencing

A Shift in Skills

Dictating letters fast and well used to be a prized business skill for executives. Likewise, the ability to take dictation fattened the paychecks of many secretaries. Then came the PC and with it the expectation that most managers would type their own letters. The competitive advantage of dictating letters and taking dictation vanished. New communication skills mattered. Knowing how to use a spell-check program or deciding when to send an e-mail versus leaving a voice mail were among the communication skills that emerged as important.

Mastering communication technology provides a powerful competitive advantage. The more powerful the medium, the more potent the advantage and the more damaging the disadvantage to those who fail to grasp the skills the technology requires. There is no medium more powerful than visual communication, as evidenced by the advent of television. Radio kept voters informed, but television changed politics. Political strategists began structuring campaigns around *photo ops*, and successful politicians learned how to deliver eight-second soundbites for the evening news. As television took hold, winning candidates were those who could communicate effectively on camera. When we heard Neil Armstrong say "One small step for man, one giant leap for mankind," the powerful words stuck with us. But not even those words could compete with television images of Armstrong walking on the moon.

Personal videoconferencing is potentially more powerful than television, because the technology is personal and interactive. Not only can we receive visual information, but we can send it. We can also use the technology to collaborate on documents, applications and whiteboards. With the advent of multicasting, personal computers are now our own mini TV stations. Even without multicasting, personal videoconferencing is an interactive broadcast with an audience of one. While general managers of larger television stations must hire the most effective communicators as their anchors or "talent," our stripped-down operation requires us to master on-camera communication and screen-to-screen collaboration.

The need to become a video communicator and a screen-based collaborator is inescapable. Communicating effectively on-camera and collaborating efficiently through the PC is to the professional of the new century what giving and taking dictation was to the 1960s business person. We must master these skills to succeed. Our ability to compete depends on our approach to communicating and collaborating. The best video communicators and collaborators will thrive in the emerging business environment. Promotions and business opportunities will go to the collabicators. Those who fail to master communication and collaboration will suffer from stalled careers and still-born businesses. Communication skills have always determined success. So has the ability to network. What has changed are the tools.

"The people who have the ability to communicate will have an advantage over people who have difficulty with interpersonal relationships," says Pete Griffin of Tandy Corporation. As people share work spaces electronically, Griffin says the ability to work closely with others becomes more important than giving and receiving orders. Tom Hall, Video Systems Manager and contractor for Hughes Aircraft, believes mastering desktop videoconferencing is critical to advancing careers. "It's usually the best communicator becomes the leader," says Hall. "Being able to use as many tools to accomplish that is important." Hall believes that mastering desktop videoconferencing and application sharing will become part of the job description "no matter what you're doing." He compares the universal nature of the tools to that of spreadsheet and presentation programs.

Desktop video: The midas touch?

Some corporate and government specialists who have sought out videoconferencing as a project to manage have seen their stars rise with the technology. When NASA Engineering Technician Bruce Gilbaugh volunteered for a pilot remote maintenance project, he still had grease under his fingernails. His value to NASA became increasingly apparent, however, as he coordinated desktop video communications between NASA clients and professionals operating the wind tunnel at NASA's base at Moffett Field, California. "There is an advantage. My willingness to explore this technology is what changed my job," says Gilbaugh. "You're going to have to know this stuff. It does open doors." At the end of his first year coordinating desktop videoconferencing, NASA created a special position for Gilbaugh that may put him on a faster track to success.

Allen Helvajian, Senior Project Manager for Wells Fargo, believes coordinating desktop videoconferencing has given him more career options. "You tend to become involved in more strategically important projects, because you are seen as forward-thinking," says Helvajian. What helps is that desktop videoconferencing is increasingly viewed as the tool that sets professionals apart. Therefore, the corporate movers and shakers seek out the technology. Whoever provides the desktop videoconferencing solution gains an advantage. "You have a higher profile. If you have a better product, people will beat a path to your door. In many cases, if you've got a tool that helps them, they'll find you," explains Helvajian.

A recruiter for a major global financial company has seen her star rise since she started using desktop videoconferencing. She uses the technology to connect with college placement professionals and also to communicate with colleagues worldwide. Using the technology effectively has allowed the recruiter to build a network of contacts inside and outside of the company. "It's a great relationship building tool. It's helping my career. Now there's a face to a name in my recruiting network," says the recruiter." Because of her use of personal videoconferencing, the recruiter says her bosses and colleagues view her as somebody who breaks the mold to accomplish something extra. "It positions you to be ahead of the pack. You find the better candidates and do a better job," she says.

Joe Jesson, staff consultant with Amoco, is communicating regularly with the company's Chief Information Officer. That's because Jesson and Amoco CIO Carl Williams both use the technology. "The CIO can call me directly and get a video conversation going. He's likely to do that because he knows he's going to get service," says Jesson. "The ability to get to an actionable decision faster by using desktop videoconferencing has certainly enhanced my career." Jesson points out that his use of the technology has slashed the time it takes him to get answers from others who have also joined the personal videoconferencing club. Also, his involvement with the technology has branded him an expert and given him recognition within Amoco.

Anthony Iorio, ITT's Director of Telecommunications, has championed the use of desktop videoconferencing for applications ranging from teletraining to strategic planning. Because of his leadership, ITT divisions have chalked up efficiency successes. The reputation for creating bottom-line results through desktop videoconferencing has given Iorio a competitive edge. "If I champion use of the technology for all of the people I work with, I become more effective. I can get much more accomplished in less time," explains Iorio. "That's visible to my boss and to the senior staff. That helps me from a career standpoint." However, Iorio points out that in the age of downsizing the benefit of desktop videoconferencing becomes more career-protecting than career-enhancing. "It helps sustain your ability to bring home a paycheck."

Coming up short

Personal videoconferencing will separate the can-do professionals from the can't-do's. Effective use of the technology can give professionals in nearly every field speed and accuracy in networking, making business deals, and completing projects. "It's going to make a huge difference in the ability of the individual to complete and create," says PictureTel Chairman and CEO Norman Gaut. Desktop videoconferencing coupled with store-and-forward video, intranets and the Internet will empower individuals with immense capabilities. The professional who declines the opportunity may get dusted. "It's like the individual who decided they were going to stay with horses when cars came in," says Gaut.

Christine Traut of Andersen Worldwide believes personal videoconferencing is essential to any relationship-based business. This would include accounting, management consulting, law, and many others. Traut feels that particularly in these fields doing without personal videoconferencing could crush a career. "I would not want to be in competition with somebody who had it when I didn't in consulting." Traut compares this kind of strategic disadvantage to finding out that the sister of the CEO of a client company just married a partner of the firm that is your biggest competitor.

Lt. Richard Stakelum, who pioneered the use of desktop videoconferencing for remote maintenance and telemedicine for the US Navy, compares the competitive advantage that personal videoconferencing offers to that of effectively using the PC itself. "For the first few years, people who could do e-mail were very powerful. They were the gods of the Internet," says Stakelum. "Knowledge is power. Video is power." Stakelum believes that unless professionals use personal videoconferencing, they fall behind. "You go out of business, because the other guy's going to learn how to do it. If you don't have the competitive edge, you get edged out." Louis Belt of Laidlaw Environmental Services also uses the PC analogy. Belt points out that those who have mastered their PCs are empowered to accomplish more and can rise through corporate ranks. "Anybody who doesn't embrace the technology falls by the wayside," insists Belt. "The technology is the tool. The person still using the horse and the plough is not going to keep up with the person on the tractor." Belt adds that those who learn to communicate and collaborate the most effectively will see their careers take off. "At some point, those who are on top with videoconferencing are in the catbird's seat. Everybody else will be scrambling to keep up."

Those who fail to use desktop videoconferencing and related technologies will end up on the periphery of organizations. Others using the technology to speed decision making, for example, will effectively exclude non-users from the fast track of solving problems and getting noticed. Stephen Scullen, the Bank of Boston's director of treasury systems, feels that high-profile players in organizations work around people who deliver results more slowly. The professional who masters personal videoconferencing can produce results faster, unlike somebody who avoids the technology or fails to use it effectively. "They will stagnate. Their name will not be thought of when someone says I want to get something done," says Scullen. The videoconferencing project manager of a major technology company agrees. "We have people in this organization who hate videoconferencing, so they ignore it," says the project manager. "I have noticed that these people slowly are being left out. Their information is not up to date."

Dale Harris of Stanford University's Center for Telecommunications believes that desktop videoconferencing along with intranets and store-and-forward video will have a democratizing effect on "the survivors," because of enhanced access to information. However, "People not so good at it may not survive," insists Harris. Harris believes that some professionals within every organization will emerge as the communication and collaboration masters. "Those skills will probably be prized pretty highly within the organization. Such individuals would become more important in a hurry." So profound is the potential impact of personal videoconferencing and other emerging communication and collaboration technologies that Harris believes those who fail to learn the necessary skills could forfeit success. "We are moving into an era that could be analogous to another era a hundred years ago when only a small amount of people could read and write," says Harris.

Tom Manley of INET Marketing believes that the sooner a professional adopts desktop videoconferencing or coordinates its use within an organization, the greater the competitive advantage. "At some point, it'll be a device like the telephone where you'll just have to pick it up and use it," says Manley. At that point, the pervasiveness of the technology will limit the competitive advantage. Meantime, however, "Understanding the technology is going to enhance someone's career. It is something they should be thinking about in terms of their role in a company. It's important to make the business case for desktop videoconferencing." Manley suggests that professionals should consider how the technology can make them and their peers more effective.

Perhaps the most important edge that desktop videoconferencing offers professionals is the ability to make decisions and solve problems faster than the next person. Speed can boost careers. While traditional communicators are calling colleagues on the phone to explain complex subjects, the collabicator is meanwhile showing and solving the problem through personal videoconferencing. Hussein ElBadaly of Consolidated Edison believes the golden egg that the technology lays is "content." "If I show you information and get the job done in a few seconds, it's more than I see you and you see me," says ElBadaly. "Desktop videoconferencing can show the status and progress of jobs and projects. The person who can show a problem and get it resolved, for example, has an advantage.

The competitive advantage that desktop videoconferencing provides relates directly to risk. The greater implementation risk a manager takes, the higher the potential payoff. With that risk, however, comes the possibility of stubbing one's toe. The cultural impact of the technology can raise eyebrows in some organizations. Unlike changing the font on forms or some other more mundane business process switch, desktop videoconferencing is a high-profile shift. Despite the risk, Anthony Iorio of ITT believes that the potential career payoff far outweighs the risk of ruffling some feathers. "If you want to become a facilitator and look for opportunities to introduce the technology into business operations and do things more effectively, that can bode well for an individual," says Iorio. "You are a change agent. And we can't do business the way we've done it in the past."

The edge changes

Two important business skills today may become eclipsed tomorrow. One is writing, and the other is public speaking. Literature-fanciers and leisure readers will always appreciate a good book or well-written article. However, the impact of writing within organizations may change. Traditionally, masters of the written word gained an edge by writing the best memos, crafting the most effective plans, and developing the most convincing proposals. As technology speeds up processes, executives and managers will increasingly make decisions based on store-and-forward video presentations and real-time video sessions. "The people who can write brilliantly are in the driver's seat right now," according to Christine Traut of Andersen Worldwide. "In the networked world, they will be less dominant and less relevant." Of course, the professional who enhances his or her writing skills with video communication and collaboration ability is better prepared to compete than those who are unable to write.

Judith Hamilton, National Semiconductor's videoconferencing project manager, also believes that on-camera communication ability could eclipse writing skills. Hamilton offers the example of an excellent technical writer who did a great job boiling down highly technical things into laymen's terms. "But when I met that person face-to-face, they were almost painfully shy. If they're painfully shy behind their monitor, it may be a hindrance to them."

Public speaking ability has traditionally turned professionals into leaders and made executives out of managers. Increasingly, face-to-face speaking ability alone will fall short. The skills required for effective video communication differ from those used in front of live audiences. Video, like television, is a far more intimate medium that places a greater premium on one-on-one communication ability. Those who lecture or do group presentations can get by face-to-face. However, this approach falls flat on video regardless of audience size. The most effective talk show hosts, news anchors, and politicians come across on television as if they are talking to an audience of one—you. Those who address the universe of television viewers encourage their audience of one to flip the channel or grab another snack from the kitchen.

The shift in communication skills has particular impact on teaching. Succeeding in distance education requires adopting one-on-one communication skills as students increasingly take courses remotely. The distance educator must compete with infinite potential distractions in the student's remote environment. That teacher must captivate his or her audience of one by hoisting the student out of his or her easy chair and taking them on an adventure in learning. Many educators worry about the shift in skills that may be necessary to keep current in their field. Some believe the technology falls short in delivering what it promises. One internationally known professor says his concern is that the technology prevents him from effectively seeing the members of his audience. "I change what I do during my lectures. If I see somebody's nodding off, I change my voice or I move forward on the stage. If I gave a lecture and I could see only one person at a time, then my presentation is canned."

Desktop videoconferencing spotlights organizational skills. The most organized professionals gain an edge in the video networked world. Talking by phone and faxing a requested document allows the disorganized professional to find the information and assemble it before sending the document. Desktop videoconferencing forbids the luxury of lag time. The professional who requires the most time to regroup ends up on the short end. Anthony Iorio of ITT agrees that communication skills become paramount in the video networked world. "You really have to stay focused," says Iorio. "I have access to everything I need in my office. Any file that I need is available. I can talk about any topic that comes up."

Learning to listen

The ability to listen actively and effectively becomes more important in a media-rich communication and collaboration environment. As professionals work together through shared spaces, success will depend as much on the input of other team members. Therefore, sharpening listening skills becomes critical. Traditionally, listening means using your ears. However, desktop videoconferencing requires users to listen with their eyes as well. Discovering objections, for example, through evaluating body language gives a professional an edge. He or she can ask a follow-up question to establish the objection, discuss it, and perhaps eliminate it. "All of us are bad listeners," says Stephen Scullen of the Bank of Boston. "Desktop videoconferencing gives us the opportunity to interact more directly. The quicker people can absorb information that others contribute, the more effective they become."

Appearance matters

Desktop videoconferencing may shift the emphasis from ideas and content to physical appearance and personality. One videoconferencing network manager for a major international bank says many people who failed to fit in the mainstream gained ground because of e-mail. Desktop videoconferencing could cause a set-back for this group of professionals. The videoconferencing manager uses computer clubs as an example. "You could see people who looked horrible. Because you had to meet them first online, you had already connected with them and didn't care as much how they looked." The videoconferencing manager believes that people who worry about being bald or about their dress and appearance may avoid desktop videoconferencing. "These things will matter, because unfortunately this is human nature. Most of us cannot stop judging people based on how they look, even though it has nothing to do with the capability of the person. While physical attributes gained at birth offer no indication of ability, the aspects of appearance that people can control may offer clues to their thinking and work habits. Somebody who fails to comb her hair or straighten his tie may indicate a lax approach to doing business. These visual clues send messages. In these cases, physical appearance includes content.

There is traditionally a gap between how others see us and how we see ourselves. Often, people never realize how others see them. This is how distracting habits develop including slow blink, lip licking, eye dart, fast blink, and face-rubbing. These habits send visual messages the way poor grammar and spelling do in written communication. The message may be a lack of confidence, nervousness or dishonesty. Therefore, the language our faces speak can have a major impact on business relationships and deals. Personal videoconferencing emphasizes bad habits, because the face usually fills the screen. However, desktop videoconferencing also provides the solution, because the technology allows people to see themselves as others see them. Martha Gorman of Bassett Healthcare believes that desktop videoconferencing will drive people to improve their communication skills. "If I can see myself, I might improve body language, the way I talk, my eye glass frames, clothes, and the colors I choose," says Gorman. "If I see that I have some mannerisms that are distracting, I'm more likely to change them." Gorman adds that she believes these changes are more than superficial, because they impact self esteem.

People who refuse to improve their on-camera communication skills may lose their edge. However, there are always exceptions. Gorman tells the story of the corporation she visited in which everybody wore dark suits. One fellow stuck out, because he was wearing an old, rust-colored corduroy jacket and cheap-looking shoes. It became quickly apparent, though, that this fellow was the brains of the organization. He could get away with sending out negative messages in his appearance, because he was a genius. Says Gorman, "The rest of us will clean up or perish."

Because companies will increasingly use personal videoconferencing to interview internal and external job candidates, on-camera presentation skills become critical to the professional seeking another position. As companies globalize, they will rely on technology even more to boost efficiency in recruiting and promoting. Kristi Moushon of Caterpillar believes video skills can determine promotions. "If I can't communicate well over video or I don't know which colors work best, that might impact career opportunities," says Moushon.

Striving to become Clark Kent...or Dan Rather

Professionals who advance will increasingly need to acquire the skills of news reporters. These skills include digging up information quickly. Professionals need to know how to use personal videoconferencing, intranets, the Internet and other emerging communication technology to access experts and collective knowledge. "It's a revolution, and so far we're seeing only the pinpricks of change," says Norman Gaut of PictureTel. Gaut believes the required shift in skills must impact education. He compares effective desktop videoconferencing and Internet skills with learning to drive. "If you're not familiar with it and if you don't feel comfortable with it as a child, you won't be able to use it effectively as an adult." Not only must children learn these skills, but also adults must do their best to acquire them.

Access and exposure

Catching the eye of senior executives is critical to any corporate player looking to advance through the ranks. Traditionally, writing effective memos and getting the nod to join high-level meetings put managers in the limelight and provided a path to promotion. Desktop videoconferencing will increasingly become the technology that plugs professionals into the advancement track. "Top people within corporations will be accessible through these technologies," says Fred Parnon of Parnon & Pratt. "If you can't use them effectively, you won't have access to top people. You'll be out."

Exposure within an organization can also fuel a career. The more visible the project, the more credit the person coordinating the project receives. Using desktop videoconferencing often spotlights both the project and the person. "Desktop videoconferencing tends to attach a name to a face and an action to a face," says Stephen Scullen of the Bank of Boston. "What this will provide to the individual is more exposure." The flip side, however, is that a failed project in which desktop videoconferencing is used may draw more attention as well.

Still, many users of desktop videoconferencing believe that video is the least important aspect of the technology. This group considers that the collaborative functions are paramount. "In the short term, they are absolutely right," according to Hussein ElBadaly of Consolidated Edison. However, "Those are the same people who in another era were attacking the phone." ElBadaly believes the video doubters need more information and vision about the potential of video links and how they can enhance collaborative functions so that problems can be solved faster.

Parnon of Parnon & Pratt feels strongly that the video doubters could fall behind. "They're wrong. They're missing the whole point about what videoconferencing is all about, which is communication among people," says Parnon. "Document sharing is fine. But when you want to talk to a person, what's better...sending documents back and forth or seeing them." Christine Traut of Andersen Worldwide insists, "There is no rational argument that video is not important." VIVO President and CEO Staffan Ericsson says, "People are grossly underestimating how much we rely on our visual senses when they say that the video is not important." For those who believe video is unnecessary or distracting, there is always the option of capping the camera lens or minimizing the video window. In some professional environments, this option may fly. In other situations, however, avoiding video may backfire. Dr. Michael Kleper of the National Technical Institute for the Deaf is practical about the impact of avoiding video. He believes that if an organization deploys desktop videoconferencing, the expectation will be that people appear on camera. "If people turned off their cameras, it would have to be on their performance appraisals," says Kleper.

Manipulating your environment

Personal videoconferencing allows a professional to unleash the power of television to achieve results. Your videoconferencing audience of one or of many only gets what you give them. That creates the opportunity to manipulate your environment and gain an advantage. With a few props and simple backdrops, an office becomes a mini television studio. The purpose of the studio is to create an illusion. A city backdrop, for example, might give a suburban-based business more panache. An official seal in the background might elevate the importance of a professional.

Steve Shao of Project DIANE tells the story of a research and development executive of France Telecom who traveled to mid Tennessee for meetings with state development officials. His trip would have forced him to cancel a speaking engagement for the 50th Anniversary of D-Day in his home country. Shao developed a solution. The man's staff brought along photographs and banners commemorating the D-Day invasion. Shao set up the desktop videoconference at his office at Tennessee State University. "There was this huge backdrop. He had a tremendous, powerful presence because he could manipulate his environment," says Shao. "It looked like he was in the office of the President of France." To the audience gathered in Paris, the presentation on a 16-foot screen looked impressive. "They didn't know he was in a small computer lab," says Shao.

Shao has also manipulated desktop videoconferencing environments to entertain children. Project DIANE has done "virtual Santa Claus" over desktop videoconferencing. To make the experience more like a visit to the North Pole, Shao and his team bought wrapping paper with the biggest design they could find. They created a powerful effect by putting paper with huge snowflakes behind Santa. "This is somewhere between TV and reality. You can use these so-called telepresences," explains Shao. Likewise, the professional who masters the technology can manipulate his or her environment to enhance a message they are communicating. A bookcase might communicate scholarly work. A photograph of a waterfall might display a commitment to the environment.

Savvy professionals can borrow a bit from event planners of political campaigns. The backdrop that appears on television is rarely an accident. Everything and everybody from the schoolchildren behind the candidate to the hard hats in front of the camera platform were placed there for effect. While too much attention to these details is overkill for desktop videoconferencing, understanding the power of the visual medium and how environments can be manipulated is critical to maintaining an edge.

Some professionals take their cues from the television industry in designing their offices. Since the typical office is poorly lit, these professionals seek out television lights. Videssence, a California company, provides lighting to compliment desktop videoconferencing. These lights are cartridges that can be attached to ceilings. Paul Costa, a former NBC News field producer, runs the company. "The great failing of video communication is that these technologies are not designed on an artistic or personal basis," says Costa. Effective personal videoconferencing communicators pay attention to how their faces are lit, regardless of whether they invest in professional lights.

At the opposite end of the spectrum from the professional wishing to convert his or her office into a mini TV studio is the environmental slob. Every organization has a few. Often they are top producers, but keeping a tidy desk and office is apparently no priority for them. A videoconferencing project manager at a major computer hardware company describes a brilliant professional who writes top-notch reports and memos. The professional structures his thoughts well in writing, and that communicates an impression that the professional is organized. However, this professional's office resembles a disaster zone. As the company deploys desktop videoconferencing and the professional's office appears on camera, the credibility of that person could nose dive if he fails to clean up his act. At the very least, sloppy desk diehards should try to keep their mess out of the camera's view.

Leveling the playing field

Desktop videoconferencing gives disabled workers, particularly those confined to a wheelchair, the ability to avoid the mobility barrier. They can work from home, while collaborating and communicating with clients and colleagues. The technology can become an equalizer by eliminating the notion that the disabled are different from the rest of the workforce. Nobody sees a wheelchair, for example, during a desktop videoconference. The Disabled professional who maximizes video communication and collaboration gains an advantage over the non-disabled worker who lags behind in adopting the technology effectively. Deaf professionals, who are unable to use the telephone, gain the ability to conduct business and communicate remotely. They know better than most that the role of e-mail as a medium is limited. "This is the way deaf people want to communicate—visually," says Michael Kleper of the National Technical Institute for the Deaf. "Typing back and forth has been wonderful, but the ideal is video face-to-face because sign language is very rich."

The Remote Management Edge

Managing distributed workers requires different skills than supervising people in adjacent cubicles. The project manager of a virtual work team faces challenges that the traditional manager never faced. The opportunity may never come to assemble the entire team in one physical location for a meeting. Therefore, the technology places a premium on communicating effectively. While mediocre communicators could survive—and sometimes thrive—as managers in the past, they will see their stock decline. "People who aren't good at communicating fear the telecommuter environment or the spread-out work group," says Peter Lee, senior telecommunications specialist with Novacor Chemicals. "Those who can't adapt will have to get rid of the idea of being a team leader." Lee believes these managers will have to accept demotions or leave organizations. Lee points out that the manager who fails to look up from paperwork while talking to a team member is communicating miserably. That approach looks even worse via the more intimate medium of video. "It makes you concentrate more on people you're communicating with, which is critical," says Lee.

The role of the virtual work team manager is more of a facilitator and coordinator. The manager encourages critical thinking and learns how to get the most from each team member. Rather than dictating policy to specialists on the team, the manager encourages team members to disagree and debate points they feel strongly about. This prevents teams from ignoring critical issues that may impact production, marketing or whatever the objective may be. According to Lee of Novacor, "You must be prepared to disagree and to defend your position to the workgroup through desktop videoconferencing."

Power Players

Personal videoconferencing coupled with virtual approaches to doing business will create a geographically-dispersed group of power players. "Those people can call the shots. They get paid based on value rather than time," insists Fred Parnon of Parnon & Pratt. These experts can provide consulting and expert input to corporations on high-impact projects. These masters of video communication and collaboration can live anywhere they wish and make good livings.

While traditionally the most able professionals had to sign up with a corporation, personal videoconferencing and other technology is giving the power player the freedom to sell his or her expertise to the highest bidder.

Therefore, these professionals may work for many corporations on a project basis. "Rather than the corporation, the single unit of effective delivery could become the individual," says Mark McClellan, Chair of Cornell's Food Science and Technology Department. "We'll move towards not associating with a particular company." McClellan uses desktop videoconferencing over the Internet to avoid a 2½ hour commute. He believes people will frequently work six months for one company and then join another team for another six months. "The advantage is the ability to customize the workforce and optimize it so you can get access to the best people," says McLellan. "The disadvantage is you become a one-man band." McLellan believes that some people may have difficulty operating in a virtual work team environment. They would either fall out of the workforce or seek retraining.

Some believe that the window of opportunity for power collabicators is short. As the technology becomes pervasive, the ability to communicate and collaborate through video will become basic. Then, there is no competitive advantage to mastering the medium. There is only a competitive disadvantage to those who fall short. "Once everyone's caught up, it will just be the way people do business," says Kyle Krajewski of Contempo Realty. "Those who do not go this route will be displaying their inability to adapt to the changing times. It will be financially constraining for them."

Fighting fear and winning

A change as profound as personal videoconferencing is scary for many people. Some feel that the immediacy of video communication and screen-to-screen collaboration could trip them up. Many professionals are insecure about their ability to actively collaborate or their ability to come across effectively through the technology. After all, personal videoconferencing is a participatory—rather than a spectator—sport. Others view the technology as a threat to their jobs. They feel that as PCs do more, people will do less. Still others believe the way they have done their jobs for years has worked fine, and "if it ain't broke, don't fix it." There are elements of both truth and hyperbole to all of these arguments. However, profound change is inevitable. Fighting desktop videoconferencing, store-and-forward video, the Internet, and intranets is futile.

Every reader of this book is capable of making the transition into the personal video age. Developing new communication and collaboration skills can turn traditional managers and professionals into 21st Century collabicators. The best way to overcome fear is to learn. Take a chance that you will flop as an on-camera communicator and screen-to-screen collaborator. Start using the technology, and make mistakes.

In many ways, the word *technology* is threatening. The word turns off many people who have limited or no computer skills. So, forget the word. Soon advanced user interfaces and features will make the technology transparent and desktop videoconferencing as easy as using the phone. The phone is certainly technology, but we rarely think of it that way. Hussein ElBadaly of Consolidated Edison suggests thinking of personal videoconferencing as "a vehicle to take you from one place to another." And the sooner we arrive at results, the more time we have for ourselves. Personal videoconferencing is one element in a palette of collabication capabilities. Through these tools, we may gain the opportunity to achieve more in our personal and professional lives.

Appendix

The application is critical to choosing desktop videoconferencing systems. So before you evaluate systems, you should have a good idea of your organization's primary and potential uses of personal videoconferencing. Next comes establishing criteria, the most basic of which include the hardware platform and the transport type. The ability to communicate both inside and outside of the organization through personal videoconferencing is key. It is also important that the system allow easy integration of emerging standards and technologies.

Personal videoconferencing systems can be grouped in two major ways, one involving the compression approach and the other relating to the transport choice. Compression categories include software-only, hardware-only, and hardware-assist. Transport categories include LAN solutions, ISDN solutions, POTS products, Internet approaches, and a solution that provides television-quality, analog video throughout a campus environment with a WAN gateway.

The following is a listing of personal videoconferencing systems arranged in the alphabetical order of vendors. These systems comply—or will soon comply—with international standards, unless otherwise noted.

Aeontech International AEON *AVShare*

Versions: N/A

Description: AEON *AVShare* is a desktop videoconferencing kit operating over the Internet, LAN/WAN and POTS.

Platform: PC

Description: Desktop videoconferencing kit operating over POTS, LAN/WAN, and the Internet

Requirements:

- 486/33 CPU
- 4 MB RAM
- 4 MB hard disk space
- Windows 3.1, Windows NT
- Microsoft Mouse
- VGA Graphics

Video Compression Type: Software

Video Codec/Resolution: N/A / 12-15 fps @ 160 × 120 at 28.8 kbps DSVD

Audio Encoding: N/A

WAN Protocols/Transmission: N/A

LAN Protocols Supported: TCP/IP

Features: Shared workspace with editing tools, two-way teletype, phone book with saved images, video mail with voice, call announce or auto answer, remote selection of video sources and image quality, file transfer, voice/data switching on single line, image capture-compression-display

Includes:

- *AVShare* software
- 1/3" CCD color camera
- video capture board
- 28.8 DSVD modem

Multipoint: Multipoint on LAN/WAN

Freeware/Shareware: N/A

Phone (sales): 886 2 914 6677

Phone (tech support): 886 2 914 6688

Fax: 886 2 914 6688

WWW: N/A

Address: 6F-1, No. 94, Pao Chung Road, Hsin Tien City, Taipei Hsien, Taiwan

Apple *QuickTime Conferencing*

Versions: Software-only, *QuickTime Conferencing Kit, QuickTime Conferencing ISDN kit* (upgrade)

Description: A desktop videoconferencing and collaboration add-on kit for Macintosh.

Platform: Mac

Requirements:

- Any Macintosh AV model or AV Power Macintosh
- 16 MB RAM
- System 7.5 or later
- PlainTalk Microphone
- ISDN service, Internet connection, or Ethernet (TCP/IP or Apple protocols)
- NT1 (for ISDN) or network adapter (for LAN)

Video Compression Type: Software

Video Codec/Resolution: Photo-JPEG, Apple Video, H.261- FCIF at 10 fps, QCIF at 13 fps

Audio Encoding: G.711, G.722, G.728, MACE
WAN Protocols/Transmission: ISDN, POTS/ up to 128 kbps

LAN Protocols Supported: TCP/IP, IsoEthernet, Ethernet, ATM, FDDI, X.25

Features: Easily extensible architecture to support video mail, medical imaging, distance learning; supports desktop broadcasting, shared whiteboard, application sharing, ability to record *QuickTime Conferencing* sessions.

Includes:

- software-only or *QuickTime Conferencing Kit*: Apple Media Conference software
- QTC system extension
- QTC Camera 100, cables

QuickTime Conferencing ISDN Kit: This is an upgrade to the *QuickTime Conferencing Kit*. It includes a NuBus expansion card which provides the ISDN connection as well as an H.320-compliant hardware codec (for compression and decompression), QTC H.320 software, a telephone handset, cables. Kit is available in NuBus and PCI versions. Nt1 slated to ship with PCI kits.

Multipoint: Over LAN and Internet, MCU needed over ISDN

Freeware/Shareware: Yes

Phone: 408-996-1010

Fax: 408-996-0275

WWW: http://qtc.quicktime.apple.com

Address: 1 Infinite Loop, Cupertino, CA 95014

AT&T *VISTIUM* (Discontinued)

Versions: *VISTIUM Personal Video 1200, Personal Video 1300*

Description: A family of products that can improve productivity by uniting and expanding the capabilities of your most powerful desktop tools—the PC and telephone.

Platform: PC

Requirements:

- 486DX/33 MHz CPU (486DX2/66 MHz recommended) for 1200
- 386/486DX/33 MHz CPU (486DX2/33 MHz recommended) for 1300
- 8 MB RAM (12 MB RAM recommended)
- 10 MB available hard disk space
- Windows 3.1
- MS DOS version 5.0
- PC-AT bus architecture (ISA bus)
- VGA or higher resolution
- Two adjacent 16-bit (AT) slots available for 1300

One 16-bit (AT) slot available for 1200 plus one additional slot for TM-BRI, SW56 or V.35 interface

Video Compression Type: Hardware

Video Codec/Resolution: FCIF (352×288) at 10-15 fps, CIF (352×240), QCIF (176×144) at 15 to 30 fps.

Audio Encoding: G.711, G.728

WAN Protocols/Transmission: ISDN-BRI, Switched 56, V.35/112 to 128 kbps

LAN Protocols: N/A

Features: Application sharing, shared whiteboard, still image (JPEG) sharing, scalable video window, multipoint capable, Picture-in-picture.

Includes:

- video codec
- ISDN interface card
- camera, speaker
- Vistium Share collaboration software. Vistium 1300 includes a PC

Multipoint: Yes

Freeware/Shareware: N/A

Phone: 1-800-VIDEO-GO

Fax: 908-658-8443

WWW: http://www.att.com

Address: 55 Corporate Drive, Bridgewater, NJ 08807

Applied Communication Concepts *Interact*

Versions: N/A

Description: Videoconferencing and collaboration add-on kit for PC's via software added to multimedia I/O capable PC's. Product is capable of working at various bandwidths, but very low cost POTS and Internet connectivity are emphasized: PC-PC through POTS network or PC-PC modem to LAN through the Internet or LAN to LAN through the Internet.

Platform: PC (Mac on special request)

Requirements:

- Pentium processor
- Windows 95 or Windows 3.x
- 8 MB RAM (20 MB RAM for better performance)

Video Compression Type: In development

Video Codec/Resolution: In development

Audio Encoding: Various

WAN Protocols/Transmission: POTS, TCP/IP

LAN Protocols: TCP/IP

Features: Unusually complete and powerful whiteboard, shared visual workspace, still image, graphics, annotations, photos, video clips, audio clips, chat, audio and video conversation, folders, application sharing, software multipoint, ability to work in modem/normal phone environments. Intuitive operation, computer skill is not required. Camera and scanner support integrated in the software. Conversion capability for popular file formats.

Includes: Software

Multipoint: Software-only multipoint through the Internet. Number of persons "present" can be very large; number of persons "active simultaneously" depends on the connected bandwidth.

Freeware/Shareware: Undecided

Phone: 919-544-9450

Fax: 919-544-9384

WWW: N/A

Address: P.O. Box 13344, Research Triangle Park, North Carolina 27709

Avistar *Collaboration System*

Versions: N/A

Description: Avistar is a family of collaboration products that includes television-quality analog videoconferencing over a separate video LAN, document conferencing and visual directory applications.

Platform: PC, Mac, Workstation
Requirements:

PC client:

- 386/33 CPU
- Windows 3.1 or Windows for Workgroups
- 4 MB RAM
- 5 MB available hard disk space
- WinSock 1.1 compliant TCP/IP stack
- Ethernet adapter
- 1 ISA slot
- Monitor or TV

Mac client:

- 68030 or greater or Power Macintosh with A/V card or one available NuBus slot
- System 7.0
- 3 MB RAM
- 5 MB available hard disk space
- Ethernet adapter
- Color monitor or TV
- Mac TCP version 2

Sun client:

- Sun SparcStation
- SunOS 4.x or Solaris 2.x
- Sun TCP/IP
- Ethernet adapter
- 1 SBus slot
- Monitor or TV

Video Compression Type: N/A
Video Codec/Resolution: Analog system for local area calls—choice of codecs over the WAN/ 30 fps NTSC or PAL and SECAM frame rate variable for local area calls.
Audio Encoding: N/A
WAN Protocols/Transmission: N/A
Features: Shared whiteboard, application sharing, file transfer, network and session management, visual directory.
Includes:

- color camera
- video LAN interface module

- audio input/microphone, Avistar switches
- patch panel and cable for server
- collaboration software
- session management software

Multipoint: Yes
Freeware/Shareware: No
Phone: 415-617-1350
Fax: 415-617-1351
Email: info@avistar.com
Address: 505 Hamilton Avenue, Palo Alto, CA 94301

BBN *Corporation Video Network Access Device (VNAD)*

Versions: N/A
Description: The *VNAD* is a PC-based platform that enables both room-based and desktop videoconferencing systems to operate over IP-based local and wide area networks.
Platform: PC
Requirements:

- Pentium Processor
- High-density 3.5 floppy drive
- Windows 95 or Windows 3.11
- 8 MB RAM
- Microsoft multicast TCP/IP protocol stack
- 16-bit ISA Ethernet board
- Synchronous HDLC board
- VNAD Videoconferencing Control Software

Video Compression Type: No compression-transport layer product
Video Codec/Resolution: Many codecs supported including PictureTel, VTEL, CLI and NEC
Audio Encoding: All supported
WAN Protocols/Transmission: TCP/IP
LAN Protocols Supported: TCP/IP, HDLC
Features: Reduces management and operation costs by leveraging existing packet-based network infrastructure, conducts multipoint videoconferencing without an external MCU, operates on a standard PC platform and interoperates with most commercial codec platforms.
Includes: The *VNAD* comes complete with full-featured software capability. A Pentium PC platform is optional

Multipoint: Implements IP multicast to provide multipoint conferencing without the need for an external MCU.
Freeware/Shareware: N/A
Phone: 800-825-4730
Fax: 617-873-5421
WWW: http://www.bbn.com
Address: 150 Cambridge Park Drive, Cambridge, MA 02140

Bitfield Oy *MediaMaster*

Versions: N/A
Description: Desktop videoconferencing and collaboration add-on kit for PCs, supporting ISDN, POTS, and LAN
Platform: PC, Mac, Sun
Requirements for PC:

- 486/66 CPU
- Windows 95, Windows 3.1
- 8 MB RAM
- VGA with 256 K color
- 2 ISA bus slots
- ISDN service
- NT1

Video Compression Type: Hardware
Video Codec/Resolution: H.263, H.261-5 frames per second at FCIF at 128 kbps or with VideoBooster daughterboard 30 fps @ FCIF at 2 Mbps
Audio Compression: G.711, G.722, G.728, G.723
WAN Protocols/Transmission: POTS, B-ISDN, P-ISDN, T1, E1up to 2 Mbps
LAN Protocols Supported: TCP/IP, Net BIOS
Features: Shared whiteboard, application sharing, file transfer.
Includes:

- camera
- codec & ISDN board
- DataBeam FarSite collaboration software
- microphone
- speakers

Freeware/Shareware: No
Multipoint: Yes

Phone (Sales):

- 310-322-9863 (USA)
- +358-0-5024 2213 (Finland)

Phone (Tech. Support): +358-0-5024 2250
Fax:

- 310-322-9867 (USA)
- 358-0-455 2240 (Finland)

WWW: http://www.bitfield.fi
Address: Ukonvaaja 2, 02130 Espoo, Finland

BT Visual Images *VC 7000*

Platform: Stand alone
Description: Stand-alone video unit for use on ISDN circuits. Capable of PC collaboration via data ports that permit PCs to be added to the link and file sharing to take place at the same time as the video without screen sharing.
Video Compression Type: Hardware-assist
Video Codec/Resolution: H.263,H.261 - 15 fps @ FCIF and 30 fps @ QCIF at 128 kbps.
Audio Compression: G.711 3.1 kHz 56 or 64 kbps, G.722 7 kHz 48, 56 or 64, G.728 3.1 kHz 16 kbps
WAN Protocols/Transmission: ISDN-BRI, POTS, Switched 56/ 56 to 128 kbps
LAN Protocols Supported: TCP/IP, Net BIOS, IsoEthernet
Features: Picture-in-picture, phone book, snapshot, video mute, hands-free or handset operation, easy installation by connecting two cables, weighs less than 40 pounds, PC-to-PC file transfers through a built-in 9.6 kbps data port.
Includes:

- single unit including color CCD camera
- 9-inch color NTSC monitor
- keypad
- microphone

Options provided by BT include:

- miniature graphics stand, 20-inch color monitor
- auxiliary camera
- switched 56 cables
- echo canceller (full duplex audio)
- protective bag

Other options supported include:

- personal computer
- slide-to-video converter
- videoprinter
- auxiliary camera

Multipoint: Yes
Freeware/Shareware: N/A
Phone: 800-778-6288
Fax: 703-709-4231
Address: 360 Herndon Parkway, Suite 2200, Herndon, VA 22070-4820

BT Visual Images *Portrait Videophone* (*VC 9000*)

Platform: Stand alone
Description: Videophone
Requirements: ISDN service, NT1
Video Compression Type: Hardware-assist
Video Codec/Resolution: 15 fps @ QCIF at 128 kbps
Audio Encoding: G.728, G.711, G.722
WAN Protocols/Transmission: 56 to 128 kbps
LAN Protocols: N/A
Features: File transfer through PC connection, portable, screen tilt, phone book, hands-free or handset operation, calling line identification display.
Includes:

- single unit including 6" liquid crystal display
- color CCD camera
- keypad
- microphone

Multipoint: N/A
Freeware/Shareware: N/A
Phone: 800-778-6288
Fax: 703-709-4231
Address: 360 Herndon Parkway, Suite 2200, Herndon, VA 22070-4820

Casio PhoneMate *LT-70P* Videophone and *Image Tel* Videophone

Versions: *LT-70P* and *Image Tel* (customized for telesurveillance)
Description: Videophone
Platform: PC or TV

Requirements:

- Analog telephone
- TV or PC (requires RGB-NTSC converter and a video capture board)
- Analog telephone line

Video Compression Type: Hardware

Video Codec/Resolution: Modified JPEG Standard resolution is 128 x 112 dots (24 kbits), high resolution is 512 x 224 dots (160 kbits)

Audio Encoding: N/A

WAN Protocols/Transmission: 14,400/9,600 (full duplex modem). Transmission time is 3.5 seconds/image for standard resolution and 30 seconds/frame for high resolution.

LAN Protocols: N/A

Features: Full-screen, high resolution color transmitter with simultaneous voice, Picture-in-picture, portable, ability to transmit images captured with camcorder or digital camera, ability to store images in internal memory or record onto VCR, ability to print images. *ImageTel* is designed for telesurveillance.

Includes:

- videophone
- wireless remote control
- modular cables
- AV cable
- AC cord
- 2 AA batteries

Multipoint: N/A

Freeware/Shareware: N/A

Phone:

- 800-DEMOVIEW
- 310-618-9910, Ext. 639

Fax: 310-212-6316

Address: 20665 Manhattan Place, Torrance, CA 90501

CINECOM Corporation *CineVideo/Direct*

Versions: N/A

Description: Desktop videoconferencing over POTS, ISDN, LAN or WAN.

Platform: PC

Requirements:

- Windows 95 or Windows NT or Windows 3.1
- 486/66 CPU

- 8 MB RAM
- 1 MB hard disk space
- VGA monitor
- 28.8 kbps modem

Video Compression Type: Software
Video Codec/Resolution: Proprietary/ 15 fps @ 160 x 120 at 128 kbps
Audio Encoding: Enhanced GSM
WAN Protocols/Transmission: ISDN-BRI, POTS, any other network supporting TCP/IP
LAN Protocols Supported: TCP/IP
Features: Text chat window, resizable viewport, supports color and black & white video, full duplex audio.
Includes:

- software
- Quickcam camera (b&w)
- microphone

Multipoint: No
Freeware/Shareware: Yes
WWW: http://www.cinecom.com
Phone (sales): 888-246-8101
Phone (tech support): 703-680-4733
Fax: 703-680-1697
Address: 15621 Neath Drive, Woodbridge, VA 22193

CLI *Desktop Video 1000*

Versions: N/A
Description: Desktop videoconferencing and collaboration add-on kit for PCs
Platform: PC
Requirements:

- Pentium/66 MHz CPU
- Windows 95, Windows 3.11, Windows for Workgroups 3.11
- 8 MB RAM
- PCI bus
- 15 MB free hard disk space
- CD-ROM drive
- VGA monitor with 64 K color

Video Compression Type: Hardware

Video Codec/Resolution: H.261/ FCIF at up to 15 frames per second, QCIF at up to 30 frames per second
Audio Compression: G.711, G.728
Transmission: 56 to 128 kbps (Model 1000)
Features: Shared whiteboard, file transfer, JPEG still image compression, G3 and G4 document compression, on-screen dial pad, on-screen phonebook, manual and auto answer, Remote/local TWAIN scanner control, Picture-In-Picture, scaleable video-in-a-window size.
Includes:

- single PCI board codec with ISDN interface
- digital video camera
- telephone handset
- software

Options include:

- headset
- speakerphone
- support for Intel ProShare Premier collaboration software

Multipoint: Yes
Freeware/Shareware: No
Phone (Sales): 408-428-6732
Phone (Tech Support): 800-767-2254
Fax: 408-922-5429
WWW: http://www.clix.com
Address: 350 Plumeria, San Jose, CA 95134-1900

CLI *Desktop Video 2000*

Versions: N/A
Description: Desktop videoconferencing and collaboration add-on kit for PCs.
Platform: PC
Requirements:

- Pentium/66 MHz CPU
- Windows 95, Windows 3.11, Windows for Workgroups 3.11
- 8 MB RAM
- PCI Bus
- 15 MB free hard disk space
- CD-ROM drive
- VGA monitor with 64K color

Video Compression Type: Hardware
Video Codec/Resolution: H.261/FCIF at up to 22 fps, QCIF at up to 30 fps
Audio Encoding: G.711, G.728
Transmission: 56 to 384 kbps (Optional add-in board and software upgrade needed to achieve 384 kbps)
Features: Shared whiteboard, file transfer, JPEG still image compression, G3 and G4 document compression, on-screen dial pad, on-screen phonebook, manual and auto answer, Remote/local TWAIN scanner control, Picture-in-Picture, scaleable video-in-a-window size.
Includes:

- single PCI board codec with ISDN interface
- digital video camera
- telephone handset
- software

Options include:

- headset
- speakerphone
- Intel ProShare Premier collaboration software

Multipoint: Yes
Freeware/Shareware: No
Phone (Sales): 408-42806732
Phone (Tech Support): 800-767-2254
Fax: 408-922-5429
WWW: http://www.clix.com
Address: 350 Plumeria, San Jose, CA 95134-1900

COM2001 *TransViewer*

Versions: *Home Edition, Office Edition, Professional Edition, Lite Edition*
Platform: PC
Description: Desktop videoconferencing and collaboration add-on kit for PCs with added computer telephony-based functionality supporting ISDN, POTS, LAN, Internet.
Requirements:

- Pentium/75 MHz
- Windows 95, Windows 3.1, NT4.0
- 16 MB RAM
- 20 MB hard disk space
- UBUS (preferred), PCI, ISA, EISA bus

- Color CCD Camera
- Video Capture Board

Video Compression Type: N/A
Video Codec/Resolution: H.261, H.263/ 30 fps @ FCIF at 128 kbps, 15 fps @FCIF at 28.8 kbps
Audio Encoding: G.711, G.722, G.728
WAN Protocols/Transmission Speed: ISDN-BRI, POTS/ up to 128 kbps
LAN Protocols Supported: TCP/IP, Net BIOS and IsoEthernet
Features: Shared whiteboard, personal notepad, speed dialer with Caller ID and stored image display, application sharing and supports shared OLE (*Office Edition*), Internet videoconferencing (*Office Edition*), COMMail video and audio mail (*Office Edition*, ability to record and playback video and audio (*Office Edition*), multipoint videoconferencing on most LANs and WANs (*Professional Edition*), choice of proprietary or H.324 codec (*Professional Edition*).
Includes:

- software
- digital camera with video capture on board via parallel port
- microphone
- ear piece
- optional high-speed modem

Multipoint: Within LAN connection
Freeware/Shareware: Yes
Phone (sales): 800-888-COM-2001
Phone (tech support): 619-638-2001
Fax: 619-638-2002
WWW: http://www.COM2001.com
Address: 9740 Scranton Road, San Diego, CA 92121

Connectix *VideoPhone*

Versions: N/A
Description: Connectix *VideoPhone* allows users to see simultaneous live video of each other, talk and share a whiteboard.
Platform: Mac, PC
Requirements:

For PC:

- 486DX2-50 CPU
- 8 MB RAM

- Windows 95, Windows 3.11, Windows for Workgroups 3.11
- VGA or SVGA with 256-color support
- Modem or network interface card
- Sound board
- Video capture card
- TCP/IP communications software (Microsoft MS/TCP-32 recommended) or Novell's IPX communications software
- Audio input, speakers
- 1 parallel port

For Mac:

- Centris, Quadra or PowerPC-based Macintosh (Except Quadra 605 or 630)
- 16 MB of physical RAM
- System 7.1.1 or later (System 7.5 recommended for full features)
- Monitor with 256-color support (thousands of colors recommended)
- Microphone
- Network interface

Video Compression Type: Software

Video Codec/Resolution: Proprietary, H.261 - 10 fps at 160 x 120 over **LAN, NSVideo:** 6 fps at 160 x 120 over 28.8

Audio Encoding: N/A

WAN Protocols/Transmission: TCP/IP

LAN Protocols: TCP/IP

Features: Shared whiteboard, file transfer, full-duplex audio, supports slide show and animations, video messaging, multicast support, phone book, recording of conferences, snapshot, can share QuickTime movies (Mac version).

Includes:

- software codec
- collaboration software
- QuickCam camera (greyscale)
- color camera optional
- QuickTime Conferencing software (with Mac version)

Multipoint: N/A

Freeware/Shareware: No

Phone:

- 800-905-5880
- 415-571-5100

Fax: 415-571-5195

Faxback: 800-571-7558
WWW: http://www.connectix.com
Address: 2655 Campus Drive, San Mateo, CA 94403

Corel *CorelVIDEO*

Versions: N/A
Description: *CorelVIDEO* is an analog switch-based video system which allows an unlimited number of connections without consuming valuable network bandwidth.
Platform: PC, Mac (for clients)
Requirements:

A standard PC serves as the *CorelVIDEO* switch. The server requires:

- 486/66 CPU (Pentium/60 recommended)
- Windows 95 for server
- 16 MB RAM (32 MB RAM recommended)
- 6 MB hard disk space (10 MB hard disk space with codec)
- 256K-color support

The client requires:

- 486/33 CPU (486/66 recommended)
- Windows 95 or Windows 3.11
- 8 MB RAM (16 MB RAM recommended)
- 4 MB hard disk space without dataconferencing
- 65 K-color support recommended

Video Compression Type: N/A
Video Codec/Resolution: H.261/Over LAN: 30 fps NTSC, PAL, SECAM (TV). Over ISDN: 12-15 fps.
Audio Encoding: G.711, G.722, G.728
WAN Protocols/Transmission: ISDN/Up to 384 kbps.
LAN Protocols: TCP/IP, NetBIOS
Features: Near broadcast quality over LAN, ISDN connectivity, multipoint conferencing, broadcast capability, datasharing, whiteboarding, call waiting, call transfer, hold feature, picture phone books, file transfer, snapshot.
Includes:

- Corel console
- Corel line card
- Corel line module
- Corel camera
- *CorelVIDEO* software

Multipoint: 3rd-party hardware required
Freeware/Shareware: No
Phone: 800-772-6735
FaxBack: 613-728-0826, ext. 3080, Document #1081
WWW: http://www.corel.com
Address: The Corel Building, 1600 Carling Avenue, Ottawa, Ontario, Canada K1Z 8R7

Cornell University *CU-SeeMe*

See White Pine Software.

Creative Labs *ShareVision*

Versions: *PC3000, Mac3000*
Description: Desktop videoconferencing kit for PC or Power Macintosh
Platform: PC, Mac
Requirements:

For PC:
- 486DX2-66 MHz CPU
- 8 MB RAM
- 3 MB hard disk space
- Windows 95 or Windows 3.1
- 32K colors
- 2 ISA slots

For Mac:
- Power Mac 7100 AV or 8100 AV
- 8 MB RAM
- 4 MB hard disk space
- 32K color
- NuBus card
- 1 slot

Video Compression Type: Hardware-assist
Video Codec/Resolution: H.263 and proprietary/ 12-15 fps @ 160 × 112 (sub QCIF) at 28.8 kbps
Audio Encoding: N/A
WAN Protocols/Transmission: POTS and ISDN (planned)/POTS up to 28.8 kbps
LAN Protocols Supported: N/A

Features: Videoconferencing with audio, shared whiteboard, snapshot, screen capture, application sharing, file transfer all in 28.8 kbps through bandwidth management.

Includes:

PC3000 includes:

- camera
- video codec card
- audio codec card
- 28.8 kbps modem
- software
- earpiece with build-in microphone

Mac3000 includes:

- camera
- audio codec card
- 28.8 kbps modem
- earpiece/microphone

(Video codec provided by Apple's AV card)

Multipoint: Through third-party multipoint service providers
Freeware/Shareware: No
Phone (sales): 800-998-5227
Phone (tech support): 405-742-6622
Fax: 408-428-6611
WWW: http:// www.creativelabs.com
Address: 1901 McCarthy Boulevard, Milpitas, CA 95035

Creative Software Technologies *CollabOrator*

Versions: *CollabOrator 1000 R2.0* (data conferencing), *CollabOrator 1000 R2.5* (data conferencing-Windows 95), *CollabOrator System 2000* (data/voice conferencing), *CollabOrator System 4000* (Data/voice/videoconferencing), *System 6000* (Data/voice/videoconferencing at high bandwidth), *System 9000* (LAN)

Description: *CollabOrator* provides an open multimedia conferencing platforms capable of supporting a wide range of both existing and evolving communication infrastructures.

Platform: PC

Requirements:

- i486 33 MHz or higher
- Windows 95 (*CollabOrator 1000 R2.5*), Windows 3.1, Windows for Workgroups 3.11

- 8 MB RAM
- 5 MB disk space
- ISA bus
- 1 expansion slot for H.320 codec card
- ISDN service, LAN/WAN support, POTS (*System 2000, 1000*), Internet (*System 2000, 1000*)
- NT1 (with ISDN service)

Video Compression Type: Software
Video Codec/Resolution: FCIF, QCIF
Audio Encoding: N/A
WAN Protocols/Transmission: POTS, ISDN, Internet/ up to 384 kbps (*System 4000*), up to 2 Mbps (System 6000)
LAN Protocols: N/A
Features: Shared whiteboard, address book, user interface that includes photo icons of conference participants, file transfer, text chat tool, snapshot.
Includes:

- software
- H.320 codec card (*System 4000*), external peripheral connector box
- color CCD camera (*System 4000*)
- headset (*System 4000, System 2000*)

Multipoint: N/A
Freeware/Shareware: N/A
Phone: 61 3 587 1444 (Australia)
Fax: 61 3 580 5381 (Australia)
WWW: http://www.cst.com.au
Address: 43 Malcolm Road, Braeside VIC 3195 Australia

DataBeam *FarSite*

Versions: N/A
Description: Windows-based document conferencing includes whiteboarding and application sharing.
Platform: PC
Requirements:

- 8 MB RAM
- 8 MB hard disk space
- Windows 95 or Windows 3.1
- LAN, WAN, ISDN or dial-up connection

Video Compression Type: Software

Video Codec/Resolution: N/A
Audio Encoding: N/A
WAN Protocols/Transmission: ISDN, POTS
LAN Protocols Supported: TCP/IP, IPX
Features: Multipoint, file transfer, application sharing, whiteboarding
Includes: Software
Multipoint: Connect with multiple sites over LAN or bridging service
Freeware/Shareware: No
Phone (sales):

- 800-877-2325
- 606-245-3500

Phone (tech support): 606-245-3530
Fax: 606-245-3528
WWW: http://www.databeam.com
Address: 3191 Nicholasville Road, Lexington, KY 40503

Datapoint *Minx NVS*

Versions: *100, 200, 300, 400, PCNVS Telecommuter System*
Description: The MINX NVS is a local video network with a WAN or long distance connection via a shared codec or codecs on the network, much like a telephone PBX with long distance trunk lines. The local video network consists of a central video switching hub which is attached to the desktop connections directly in a star topology much like a telephone PBX switch is connected to phones in each location from the central switch. This connection does not run over the LAN as compressed video, but can run across UTP category 3,4, and 5 wiring and may be the unused 2 pair in 10BaseT wiring or it could be coaxial cabling.
Platform: Any that supports a video overlay interface which allows for NTSC or PAL composite video input. Also runs on television sets.
Requirements:

- Windows 95, Windows 3.1, Windows NT or OS/2 for Windows
- 1 ISA slot for video overlay board

Video Compression Type: Hardware
Video Codec/Resolution: H.261/ FCIF at 30 fps
Audio Encoding: G.711, G.722, G.728
WAN Protocols/Transmission: ISDN and switched digital services from 56 kbps to 2 Mbps

Features: Independent video network that uses unused wiring in the LAN wiring scheme, full-motion and uncompressed TV-quality video throughout campus environment.

Includes:

- hub
- interface card
- codec boards

Optional FeaturePAKs including camera with built-in microphone-video overlay card-Sony speakers. Optional collaboration software.

Multipoint: The MINX system is inherently multipoint and Datapoint holds several patents associated with this capability. Supports over 1000 local or campus connections and delivers TV-quality video.

Freeware/Shareware: No

Phone: 1-800-DPT-MINX

Fax: 210-593-7518

WWW: http://www.datapoint.com

Address: 8410 Datapoint Drive, San Antonio, TX 78229

Ericsson *Multimedia Workgroup System*

Versions: *Multimedia Workgroup System* (complete solution), *Multimedia Station Kit* (desktop product)

Description: MWS is a set of products including desktop and network equipment. MSK is a desktop videoconferencing and collaboration upgrade kit for PCs for operation over LAN. Network components include a multimedia LAN hub and a server which acts as a network LAN to WAN gateway.

Platform: N/A

Requirements:

For both multimedia stations and call control server

- Intel 486 processor
- Windows
- 16 MB RAM
- 250 MB disk space
- ISA bus
- 15" monitor
- two free card slots

Type of Video Compression: Hardware-assist

Video Codec/Resolution: H.261/ 30 fps @ QCIF at 128 kbps, 15 fps @ FCIF at 128 kbps

Audio Encoding: G.722, G.728, G.711

WAN Protocols/Transmission: ISDN-PRI/up to 768 kbps

LAN Protocols: TCP/IP, IsoEthernet

Features: H.320 video over isoEthernet LANS, shared whiteboard, document conferencing, application sharing, sizable video display capability up to full screen, phone book, user-controlled bandwidth allocation audio-video-data, user-selected line speed for each call, developer's kit available.

Includes:

- Multimedia station kit includes ProShare Premier collaboration software
- isoEthernet adapter card
- codec board
- camera with microphone
- speakers
- telephone set

Call control server kit includes server software, isoEthernet adapter card, 2-port ISDN PRI card (E1 or T-1 with BONDING Mode 1), user guide.

Multipoint: Requires MCU. Collaboration for up to 8 users supported

Freeware/Shareware: No

Phone: 800-374-2776 (USA)

Fax: N/A

WWW: http://www.ericsson.se/isoEthernet/

Address: S-131 89 Stockholm, Sweden (Hdq)

One Triangle Drive, Research Triangle Park, NC 27709 (USA)

EyeTel *InSight*

Versions: *100, 200, 300*

Description: Desktop videoconferencing and collaboration add-on kit for PCs running over WAN and LAN.

Platform: PC

Requirements:

For *100*:

- Pentium CPU
- Windows 95 or Windows 3.1
- 256-color VGA monitor
- 28.8 baud modem
- 1 ISA slot

For *200*:

- Pentium 90 CPU
- 8 MB RAM
- 6 MB hard disk space
- Windows 95 or Windows 3.1
- VGA graphics card (1 MB Stealth 64)
- 1 PCI slot
- NT1 (for ISDN-BRI) and/or LAN adapter

For *300*:

- 486/66 CPU
- Windows 95 or Windows 3.1
- 3 ISA slots
- VGA display with graphics card
- NT1 (for ISDN-BRI) and/or LAN adapter

Video Compression Type: Hardware

Video Codec/Resolution: H.261, Proprietary for POTS/ *Insight 100*: 10 fps at 160x120 at 28.8 kbps *Insight 200*: 20 fps at FCIF *Insight 300*: 25 fps at FCIF at 384 kbps or higher

Audio Encoding: G.711, G.722, G.728

WAN Protocols/Transmission: All

LAN Protocols: TCP/IP, NetBIOS, BUI

Features: Picture-in-picture, application sharing, file transfer, shared white-board, multipoint.

Includes:

- camera
- headset
- inVIEW collaboration software
- single board

Multipoint: No

Freeware/Shareware: Yes

Phone: 800-923-7393

Fax: 941-434-7613

WWW: http://www.eyetel.com

Address: 501 Goodlette Road N., D-306, Naples, FA 33940

Fiber & Wireless *Mediafone/Fonewatch*

Versions: *Mediafone*

Description: Videoconferencing PC upgrade kit or software-only.

Platform: PC
Requirements:

- 486 DX 33 MHz
- 4 MB RAM (8 MB recommended)
- 256K external cache
- 12 MB hard disk space
- VGA monitor
- High density floppy drive
- 14,400 or higher modem
- Camera

Video Compression Type: Software
Video Codec/Resolution: Proprietary Motion JPEG/ up to15 fps at 80 x 60 at 28.8 kbps
Audio Encoding: N/A
WAN Protocols/Transmission: POTS, ISDN, LAN, Internet
LAN Protocols Supported: TCP/IP
Features: Shared whiteboard, application sharing.
Includes:

PC upgrade kit includes :

- *Mediafone/Fonewatch* software
- video capture and VGA board
- feature connector and AV/VGA cable

Also available is a laptop system.
Multipoint: N/A
Freeware/Shareware: No
Phone: 310-787-7097
Fax: 310-787-7099
Email: FiberWire@aol.com
Address: 370 Amapola Ave., #100, Torrance, CA 90501

GPT Video Systems *FOCUS PC*

Versions: Focus 10, 10+, 20 and 30
Description: *FOCUS PC* is an upgrade kit for IBM compatible PCs. The product utilizes a basic rate ISDN network connection.
Platform: PC
Requirements:

- 386/33 CPU
- 8 MB RAM

- 120 MB hard disk
- Windows 3.11
- 1 available ISA slot
- VGA display with 256K colors
- NT1

Video Compression Type: Hardware
Video Codec/Resolution: H.261/ 15 fps at FCIF, 30 fps at QCIF
Audio Encoding: G.711, G.722, G.728
WAN Protocols/Transmission: ISDN-BRI/ up to 128 kbps
LAN Protocols: N/A
Features: Telephone directory, flexible call manager, standard and advanced OLE shared whiteboard, unanswered call log, mute video and audio, file transfer, up to full-screen video window, picture-in-picture, variable picture quality, notepad.
Includes:

- codec card
- camera (several options)
- audio adapter or station
- software

Multipoint: via H.320 MCU
Freeware/Shareware: No
Phone: 203-882-6287
Fax: +44 1628 772266
WWW: http://www.gpt.co.uk
Address: 6 Roxborough Way, Foundation Park, Maidenhead, Berkshire SL63UD (UK)

Hewlett Packard Boeblingen *Multimedia Collaboration (MMC)*

Versions: N/A
Description: LAN-based videoconferencing and application sharing.
Platform: HP workstations
Requirements:

- HP 9000- 712/60
- 32 MB RAM
- 1 GB hard disk space
- HP-UX 9.0x
- HP DVC-Box

Video Compression Type: Hardware

Video Codec/Resolution: H.261, M-JPEG/ Up to 25 fps @ 768 x 576 (PAL), up to 30 fps @ 640 X 480 (NTSC)
Audio Encoding: G.711, G.722, G.728
WAN Protocols/Transmission: N/A
LAN Protocols Supported: TCP/IP
Features: Powerful application sharing (any number of applications at any time, shares almost every application running on X11, token mode and free mode), powerful conference management (open/closed conferences, different roles—chair-vice chair-observer), high quality video and audio, multipoint limited only by the network.
Includes:

- Video/audio and collaboration software
- software decompression for H.261 and M-JPEG

Multipoint: Yes
Freeware/Shareware: No
Phone: ++49- (0)30-31421238
Fax: ++49- (0)30-31421114
WWW: http://www.prz.tu-berlin.de/docs/html/MMC/
Address: Technical University Berlin, MMC Project, Sekr: MA073, Strasse des 17. Juni 136, 10623 Berlin, Germany

Incite *Conversational Media* with *Multimedia Package and Hub*

Versions: N/A
Description: Desktop videoconferencing add-on kit for PCs with network server architecture for integrating video, voice and data on LANs with WAN gateway. Ideal for call center applications.
Platform: PC
Requirements:

- 486/66 CPU
- Windows 3.1 (Windows 95 recommended)
- 2 available ISA slots
- SVGA display with 256-color video board

Hub/Server:

- 486/66 CPU
- Windows NT v3.5.1
- 10BaseT network interface card
- NT1

Video Compression Type: Hardware

Video Codec/Resolution: H.261/ 30 fps @ FCIF at 384 kbps and above
Audio Encoding: N/A
WAN Protocols/Transmission: ISDN-BRI, ISDN-PRI
LAN Protocols: IsoEthernet
Features: Shared whiteboard, file transfer, application sharing, video-voice-data on LANs and WANs via gateway.
Includes:

- collaboration software
- call management software
- IsoEthernet network adapter
- codec board
- camera
- speakerphone
- PBX network interface card

Multipoint: Yes
Freeware/Shareware: No
Phone: 800-946-2483
Fax: 214-447-8205
WWW: http://www.incite.com
Address: 5057 Keller Springs Road, Dallas, TX 75248

INRIA *Inria Videoconferencing System (IVS)*

Versions: N/A
Description: Software system to transmit audio and video data over the Internet using standard workstation.
Platform: SUN, Silicon Graphics, DEC, HP
Requirements:

- SPARC stations with Parallax, SunVideo, VideoPix and Vigrapix
- Silicon Graphics stations with IndigoVideo, GalileoVideo and VinoVideo
- PC/Linux with SCREENMACHINE II
- DEC 5000 stations with VIDEOTX
- DEC ALPHA stations without video capture
- PC/FreeBSD2.0 stations without video capture
- HP stations with VideoLive

Video Compression Type: Software
Video Codec/Resolution: H.261/ Depends on platform
Audio Encoding: G.711, ADPCM, GSM 06.10

WAN Protocols/Transmission: UDP/IP
LAN Protocols Supported: UDP/IP
Features: *IVS* includes a congestion control algorithm which adapts the output rate control of the coder according to the network conditions. An option is also available to manually tune the output video rate. *IVS* can be used in point-to-point mode or in point-to-multipoint on top of the MBone. *IVS* is an RTP-based videoconferencing tool.
Includes: Audio/Video software codec and session tool.
Multipoint: Yes, using IP multicast extensions
Freeware/Shareware: Yes
WWW: http://www.inria.fr/rodeo/ivs.html
Phone: N/A
Fax: +33 93 65 77 65
Address: INRIA U.R. de Sophia Antipolis 2004, Route des Lucioles BP 93, 06902 Sophia Antipolis CEDEX France

InSoft (Netscape) *Communique!*

See Netscape Communications Corp.

Intel *ProShare Conferencing Products*

Versions: *ProShare Video System 150* (LAN), *ProShare Video System 200* (ISDN), *ProShare Premier* (Collaboration only), *ProShare Presenter* (Desktop broadcasting)
Description: Desktop videoconferencing and collaboration over ISDN and LAN The *Video System 150* is a LAN-only product.
Platform: PC
Requirements:

- IntelDX2™ 66 MHz processor
- Windows 95 or Windows 3.1
- 16 MB RAM
- 32 MB hard disk space
- VGA display with 256 colors or higher (no feature connector required
- 2 ISA slots (1 full-length ISA slot for Video System 150)
- For ISDN use (*Video System 200*): NT1 adapter, ISDN service
- Intel LANDesk Conferencing Manager R1.9 (for use with LAN-based conferencing)

Requirements for ProShare Presenter:

Presenter side requires:

- *ProShare Video System 150* or *200*
- Pentium Processor
- Windows 95, Windows 3.1, Windows 3.11
- 16 MB of available RAM
- 32 MB hard disk space available
- VGA display with 16-bit colors
- 1 full-length ISA slot
- 16-bit network interface card
- One of the following network stacks:

  For MAC multicast:

  - Novell ODI
  - Microsoft NDIS2-based network stack or Microsoft NDIS3-based network stack

  For IP Multicast:

  - FTP Software OnNet TCP/IP 1.2 or later (Windows 3.1, Windows 3.11 only) or Microsoft Windows 95 TCP/IP

Participant side requires:

- Intel 486TM DX2 66 MHz CPU or better
- Windows 3.1, Windows 3.11 or Windows 95
- 8 MB of available RAM minimum, 12 MB for Windows 95
- 10 MB hard disk space available
- VGA display with 256 colors or better
- 16-bit network interface card
- One of the following network stacks:

  For MAC multicast:

  - Novell ODI
  - Microsoft NDIS2-based network stack or Microsoft NDIS3-based network stack

  For IP Multicast:

  - FTP software OnNet TCP/IP 1.2 or later (Windows 3.1, Windows 3.11 only) or Microsoft Windows 95 TCP/IP
- Headset or speakers and microphone
- WAV compatible sound card (or *ProShare* Video System 150 or 200)

NOTE: *ProShare Presenter* Total Starter Package includes:

- *ProShare Video System 150*
- *ProShare Presenter* Sender software

- *ProShare Presenter* Participant software for up to 50 users
- LANDesk Personal Conferencing ManagerVideo Compression Type: Hardware-assist

Video Codec/Resolution: H.261, Proprietary (Indeo)/10 fps at QCIF (*Video System 200* only). Indeo over ISDN: 15fps in a 160x120 window, 7.5 fps in a 320x240 window Over LAN (*Video System 150*): 15fps in 160X120 and 320x240 windows. *Video System 200* will receive and display FCIF.

Audio Compression: G.711 and G.728

WAN Protocols/Transmission: ISDN-BRI/128 kbps, Switched 56 (with Telesynch adapter)

LAN Protocols Supported: TCP/IP, IPX

Features: Shared whiteboard, application sharing, snap shot, phone book, speed dialing, conference manager displays meeting participants in office-conference room or auditorium depending on number of participants, access *ProShare* from any open Windows application, software-controlled zoom and pan, optimize video for motion smoothness or picture sharpness.

Includes:

- software
- *ProShare Premier* collaboration software
- video input board
- SDN/audio board
- color camera
- headset/microphone

Multipoint: Yes, using H.320/T.120 compliant MCUs. Data conferencing on the LAN (5-way, peer-to-peer)

Freeware/Shareware: No

Phone (sales):

- 800-538-3373 (North America)
- 503-264-7354
- +44-1793-431155 (Europe)

Phone (tech support): 503-264-7000

FaxBack:

- 800-525-3019
- 503-264-6835
- +44-1793-432509 (Europe)

WW W: http://www.intel.com/comm-net/proshare/index.html

Address: 2200 Mission College Blvd., P.O. Box 58199, Santa Clara, CA, 95052-8119 USA

Intel *Video Phone* with *ProShare technology*

Versions: N/A
Description: *Video Phone* software application for PC Original Equipment Manufacturer (OEM) integration. Supports H.324 standard for placing video phone call over POTS.
Platform: PC
Requirements:

- 133 MHz Intel Pentium Processor (120)MHz for receive-only)
- 16 MB RAM
- Windows 95
- Videophone-ready 28.8 kbps modem
- Any video capture card that supports YUV-12 image format

Video Compression Type: Software
Video Codec/Resolution: H.263/4-12 fps@ QCIF at up to 28.8 kbps
Audio Encoding: G.723
WAN Protocols/Transmission: POTS
LAN Protocols: N/A
Features: Voice-call first, snapshot mode for still image transfer, image quality slider, completely software-based.
Includes: Software on CD ROM. PC OEM supplies hardware.
Multipoint: No
Freeware/Shareware: No
Phone: N/A-Contact PC OEM
Fax: N/A
WWW: N/A
Address: N/A

Intelligence at Large *BeingThere*

Versions: N/A
Description: Desktop videoconferencing and collaboration software for Macintosh and Windows platforms. Designed for Internet use, *BeingThere* can be used over POTS, ISDN, LAN and WAN connections.
Platform: Mac, PC
Requirements:

For Mac:

- Power Mac
- 16 MB physical RAM
- 3 MB hard disk space

- A LAN, WAN or Internet connection. An ISDN connection is required to send and receive video
- Mac OS 7.5.1 or later

For PC:

- Pentium Processor
- 16 MB RAM
- 4 MB hard disk space

Video Compression Type: Software or hardware
Video Codec/Resolution: H.261, QuickTime, NSVideo 3.0 (software codecs). Hardware codecs available from SAT-Sagem./ Software: 15 fps @ 120 x 160 over Ethernet, 10 fps @ 120 x 160 at 128 kbps
Audio Encoding: Software- QuickTime, Lernout & Housepie, G.723; Hardware- G.711, G.722, G.728 hardware codec from SAT-Sagem
WAN Protocols/Transmission: All WAN protocols supported
LAN Protocols Supported: TCP/IP
Features: Chat window, file transfer, application sharing, clipboard transfer, high resolution window sharing, multiple window sharing, broadcast. Supports LAN and WAN connections using AppleTalk and TCP/IP.
Includes:

- software codec
- collaboration software

Multipoint: Capable over 128 kbps or faster Internet connection
Freeware/Shareware: No
Phone (sales):

- 215-387-6002
- 800-425-7638

Phone (tech support): 215-387-6002
Fax: 215-387-9215
WWW: http://www.beingthere.com
Address: 3508 Market Street, Philadelphia, PA 19104-3316

Mentec *MXV-1000/2000*

Versions: N/A
Description: Desktop video codec (ISA or PCI) for the OEM market
Platform: PC
Requirements:

- 386 CPU
- Windows 95, Windows 3.1 or Windows for Workgroups 3.11

- ISA bus
- SVGA or VGA monitor
- SVGA or VGA adapter with feature connector
- Camera
- Microphone

Video Compression Type: Hardware
Video Codec/Resolution: H.261/ 15 fps @ FCIF at 128 kbps, 22 fps @ FCIF at 384 kbps, 30 fps @ QCIF at 128 kbps
Audio Encoding: G.711 300-3.4 Khz at 6.4 kbps, G.722 50-7.0 Khz at 48/56 kbps, G.728 300-3.4 Khz at 16 kbps
WAN Protocols/Transmission: ISDN-BRI/ up to 384 kbps (up to 2 Mbps over LAN)
LAN Protocols Supported: TCP/IP
Features: Picture-in-picture, flexible software development environment, ease of installation.
Includes:

- single board video codec
- MVIP cable to communications interface
- cable harness for audio/video connections
- software development and integration libraries
- Windows application

Multipoint: Supported via standards-based MCU
Freeware/Shareware: No
Phone (sales):

- 508-970-3600 (US)
- 800-338-2585
- +353-1-285-8444 (Ireland)

Phone (tech support):

- 508-970-3600
- 800-338-2585

Fax:

- 508-970-3400 (US)
- +353-1-285-8005 (Ireland)

WWW: http://www.mentec.com
Address:

- 55 Technology Drive, Lowell, MA 01851 (USA),
- Mentec House, Dun Laoghaire Industrial Estate, Dun Laoghaire, Co Dublin (Ireland)

Mosaic Information Technologies *DV*

Versions: *DV100, DV100R, DV200, DV200R*

Description: Desktop videoconferencing product that uses motion JPEG compression technology over the LAN and TCP/IP-based.

Platform: PC, UNIX, Mac

Requirements:

For Mac:

- PowerMac A/V
- System 7.5
- Monitor with support for 256-color

For PC:

- 486/33 CPU
- 16 MB RAM
- 5 MB hard disk space
- 1 Isobus slot

Video Compression Type: Software and hardware

Video Encoding/Resolution: Motion JPEG, H.261 (some models)/ 30 fps at QCIF, 15 fps at FCIF

Audio Compression: ADPCM

WAN Protocols/Transmission: All/From 64 kbps to 768 kbps

LAN Protocols Supported: TCP/IP, IsoEthernet

Features: Multiple simultaneous images with Continuous Presence (*DV200, DV200R*), Shared whiteboard, file transfer, application sharing, fully resizable video window

Includes:

- WAN-based Codec board
- WAN-based communications board (*DV100R, DV200, DV200R*)
- LAN-based codec board set (*DV100*)
- Desktop Workstation Interface Board (*DV200, DV200R*)
- collaboration software
- call management software
- camera
- microphone
- speakers

Multipoint: MCU functionality built into software

Freeware/Shareware: No

Phone: 212-604-9630

Fax: 212-604-9640

WWW: http://www.videoconferencing.com
Address: 130 Fifth Ave., 9th Floor, New York, NY 10011

MRA Associates *VidCall*

Versions: N/A
Description: Video/audio/document conferencing software for PCs using POTS, Internet (TCP/IP) and LAN/WAN
Platform: PC
Requirements:

- 486/66 CPU
- Windows 3.1, Windows for Workgroups, Windows NT, Windows 95
- 4 MB RAM
- 2 MB available disk space
- 14.4 or higher modem
- Camera
- VGA graphics card 256 colors (hi-color recommended)
- Video capture card

Video Compression Type: Software
Video Codec/Resolution: Proprietary/ 10 fps at 80x60 over POTS
Audio Encoding: Proprietary
WAN Protocols/Transmission: POTS, ISDN-BRI, TCP-IP
LAN Protocols Supported: TCP/IP, IPX
Features: LAN/WAN multipoint, shared whiteboard with editing tools, two-way teletype dialogue, phone book with saved images, video mail, auto answer, remote selection of video sources and image quality, voice/data switching on single line, file transfer.
Includes:

- software codec
- network management software
- collaborative software

Multipoint: Supports up to 10 participants in LAN/WAN conference
Freeware/Shareware: Yes
Phone: 703-448-5373
Fax: 703-734-9825
WWW: http://www.access.digex.net/~vidcall/vidcall.html
Address: 2102B Gallows Road, Vienna, VA 22182

MultiMedia Access Corp. *Viewpoint*

Versions: *Viewpoint FamilyFone, Viewpoint Pro, Viewpoint Viewcaster* (multicast video), *Viewpoint LiveSwitch/LiveFone.*

Description: Desktop videoconferencing add-on kit for PCs.

Platform: PC

Requirements:

Viewpoint FamilyFone:

- 486/66 CPU
- Windows 95
- 8 MB RAM
- 1.3 MB hard disk space
- 1 PCI slot
- 28.8 kbps modem

Viewpoint Pro:

- 486/66 CPU
- Windows 3.1
- 8 MB RAM
- 1 MB hard disk space
- 1 ISA slot
- Ethernet

Viewpoint LiveSwitch/LiveFone:

- 486/33 CPU
- Windows 95 or Windows 3.1
- 4 MB RAM
- 500K hard disk space
- Ethernet or Token Ring for control
- Optional video overlay board, sound card

Video Compression Type: *FamilyFone* and *Pro-* hardware, Viewcaster-hardware-assist

Video Codec/Resolution: H.263, H.261 with software upgrade (FamilyFone), CPV for *Pro*, *Viewcaster*. *LiveSwitch/LiveFone* provides uncompressed analog video./ 15 fps @ FCIF at 28.8 kbps (*FamilyFone*), 30 fps @ 256 x 200 at 640 kbps (*Pro* and *Viewcaster*), 30 fps NTSC video (*LiveSwitch/LiveFone*),

Audio Encoding: G.723, G.728 with software upgrade (*FamilyFone*), CPV for *Pro* and *Viewcaster*.

WAN Protocols/Transmission: *FamilyFone*: POTS, ISDN-BRI/ 128 kbps; Pro: Ethernet routers; *Viewcaster*: Ethernet multicast routers; *LiveSwitch/LiveFone*: ISDN-BRI, ISDN-PRI, Fractional T1, POTS, DS3

LAN Protocols Supported: TCP/IP for all versions. LiveSwitch/LiveFone also supports NetBIOS, IPX (LAN used for control only)

Features: *FamilyFone*: address book, frame grab with video, scrapbook, logs, speed dial, file transfer, video mail, voice mail, fax.

Pro: Multipoint conferencing, IP multicast, application sharing

Viewcaster: IP multicast receive

LiveSwitch/LiveFone: TV-quality video/audio, 3500′ loop length on Cat. 5 UTP, 7 port conference, speed dial, H.320 trunk, NTSC source, 96 non-blocking ports, coaxial UTP wiring.

Includes:

FamilyFone:

- codec card
- software
- optional camera

Pro:

- codec card
- camera
- collaboration software
- 10-user Viewcaster site license

Viewcaster:

- software

LiveSwitch/LiveFone:

LiveFone (client):

- camera
- video overlay board
- transceiver
- software

LiveSwitch (PBX):

- server
- software
- livecards.

Multipoint: Yes

Freeware/Shareware: Yes (*FamilyFone*)

Phone (sales):

- 214-488-7103 (*FamilyFone*)
- 214-488-7193 (*Pro*)
- 214-488-7193 (*Viewcaster*)
- 970-586-4660 (*LiveSwitch/LiveFone*)

Phone (tech support): 214-488-7100
Fax: 214-243-0635
WWW: http://www.mmac.com
Address: 2665 Villa Creek Dr., Suite 100, Dallas, TX 75234

Netmanage *InPerson* for Windows

Versions: N/A
Description: Windows version of Silicon Graphics videoconferencing product.
Platform: PC
Requirements:

- 486/66 CPU recommended
- Windows 95, Windows 3.1,3.11 or NT
- 16 MB RAM
- 20 MB available hard disk space
- 256-color video
- Compatible video capture card
- Audio card with record and playback capability
- Color CCD camera

Video Compression Type: Software
Video Codec/Resolution: Proprietary/1-10 fps adjustable rate
Audio Encoding: N/A
WAN Protocols/Transmission: TCP/IP
LAN Protocols Supported: TCP/IP
Features: Compatible with Silicon Graphics *InPerson*, shared whiteboard, multipoint, custom phone book, highly configurable frame rate and compression. Whiteboard displays each page with scroll bars. Dial-up users can connect with LAN-based users.
Includes:

- software codec
- collaboration software

Multipoint: Yes, using multicasting.
Freeware/Shareware: No
Phone: 408-973-7171
Fax: 408-257-6405
WWW: http://www.netmanage.com
Address: 10725 N. DeAnza Blvd., Cupertino, CA 95014

Netscape Communications Corporation *Communique!*

Versions: N/A

Description: *Communique!* is the industry's first desktop videoconferencing product able to conference between Windows 3.1, Windows 95 and Windows/NT and any of the five major UNIX platforms (HP-UX, AIX, IRIX, SunOS/Solaris and Digital UNIX). *Communique!* is based on a software architecture which allows desktop conferences, application sharing, and digital video to be distributed across any network (frame relay, ISDN, ATM, Ethernet, FDDI, SMDS, etc.) and between various video compression/decompression algorithms (H.261, JPEG, DellB, Indeo, etc.).

Platform: PC, Workstation

Requirements:

- 16 MB RAM
- 10 to 15 MB temporary space
- 15-inch display
- Bus and number of slots depend on platform

Video Compression Type: Software

Video Codec/Resolution: H.261, H.263, JPEG, CellB, Indeo, DVE2/Resolution depends on network, platform and video board...fully scalable from 0-320 fps.

Audio Encoding: GSM, G.711, G.723

WAN Protocols/Transmission: ISDN via GlobalConference Gateway. Works with Lucent Technologies MMCX for PBX to LAN conferencing.

LAN Protocols Supported: TCP/IP

Features: Bandwidth allocation, multipoint and point-to-point flexibility, a Virtual Conference Room environment, automated installation and system configuration, conference manager icons, business card editor, shared graphics and images in shared whiteboard, imager tool for online slide presentations, chat tool and shared application capability.

Includes:

- kit sold with software and choice of type of camera
- video board
- speakers and microphone

Multipoint: Number of points in a conference dependent on network and system infrastructure.

Freeware/Shareware: No

Phone: 415-254-1900

Fax: 415-528-4124

WWW: http://home.netscape.com

Address: 501 Middlefield Road, Mountain View, CA 94043

Osprey Technologies (Multimedia Access Corp.) *Osprey-1000*

Versions: *1000, 1004, 320/2, 320/6, 1100, 1104*
Description: Video/audio codec for desktop video applications
Platform: PC, Sun Workstation
Requirements:

For PC:

- Pentium 90 MHz
- 2 MB hard disk space
- Windows 95, Windows NT, Windows 3.11
- Available PCI 1/2 slot
- 256-color display adapter
- Network connectivity adapters
- Audio input, output

Video Compression Type: N/A
Video Codec/Resolution: H.261, H.263, Lossless JPEG, MPEG-1./ frame rates depend on codec and bandwidth
Audio Encoding: G.711, G.722, G.728, G.723, AEC
WAN Protocols/Transmission: ISDN-BRI, POTS
LAN Protocols Supported: TCP/IP, UDP, RTP (via partners)
Features: multialgorithm codec board, cross-platform support, uncompressed video capture.
Includes:

- 1 PCI slot multicodec board
- configuration software
- developer's API

Multipoint: Provided by 3rd-party application software
Freeware/Shareware: No
Phone (sales):

- 919-319-9200
- 415-579-6680

Phone (tech support): 919-319-9200
Fax: 919-319-9814
WWW: http://www.osprey.mmac.com
Address: 1150 SE Maynard Rd., Suite 110, Cary, NC 27511

Panax *VideoTwist*

Versions: *VTW 3240, VTW 6080*

Description: The VTW System distributes interactive video and audio over UTP and interfaces to any vendor's codec. The video is analog and uncompressed.
Platform: PC
Requirements:

- 386/33 CPU
- 4 MB RAM
- 1 MB hard disk space
- Windows 95 or Windows 3.11
- VGA monitor with 256-color support
- Camera
- Microphone
- Speaker

Video Compression Type: Software
Video Codec/Resolution: 30 fps full-frame NTSC, PAL or SECAM (TV) video over LAN. Frame rate over WAN depends on codec
Audio Encoding: N/A
WAN Protocols/Transmission: All/ at any speed, bandwidth
LAN Protocols Supported: Proprietary protocol, DX
Features: Full-motion and uncompressed video, stereo audio, messages, remote control of source devices (VCR, laser disk, etc.), source channel control (CNN, C-Span, etc.), videoconferencing, polling of security cameras. UTP up to 4000', *3240* and *6080* can be coaxial or fiber bused together—distance not an issue.
Includes:

- central switching matrix
- master software
- PC software

Requires a video capture board, camera, and speakers.
Multipoint: LAN multipoint up to four location may be connected for a videoconference.
Freeware/Shareware: No
Phone (sales): 502-587-2830
Phone (tech support): 502-339-9966
Fax: 502-339-9494
WWW: N/A
Address: 320 Whittington Parkway, Suite 216, Louisville, KY 40222

Paradise Software *Simplicity*

Versions: N/A

Description: *Simplicity* is videoconferencing and shared whiteboard software for Sun, HP and IBM Unix platforms.

Platform: Sun, HP, IBM PowerPC Workstations

Requirements:

For Sun SPARCstation:

- Parallax Graphics Power Video/XVideo board with software version 3.0.6 (Sun OS) or 3.4 (Solaris)
- Runs onSunOS 4.1.3.U1 or greater, OpenWindows 3.X or X11R5/Motif 1.2

For HP 9000/700:

- Parallax Graphics Power Video/XVideo board with software version 9.1 or greater
- Runs on HPUX 9.0.3 or greater, X11R5/Motif1.2

For IBM PowerPC:

- Parallax Graphics Power Video/XVideo board with software version 1.0
- Runs on PowerPC 40P hardware, AIX 4.1, X11R5/Motif 1.2 software

Video Compression Type: Hardware

Video Codec/Resolution: Parallax Graphics PVC or VIO (M-JPEG)/ 30 fps at 320x240 over T1, 15 fps at NTCF/PAL over 10 Mbps LAN

Audio Encoding: G.711

WAN Protocols/Transmission: via Simplicity H.320 bridge

LAN Protocols Supported: IP and ATM

Features: Shared whiteboard, file transfer

Includes: Videoconferencing and whiteboard software-only or *Simplicity* kit which includes:

- codec board
- camera
- microphone
- videoconferencing
- whiteboard software

Multipoint: Yes

Freeware/Shareware: No

Phone: 609-655-0016
Fax: 609-655-0045
WWW: http://www.paradise.com
Address: 7 Centre Drive, Suite 9, Jamesburg, NJ 08831

PictureTalk *PictureTalk Communicator* and *Conference Server*

Versions: N/A
Description: Visual communication software for real-time collaboration
Platform: Mac, PC, UNIX Workstations
Requirements:

For PC:

- 386/25 MHz CPU
- 4 MB RAM
- 14.4 kbps modem or better

For Mac:

- 68030 or PowerMac
- 4 MB RAM
- 14.4 kbps modem or better

Video Compression Type: N/A
Video Codec/Resolution: N/A
Audio Encoding: N/A
WAN Protocols/Transmission: TCP/IP Any speed
LAN Protocols Supported: TCP/IP Any speed
Features: Users can collaborate in real-time using any existing or new application.
Includes: Attend-mode and present-mode capabilities in free client software.
Multipoint: Yes. *Conference Server* adaptively balances communication workload to clients.
Freeware/Shareware: Yes (client software)
Phone (sales): 510-467-5300
Phone (tech support): 510-467-5300
Fax: 510-467-5310
WWW: http://www.picturetalk.com
Address: 4234 Hacienda Drive, Suite 200, Pleasanton, CA 94588-2721

PictureTel *Live*

Versions: *Live 100, Live 50, Live 200i, Live 200p*
Description: Complete H.320 desktop videoconferencing add-on solution for ISA or EISA bus PCs. *Live* 200p supports PCI bus.
Platform: PC
Requirements:

Live 100, Live 50:

- 386/25 or faster CPU
- Windows 95, Windows 3.1
- 8 MB RAM
- 20 MB disk space
- ISA or EISA bus
- SVGA or VGA monitor
- VESA Advanced Feature Connector (PCS 50)

Live 200i:

- 486/33 or faster CPU
- Windows 95
- 16 MB RAM
- 20 MB disk space
- ISA or EISA bus slot
- SVGA or VGA monitor
- VESA Media Channel (VMC) video graphics subsystem (PCI or VLB)

Live 200p:

- 486/66 or faster CPU
- 16 MB RAM
- Windows 95
- 20 MB hard disk space
- PCI bus slot
- 32-bit high performance PCI graphics controller with a minimum of 2 MB graphics memory
- SVGA monitor

Video Compression Type: Hardware-assist
Video Compression/resolution: H.261/ 15 fps @ FCIF, up to 10 fps @ QCIF regardless of network bandwidth
Audio Compression: G.711 64 kbps with response from 300 Hz to 3.4 KHz, G.728 16 kbps with response from 300 Hz to 3.4 KHz, G.722 48 or 56 kbps with

response from 50 Hz to 7.0 KHz, PT724 24kbps with response from 50 Hz to 7.0 KHz

WAN Protocols/Transmission: ISDN-BRI, Switched 56 (*Live 100*, *Live 50*)/ 56-384 kbps (*Live 100*), 56-128 kbps (*Live 50*,*Live 200i*). Option allows *Live* 50 to operate up to 384 kbps

LAN Protocols Supported: N/A

Features: *Live 100*: Camera that mounts on top of monitor or on desk stand (*Live 100*), snapshot of local or remote video window (*Live 100*, *Live 50*), Far-end camera control (*Live 100*, *Live 50)*, phone directories, call log, application sharing, shared whiteboard, file transfer, shared clipboard, messaging, manual and auto answer. *Live 200* family features intuitive user interface, flexible address book that can be used independently of PictureTel application, Caller ID.

Includes:

Live 100:

- video/audio/graphics/ISDN two-board set
- adjustable color Y/C) camera
- full duplex hands-free speakerphone
- LiveShare Plus collaboration software

Options include:

- additional camera
- headset
- additional network interfaces

Live 50:

- Video/audio board with ISDN BRI I/F
- color composite camera
- headset
- LiveShare Plus collaboration software

Options include:

- graphics board with VAFC Interface
- speakerphone
- color composite camera

Live 200i and *Live 200p*:

- Video/audio board with ISDN BRI I/F (ISA), color composite camera
- headset
- multimedia speakers

- LiveWare collaboration software
- VMC graphics sub-system (*Live 200i*)

Multipoint: H.320 multipoint supported with voice activation
Freeware/Shareware: No
Phone (sales): 800-716-6000
Phone (tech support): 800-874-2835
Video: 700-730-5271 twice
Fax: 508-762-5245
WWW: http://www.picturetel.com
Address: The Tower of Northwoods, 222 Rosewood Drive, Danvers, MA 01923

RSI Systems *Eris*

Versions: *Eris 1000*
Description: Eris is an SCSI base computer peripheral that enables any host computer to function as a desktop H.320 device. It is a self-contained portable videoconferencing system. The initial product is ISDN, SW56, RS449 or DDS. A software upgrade allows *Eris* to function without the need of a PC host computer.
Platform: PC, Mac, Unix
Requirements:

For PC:

- 486 CPU
- Windows 3.1
- 8 MB RAM
- 2 MB Video RAM
- Video card supporting 64,000 colors
- Standard SCSI or PCMCIA interface
- color camera
- NT1 (if using ISDN)
- ISDN service or POTS

For Mac:

- System 7.0 Mac OS
- 68040 or better processor
- 8 MB RAM
- 16-bit color ("Thousands of Colors")
- CCD camera

- NT1 (if using ISDN)
- ISDN service or POTS

Video Compression Type: Hardware
Video Codec/Resolution: H.261/ 15 fps @ FCIF at 128 kbps
Audio Encoding: G.711, G.722, G/728 with AEC
WAN Protocols/Transmission: ISDN-BRI, SW56, RS 449 and DDS (POTS pending)/ up to 128 kbps (384 kbps enhancements pending)
LAN Protocols Supported: N/A
Features: Picture-in-picture, full screen or fully resizable video window, document conferencing, file transfer, photo-based phone book, 5.5 pound portable (can be used with laptops), input jack for auxiliary camera
Includes:

- audio/video codec
- ISDN terminal adapter
- cabling software
- external microphone
- collaborative software

Multipoint: Can interoperate with standards-based MCUs
Freeware/Shareware: No
Phone:

- 800-496-4304, 612-896-3020 (USA)
- 44 (0) 1924 840446 (UK)
- 61 (8) 233 5866 (Australia)

Fax:

- 612-896-3030 (US)
- 44 (0) 1924 840812 (UK)
- 61 (8) 233 5858 (Australia)

WWW: http://www.rsisystems.com
Address: 7400 Metro Boulevard, Suite 475, Edina, MN 55439

SAT-SAGEM *MeetMe*

Versions: *MeetMe, MeetMe PC, MeetMe PCI*
Description: Desktop videoconferencing and collaboration kit for Mac and PC for use over ISDN (H.320 compliant).
Platform: Mac, PC
Requirements:

For Mac:

- Power PC compatible MAC with Apple AV card

- Open Nubus slot
- 12 MB RAM (16 MB RAM recommended)
- System 7.5
- Camera

For PC:

- 386 CPU
- 16 MB RAM
- Windows 3.1
- 1 open ISA slot

For PCI:

- Any PCI Macintosh with AV bus

Video Compression Type: Hardware
Video Codec/Resolution: H.261/ 12.5 fps @ FCIF at 128 kbps, 15 fps @ QCIF at 128 kbps
Audio Encoding: G.711, G.722, G.728
WAN Protocols/Transmission: ISDN BRI/ up to 128 kbps
LAN Protocols Supported: N/A
Features: Shared whiteboard, snapshot, drag-and-drop file transfer, hands-free or telephone handset audio, high-speed Internet access.
Includes:

For Mac:

- H.320 NuBus-format codec with ISDN daughterboard
- telephone handset
- CCD color camera
- camera connector and power supply
- software
- NT1

For PC:

- ISA-format codec with built-in ISDN interface (1 slot)
- telephone handset
- color camera with integrated microphone
- camera connector and power supply
- external speakers
- collaboration software
- videoconferencing software

Multipoint: Yes
Freeware/Shareware: No

Phone (sales): 408-446-8690
Phone (tech support): 408-446-8693
Fax: 408-446-9766
WWW: http://www.satusa.com
Address: 20370 Town Center Lane, Suite 255, Cupertino, CA 95014

Silicon Graphics *InPerson*

Versions: *InPerson*, *InPerson* for Windows (See NetManage)

Description: Multipoint LAN and Internet-oriented videoconferencing and collaboration software. Works over any TCP/IP network (LAN or WAN) with at least 100 kbps/second bandwidth. Also works over ISDN using PPP-based point-to-point IP connections.

Platform: Silicon Graphics workstation (collaboration software available for PC through NetManage)

Requirements:

- Any Indy, Indigo, Indigo2 or Onyx workstation running IRIX 5.3 or IRIX 6.2
- 32 MB RAM
- 5 MB available hard disk space
- For audio: any AL (Audio Library) supported audio device
- For video: any VL (Video Library) supported video capture device

Video Compression Type: Software (*InPerson* Option hardware is available for the SGI Indy workstation that provides acoustic echo cancellation and audio compression)

Video Codec/Resolution: H.261, HDCC, and "Uncompressed" (256 color) (for use on FDDI or ATM links)/ 10 fps @ FCIF over 128 kbps, 15 fps @ 320 x 240 over Ethernet, 30 fps @ 320 x 240 over FDDI or ATM. On a SGI Indigo2 with optional Indigo2Video card: 10 fps @ all bandwidths.

Audio Encoding: DVI 16, DVI 8, ulaw, GSM and G.728 (with *InPerson* option board), "uncomp16" (uncompressed 16 kHz) and "uncomp44" (uncompressed 44.1 kHz.

WAN Protocols/Transmission: Any WAN capable of carrying TCP/IP packets with at least 100 kbps/second bandwidth. This includes ISDN-BRI, T1, E1, T3, packet-relay, etc.

LAN Protocols Supported: TCP/IP

Features: Multiway, multiline, hold function, Phone book, personal directories, display showing current calls in progress, shared whiteboard, unlimited whiteboard pages, file sharing, application sharing, snapshots, video size choice, video and still image settings, automatic and manual network utilization-video resolution-compression algorithm selection, congestion sensing snapshot.

Includes:

- software codec
- collaboration software

All necessary audio and video hardware comes standard with the Indy, including camera.

Multipoint: Supports multipoint using UDP multicasting, except over ISDN where calls are limited to point-to-point. Supports as many people as desired, limited only by CPU type and network bandwidth. New participants can be invited in at any time during an established call.

Freeware/Shareware: No

Phone (sales): 800-800-7441 (US), 415-960-1980, (41) 22-798.75.25 (Europe)

Phone (tech support): 800-800-4744

Fax: 415-933-0926

WWW: http://www.sgi.com/Products/software/InPerson/ipintro.html

Address: 2011 N. Shoreline Boulevard, Mountain View, CA 94043

SMART Technologies *SMART 2000 Conferencing*

Versions: *SMART 2000 Conferencing, SMART Conferencing for Macintosh*

Description: Delivers real-time, interactive data conferencing via desktop computers or a SMART Board. Connects multiple locations over standard phone lines, ISDN or LAN/WAN, allowing users to share applications and edit or annotate documents in real time. *SMART Conferencing for Macintosh* is cross-platform data conferencing software compatible with Intel ProShare (shared notebook only).

Platform: PC, Mac

Requirements:

For PC:

- 386 CPU (486 CPU recommended)
- Windows 3.1
- 4 MB RAM (8 MB RAM recommended)

For Mac:

- Any Macintosh with 68020 or greater processor (68030 recommended)
- 4 MB RAM (8 MB RAM recommended)
- 4 MB available hard disk space
- System 7 or higher

Video Compression Type: N/A
Video Codec/Resolution: N/A
Audio encoding: N/A
WAN Protocols/Transmission: ISDN, POTS
LAN Protocols Supported: TCP/IP, Novell IPX, NetBIOS, Banyan Vines
Features: Shared whiteboard (Notepad), application sharing, electronic pens and highlighters, Print Capture allows printing any file directly to Notepad, slide sorter, *SMART* Scribe for minute-taking and broadcasting, address book, screen capture (partial or full), support for all TWAIN scanners, compatible with *SMART*'s touch sensitive whiteboards and *SMART* Board and Rear Projection *SMART* Board for remote group meetings. *SMART Conferencing for Macintosh* supports cross-platform conferencing to Intel ProShare.
Includes: Software
Multipoint: *SMART 2000* supports up to 64 locations in a single meeting over LAN or WAN. For conferences using modems, *SMART 2000* is compatible with the *SMART* Bridge which supports up to 32 users. *SMART Conferencing for Macintosh* supports up to 8 participants in a single meeting over LAN or WAN.
Shareware/Freeware: No
Phone: 403-245-0333
Fax: 403-245-0366
WWW: http://www.smarttech.com
Address: 1177-11th Avenue SW, Suite 600, Calgary, AB, Canada T2R 1K9

Specom Technologies *VisionTime*

Versions: *VisionTime Pro, VisionTime Gold, VisionTime Platinum, VisionTime Diamond, Internet Video Phone*
Description: Desktop videoconferencing software and hardware accessories running over ISDN, POTS, Internet, LAN, cable modem.
Platform: PC
Requirements:

- 386 CPU
- Windows 3.1
- DOS 6.0
- 4 MB RAM
- 8 MB available hard disk space
- VGA display with 256-color support
- Video capture card (ISA/PCI)

- Network interface card for LAN
- 2 available ISA slots
- NT1 or 9600 or faster modem

Video Compression Type: Software
Video Codec/Resolution: Proprietary/5 fps at 160x120 at 128 kbps
Audio Encoding: Proprietary
WAN Protocols/Transmission: POTS, ISDN-BRI, Internet
LAN Protocols Supported: Internet Video Phone supports TCP/IP
Features: Vision mail enabling user to create postcard-like images with multiple video capture, Post card-like images can be sent electronically, shared whiteboard, phonebook, draw, type with choice of fonts and colors.
Includes:

VisionTime Gold includes:

- *VisionTime Pro* software and video capture card

VisionTime Platinum includes:

- software
- video capture card and DSVD modem

VisionTime Diamond includes:

- software
- video capture card
- DSVD modem
- color video camera

Multipoint: *VisionTime Pro* capable of multipoint broadcasting up to 64 sites
Shareware/Freeware: No
Phone: 408-982-1880
Fax: 408-982-1883
WWW: http://www.specom.com
Address: 2322 Walsh Ave., Santa Clara, CA 95051

Sun Microsystems *ShowMe*

Versions: N/A
Description: *ShowMe* is a complete LAN-based desktop videoconferencing solution.
Platform: Sun Workstation
Requirements:

- Any SPARC-based system
- 1 SBus slot for SunVideo board

- SunMicrophone or equivalent
- Solaris 2.3 or higher operating system
- 32 MB of main memory
- 35 MB hard disk space

Video Compression Type: Hardware-assist

Video Codec/Resolution: JPEG, CellB/ 30 fps @ 320x240 at 1.25 Mbps or 10 fps @ 640 x 480 at 1.5 Mbps

Audio Encoding: G.711

WAN Protocols/Transmission: N/A

LAN Protocols Supported: TCP/IP and IP Multicast

Features: Comes with a shared whiteboard and application-sharing capability, multiple users can share common whiteboard and interact with a live application in real time, users can manually adjust the frame rates to optimize bandwidth usage, picture-in-picture, full duplex mode, each participant has color-coded on-screen marker, annotation tools, address book, *ShowMe* TV option allows IP multicast.

Includes:

- color camera with tilt stand
- codec/video capture board
- software codec
- SharedApp and Shared Whiteboard collaboration software
- *ShowMe* Video
- *ShowMe* Audio

Multipoint: Supports many-to-many and one-to-many multipoint

Shareware/Freeware: No

Phone (sales and tech support):

- 800-821-4643
- 415-960-1300

Faxback: 800-873-7869

Fax: 415-969-9131

WWW: http://www.sun.com

Address: 2550 Garcia Ave., Mountain View, CA 94043-1100

Systems of Excellence *SEI DeskTop Video Teleconferencing System*

Versions: *3000 ULTRA*

Description: Full-color, full-motion (30 fps) and audio up to 8,000 feet to the desktop over a campus local video network (LVN) using existing unshielded twisted pair (UTP, fiber, or coaxial cable. Interfaces directly to proprietary and all H.261 standard codecs outside of the LVN.

Platform: PC, Mac, SUN, other UNIX platforms

Requirements:

- 386/486 CPU and 16-bit bus connections
- 4-16 MB RAM
- MS-DOS or PC-DOS Rev. 3.1 or greater
- Windows 3.0 or greater
- VGA with VESA feature connector

Video Compression Type: N/A

Video codec/resolution: H.261-compatible through WAN gateway/ Within campus: full-color, full-motion 30 fps. Scaleable to full screen. Frames-per-second in WAN environment depend on codec and transmission speed.

Audio encoding: G.711, G.722, G.728

WAN Protocols/Transmission: ISDN-BRI, ISDN-PRI, Switched 56, Fractional T1, T1, microwave, satellite

LAN Protocols Supported: Switching and control software compatible with TCP/IP and Net BIOS

Features: Broadcast TV quality video/audio, operates over existing premise wiring, multi-platform, complete video/audio synchronization, partial/full screen at 30 fps high resolution, freeze frame, frame capture, simultaneous multipoint conferencing in both LVN and WAN environments, collaborative computing, distributed video/audio processing, cascadable switching.

Includes:

- integrated camera-speaker-microphone
- multimedia PC card
- video/audio transmission drivers
- display software
- *SMART 2000* collaborative software (T.120 compatible)
- cabling

Multipoint: LVN Multipoint Desk Top Conferencing provides constant presents with all conference participants and other switched video with SEI's Quad Video Multiplexer(s) and N-1 audio bridging.

Freeware/Shareware: N/A

Phone: 703-734-9200

Fax: 703-883-1434

WWW: http://www.seivideo.com

Address: Tyson's Dulles Plaza, 1420 Spring Hill Road, McLean, VA 22152

Target Technologies *C-Phone*

Versions: N/A

Description: Desktop videoconferencing systems that provide full-screen, TV-quality video at 30 frames per second over the LAN and fully compatible with H.320 video over ISDN. Can also send video over T1, fiber.

Platform: PC

Requirements:

- 386/25 CPU
- Windows 95, Windows 3.11, Windows for Workgroups
- 8 MB RAM
- 4 MB hard disk space
- VGA with VESA Feature Connector
- VGA monitor with 256-color support
- 1 available ISA slot
- Novell Netware
- NetBIOS compatible networks
- LANtastic

Video Compression Type: Hardware

Video codec/resolution: Over LAN: H.261 over WAN via WAN server/ 30 fps full frame NTSC (TV) over LAN. Over WAN: 12-15 fps @ FCIF at 128 kbps, 20-24 fps @ FCIF at 384 kbps

Audio Encoding: G.711, G.722, G.728

WAN Protocols/Transmission: ISDN-BRI, ISDN-PRI, T1

LAN Protocols Supported: TCP/IP, NetBIOS, IPX/SPX

Features: supports both LAN and WAN networks, call transfer, call forwarding, call screening, hold feature with music or message, answering machine features, broadcast mode, simultaneous multipoint capability on both LAN and WAN, photo-icon based dialing directory with cross-referenced call up, video playback, file transfer. Optional multipoint control unit features 4 simultaneous video streams.

Includes:

- software
- video/audio/system controller board
- color CCD camera
- speaker
- microphone unit
- handset
- power supply
- Video Interface Module (VIM)

Optional hardware includes:

- WAN server
- C-Bridge connection for multiple workgroups
- multipoint controller
- C-TV TV and cable interface module
- document camera

Multipoint: Proprietary multipoint enables 4 or more people from local or remote locations to be displayed on one screen.
Freeware/Shareware: No
Phone:

- 910-395-6100
- 800-666-2496

Fax: 910-395-6108
WWW: http://www.cphone.com
Address: 6714 Netherlands Drive, Wilmington, NC 28405

Technical University of Berlin

See Hewlett-Packard Boeblingen

Teles *Vision*

Versions: *B-1* (Basic), *B-2*, *P-2* (Personal), *MTM-1* (Manager+True Multipoint), *MTM-4*, *Vision LAN*, *Vision POTS*
Description: Desktop videoconferencing add-on kit for PCs
Platform: PC
Requirements:

For *Vision* Basic models (Software encoding and decoding):

- Pentium 90 MHz
- Windows 95 or Windows 3.1
- DOS 5.0
- 16 MB RAM
- 1 available ISA slot
- PCI graphics card with 64K colors
- One free interrupt
- Frame Grabber card (for B2)
- Additional ISDN interface (for B2)

For *Vision* Personal (Hardware encoding and software decoding) models:

- Pentium 60 MHz
- 16 MB RAM
- 1 available ISA slot
- PCI or VLB graphics card with 64K colors
- 1 free interrupt

For *Vision-MTM-1*(Hardware encoding and decoding):

- 486 33 MHz CPU
- 16 MB RAM
- Windows 3.1 or 3.11
- DOS 6.2
- ISA-VGA board with feature connector (PCI or VLB applicable with special options)
- ISA bus slot (16 bit) for Teles.BRI/TR card

Video Compression Type: Basic: Software, Personal: Hardware-assist

Video Codec/Resolution: H.261/ Basic: FCIF at 15 fps, Personal: FCIF at 30 fps, MTM: FCIF at 22 fps, QCIF at 30 fps

Audio Encoding: G-722, G-711, G-728 (MTM-4)

WAN Protocols/Transmission: ISDN-BRI

LAN Protocols Supported: N/A

Features: Shared whiteboard, file transfer, application sharing, fax, picture-in-picture (MTM), TELES.COM collaboration software, multipoint.

Includes:

- software codec (except MTM)
- TELES.COM collaboration software

Some models include:

- camera
- rame Grabber card
- analog telephone

Multipoint: N/A

Freeware/Shareware: No

Phone (sales):

- 415-652-9191, 800-70TELES (USA)
- (+49)30/399 28 00 (Germany)

Phone (tech support): 415-652-9191 (USA)

Fax:

- 415-652-9192 (USA)
- (+49)30/399 28 01 (Germany)

WWW: http://www.teles.de
Address:

- 1818 Gilbreth Road, Suite 211, Burlingame, CA 94010 (USA)
- Dovestr. 2-4, 10587 Berlin, (Germany)

VCON *ARMADA*

Versions: *ARMADA Cruiser 100, ARMADA Cruiser 50, ARMADA Escort* LAN/WAN system, *ARMADA PT System* (POTS)
Description: Desktop videoconferencing add-on kit for PCs
Platform: PC
Requirements:

- 486/66 CPU
- Windows
- 8 MB RAM
- SVGA monitor
- PCI bus interface
- PCI-VGA card

Video Compression Type: Hardware
Video Codec/Resolution: H.261/15 fps at FCIF, 30 fps at QCIF
Audio Encoding: G.711, G.728, G.722
WAN Protocols/Transmission: 56 to 384 kbps (*Cruiser 100* with optional add-in board to achieve 384 kbps), 56 to 128 kbps (*Cruiser 50*).
LAN Protocols Supported: IsoEthernet, ATM
Features: Picture-in-picture, Shared whiteboard, image phonebook, snapshot, scaleable video window up to full screen, JPEG still image compression, remote laser printer control, G3 and G4 document compression, audio-only conferencing.
Includes:

- codec card with ISDN interface
- color CCD camera
- telephone handset
- Win2Win collaboration software

Options include:

- application sharing
- electronic business card exchange
- video and audio answering machine
- Ethernet LAN support up to 384 kbps
- MPEG-1 playback from CD-ROM or file or MVIP

- high-speed remote Internet access
- high-speed remote LAN access
- dual video input (NTSC/PAL or digital)

Multipoint: N/A
Freeware/Shareware: No
Phone:

- 214-735-9001 (USA)
- 49-6074-858-103 (Germany)
- 972-9-567-233 (Israel)

Fax:

- 214-735-9099 (USA)
- 49-6074-858-137 (Germany)
- 972-9-567-244 (Israel)

WWW: N/A
Address: 17130 N. Dallas Parkway, Suite 210, Dallas, TX 75248

VCC *TeleView Plus*

Versions: N/A
Description: The product is a software codec for ISDN and POTS.
Platform: PC
Requirements:

- 486/66 CPU
- 1.7 MB hard disk space
- Windows 95, Windows 3.1 or Windows NT (Intel only)
- VGA card 256 color (16 bit or 24 bit recommended)
- MNP/V.42 14.4 modem minimum for POTS
- Video Source: ATI VideoBasic or VideoLogic Captivator
- Audio card

Type of Compression: Software
Video Codec/Resolution: H.261, H.263 (with hardware-assist) /15 fps @ 352 X 288 on POTS, 21 fps @ QCIF at 128 kbps.
Audio Encoding: G.711
WAN Protocols/Transmission: ISDN, POTS
LAN Protocols Supported: N/A
Features: Shared whiteboard, application sharing, auto answer or announced calls, remote selection of image quality and video source, integrated phonebook with image of person, two-way chat box for users without sound abilities.

Includes:

- software codec
- collaboration software

Multipoint: No
Shareware/Freeware: No
Phone:

- 714-452-0800
- 888-284-3364 (USA)
- 422-439-134 (Czech Republic)

Fax:

- 714-581-9271
- 422-439-134 (Czech Republic)

WWW: http://www.videoconf.com
Address:

- 1615 N. El Camino Real, Suite G, San Clemente, CA 92672 (USA)
- Ve Svahu 1067/33, 147 00 Praha 4 (Czech Republic)

VDOnet *VDOPhone*

Versions: N/A
Description: PC desktop videotelephony tool for the ordinary user
Platform: PC
Requirements:

- Pentium 75 MHz CPU
- 16 MB RAM
- Windows 95 or Windows NT
- Sound card (For full duplex audio: a full duplex-capable, sound blaster compatible, sound card with supporting drivers)
- Microphone
- Earphone or speakers
- Video capture card supported by *VDOphone*
- Camera compatible with video capture card

Video Compression Type: Software with options for hardware-assist
Video Codec/Resolution: H.263/ 20 fps @ QCIF at 28.8 kbps.
Audio Encoding: G.723
WAN Protocols/Transmission: TCP/IP
LAN Protocols Supported: TCP/IP
Features: User directory showing who is on-line currently.

Includes: Software
Multipoint: No
Shareware/Freeware: No
Phone: 415-846-7700
Fax: 415-846-7900
WWW: http://www.vdophone.com
Address: 4009 Miranda Ave., Suite 250, Palo Alto, CA 94304

VIC Hi-Tech *GlobalPhone*

Versions: *1.5 Turbo A/V Complete*
Description: Desktop videoconferencing and collaboration add-on kit for PCs. Available in software-only, various add-on kits, and full turnkey systems. *Global Phone* runs over POTS, TCP/IP LAN and the Internet. ISDN connection is available with ISDN modems.
Platform: PC
Requirements:

- 486DX-33 MHz CPU
- 8 MB RAM
- 2 MB hard disk space
- Windows 95 or Windows 3.1 or Windows NT
- 1 ISA or PCI slot for video card
- 32-bit PCI bus and 16-bit ISA bus

Video Compression Type: Software
Video Codec/Resolution: Motion JPEG/ Over POTS: 10 fps @ 120x90; Over LAN: 30 fps @ QCIF
Audio Encoding: As required
WAN Protocols/Transmission: POTS, ISDN, TCP/IP
LAN Protocols Supported: TCP/IP
Features: High-resolution whiteboard with multi-color editing functions, teletype, local and remote snapshots, full screen video, TWAIN device support, file transfer, voice/data switching between phone and videoconference modes, video hardware configuration within program without restarting program or system, video quality range selectable from 1-100, picture-in-picture, phonebook, auto answer or announce, remote selection of video sources-image size-image quality, ability to scan images in to the shared whiteboard.
Includes:

- *Global Phone* software
- Video Packer Turbo card (a PCI-bus SVGA and video capture card in one with 2 MB DRAM standard)

- 28.8 kbps DSVD modem
- color CCD camera
- collaboration software

Multipoint: Up to 8 remote simultaneous multipoints over LAN and Internet. Each remote site is in its own window with simultaneous video movement.
Freeware/Shareware: No
Phone: 310-643-5193
Fax: 310-643-7572
WWW: http://www.vic-corp.com
Address: 2221 Rosecrans Ave #237, El Segundo, CA 90245

Videoconferencing Systems, Inc. (VSI) *Omega MVP*

Versions: N/A
Description: Desktop videoconferencing add-on kit for PCs running over ISDN or Switched 56.
Platform: PC
Requirements:

- 486/66 MHz CPU
- 8 MB RAM
- Windows 95, or Windows 3.1, or Windows for Workgroups 3.11
- Standard PC/AT ISA bus full-length card slot

Video Compression Type: Hardware
Video Codec/Resolution: H.261/15 fps @ FCIF at 384 kbps, 30 fps at QCIF as 128 kbps
Audio Encoding: G.711, G.722, G.728
WAN Protocols/Transmission: ISDN-BRI, Switched 56/ISDN-BRI up to 128 kbps (up to 384 kbps with IMUX board), Switched 56 up to 112 kbps
LAN Protocols Supported: Under development
Features: Numerous collaboration packages supported, FCIF still image transfer, superior audio with echo cancellation, chat.
Includes:

- codec board
- software
- video/audio peripherals

Multipoint: Compatible with H.320 MCUs
Freeware/Shareware: No
Phone (sales): 800-423-0769
Phone (tech support): 800-551-1109

FAX: 770-242-5730
WWW: http://www.vsin.com
Address: 5801 Goshen Springs Road, Norcross, GA 30071

VideoLAN *VL2000*

Versions: N/A
Description: Television-quality analog videoconferencing over campus video network with WAN gateway.
Platform: PC
Requirements:

- 386 CPU
- Windows 3.1
- DOS 5.0
- 4 MB RAM
- 5 MB hard disk space
- VGA card
- ISA, VL or PCI bus

Video Compression Type: N/A
Video Codec/Resolution: On campus- Uncompressed NTSC composite video (TV). Wide area- H.261
Audio Encoding: Wide area- G.711, G.722, G.728
WAN Protocols/Transmission: T1, ISDN PRI, ISDN BRI up to 384 kbps
LAN Protocols Supported: N/A
Features: Uncompressed broadcast-quality video on campus, 2 real-time full-spectrum audio signals (20 Hz - 20 Khz) for each session, video switching on demand, video connections to and video control of remote devices, application sharing, "Quadrature" option for multipoint conferences-up to four parties can be displayed on a four-way split screen, reception and broadcast of video feeds from cable networks and other sources.
Includes:

- one or more broadband switching modules- each with 16 ports for user and device connection (modules interconnect and stack to operate as a unitary switch)
- wide area video gateway(s)
- Metallic-Fiber Modem (PC cards that contain VideoLan's proprietary twisted-pair transmission technology)
- video overlay cards
- microphones

- headsets or external speakers
- remote stand-alone video workstations

Multipoint: N/A
Freeware/Shareware: No
Phone: 502-895-4858
Fax: 502-895-1680
WWW: N/A
Address: 100 Mallard Creek Road, Suite 20, Louisville, KY 40207

ViewPoint Systems

See MultiMedia Access Corporation

VistaCom *VCI*

Versions: *VCI 100, VCI 10, PowerDESK, VCI-10.5*
Description: VistaCom supplies high-performance H.320/H.324 video codec for desktop applications. The *VCI-100* board set supports communication up to T1 (1.5 Mbps)/E1 (2 Mbps). The single board *VCI-10* supports rates up to 384 kbps. Both products mount onto the industry standard PC/AT bus (ISA/EISA). *VCI-10* and *VCI-100* facilitate the development of complete codecs for virtually any digital network. Both codecs can operate with multiple lines, e.g. 6 ISDN BRI solutions are available. The codecs can also be used in broadcast mode.
Platform: PC
Requirements:

- 386/33 CPU
- Windows 95 or Windows 3.1
- Camera
- *VCI-10*: 1 available ISA/EISA bus slot
- *VCI-100*: 3 available ISA/EISA bus slots
- Audio input and output
- VGA monitor with 256-color support
- NT1

Video Compression Type: Hardware
Video Codec/Resolution: H.261/ 30 fps @ FCIF at 1.5 Mbps, 15 fps @ FCIF at 128 kbps to 384 kbps.
Audio Encoding: G.711, G.722, G.728

WAN Protocols/Transmission: VCI 10: ISDN-BRI (up to 3 BRI), VCI 100: ISDN-PRI, T1

LAN Protocols Supported: TCP/IP

Features: N/A

Includes:

- board
- Application Programming Interface (API)

The user-friendly VistaAir graphical user interface is available for both codec board families.

Multipoint: N/A

Freeware/Shareware: No

Phone: 408-253-5165

Fax: 408-253-5170

WWW: http://www.vistacom.fi

Address: 20431 Stevens Creek Blvd., #240, Cupertino, CA 95014

VIVO *320/TeleWork-5*

Versions: N/A

Description: Desktop videoconferencing and collaboration add-on kit for Pcs. Enables 5 high-speed ISDN-based applications: H.320 videoconferencing, document and application sharing, high-speed Internet access, remote LAN access, analog fax/modem emulation.

Platform: PC

Requirements:

- Pentium 90 MHz with L2 cache
- Windows 95 or Windows 3.1
- 12 MB RAM
- 5 MB hard disk space
- 8-bit or greater Local-bus (PCI or VLB)
- Video display (with PCI or VLB accelerator for best results)
- 2 ISA slots--one full-length, one 3/4-length
- DCI capable graphics card (for full-screen video)

Type of Compression: Software

Video Codec: H.261/Transmits: 15 fps @ QCIF at 128 kbps on a Pentium 133, Receives: 30 fps @ FCIF at 128 kbps.

Audio Encoding: G.711, G.722

WAN Protocols/Transmission: 112 or 128 kbps with dynamic rate adaption

LAN Protocols Supported: N/A

Features: DataBeam FarSite collaboration software, Supports any application-sharing product, ScreenView™ presentation software transmits any portion of Windows desktop as live FCIF video to any H.320 far-end, drag-and-drop file transfer, fax/modem software without need for additional hardware, ISDN Internet access capability, High-speed remote LAN access.

Includes:

- videoconferencing software
- Logitech VideoMan digital video camera
- microphone
- op-of-monitor camera stand
- desktop camera stand
- speaker for hands-free operation
- earpiece
- Logitech MovieMan ISA-bus video capture card
- IBM WaveRunner ISA-bus ISDN terminal adapter card
- drivers

Multipoint: Can participate in H.320 multipoint calls over MCU bridges

Freeware/Shareware: No

Phone:

- 800-848-6411
- 617-899-8900

Fax: 617-899-1400

WWW: http://www.vivo.com

Address: 411 Waverley Oaks Road, Waltham, MA 02154-8414 USA

VTEL DeskMax *115S* and *117S*

Versions: *115S* and *117S*

Description: Complete desktop videoconferencing solution.

Platform: PC

Requirements:

- NT-1
- ISDN service

Video Compression Type: Hardware

Video Codec/Resolution: FCIF at 15 frames per second, QCIF at 30 frames per second

Audio Encoding: G.711 64 kbps with response from 50 Hz to 3.4 kHz, G.722 64 kbps with response from 50 Hz to 7 kHz, G.728 16 kbps with response from 50 Hz to 3.4 kHz

WAN Protocols/Transmission: 56 kbps to 384 kbps
LAN Protocols Supported:
Features: Picture-in-picture, shared whiteboard, document conferencing, application sharing, snapshot, software-upgradable, privacy feature, in-band audio.
Includes:

- Intel 486 computer
- Windows 3.11
- 540-Mbyte hard disk drive
- CCD color camera with integrated microphone
- headphone/headset
- microphone internal to camera module
- 17" SVGA color monitor (*117S*)
- 15" SVGA color monitor (*115S*).

Multipoint: N/A
Freeware/Shareware: N/A
Phone: 800-299-VTEL (North America), +44(0)1734 560915 (UK)
Fax: 512-314-2792
WWW: http://www.vtel.com
Address: 108 Wild Basin Road, Austin, Texas 78746 USA

VTEL *Personal Collaborator*

Versions: N/A
Description: Desktop videoconferencing and collaboration add-on kit for PCs.
Platform: PC
Requirements:

- 486/33 MHz or higher
- Windows 95
- 8 MB RAM
- 1 ISA or PCI slot
- VGA card with Feature Bus connector or multimedia-capable PCI display card
- NT-1 adapter
- ISDN service

Video Compression Type: Hardware
Video Codec/Resolution: H.261/ 15 fps @ FCIF at 128 kbps
Audio Encoding: G.711 64 kbps, G.722 64 kbps, G.728 16 kbps

WAN Protocols/Transmission: ISDN-BRI 56 kbps to 384 kbps (optional card needed for rates above 128 kbps)

LAN Protocols: N/A

Features: Same user interface as VTEL room systems, file transfer, object sharing (selected objects within files), full-screen feature, picture-in-picture, drag-and-drop functionality, multipoint-ready, still image capture, VTEL echo canceller on audio, address book, ISDN Internet access capability, High-speed remote LAN access, ability to integrate Internet access into a videoconference, snapshot.

Includes:

- ISDN codec card with built-in IMUX
- desktop speakers
- camera/microphone and software

Multipoint: Provides multi-way video communications when used with VTEL MCUII controller

Freeware/Shareware: No

Phone (sales):

- 800-299-VTEL
- 508-358-4432 (North America)
- +44(0)1734 560915 (UK)

Phone (tech support): 512-314-3654

Fax: 512-314-2748

WWW: http://www.vtel.com

Address: 108 Wild Basin Road, Austin, Texas 78746 USA

White Pine *Enhanced CU-SeeMe*

Versions: N/A

Description: Desktop videoconferencing software for real-time, person-to-person or group conferencing and collaboration that operates over the Internet, TCP/IP network or standard telephone line. Runs over a 28.8 kbps modem or better. Offers full-color video, audio, chat window and whiteboard image collaboration.

Platform: PC, Mac

Requirements:

For Mac:

- Power Macintosh, 68020, 030, 040
- 4 MB RAM
- System 7.0 or greater

For PC:

- 486 CPU
- 8 MB RAM
- Windows 95, Windows 3.1, Windows NT

Video Compression Type: Software
Video Codec/Resolution: H.261
Audio Encoding: G.711, G.722, G.728
WAN Protocols/Transmission: POTS, ISDN, T1
LAN Protocols Supported: TCP/IP, SLIP/PPP
Features: Cross-platform, full-color video, audio, chat window, shared whiteboard, 24-bit true color support, broadcasting and multicasting, reflector support for UNIX and Windows NT, 24-bit true color support.
Includes: Software
Multipoint: N/A
Shareware/Freeware: Yes
Phone (sales):

- 603-886-9050
- 800-241-PINE

Phone (tech support): 603-594-2804
Fax: 603-598-0962
WWW: http://www.cu-seeme.com
Address: 40 Simon St., Nashua, NH 03060-3043

Winnov *Videum*

Versions: N/A
Description: Video/audio capture board supporting multiple codecs, transports, applications.
Platform: PC
Requirements:

- 486/66 processor (Pentium 120 MHz for TV capability)
- Windows 95 or Windows 3.1 or Windows NT
- 16 MB RAM
- Monitor with 256-color support
- 1 ISA slot

Video Compression Type: On-board hardware compression for performance through the ISA bus.
Video Codec/Resolution: Codec independent. Also supports integrated AVI formats and RGB formats.

Audio Encoding: Codec independent
WAN Protocols/Transmission: Transport independent
LAN Protocols Supported: Independent
Features: Video and audio capture board that is transport independent, codec independent, application independent. 3 separate video inputs (composite, SVHS, multimedia port), full-duplex audio (both multiples of x8 kHz and x11 kHz up to 48 kHz), "No video-overlay" TV capable on DCI enabled Pentium systems.

Includes:

- 1/2 size ISA-based board
- drivers
- applet for video-audio-picture clips
- real-time Video Preview application for DCI equipped Pentium systems
- samples of programs using *Videum's* API. Kit includes camera, trial versions of several software codecs and other related applications on CD ROM, plus the other items.

Multipoint: Depends on application
Shareware/Freeware: Yes
Phone: 408-733-9500
Fax: 408-733-5922
Video: 408-733--0398 (x2)
WWW: http://www.winnov.com
Address: 1150 Kifer Road, Suite 201, Sunnyvale, CA 94086

Workstation Technologies *Chameleon*

Versions: N/A
Description: Single card codec that combines video and audio compression with options including on-board ISDN interface, composite video input/output and a variety of host interfaces.
Platform: PC
Requirements:

- 486/33 CPU
- 8 MB RAM
- Windows 3.1
- 1 ISA or PCI slot
- VGA card with Feature Bus connector or PCI multimedia capable display card

Video Compression Type: Hardware
Video Codec/Resolution: H.261, H.263/ H.261: 5-15 fps at FCIF, 30 fps at QCIF
Audio Encoding: G.711 (64 kbps), G.722 (32 kbps), G.728 (16 kbps), CELP (4.8 kbps)
WAN Protocols/Transmission: POTS, ISDN-BRI, ISDN-PRI
LAN Protocols Supported: N/A
Features: Single card codec. Options include on-board ISDN interface, composite video input/output and variety of host interfaces to form flexible base for multimedia and video communication systems.
Includes:

- single card codec only
- optional camera

Multipoint: N/A
Shareware/Freeware: No
Phone: 714-250-8983
Fax: 714-250-8969
WWW: N/A
Address: 18010 Sky Park Circle, MS 155, Irvine, CA 92714

Index